ICON, LIBERTINE, LEADER

ICON, LIBERTINE, LEADER

The Life and Presidency of John F. Kennedy

Mark White

BLOOMSBURY ACADEMIC
LONDON • NEW YORK • OXFORD • NEW DELHI • SYDNEY

BLOOMSBURY ACADEMIC
Bloomsbury Publishing Plc
50 Bedford Square, London, WC1B 3DP, UK
1385 Broadway, New York, NY 10018, USA
29 Earlsfort Terrace, Dublin 2, Ireland

BLOOMSBURY, BLOOMSBURY ACADEMIC and the Diana logo are trademarks of Bloomsbury Publishing Plc

First published in Great Britain 2024

Copyright © Mark White, 2024

Mark White has asserted his right under the Copyright, Designs and Patents Act, 1988, to be identified as Author of this work.

For legal purposes the Acknowledgements on p. ix constitute an extension of this copyright page.

Cover design: Adriana Brios
Cover image: President John F. Kennedy, 1961. (© The Estate of Jacques Lowe/ Getty Images)

All rights reserved. No part of this publication may be reproduced or transmitted in any form or by any means, electronic or mechanical, including photocopying, recording, or any information storage or retrieval system, without prior permission in writing from the publishers.

Bloomsbury Publishing Plc does not have any control over, or responsibility for, any third-party websites referred to or in this book. All internet addresses given in this book were correct at the time of going to press. The author and publisher regret any inconvenience caused if addresses have changed or sites have ceased to exist, but can accept no responsibility for any such changes.

A catalogue record for this book is available from the British Library.

Library of Congress Cataloging-in-Publication Data

Names: White, Mark J., author.
Title: Icon, libertine, leader : the life and presidency of John. F. Kennedy / Mark White.
Description: London ; New York : Bloomsbury Academic, 2024. | Includes bibliographical references.
Identifiers: LCCN 2024012516 (print) | LCCN 2024012517 (ebook) | ISBN 9781350426115 (hb) | ISBN 9781350426122 (pb) | ISBN 9781350426139 (epub) | ISBN 9781350426146 (ebook)
Subjects: LCSH: Kennedy, John F. (John Fitzgerald), 1917-1963. | Presidents–United States–Biography. | United States–History–1953-1961.
Classification: LCC E842 .W524 2024 (print) | LCC E842 (ebook) | DDC 973.922092–dc23/eng/20240708
LC record available at https://lccn.loc.gov/2024012516
LC ebook record available at https://lccn.loc.gov/2024012517

ISBN: HB: 978-1-3504-2611-5
PB: 978-1-3504-2612-2
ePDF: 978-1-3504-2614-6
eBook: 978-1-3504-2613-9

Typeset by Deanta Global Publishing Services, Chennai, India
Printed and bound in Great Britain

To find out more about our authors and books visit www.bloomsbury.com and sign up for our newsletters.

In memory of Bernard Talbot and Jocelyn Armstrong

CONTENTS

List of Figures	viii
Acknowledgements	ix
INTRODUCTION: JAMES BOND IN CAMELOT	1
Chapter 1 BEGINNINGS	7
Chapter 2 RISE TO POWER	35
Chapter 3 A YEAR OF CRISIS	59
Chapter 4 MICHAEL CARTER AND THE MISSILE CRISIS	97
Chapter 5 ENDGAME	123
Chapter 6 THE CHARACTER QUESTION	157
Chapter 7 HOLLYWOOD ALLURE	193
Chapter 8 WITHOUT DALLAS	215
CONCLUSION	231
Notes	235
Selected Bibliography	263
Index	265

FIGURES

1.1	A fourteen-year-old JFK at home in Hyannisport. His early years would be marked by a long struggle with ill-health.	12
2.1	The role played by John Kennedy's mother Rose and sisters Eunice, Patricia and Jean was a significant factor in his successful bid for the US Senate in 1952. Here they join the candidate for a TV appearance during the campaign.	38
2.2	Kennedy with his bride Jacqueline Bouvier at their wedding in Rhode Island in September 1953. Over time, her glamour, role as wife and mother, and extensive cultural interests bolstered JFK's image.	40
2.3	Kennedy's performance in his first TV debate with Richard Nixon, including his superior visual impact, was crucial to his victory in the 1960 presidential election.	56
3.1	Kennedy's acrimonious encounter with Soviet leader Nikita Khrushchev in Vienna in June 1961 triggered the Berlin crisis that dominated his first summer in the White House.	74
4.1	Kennedy with his secretary of defense, Robert McNamara, in an ExComm meeting as the Cuban missile crisis drew to a close. Defusing the most dangerous crisis in the Cold War era represented a key achievement of the Kennedy presidency.	120
6.1	John and Robert Kennedy chat with Marilyn Monroe at a New York party following her famous rendition of 'Happy Birthday' on the occasion of JFK's birthday celebrations at Madison Square Garden in May 1962. His affair with her would contribute to the emphasis placed by some historians on his private life and character.	182
7.1	JFK attends a ball held on the occasion of his inauguration as president on 20 January 1961. His sartorial elegance reflected the Hollywood style that would characterize his time in the White House.	196
7.2	The American people were bombarded by images of familial bliss in the White House during the Kennedy years. Here his children Caroline and John Jr. play with JFK in the Oval Office.	201
8.1	John F. Kennedy lying in state in the Capitol Rotunda, following the assassination in Dallas. In the years which followed, many Americans pondered the price paid for this tragedy in terms of the future direction of the country, including US policy in Vietnam.	226

ACKNOWLEDGEMENTS

I would like to thank Iwan Morgan, Robert Green and John Dumbrell for reading parts of the manuscript for this book. Their suggestions were invaluable. I wish to express my gratitude to the journal *American Diplomacy* for permission to make use of material in Chapter 8 that was published originally in its November 2020 edition. Thanks to my wife Amanda for her unstinting support. Thanks also to Atifa Jiwa and Nadine Staes-Polet who have provided generous assistance at Bloomsbury.

INTRODUCTION

JAMES BOND IN CAMELOT

On a spring day in 1960 John F. Kennedy strolled down a street in Washington with his wife Jackie. It was a rare interlude of tranquillity amidst his frenetic campaign for the presidency. Suddenly a car driven by his friend Marion Leiter, who was to be dining with the Kennedys that evening, pulled over. Leiter had with her a famous passenger, Ian Fleming, writer of the James Bond novels. Leiter asked if Fleming could join them for dinner. The presidential candidate shook hands with the celebrated author and said, 'James Bond? But, of course, by all means – do please come.'[1]

At that dinner Fleming advised Kennedy on how best to handle one of the thorniest problems facing America: the challenge posed by Fidel Castro. US policy, Fleming confidently asserted, should be based on an understanding that Cubans were obsessed with three things: sex, money, and religion. The CIA, therefore, should disrupt Cuba and undermine Castro by dropping money over Havana, painting crosses in the sky, and spreading disinformation that US nuclear testing had poisoned the Cuban atmosphere with radioactivity, which stayed longest in men's beards. Hence Cuban men would shave their beards, Fleming explained to Kennedy, thus ending their interest in revolution. JFK listened to the writer with unwavering concentration.[2]

The attention paid by Kennedy to these outlandish proposals reflected his admiration for Fleming. Jackie had introduced her husband to Fleming's novels, and CIA director Allen Dulles discussed them with the young Democrat. Soon Kennedy became an avid fan of the James Bond stories. When two months into his presidency *Life* magazine asked Kennedy to reveal his top ten books, he included on his list Fleming's *From Russia with Love*. From then on, the press would often comment on JFK's fondness for James Bond. Even overseas the Kennedy–Bond connection elicited much comment. After Kennedy had ordered the CIA to carry out the Bay of Pigs invasion in April 1961, the London *Times* mused that James Bond was influencing US foreign policy, with the new president convinced that clandestine operations could undo tyrants like Castro. The admiration between JFK and Fleming was mutual. In his 1965 novel *The Man with the Golden Gun* one of the books in Bond's library is Kennedy's *Profiles in Courage*.[3]

Right up to his assassination in November 1963, Kennedy's life would be oddly entwined with the character of James Bond. Two days before that tragic day in

Dallas, he watched the last film he would ever see: a private screening of *From Russia with Love* with Sean Connery in the lead, the second movie in the Bond franchise. A certain Lee Harvey Oswald also admired that Ian Fleming novel, having borrowed it from the New Orleans Public Library precisely three months before he murdered the president.[4]

The London *Times* proved to be right: on reaching the White House Kennedy did resort to James Bond–type tactics in dealing with Castro. Early in his presidency he sanctioned the Bay of Pigs, the top-secret Operation Mongoose, and even assassination plots to rid the Western Hemisphere of the Cuban revolutionary. But the responsibility for pulling America and the world back from the brink of nuclear war in the Cuban missile crisis of October 1962 changed Kennedy. Thereafter he made diplomacy and reconciliation the motifs of his foreign policy. In his speech at American University in June 1963 he urged his countrymen to adopt a more tolerant attitude towards the Russians, saying, 'No government or social system is so evil that its people must be considered as lacking in virtue.' That summer Kennedy agreed to the establishment of a 'hot-line' between the White House and the Kremlin to permit the sort of speedy superpower communication that could not have taken place during the missile crisis. He also signed the landmark Nuclear Test Ban Treaty. In the final weeks of his life he contemplated further avenues of cooperation with Cuba and Russia, including a Soviet–American moon project.[5]

The change and growth evident in Kennedy's approach to the Cold War was also apparent in his quest for a more equal society at home. In June 1963 he became the first president in the twentieth century to declare that civil rights constituted a moral issue, not just a legal and political one, and to introduce major legislation that would end racial segregation in the South. Change and growth in the way John Kennedy met the political challenges of his presidency represent key themes in this biography.[6]

To focus on Kennedy's political career, however, tells only part of his story. It is recognized that he had an extraordinary appeal, an image unprecedented for its seductive power. As journalist David Halberstam remarked, he was able to come across to the American people 'not just as leader, but as star'. Aspiring for, then attaining high office, Kennedy inhabited the world of politics. But more than any previous president, he was a part of popular culture too. To some degree, this was beyond his control. Youthful, handsome and the son of a famous father, he inevitably attracted enormous attention from the media and the public. But it was also the case that he actively engaged with popular culture. As the son of a Hollywood producer, he grew up with an appreciation of image, performance and presentation. His friend Charles Spalding noticed that when JFK visited him in Los Angeles in 1946, he

> was beginning to notice the parallels between people out there, like personalities drawing crowds. Why did [Gary] Cooper draw a crowd? And the other people out there: Spencer Tracy and Clark Gable and others who were floating through that world . . . he was always interested in seeing whether he had it – the magnetism – or didn't have it. We'd spend hours talking about it.

His subsequent friendship with Frank Sinatra and fascination with Marilyn Monroe showed how Kennedy continued to be immersed in popular culture. His penchant for the exploits of James Bond revealed the same thing.[7]

Kennedy's interest in crooners, movie stars and popular fictional characters was not trivial. It contributed to his understanding that fashioning a dazzling image was crucial to the pursuit of his political ambitions. And Kennedy was right: image did matter. Indeed it is impossible to understand his meteoric rise, election as president and popularity in the White House without considering his beguiling image. In other words, a number of the major questions concerning Kennedy can be answered only by reference to his image. An account of his political role alone does not suffice. Yet in the biographies of Kennedy, image is a theme that has been touched on but not rigorously explored. This book is based on the belief that a close examination of JFK's image is crucial to an understanding of his political success and historical significance.

One reason why the character of James Bond so resonated with Kennedy was surely self-recognition: Bond's guilt-free attitude towards sex mirrored his own. Joseph P. Kennedy's brazen infidelities influenced his son, but JFK also absorbed the nonchalant pleasure-seeking ethos of upper-class England, James Bond's world, during the time he spent in London in the late 1930s when his father was Franklin Roosevelt's ambassador at the Court of St. James. Kennedy's relentless quest for new sexual partners and experiences continued even after his marriage to Jacqueline Bouvier in 1953. His conquests would include Judith Campbell, who was close to Chicago crime boss Sam Giancana, and bohemian socialite Mary Meyer, with whom he smoked marijuana. It was these sorts of escapades that make the Kennedy years seem at times like the history of the early Roman emperors.[8]

Information about Kennedy's philandering, drug-taking and possible Mafia connections emerged in the 1970s. These revelations were too juicy to ignore. Not surprisingly, writers such as Garry Wills, Thomas Reeves and Seymour Hersh highlighted Kennedy's scandalous private behaviour in their biographies. Camelot now seemed a world of tawdry excess rather than noble, chivalric ideals.[9]

It could be argued that JFK's personal life should be of no concern to the responsible historian. His adventures between the sheets are titillating but not relevant to his role as president. But Kennedy scholars should feel obliged to respond to the historical debate on him, and the fact of the matter is that since the 1980s Kennedy's private life has been a major theme in the literature. Moreover, his conduct behind closed doors *does* raise important issues that writers such as Seymour Hersh have been justified in mulling over. His sexual relationship with West German prostitute Ellen Rometsch in the last year of his life – to take but one example – was not a trifling indiscretion because, unbeknownst to JFK, she had originally come from East Germany, where she had been a member of communist party organizations. Blackmail was a possibility. To dismiss Kennedy's promiscuous lifestyle as insignificant, therefore, is not credible. Indeed the only way to determine whether Kennedy's critics have been right to cast aspersions on his character is to dwell on the private JFK. Argument by assertion, simply saying that Kennedy's sexual history did not affect his presidency, is not sufficient. Hence

Kennedy's personal life – in other words, Kennedy the man – will be a key topic in this work. At the same time this book will challenge the twin ideas propagated by his detractors that his character was gravely flawed and that his personal life damaged his presidency.[10]

What this work provides, therefore, is a unique triple history of John Kennedy. It dissects all of the following: his political career, private life and his status as a cultural icon. In addition, this book considers the important hypothetical issue of what would have happened to Kennedy's presidency had he not been assassinated. Biographers often speculate on what would have happened to JFK had he not been murdered. His detractors say he would have taken America into a disastrous war in Vietnam, as Lyndon Johnson did, failed to pass his civil rights bill and perhaps been impeached as his sordid private life may have become public knowledge. His supporters suggest otherwise. Rather than skimming the surface of the hypothetical issue, this study devotes a chapter to a detailed examination of what would have happened to Kennedy's presidency and to America had he not been murdered.

This book does not seek to provide a comprehensive, blow-by-blow history of the Kennedy years. Anyone interested in, say, his record in Laos or aspects of his legislative agenda or his role in the space race will need to look elsewhere. But in terms of presidential policy, I explore many of the salient issues of his time in the White House: the Bay of Pigs invasion, the Cuban missile crisis, the Berlin crisis, Vietnam and civil rights – particularly with the Freedom Rides and his response to the Birmingham crisis in 1963. The core narrative begins in 1940 when the twenty-three-year-old JFK became a public figure with the publication of his first book, *Why England Slept*.

Fundamentally, what I seek to do in this book is to answer what seem to me the key questions concerning JFK's life and presidency: How did he rise to power in American politics, and specifically to what extent was this due to the influence of his father? How did he handle the major issues of his presidency, and did he change as leader during his time in the White House? How did he construct such a remarkably powerful image, and what was the significance of this for his political career? How should his character be defined, and how did his character and private life affect his presidency? What would have happened to a Kennedy presidency had the assassination in Dallas not taken place? In framing answers to these questions, I hope to contribute to our understanding of one of the most iconic leaders in modern history.

Any historian is indebted to the preceding scholarship, and that is the case here. For a decade after his assassination the dominant interpretation of Kennedy was the Camelot school, with Arthur Schlesinger and Theodore Sorensen examining his presidency and William Manchester his death to make the case that he was not just a good but a great president. The interview given by Jacqueline Kennedy to journalist Theodore White for *Life* magazine a week after the assassination was a key influence in shaping this initial scholarship. Worried that historians would interpret JFK's presidency uncharitably, she deliberately used the power of myth to help ensure that the American people would always view Kennedy kindly, whatever biographers might say. She mentioned that she and JFK had liked to listen at night to a record of the hit musical *Camelot* about King Arthur and the Knights of the Round Table. Manchester saw his lead and wrote up the article putting the Kennedy years in the context of the Arthurian legend. What he was suggesting was that JFK had been such a noble, outstanding leader it was appropriate to think of him in mythological terms. Sorensen and Schlesinger wrote their works with editorial input from Jackie, who used more coercive, legalistic methods to ensure Manchester's work was to her liking – she took him to court. That the Camelot school had put the debate on Kennedy at the interpretative extremes was perhaps most apparent from Sorensen's argument that he should not be rated below any other twentieth-century president, including Franklin D. Roosevelt who had been elected four times, pulled America out of the Great Depression, built a welfare state and defeated fascism in the Second World War – and has been the one twentieth-century president judged consistently as great by historians.[11]

As the Camelot school had been so extreme in its praise for Kennedy, it was inevitable that there would be a backlash, and that is precisely what occurred. More critical scholars felt they had to be savage rather than measured in their attacks as Schlesinger and Sorensen et al. had built the ramparts of Camelot so deep and so high. This revisionist or counter-Camelot interpretation began to emerge in the 1970s and was full-blown by the 1980s and 1990s. Revelations about Kennedy's infidelities, use of drugs and possible dealings with the Mob surfaced. In addition, it was clear by the mid-1970s, as South Vietnam fell to the communists, that US policy in Vietnam had been a disastrous failure, and as JFK had escalated US involvement in South Vietnam, he appeared to bear some of the responsibility for that calamity. In the 1980s and 1990s works by three major writers – Garry Wills, Thomas Reeves and Seymour Hersh – came to define the counter-Camelot school. Two key arguments were central to their effort to challenge the rose-tinted view propagated by Schlesinger, Sorensen and others: first, that his character was flawed, as demonstrated by his reckless private life, and this had damaged his presidency; and second, he had been an aggressive Cold Warrior as revealed by such policies as his drive to topple Castro, his escalation in Vietnam and the increase in military spending he authorized. The counter-Camelot school also emphasized, in a negative way, Joseph Kennedy's role. He was portrayed as an amoral influence, inculcating into JFK and his brothers a win-at-all-costs attitude in their approach to life and politics and a disrespectful view of women in their private lives.[12]

Historical debates are often triangular: an established view followed by a diametrically opposed interpretation followed by a third wave of scholarship that seeks to occupy the middle-ground. This was the case with the debate on Kennedy. At the start of the 1980s Herbert Parmet produced a two-volume biography that was generally positive about JFK but avoided Camelot hyperbole. For the depth of archival research – he had mined materials at the John F. Kennedy Library – it was pathbreaking. A decade later James Giglio in a wonderfully lucid and insightful work on the Kennedy presidency staked out roughly the same ground as had Parmet. Another work of importance at the start of the 1990s was written by distinguished biographer Nigel Hamilton. Despite its title, *JFK: Reckless Youth*, it was even-handed and in places positive about Kennedy. Taking the story up to 1946, it was the most authoritative account of the young Kennedy that had been written.[13]

Since the turn of the millennium the two most important works on Kennedy have been penned by Robert Dallek and Fredrik Logevall, two scholars with a formidable and award-winning body of work on US foreign relations and the modern presidency. Dallek's *John F. Kennedy: An Unfinished Life, 1917-1963* (2003) was a richly detailed work, based on the most recently released archival material, that blended praise and criticism. In one respect it was truly pathbreaking: for the light it shed on a crucial issue in JFK's life, his ill-health. Documents on this had long been sealed, but Dallek was the first scholar to be able to examine his declassified medical records. He argued persuasively that Kennedy's illnesses and the medications he received for them did not impair his presidential leadership. His revelation of an affair between Kennedy and a White House intern (who turned out to be Mimi Beardsley) received a lot of press attention at the time of publication. Logevall's superb *JFK* (2020) examined Kennedy's early years and entry into American politics, taking the story up to 1956. It is the first in a planned two-volume life, and for its thematic sophistication in connecting Kennedy to the broader themes of modern American history, and its perceptive arguments such as how JFK was both part of and independent from his family, it promises to be a key study of Kennedy's life and presidency.[14]

As well as stirring Kennedy's imagination, reflecting his interest in popular culture, and creating a character whose hedonism matched his own, there was one other way in which the James Bond stories resonated with JFK: the background of the author. Like Ian Fleming, the man he had got to know during the 1960 presidential campaign, JFK owed his start in life to the success of a father who had prospered in the world of banking. The story of John Kennedy's rise to power is linked therefore to the role played by the family patriarch, Joseph P. Kennedy. This book will begin with an examination of John Kennedy's early years, including the important issue of whether his rise to power was due more to the influence of his father or his own talents and achievements.[15]

Chapter 1

BEGINNINGS

John Fitzgerald Kennedy, son of Joseph and Rose, was born in Brookline, Massachusetts, on 29 May 1917. For someone who would go on to fashion American foreign policy at a critical juncture in twentieth-century history, the timing of his birth was noteworthy for it coincided with a pivotal moment in US history: only weeks earlier President Woodrow Wilson secured congressional approval to take the United States into the First World War. That would prove a milestone on the road to the superpower status that would become JFK's inheritance on winning the presidency in 1960.

Twenty-three years after his birth as the second son of Joe and Rose – and twenty years prior to his presidency – JFK became a public figure with the publication in 1940 of a successful book, *Why England Slept*, the initial part of the process by which he developed a dazzling image that would help him win elected office six years later in his campaign for the House of Representatives.

Several factors shaped the first two decades of Kennedy's life. Chronic ill-health – more on this anon – plagued his early years. This furnished him with a profound sense of the potential brevity of life, which would intensify his determination to rise rapidly up the political ladder, and create a desire to enjoy life romantically and carnally while he was around to do so. It is easy to think of John Kennedy, extrapolating back from his self-assured public performances during the 1960 campaign and his presidency, as a confident individual; but an early sense of his own physical frailty must have created pockets of insecurity that co-existed with the social confidence he felt as a result of his wealthy, privileged background. Revealingly, Judith Campbell, his lover in the early 1960s, would be surprised how often he needed her confirmation that he 'looked just right' when appearing in public. His early feelings of inadequacy were amplified by the competitive relationship he had with his bigger, stronger, short-tempered, opinionated elder brother Joseph Jr., with that rivalry evident in the various sporting activities that constituted a major part of Kennedy family culture.[1]

This sense of weakness and inadequacy had a positive consequence: the development of attributes that could impress people in other ways, including wit and charm. Long-term, those would prove to be professional assets, making for a charismatic political persona. At the same time, the enforced solitariness of all those days laying in a hospital bed nurtured a bookishness. He liked to read history and biography, but he also devoured Robert Louis Stevenson, Rudyard Kipling, John Bunyan and Harriet Beecher Stowe. He read far more widely than, for example, his younger brother Robert. Although JFK's academic performance underwhelmed before he went to Harvard, often playing the role of prankster when at Choate, his early reading lay the foundation for his subsequent intellectual development, of which *Why England Slept* would be the first conspicuous sign.[2]

The parlous health of John, or Jack as he was often called, was, of course, of deep concern to his parents. Our understanding of his relationship with Rose and Joe Sr. has changed over the years. The general view, furthered in part by her polished performances when campaigning for her sons and by her 1974 autobiography *Times to Remember*, used to be that Rose was the model matriarch who skillfully raised these fantastically successful children. As the extent of Joe Sr.'s philandering was revealed in the years after his death in 1969, including an affair with screen siren Gloria Swanson, it seemed clear that her forbearance had been essential in keeping the family together. Joe's waywardness was also evident in a political sense with his notorious stance as Franklin D. Roosevelt's ambassador in London in favour of US isolationism and the appeasement of Adolf Hitler. Biographer Nigel Hamilton's excellent 1992 study of the young John Kennedy, *JFK: Reckless Youth*, was an important part of the process by which a sounder view emerged of JFK's relationship with his parents. In fact he had a frosty relationship with a mother who was detached, obsessed as she was with the seemingly contradictory pursuits of religious faith and fashion. She dealt with marital pressures caused in part by a philandering husband by travelling for long periods, to Paris and elsewhere. It was Rose herself, in her autobiography, who revealed how a five-year-old Jack reacted to one such absence: 'Gee, *you're* a great mother to go away and leave your children all alone.' In later years his assessment of Rose was even more severe, describing her as a 'nothing'. Rose was not some sort of caricatured ogre. Of course she cared about her children, and had a studious interest in their development, evident in the file cards she bought from a local stationery store on which, as she put it, she 'set to work cataloguing names, dates and events in a systematic way'. Information such as church of baptism, names of godparents, body weight and vaccination records was recorded. 'I did little diaper-changing, but I had to be sure there were plenty of good-quality diapers on hand,' perhaps showed less practical attentiveness. With his affair in his early twenties with Inga Arvad, there is very much the sense that JFK was so enamoured of her not just because of her physical beauty and erotic appeal, but also a sort of maternal *warmth* he had not previously experienced.[3]

As a parent, Joe was different. Domineering, as in all facets of his life, he was nevertheless consistently affectionate towards his children, including Jack. Whenever there were problems, he would be attentive. He possessed the gift of encouragement. 'You know I really think you are a pretty good guy,' he wrote to the teenage Jack, 'and my only interest is in doing what is best for you'. In later years JFK would recall how one of his dad's best attributes was his ability to turn a negative into a positive. If ever Jack seemed to have experienced a setback, Joe would tell him it was actually the best thing that could have happened and that it in fact represented a valuable opportunity. Family friends noticed that Joe was at home more than they expected, given his status as a titan of American business, organizing the household. Unlike Rose, he was demonstrative in his affection, tactile. Rose recalled how 'He would sweep them [the children] into his arms and hug them, and grin at them and talk to them'. He did not administer spankings to the children; Rose did, often using a coat-hanger. That is not to say that JFK's relationship with his father was without strain or complexity, and in particular his domineering tendencies grated on a boy who was naturally independent (rebelling, for instance, against the family's strict time-keeping ethos). In a 1965 interview for the Kennedy Library, Priscilla Wear – a White House staffer and presidential lover who spent a lot of time with JFK – opined that Jack's 'relationship with his father was very strained. He once said that he could never be around his father for more than three days without having to get away. His father was terribly dictatorial, always giving him advice on things. I think he just never felt relaxed around him.' Still, the emotional reality remained that he was closer to his father than his mother.[4]

The nature of Joe's relationship with Jack has received much attention from biographers. To his detractors, JFK, his political career in particular, was in the main the creation of a ruthlessly driven father determined to place one of his sons in the White House, once he had failed himself to reach the pinnacle of power in America. Puppet and puppet master was, allegedly, the essential dynamic. This work argues that JFK's political success was due largely to his own gifts and accomplishments. In other words, JFK's own agency in his rise to power should be emphasized.[5]

That is not to suggest that Joe Kennedy was unimportant to Jack's rise; it is a question of the significance of paternal influence in relation to JFK's own. In what ways did Joe influence Jack's rise? In short, four things: money, ambition, Hollywood connections and political engagement. 'Money is the mother's milk of politics' is a famous maxim, and JFK's campaigns would always be exceedingly well financed thanks to Joe's fabulous wealth, much of it made on the unregulated Wall Street market of the 1920s, with that wealth preserved and extended by having the nous to offload stocks prior to the Crash in 1929. That money did not guarantee electoral success, but it certainly helped.[6]

Joe's ambition was vast, and he inculcated it into his children, especially his sons. Despite quickly constructing a life of wealth and privilege – one of the richest men in America by the 1930s – he harboured a very strong sense of outsider status which derived from his Irish Catholicism. He had been excluded from the most prestigious clubs on campus when attending Harvard due to that prejudice and snobbery. This left him with a deep and abiding resentment against WASP condescension. 'I was born here,' he once exclaimed. 'My children were born here. What the hell do I have to do to be an American?' Even his entry into the world of banking and finance took place against the backdrop of WASP-Irish distrust. Vexed by the control exerted by old money over Boston's financial institutions, Joe's father Patrick J. Kennedy and other Irish businessmen established an independent bank, the Columbia Trust Company, that had endured for two decades. When a large Boston bank attempted to buy it out, Patrick Kennedy asked his son, who by this time had become a state bank examiner and in this capacity had visited banks across eastern Massachusetts, to lead the effort to prevent the takeover. Joe Kennedy won that battle, and at only twenty-five years old became the president of Columbia Trust, reputedly the youngest bank president in the country. That intense immigrant drive, that determination not to allow any barriers, social or otherwise, to bar his rise was passed on by Joe to his children, including Jack. With JFK, his charm and affability would often conceal that ferocious drive, but it was there and would become particularly evident when running for office.[7]

As well as accumulating a fortune on Wall Street, Joe Kennedy made money as a Hollywood producer in the 1920s, making for the most part safe, commercial movies. It was during this period that he embarked on a tempestuous affair with Hollywood siren Gloria Swanson. This phase in his career left Joe with a deep understanding of the importance of image. In time he would see the similarities between projecting the image of a showbiz star and of a politician – not least in terms of good press. That consideration was why Joe would come to pay *New York Times* journalist Arthur Krock in order to keep his name in the headlines. A young JFK observed all of this, developing his own fascination with Hollywood, where he spent time as a young man. Affairs with stars such as Gene Tierney, Marilyn Monroe and other actresses would be a part of this, and when his sister Patricia married actor Peter Lawford in 1954, those ties became stronger still. The key point is that more than any other politician of his generation JFK had a deep, Hollywood-style understanding of the importance of image in politics. He developed his own, more considerable expertise on the construction of image, but the spark for his preoccupation with image came from his father. And this factor is crucial to an understanding of JFK's rapid rise in American politics.[8]

Joe also nurtured in Jack a fascination with politics. Joe understood that the election of Franklin Roosevelt in 1932 had changed the United States, that whereas in the 1920s the movers and shakers on Wall Street in an era of supine presidents were the most important people, power had now shifted to Washington DC with a charismatic leader, revitalized presidency and activist federal government. Hence, Joe moved into the political arena, and did so by striving to get close to Roosevelt. He contributed money to FDR's 1932 presidential campaign and backed his re-election campaign four years later by releasing a book, *I'm for Roosevelt*. The quid pro quo sought by Joe was a prominent position in the New Deal. No Cabinet post was forthcoming, but in 1934 FDR appointed him chair of the Securities and Exchange Commission to regulate Wall Street. Later he was appointed as chair of the U.S. Maritime Commission and then US ambassador in London, a plum diplomatic assignment viewed by Joe as a stepping-stone to the presidency. His controversial commitment to a policy of appeasement and US isolationism would thwart that ambition, but his engagement with politics stimulated JFK's own. Politics was often the focus of family dinner-time conversations. Jack and his brothers absorbed their father's lofty political ambitions. Deepening Jack's burgeoning interest in politics was his wider family connections to the political world. Joe's father, Patrick J. Kennedy, had been a ward boss in East Boston and served in the Massachusetts House of Representatives and Senate. Joe's father-in-law John F. 'Honey Fitz' Fitzgerald had been Mayor of Boston, remained a prominent political figure thereafter and, when JFK ran for Congress in 1946, Honey Fitz was still around to support his grandson.[9]

As a young JFK negotiated complex family dynamics, he had to battle with serious ill-health. The sickness was perennial – most of the days of his life were lived in pain, often acute. On several occasions he was either at death's door or perceived to be. The impact of his ill-health on his mindset is clear: it enhanced the pleasure-seeking ethos based around sexual gratification that he had learned from a father who – JFK once recalled – encouraged his sons 'to get laid as often as possible'.[10]

The significance of Kennedy's appalling health for his character development needs to be considered as critics – even at the time, notably aides to presidential rival Lyndon Johnson – have accused him of deceiving the American people by covering it up, particularly by lying about his Addison's disease in the 1960 presidential campaign. But as *the* authority on JFK's medical issues Robert Dallek has argued, Kennedy was hardly the first president to be less than forthcoming about his health. William Henry Harrison, Zachary Taylor, Grover Cleveland, Woodrow Wilson, Calvin Coolidge, Franklin Roosevelt and Dwight Eisenhower all concealed their maladies. That most Americans did not even know that FDR was disabled has not prevented historians from judging him to be the one great president in twentieth-century American history. Nor has Eisenhower's concealments deterred revisionist scholars from waxing lyrical about his leadership. Hence, it would be a double standard to castigate Kennedy for a lack of candour that has not been considered crucial to assessments of his presidential predecessors.[11]

Rather than displaying a lack of character, JFK's response to the sequence of medical crises in his life revealed courage, stoicism, a remarkable humour in the face of adversity and a determination that his ill-health would not prevent him from playing an active role in the nation's affairs. How many young men in his situation of privilege and wealth would have resisted the temptation to forsake the pressures of public life for the cosseted comforts of Palm Beach and Hyannisport? That he did so reflects well on both his courage and his public-spiritedness. In short, JFK displayed enormous character in combatting ill-health.

At the age of two Kennedy had a life-threatening case of scarlet fever. For over two months he struggled to recover in a hospital and then in a sanatorium. In the 1920s he endured numerous illnesses, including bronchitis, ear infections, German measles and whooping cough. As a teenager, things went from bad to worse. He had difficulty in putting on weight. In 1931 he collapsed due to acute stomach pain. He had an operation for appendicitis, but by the autumn of 1932 he was again experiencing abdominal discomfort. By the winter of 1934, at the age of seventeen, he was extremely ill, losing weight and suffering from hives. Doctors suspected leukemia and hence that his life was in danger. 'It seems that I was much sicker than I thought I was,' he told his Choate classmate K. LeMoyne Billings, 'and am supposed to be dead.'[12]

By the mid-1930s the underlying condition that accounted for these abdominal problems was finally diagnosed: it was colitis. The standard treatment for colitis at the Mayo Clinic in Rochester, Minnesota, which began to treat JFK in 1934, included a careful diet and stress reduction. By the late 1930s, however, a new, potentially effective treatment emerged: corticosteroids, created from adrenal

Figure 1.1 A fourteen-year-old JFK at home in Hyannisport. His early years would be marked by a long struggle with ill-health. (*Source*: Wikimedia, public domain, Search media – Wikimedia Commons.)

extracts. The use of steroids as a treatment became possible when a technique to implant steroid pellets under the skin was devised. It has long been known that Kennedy took steroids after being diagnosed with Addison's disease in 1947. But it may well have been the case that he was receiving steroid treatments as early as 1937 for his colitis. There is a solid account of JFK implanting a pellet in his leg, as would be done with steroids, in 1946 – that is, before his diagnosis for Addison's disease.[13]

Colitis, along with back problems and Addison's disease (the malfunctioning of the adrenal gland), was the major health issue afflicting Kennedy. It was not known when steroids were developed that their side effects included degeneration of the lumbar region and damage to adrenal function. The steroids administered for his colitis, then, may have caused or at least exacerbated Kennedy's spinal problems and Addison's disease.[14]

By 1938 Kennedy was suffering from 'an occasional pain in his right sacro-iliac joint'. While playing tennis in late 1940, he felt severe pain in his lower right back and was hospitalized for ten days. A back support helped ease the discomfort, but he continued to suffer from periodic back pain. His wartime service in the Pacific thus aggravated but did not cause his spinal problems. With the side effects of the steroids (which he probably took for his colitis) continuing to damage his back, he had a spinal operation in 1944 that revealed osteoporosis and removed 'some abnormally soft disc interspace material'. Were bone loss to persist, Kennedy's back problems would continue in the future. That proved to be the case, and a decade later, major spinal surgery would take him to death's door.[15]

After his election to the House of Representatives in 1946 Kennedy's health deteriorated, for the following year during a trip to Ireland he fell ill. An English doctor diagnosed Addison's disease, telling Winston Churchill's daughter-in-law Pamela, 'That young American friend of yours, he hasn't got a year to live.' On the voyage back to the United States he became so ill that on his arrival a priest came aboard to administer the last rites. Regular oral doses of cortisone would be used to treat his Addison's disease. But he would suffer from the condition for the rest of his life. His back pain became more consistent and severe too. By 1950–1 the bones bearing the weight of his spinal column were collapsing and there were compression fractures in the lower spinal area. He had to use crutches to ascend a flight of stairs. His back problems would reach a crisis point in 1954, just as he was grappling with a political crisis triggered by the fall of Republican senator Joseph McCarthy. In addition to these severe medical challenges, JFK – it should be noted – had to learn to live with a series of terrible family tragedies: the institutionalization of his sister Rosemary, who had mental health issues, after Joe Sr. authorized a lobotomy in 1941 that rendered her permanently incapacitated; the death of Joe Jr. in combat in 1944 and the death of his sister Kathleen, whom he adored, in a plane crash in France in 1948. The death of Joe Jr. had particular implications for JFK's life in politics. It is clear from what he said to Inga Arvad and others that he harboured political ambitions prior to his elder brother's demise. It was not a case of JFK embarking on a political career he would never have considered had his elder brother not died. After 1944, however, he was the eldest remaining Kennedy son, and so the focus of the family would be on his rise to power.[16]

Despite his severe ill-health, Kennedy became a public figure in July 1940, six years before he entered politics by running for Congress. That month his first book, *Why England Slept*, was published. In any account of Kennedy's rise to power, *Why England Slept* should figure prominently. It established key parts of an image so appealing that it would help take him to the White House. *Why England Slept* defined his early ideas on American foreign policy. These ideas shaped his thinking on international affairs throughout his political career. Hence, a full understanding of Kennedy's approach as president to foreign policy cannot be achieved without considering *Why England Slept*. JFK's book also demonstrated his capacity to think independently of his overbearing father. Unlike his elder brother Joe Jr., Jack rejected the isolationist views of Joe Sr., even though he was Franklin Roosevelt's ambassador at the Court of St. James at the time. Appeasing Hitler, as his father had urged FDR to do, was a fool's errand, realized the young JFK, and so America needed to rearm with alacrity in confronting the Nazi menace. The maturity and intellectual independence he showed in distancing himself from Joe Kennedy's response to Hitler was impressive and reflected well on his character. He was hardly the only young American to reach the conclusion in 1940 that the Nazi threat required something more robust from the United States than the supine approach advocated by the isolationists. But it was far more difficult to do so with a father as powerful, intimidating and dogmatically convinced of the wisdom of isolationism as Joe Kennedy. This highlights a broader theme of this study: although Joe Kennedy's role in driving his son to the White House has often been seen as crucial, of greater importance than that paternal influence was John Kennedy's own talents.

Why England Slept was a reworking of JFK's undergraduate thesis at Harvard, entitled 'Appeasement at Munich', which examined the British appeasement of Nazi Germany. The impulse for Kennedy's study was the time he spent in England in the late 1930s after his father's appointment by FDR as the US ambassador to Britain. This period saw the young JFK mixing with the social and political elite, which furnished him with a lifelong admiration for the way the British upper class combined a commitment to public service with the private pursuit of pleasure. His stay in England meant he was close at hand as the appeasement policy championed by Prime Minister Neville Chamberlain was applied, most infamously at the 1938 Munich conference, and failed, as the outbreak of the Second World War at the start of September 1939 made clear. When deciding on a topic for his Harvard thesis, he turned to the subject already preoccupying him: the British response to Hitler. He studied harder than he ever had, but with the support of a researcher and stenographers. In their evaluation of his thesis, Harvard faculty identified various shortcomings, including JFK's stylistic idiosyncrasies. But they generally admired Kennedy's examination of British appeasement, and that summer he graduated cum laude in political science.[17]

It was at this juncture that Joe Kennedy played an important role in raising his son's profile: he put JFK in touch with his journalist friend Arthur Krock who read the thesis. Believing that 'it would make a very welcome and very useful book', Krock found a publisher, Wilfred Funk, via his own agent, edited the text and gave the book the title of *Why England Slept*. Joe Kennedy also arranged for the media tycoon Henry Luce to write a gushing introduction to the book. In July 1940, *Why England Slept* came out. John Kennedy had become a published author at the age of only twenty-three.[18]

To be sure, Joe Kennedy's connections were important in ensuring that his son's thesis was published, but at the same time *Why England Slept* was the product of JFK's rapid intellectual development at Harvard. A common misconception about his ability has arisen as a result of the comparison with his bright, popular, outgoing elder brother, Joe Jr., already a figure of note on the campus by the time JFK arrived at Harvard. The younger Kennedy contributed to this impression of intellectual inferiority. When he met Assistant Professor of Government Payson Wild at Winthrop House, the new student told him, 'I want you to know I'm not bright like my brother Joe.' But the recollections of Wild (who knew Joe Jr. well and was a major influence on JFK) are instructive. Jack, he observed, was a 'far more thorough' student than his brother, and was 'genuinely interested in political problems and in international affairs'. A comment made by the chief dining room stewardess, who became a mother-figure to many of the students, struck Wild: 'Now don't be too enraptured by older boy Joe, who's a handsome, wonderful fellow, but it's his brother Jack who is really the diamond in the rough and who is the one who is the deeper thinker.'[19]

More than he ever had, JFK applied himself. Edward Crane, an undergraduate who worked at Harvard's Union Library, noticed that Kennedy along with two other undergraduates were 'obviously the voracious readers'. When the library closed at 10 p.m., he continued reading by taking out books that had to be returned by 9 a.m. the following day. Crane also learned of Kennedy's early political ambitions over a late-night bowl of soup when he said: 'Well, the big decisions of the future are all going to be made at Washington, D.C.' Payson Wild, too, noted JFK's serious-minded diligence. He was genuinely interested in political theory, including the ideas of Aristotle and Plato. Soon Kennedy's grades improved. He started at Harvard as a C student. By his senior year he achieved a B+ average, making him eligible to research an honours thesis, which led to *Why England Slept*. Kennedy's impressive application at Harvard suggested that he was ambitious; and the quality of the thesis, that he was smart. It confirmed what his parents already knew to be the case. Much to their surprise, tests from his schooldays showed that Jack's IQ was higher than that of the supposedly brilliant Joe Jr. *Why England Slept*, then, was the product of not only his father's influence in high places, but JFK's own ability and diligence.[20]

Once the book was out, Jack promoted it energetically to help ensure its success. As the son of America's ambassador in London, *Why England Slept* was bound to attract attention. But JFK did not leave it to chance. He gave radio interviews, signed copies and sent them out, and called bookshops to check on *Why England Slept*'s progress. His father promoted the book too, and rumours spread that he secretly purchased many copies – though there is no hard evidence to substantiate that theory. If the story is true, the book (in reality) sold 50,000 copies by spring 1941; if it is not, the figure was 80,000. Either way, sales were substantial. The reviews, in *The New York Times* and elsewhere, were favourable. Even FDR was impressed, writing to Jack to praise his work as 'a great argument for acting and speaking from a position of strength at all times'. By twenty-three, JFK had become a bestselling and much praised author. That is how many Americans became aware of him.[21]

This was important as the success of *Why England Slept* established a key component of the image that has seduced America ever since: he was a man of letters. When he was in Congress, his literary credentials set him apart from most other politicians, making him appear more sophisticated. Sixteen years later his second book, the Pulitzer Prize–winning *Profiles in Courage*, would enlarge his reputation as a literary figure.

As well as initiating the construction of his potent image, the writing of *Why England Slept* enabled Kennedy to define his views on American foreign policy. These ideas would continue to shape his thinking on international affairs once he entered politics. The major themes of his book were the differences between democracies and dictatorships, and the importance of military preparation. In highlighting the necessity of military readiness in a dangerous, unpredictable world, JFK was in agreement with his father whose diplomatic dispatches back to the State Department bemoaned Blighty's elephantine rearmament. But the conclusion drawn from that concern differed between Joe and Jack. Isolationist

Joe argued that Britain's military weakness meant that the United States must not enter the war as it would be backing a nation that Hitler would easily defeat. Jack, however, asserted that the lessons of British appeasement were that the United States must rearm quickly, engage with world politics and be prepared to go to war with Nazi Germany. 'We must always keep our armaments equal to our commitments. Munich should teach us that; we must realize that any bluff will be called. We cannot tell anyone to keep out of our hemisphere unless our armaments *and the people behind these armaments* are prepared to back up the command, even to the ultimate point of going to war.' A strong national defence and resilience in dealing with aggressive dictators would remain core ideas in JFK's thinking on US foreign policy when the Cold War began.[22]

Distancing himself from his father in the national debate on how to respond to Hitler was no easy matter for Jack, especially given his father's prominent role as FDR's ambassador in London. But he was frank about his disagreement with his dad, though he was never disrespectful about him. Wild recalled that JFK 'made it clear to me that he did not follow his father's line' on Nazi Germany. That demonstrated a capacity for independent thinking and sound judgement that were impressive character traits, particularly given his father's domineering proclivities.[23]

Jack's commitment to a strong national defence deepened as he considered the differences between democracies and dictatorships. Based, as it was, on respect for the individual, democracy was a better system than totalitarianism, he said. But democratic governments were at a disadvantage when it came to military spending as they had to take public opinion on board, unlike dictatorships such as Nazi Germany. In Britain various groups, including unions and pacifists, had opposed the military build-up that Nazi aggression made essential. The lesson for America's leaders, said Kennedy, was the need to press ahead with increases in defence spending even if that meant ignoring public pressure.[24]

That *Why England Slept* signalled a lifelong commitment on Kennedy's part to high levels of military spending is well known. A subtler influence is how it made him ambivalent towards the public when it came to policy-making. Once his political career began, he displayed a remarkable ability to charm, seduce and inspire the American people. But his reflections on appeasement led to a simultaneous distrust of the public, a belief that leaders should sometimes do things in secret so that their actions were not subject to the whims of public opinion. It was important, he thought, that the national interest be uncompromised by a public opinion that might well be wrong-headed, as it had been in the case of the British people's attitude towards rearmament in the 1930s. At root, Kennedy's was an elitist view, a belief that a talented coterie of public-spirited leaders knew better than the people what was in their best interests. That elitism reflected in part the social privilege of his early life but also his experience of mixing with the English upper class during his father's ambassadorship.

Why England Slept thus furnished JFK with an acute sense of the importance not only of military preparation but of the need at times for *secrecy* in policymaking. This represents an interesting parallel with the way he approached his private affairs in which clandestine conduct was a prerequisite for his philandering. More importantly, in time his wariness over the public's influence made him believe that he should often use the CIA to achieve foreign policy objectives. There is a sense in which the roots of the Bay of Pigs and Operation Mongoose go back to *Why England Slept*. This fascination with the intelligence world would also be apparent in his fondness for the James Bond stories of Ian Fleming.

Why England Slept, therefore, had a manifold significance to Kennedy's rise. It initiated the process by which his dazzling image was formed, establishing the idea that he was a man of letters. It signified an impressive independence from a father whose judgement on foreign policy was less sound than his own. It defined his early thinking on international affairs. His belief in military preparation and steel in confronting dictators influenced his approach to foreign policy right up until Dallas. On this, the first great political challenge of his life – how to handle Hitler – he had got it right. But he had overlearned the lessons of appeasement, for as the Cold War emerged he was so committed to a policy of military toughness that he was somewhat sympathetic even to the outlandish criticisms of US foreign policy made by Joe McCarthy. His distrust of the public's influence on foreign policymaking would in time help make him an ardent proponent of CIA activism; the consequences of that penchant for the covert would sometimes turn out to be damaging. The long-term challenge for Kennedy was whether he would be able to refine his thinking on American foreign policy on the basis of observation and experience so as to fashion a more nuanced, flexible and potentially effective approach. In particular, would he come to a greater appreciation of the merits of diplomacy in managing the Cold War?

Why England Slept had yet one further significance. Kennedy's first book, in effect, started a narrative on the need for heroic leadership. The United States required a president with the wisdom and strength to stand up to Hitler – in short, an American Churchill. In the rest of his life – including his wartime service, his speeches in Congress and his second book, *Profiles in Courage* – he continued this narrative. What was suggested was that he himself was the wise, courageous leader which America needed in meeting the great challenges that lay ahead. In October 1962, facing down the Russians in the Cuban missile crisis, Kennedy would be able to complete this narrative on his potential greatness as the nation's leader.

Dwelling on profound issues of war and peace did not distract Kennedy from the pursuit of pleasure in his private life. Influenced by his father's brazen promiscuity, JFK became the archetypal playboy, intent on guiltless sexual conquests – the more the better and with little emotional involvement. Then came Inga Arvad. His brief, but intense, affair with her over the winter of 1941–2, as Pearl Harbor propelled America into war, had a significance characteristic of none of his previous dalliances. For one thing, the FBI suspected that the Danish beauty was a Nazi spy. Given that Kennedy had been working in naval intelligence since October 1941, his affair with her seemingly had national-security implications. For another, the way J. Edgar Hoover's agents collected information on the Kennedy–Arvad affair – intercepting their mail, tapping her telephone, tracking their movements – meant that when Kennedy was elected president, Hoover was in possession of an incriminating file on his sexual life that stretched back two decades. That gave Hoover a certain power over the young president, which probably explained Kennedy's decision to retain his services as FBI director while appointing brother Bobby as attorney general to keep an eye on the nefarious intelligence chief. More broadly, Kennedy's affair with the woman he called 'Inga Binga' raises the issue of character that has become so central to the critique of historians determined to demolish the claim that JFK was a great man and leader.[25]

Kennedy's relationship with Inga Arvad also sheds light on the extent to which his father shaped his early life, facilitating his rise to power. Specifically, did Joe Kennedy compel his son to end an affair that made him happy but which jeopardized his future political career? More important than all of this to an understanding of Kennedy, to the emotional fabric of his life, is the depth of his feelings for Arvad: he loved her, really loved her. Nigel Hamilton has argued that she was *the* love of his life, not Jacqueline Bouvier. Only Mary Meyer, the bohemian artist who became Kennedy's lover during his presidential years, and Jacqueline Bouvier as the mother of his children could have challenged Arvad's pre-eminent place in his heart.[26]

It is noteworthy that the biography of Arvad shared certain similarities with Meyer's. Both were worldly women with husbands and lovers in their past. Kennedy couldn't trivialize or patronize them as if they were inexperienced debutantes. And, crucially, both knew him for what he was – a flawed and damaged hedonist – and yet still loved him. It was that authentic knowledge of him that accounts for the depth of his feelings for them. He did not have to hide who he was. But whereas Meyer used that intimate knowledge of Kennedy to urge him to examine himself critically, Arvad usually dwelt on his admirable characteristics and in the process boosted his self-esteem.[27]

For a man who would later be associated with James Bond, his favourite fictional character, it was fitting that the first great love of his life should have had an exotic and glamorous backstory that could have been conceived by Ian Fleming for one of his 'Bond girls'. Born in Copenhagen, she trained as a dancer at the Royal Theatre there, won the title of Beauty Queen of Denmark, eloped with an Egyptian diplomat, travelled to Egypt, divorced, starred in an MGM movie and married its director Paul Fejos – all by her early twenties.[28]

Soon estranged from Fejos, she worked in the mid-1930s in Berlin for a Danish newspaper. It was this period of her life that would later arouse the suspicions of the FBI and doom her relationship with JFK. She met and apparently charmed a good many of the most prominent leaders in Nazi Germany – not only Goering, Goebbels and Himmler, but Hitler himself, whom she interviewed twice. Her impressions of Hitler were hardly unfavourable: 'he is not evil as he is depicted by the enemies of Germany. He is without doubt an idealist, he believes that he is doing the right thing for Germany'. For his part Hitler invited her to join him in his box at the 1936 Berlin Olympics, describing her as 'a perfect example of Nordic beauty'. Arvad later claimed that she spurned an offer in 1940, made during her final visit to Berlin as she was about to go to America, to join the German Propaganda Ministry.[29]

Once in New York she studied at the Columbia School of Journalism. By charming Arthur Krock she secured a job at the conservative *Washington Times-Herald,* where she wrote a column called 'Did You Happen to See?' for which she interviewed the movers and shakers of the nation's capital. Arvad became friends with JFK's favourite sister, Kathleen, who also worked for the paper, and it was through 'Kick' that Inga met Jack. Arvad would later recall the impression he made on her: 'He had the charm that makes birds come out of their trees. He looked like her [Kathleen's] twin, the same thick mop of hair, the same blue eyes, natural, engaging, ambitious, warm and when he walked into a room you knew he was there, not pushing, not domineering but exuding animal magnetism.'[30]

As the author of *Why England Slept*, Kennedy was already newsworthy, and so Arvad's boss asked her to secure an interview with him. She did so and the article appeared in late November 1941. It was gushing. She cited his Harvard education, bestselling book, prominent father and his limitless charm. 'He is the best listener I have come across between Haparanda and Yokohama,' she said. 'Elder men like to hear his views, which are sound and astonishingly objective for so young a man.'[31]

Arvad's admiration for Kennedy was ardent. The feeling was reciprocated. Soon they were lovers. While in Washington, Jack and Inga double-dated with Kathleen and her colleague at the *Times-Herald* John White. Once, as JFK put it, 'They shagged my ass down to South Carolina because I was going around with a Scandinavian blonde, and they thought she was a spy,' Arvad would take the long train journey to Charleston so they could continue to see each other. The affair was passionate. During their three-night stay at Charleston's Fort Sumter Hotel in February 1942, the couple engaged 'in sexual intercourse on a number of occasions', reported an FBI agent. Arvad's son Ronald McCoy (from her subsequent marriage to cowboy actor Tim McCoy) revealed his mother's recollections about JFK's constant sexual demands: 'If he wanted to make love, you'd make love – now. They'd have fifteen minutes to get to a party and she'd say she didn't want to. He'd look at his watch and say we've got ten minutes, let's go. There was a certain amount of insensitiveness, an awful lot of self-centeredness.'[32]

For JFK, a major part of her appeal was pure physical attraction. Arvad was gorgeous. As John White put it, she was, 'beautiful. Truly sexy. . . . Luscious, really luscious.' Sexually experienced, she no doubt satisfied, indeed thrilled Kennedy between the sheets. Like Kennedy, she was a sexual hedonist. She may have been unfaithful to him in February with her ex-boyfriend Nils Blok. But in addition to her erotic experience and skills, she was enormously charming. Her son said, 'She had a magnetic personality. She could walk into a room and everybody would know she was there. She was brilliant. Witty. A genius at getting to know people and getting them to talk.' But she was also loving and affectionate. In her letters and phone conversations with JFK, she left him in no doubt as to her feelings for him. 'Wherever in the world I may be, drop in,' she said. 'I think I shall always know the right thing for you to do. Not because of brains. Not because of knowledge. But because there are things deeper and more genuine – love my dear.' 'Loving,' she wrote on another occasion, 'knowing it, being helpless about it, and yet not feeling anything but complete happiness. At last realizing what makes Inga tick.' She listened encouragingly to his already-forming presidential ambitions. She massaged his bad back. She lavished him with praise for his strong character and whole-hearted approach to life. The affection she showed and expressed for Kennedy was genuine. She later told her son that she had always loved JFK. More than any of his other affairs, Kennedy – with Inga Arvad – was dealing with someone very much like himself: a very attractive, infinitely charming sexual adventurer. The difference lay in her greater ability to show affection.[33]

Not surprisingly, Kennedy fell in love with her; he was not accustomed to the feeling, influenced – as he was – by his father's view of women as nothing more than disposable sex objects. He may even have contemplated marriage. On 6 February an FBI official reported to J. Edgar Hoover that Kathleen Kennedy had been overheard speculating that her brother might marry Arvad. Her father, she predicted, would oppose the match. On the other hand Arvad's husband told her (according to his sources) that Kennedy had said to his father, as Arvad herself reported it to JFK, he had no interest in marrying her and was not that besotted with her anyway. In later conversations, for instance in a 23 February discussion in their hotel bedroom, bugged by the FBI, he said very little when she raised the issue of annulling her marriage to Fejos. It is difficult to gauge the extent to which Joe Kennedy influenced Jack's wariness about marrying Inga, but a safe assumption is that despite his ardour for her, his commitment to a pleasure-seeking life, prior to the start of his political career when marriage acquired a public-relations utility, meant that even without input from Joe Kennedy, who probably did accelerate the relationship's demise, JFK would have avoided marriage with her.[34]

The Arvad affair came at a political price for JFK. Her colleague at the *Times-Herald* Page Huidekoper claimed that a friend had seen a photograph of her in Hitler's box at the Berlin Olympics, and hence that Arvad might be a spy. This was a serious matter in the febrile days following Pearl Harbor and America's entry into the Second World War. Her boss at the paper sent Huidekoper and Arvad to the FBI. Arvad strenuously denied the allegation before the FBI agent and demanded unsuccessfully a letter confirming that she was not a spy. Informed of this development, Hoover ordered 'a discreet investigation . . . to determine the truth of the allegations against Miss Arvad'. Soon the Office of Naval Intelligence confirmed a report that Arvad had been conducting an affair with John Kennedy. By 21 January 1942 Hoover, whose agents had already been keeping tabs on Arvad for some months, had requested authority from Attorney General Francis Biddle to 'install a technical surveillance on the telephone of . . . Inga Arvad', as she had charmed Hitler, was sleeping with a naval officer (Kennedy), and so might be 'engaged in a most subtle type of espionage activities against the United States'. Biddle approved the request. Hoover made clear to his subordinates that he wanted the Arvad and, by implication, Kennedy matter to 'receive continuous attention' – as indeed did FDR who told Hoover so. What followed was an elaborate intelligence operation to tap her phone, intercept their mail and bug the rooms where they slept together. The FBI would uncover no evidence that she was a spy. The regular reports on her encounters with JFK revealed that she rarely asked him anything to do with his work assignments in the navy. As

Arvad was clearly no spy, Kennedy's affair with her constituted no risk to US national security interests. He had simply fallen in love with a woman who had met and interviewed prominent German officials in doing work for the Danish press. Nevertheless, the Arvad affair meant that long before he had entered the political arena Kennedy was beholden to Hoover who had a detailed record of his relationship with a suspected spy. That would have implications for Kennedy's presidency.[35]

Kennedy worried that the press, as well as the FBI, knew about his affair with Arvad. Once his relationship with a woman of concern to the FBI had been established, the chief of naval operations ordered that JFK be transferred away from Washington. But what seemed to expedite the carrying out of that order was a piece penned in the press by syndicated gossip columnist Walter Winchell, which revealed, 'One of Ex-Ambassador Kennedy's eligible sons is the target of a Washington gal columnist's affections. So much so she has consulted her barrister about divorcing her exploring groom. Pa Kennedy no like.' Hoover was probably Winchell's source for the story. In any case, JFK was booted out of Washington within twenty-four hours. He was sent to the naval base in Charleston. Rumours that *Life* magazine was about to report on his affair with Arvad also troubled Kennedy. The paradox of the Arvad affair was that Kennedy's private life was more susceptible to press intrusion than it would be when president. The unofficial rule followed by the nation's scribes in not reporting on politicians' sexual shenanigans did not apply in this case as Kennedy was a mini-celebrity as the author of a bestseller and son of one of America's best-known businessmen, but not yet a political figure. In terms of the likelihood that press coverage of his private life would tarnish his public reputation, he was rarely more vulnerable than he was in the early days of 1942.[36]

Madly in love but pursued by the FBI and sparking media interest, Kennedy flew to Washington to end his relationship with Arvad but also to spend one last night with her on 28 February–1 March. Joe Kennedy played a role in JFK's decision. When Arvad made that assertion in a later phone conversation, JFK acknowledged: 'I talked to him Sunday night and he spoke to me about it. He said he got the [FBI] report. He said . . . things aren't quite right up there.' The FBI had been in touch with Joe Kennedy, and this conversation with Arvad indicated that JFK's father had told him about the FBI's concern over her past connections to Nazi Germany. 'Maybe there is some background on you,' JFK informed Inga. 'You can see that.'[37]

It was not just Joe Kennedy who influenced Jack's decision to part from Inga, for that decision was preceded by a troubling letter from his pal Lem Billings, saying that a family acquaintance had said to his (Billings') mother, 'you must have heard about the big Romance that has been rocking Washington circles – that one of the Kennedy boys is madly in love with a very beautiful & ravishing Danish reporter – but that fortunately the gal has been married several times – so that it will be difficult for her to marry him.' That his affair had become grist to the mill of Washington gossips must have disturbed Kennedy, and the timing of Billings's letter suggests it was a factor in his decision to leave Arvad.[38]

As with many of the major episodes in his early life – including *Why England Slept* and his celebrated wartime exploits – JFK's affair with Arvad sheds light on the degree to which Joe Kennedy fashioned his life and career. Was it the patriarch who was basically responsible for his rise to power, protecting his reputation at times, as in the case of Inga Arvad, boosting it on other occasions? Joe Kennedy's impact, important as it was, has often been exaggerated. There have been plenty of the rich and privileged who have aspired to high office and failed. Consider the elections lost by media tycoon William Randolph Hearst. Most of what JFK achieved was the result of his own talents and endeavours. He would emerge as an exceptionally gifted politician, far more so than his father who had bungled spectacularly over appeasement and the Nazi threat. Even in the Arvad affair, Joe Kennedy's intervention was only one of several factors, which included Billings's letter and his own inclination as a young man to avoid marriage, to influence his decision to end their relationship.

Ending that relationship, however, was no easy matter for Kennedy as he remained besotted with her. Only five days after jilting Arvad, he phoned her. 'Surprised to hear from me?' he asked. 'A little maybe,' she replied. JFK wanted to see her again.

Kennedy: Why don't you come [to Charleston]?
Arvad: What a question. Don't you remember that we talked it over Sunday? . . . . You're not giving up what we promised last Sunday, are you?
Kennedy: No, not till the next time I see you. I'm not too good, am I?
Arvad: I think you're perfect, dear. We'll probably meet again.
Kennedy: You mean, next week.
Arvad: I'm not coming. I don't know. I'm not trying to be stubborn. I'm only trying to help you. You know that, don't you. . . . Did you think I was coming to Charleston?
Kennedy: I had big hopes.[39]

Arvad's resolve to be sensible, rather than follow her own desires, had dashed those hopes. As she wrote in a letter to JFK, 'It took me the F.B.I., the U.S. Navy, nasty gossip, envy, hatred and big Joe,' to make her understand that she had to play it safe and abandon forever the delirious happiness she had felt with JFK over the winter months. As Kennedy moved forward in his life without Inga, their relationship became one of sporadic, but affectionate, correspondence.[40]

As the years went by, memories of the Arvad affair haunted him, especially once he launched his political career after the Second World War. If the public were to learn that he had consorted with a woman suspected by the FBI of spying for Hitler, his credibility would be damaged. According to his friend and legislative aide Langdon Parker Marvin, Jr., Kennedy sought to prevent that by procuring the FBI evidence. 'When Jack came to Congress,' said Marvin, 'one of the things on his mind was the Inga-Binga tape in the FBI files – the tape *he* was on. He wanted to get the tape from the FBI.' Although Marvin discouraged him from attempting this, Kennedy again expressed his determination to get this material after his election to the Senate. He was right to suspect that he would never entirely be able to break free from the danger of the Arvad affair. When he secured the Democratic presidential nomination in July 1960, Hoover ordered the FBI file on Arvad to be brought to his office. He understood the power it gave him over the man who might soon be president.[41]

Dirty secrets were Hoover's stock in trade, and no doubt that was the shoddy way he regarded Kennedy's fling with Inga Arvad. It was typical of *his* lack of moral imagination – his lack of character. But his affair with Arvad did *not* represent a lack of character on Kennedy's part. All he had done was fall deeply in love with a beautiful, charming, intelligent, affectionate woman. It was as simple and yet as profound as that. He did not know that she was a suspected spy when he began the affair. Despite his intense feelings for her, he broke it off shortly after learning of the concerns about her past. There is nothing in the Arvad affair to support the claim that he lacked character. He would soon demonstrate in the Pacific the impressive character which he did possess.

After the pleasures of the flesh as the lover of Inga Arvad, Kennedy put his body on the line, serving his nation in a time of war. As with many young Americans after Pearl Harbor, he craved action in battle. He sought therefore to replace his mundane desk job in naval intelligence with active service in the navy. He went to Evanston, Illinois, attending Northwestern University's Midshipmen's School for officer training. After that he was based in Rhode Island at a training school for PT boats, the light, fast craft popular with young men from the social elite whose families were members of yacht clubs. After becoming a PT instructor for a time, Kennedy was dispatched to the South Pacific in March 1943, where he took command of *PT 109*. It was Kennedy's leadership of *PT 109* in the early days of August 1943, after a Japanese destroyer rammed his boat, which made him a war hero, adding military valour to literary flair as key attributes in his emerging public persona. Even before he got to the Pacific, the press responded to his enlisting in the navy by describing him as 'author, scholar and warrior'. In an important sense his *PT 109* leadership reinforced the impression made by *Why England Slept*. His book had called for courageous leadership in confronting the Nazi threat; three years later, in the South Pacific, he displayed a courageous brand of leadership himself in saving his crew. In text and wartime deed what Kennedy became associated with was heroic command.[42]

Of all the misconceptions propagated by revisionist historians intent on tarnishing Kennedy's reputation, the most absurd is the claim that Kennedy's command of *PT 109*, despite the praise and military honours he received at the time, was reckless and incompetent. A reconstruction of the circumstances and precise events during and after the Japanese attack on *PT 109* shows that Kennedy's leadership in the Solomon Islands was brave, selfless, adroit and effective – and it helped save the lives of his crew who, not surprisingly, idolised him thereafter.[43]

On the evening of 1 August *PT 109* was dispatched with other PT boats to Blackett Strait, where they were ordered to fire on the 'Tokyo Express', Japanese destroyers on their way to resupply Japanese forces to the south. Around 2.30 am some sort of dark shape appeared a few hundred yards away. With visibility poor and with no radar, the crew of *PT 109* assumed that they were looking at other PT boats. When they realized it was in fact a Japanese destroyer, *Amagiri*, Kennedy tried to turn *PT 109* so that its torpedoes could be fired. Before that could happen the Japanese destroyer had rammed Kennedy's boat. 'This is how it feels to be killed,' he thought. A fire broke out. All the crew ended up in the water. Two were never seen again. Another, Patrick McMahon, had severe burns. As skipper of *PT 109*, it was Kennedy's responsibility to lead his crew to safety. Miles from shore and with the strong possibility of interception by the Japanese, their prospects looked bleak.[44]

As no PT boat had ever been rammed by a Japanese destroyer and General Douglas MacArthur was reported as saying that JFK should have been court-martialled for his negligent leadership of *PT 109*, Kennedy critics have claimed that he was, metaphorically, asleep at the wheel on the night of 1–2 August 1943; and hence that the story of *PT 109* was another myth which exaggerated Kennedy's virtues and obscured his failings. Various criticisms have been articulated. Why did Kennedy fail to order his crew to take evasive action so as to avoid the *Amagiri*? Linked to that, why did he have only one engine running, and not all three, thereby making it difficult for *PT 109* to move away quickly once the destroyer had been seen? Running only one engine was in fact standard practice as it meant less water was churned, reducing the wake that might be spotted by Japanese planes. The night of 1–2 August was pitch black. Adding to the difficulty in identifying the Japanese destroyer was the fact that *PT 109* was one of the PT boats that had no radar and also no contact with PT boats that did. In truth, Kennedy was attentive, not lackadaisical, in his leadership of *PT 109*. He reacted quickly once the Japanese destroyer had been seen. Engulfed in darkness, with no radar protection and with the *Amagiri* moving at great speed, a little more than ten seconds elapsed between the time the destroyer was spotted and when it rammed *PT 109*. The idea that negligent leadership on Kennedy's part was responsible for *PT 109* being rammed is a chimera.[45]

Kennedy's conduct after the attack was admirable, displaying fortitude, tenacity and altruism. Kennedy, bad back and all, swam out to the members of his crew who were a hundred yards away. He towed the badly burned McMahon to the boat, returning to help another man back to *PT 109*. As the boat began to sink, Kennedy took decisive action, ordering his crew to begin the three-and-a-half-mile swim to an island to the southeast. Remarkably, Kennedy used a kapok in his teeth to tow McMahon the entire distance. Kennedy then set out himself for Ferguson Passage in the hope of encountering a PT boat. He saw none. He headed back to Plum Pudding Island. The currents were very strong. He only just made it.[46]

On 4 August he ordered his crew to swim to Olasana Island; he again towed McMahon with the kapok between his teeth. The next day he swam out with a member of his crew to another island, Naru, where they saw in the distance a canoe with two native islanders. On their return JFK was surprised to see those two islanders with the crew of *PT 109*. The islanders, who were working as scouts for the Allies, agreed to convey a message, part of which was written by JFK on a coconut shell:

NAURO ISL COMMANDER NATIVE KNOWS POSIT HE CAN PILOT 11 ALIVE NEED SMALL BOAT KENNEDY.

This message was received by Australian coast-watcher Reginald Evans who dispatched his scouts to Olasana Island to collect Kennedy and his crew. Through a combination of courage, stamina, selflessness, doggedness and ingenuity, Kennedy had returned the crew of *PT 109* to safety. The best-informed view of Kennedy's leadership in the Solomons was that of his crew, and they would always sing his praises. When Kennedy received the Navy and Marine Corps Medal for his bravery, it was entirely merited. Only he could have known what it took to push his body, emaciated by lifelong illness, spinal weakness and probably incipient Addison's disease, through this week-long ordeal.[47]

The significance of the *PT 109* episode lies in not only what it revealed about Kennedy's tenacious character but also its impact on his image. A front-page story in *The New York Times* as well as articles in other major newspapers reported his wartime exploits to the public. Then *Life* magazine's John Hersey became intrigued by the *PT 109* story. Interviewing Kennedy and his crew, he wrote a fluent, powerful account, entitled 'Survival', for the *New Yorker* magazine. Joe Kennedy intervened to ensure the story had a wider impact. He worked behind the scenes to cajole the *Reader's Digest*, with its vast leadership, to print a shorter version of Hersey's article in August 1944.[48]

Two years before JFK ran for Congress, he had already established an image as a man of letters and a war hero. Not only had he written the timely and bestselling *Why England Slept*, he had displayed a valour in the Pacific that was now known to millions. What this suggested about his intellect and character would prove to be a major asset in the future. The story of *PT 109*, in particular, strengthened his political appeal. That *Reader's Digest* article was invariably distributed to voters when he ran for office. It presented Kennedy as the embodiment of the heroic brand of leadership called for in *Why England Slept*. If he could demonstrate such leadership on the high seas, then he could do so again in the political arena. He had undoubtedly shown the sort of courage he would extol in his second book, *Profiles in Courage*.

Joe Kennedy furthered the publicity surrounding his son's leadership of *PT 109*. But it was not Kennedy senior who had put his body on the line in the Pacific. Indeed John Kennedy's record in the Second World War stands in stark contrast to his father who had dodged the draft in the First World War. The achievement in the Solomons in August 1943 was JFK's, and his alone. The attention paid to his wartime exploits was not unwarranted. It reflected the admirable courage that he had in fact displayed.[49]

After a brief stint as a journalist at the end of the Second World War, JFK entered politics by running for Congress in 1946. He sought to represent the Eleventh Congressional District of Massachusetts, announcing his candidacy in the spring. There is an old narrative on the way this decision was made, which emphasizes the decisive role played by Joe Kennedy: the patriarch had intended for Joe Jr. to be the son who would go into politics and become the first Catholic president. But with his tragic wartime death in 1944, Joe Sr. turned instead to his second son, John, and demanded that he run for Congress.[50]

Joe Sr. was a formidable personality who usually got his way, but to trust this traditional account of how JFK began his political career is to deprive him of agency. It was clear from his private comments to Inga Arvad that he harboured ambitions to go into politics, even to become president, before Joe Jr.'s demise. Journalist and close friend Charles Bartlett, who met JFK as he was running for Congress, recalled, 'Sometimes you read that he [Jack] was a reluctant figure being dragooned into politics by his father. I really didn't get that impression at all. I gathered that it was a wholesome, full-blown wish on his own part.' While he was influenced by his father's pressure to run in 1946, that served only to reinforce his own ambitions.[51]

With the campaign itself, it was all about the Democratic primary. In an overwhelmingly Democratic district, winning the June primary guaranteed victory in November. Joe Kennedy did play an active role in the campaign. Mark Dalton, who was the official manager of JFK's campaign, has said in reality it was probably Joe Kennedy who held that position, such was his influence. Although some in Massachusetts politics believed that Joe Kennedy's role was limited, he was active behind the scenes in dispensing advice and funds far in excess of those usually spent on a congressional campaign – though, as Fredrik Logevall has argued, it is not certain that the amount spent was as vast as has sometimes been claimed.[52]

The most disreputable feature of Joe Kennedy's involvement was the entry of a second Joseph Russo into the Democratic primary. The Kennedy campaign team were concerned that the many Italian Americans in the Eleventh District would vote for the Italian-American candidate in the field, Joseph Russo. Suddenly a second Joseph Russo entered the race. If it were not skulduggery it must have been the most improbable coincidence. This was evidently an attempt to split the Italian-American vote, thereby increasing JFK's chances of victory. Mark Dalton later said that this second Joseph Russo must have been found, persuaded to run and paid in cash. The most plausible explanation is that this ploy was the handiwork of Joe Kennedy and his minions. It is feasible given the flexibility of his own moral compass and his control of the purse strings. Perhaps the patriarch would have informed his son of these underhand tactics, but there is evidence of the young candidate trying to run a 'clean' campaign and so declining the opportunity to use 'dirt' on other candidates when presented with it. This was the case when a journalist-friend showed him documentation pertaining to a rival candidate's military service. As the journalist recalled, Kennedy 'took one look at it and threw it in the wastebasket. He said it was going to be a clean campaign, no matter what'. The Joseph Russo story, therefore, probably says more about Joe Kennedy's character than JFK's.[53]

Joe Kennedy was a major influence, but the most important factor in JFK's victory in 1946 was his own considerable ability as a candidate. There are numerous examples of wealthy, privileged candidates seeking political office and failing. In-built advantages such as money and connections are exceedingly helpful but not always of decisive importance. What was vital was JFK's precocious ability on the campaign trail. 'He was a prodigious worker,' said one local politician. 'He'd go out of his way at almost any hour or any time to get to meet someone, even though he was basically, in my opinion, kind of on the shy and retiring side at that stage of the game.' 'I don't know where he got the strength he displayed,' said his campaign adviser Thomas Broderick, who recalled a night when Kennedy went through a trolley car and then a subway train, introducing himself and shaking hands with everyone. His friend LeMoyne Billings noticed that JFK was 'working as close to twenty-four hours a day as a man can work. He never let up during the entire campaign. Many healthy men could not have kept up that pace'. Driven, competitive, energetic, charismatic and charming, these were admirable traits in an aspiring politician. He was also strong in debate, and – although not the fine orator he would become – a promising speaker.[54]

Kennedy's relentlessness on the campaign trail was even more impressive given his continuing medical battles. His colitis caused abdominal discomfort. His back problems persisted. He struggled to gain weight. Emaciated and in pain, Kennedy drove himself on in the 1946 campaign with courage and determination.[55]

Kennedy's campaign was well organized and exceptionally well resourced. It was slick in a modern-PR sense, with teams of advertising agents and billboard specialists recruited to raise his profile. He had talented staffers committed to his cause. But his gifts as a campaigner meant that they had a politician who was easy to promote. As Billings explained, 'in the advertising business I've had to do a lot of selling. If you have a good product and you are able to expose that product properly, then you can be successful. That's really the whole secret of marketing – in Jack Kennedy, we found we had a good product that, if properly exposed, would convert voters to his side.'[56]

Three other factors made Kennedy a formidable candidate: sex appeal, family support and his wartime heroism. It is easy to assume that Kennedy's status as a sex symbol was achieved when he ran for president and reached the White House. Yet it is clear from accounts of the 1946 campaign that his good looks elicited much comment from the start of his political career. A journalist noticed how Kennedy 'had the edge' visually over the other candidates. 'You open the door and there is this swell-looking young guy.' 'There was a glamour to Jack as a candidate,' agreed one Kennedy aide. His friend Paul 'Red' Fay accompanied him on campaign stops at women's colleges where JFK would 'come in there like Frank Sinatra in the early days. They would scream and holler and touch him – absolutely, in 1946. I mean, these girls were just crazy about him'. A Cambridge councilman was struck by how at campaign house parties 'the minute he [JFK] came into a room where there was one or more women, the females that were in the room forgot everything else. . . . They gravitated towards him. And that would happen many times.' More than any previous politician in American history, the young Kennedy was making sex a public-relations asset. It made him appealing, exciting, masculinized – and so, significantly, not a 'soft' liberal.[57]

The process of making a political star and creating a Hollywood star were merging. Kennedy understood that this was the case – that the attributes of a movie star could and should be cultivated in the political arena. The time he had spent visiting Los Angeles, when he could observe movie stars first-hand, deepened that understanding. His knowledge of Hollywood stardom would become even more intimate in that summer of 1946 as he embarked on an affair with the beautiful and recently Oscar-nominated star of the big screen Gene Tierney. Charmed by JFK, the affair nevertheless proved ephemeral. For one thing, Tierney had been married and that made any long-term relationship with her a non-starter for the Democratic nominee for Congress.[58]

Family was also a prominent feature of JFK's 1946 campaign. As with his subsequent campaigns, there was an important mathematical reality to his quest for a seat in the House of Representatives: there were simply so many Kennedys campaigning for him. His controversial father kept a low profile, but his reputation as one of the nation's foremost businessmen was widespread. Otherwise the clan was out in force. His mother Rose, as the daughter of a mayor of Boston, was an asset for JFK on the campaign trail. His sisters Eunice, Patricia and Jean campaigned energetically for him. Those famous teas, when the Kennedy women would greet large numbers of female voters – often seen as an important factor in his victory in the 1952 Senate race – in fact began in 1946. Even young Bobby Kennedy, just out of the navy, worked hard to win support for his brother in East Cambridge. Right from the outset of his career in politics, JFK had an unusual resonance as a familial symbol. The public looked at him and saw not a lone politician but the scion of a notable family. Jackie Kennedy's cultural stardom and Bobby and Edward Kennedy's political stardom would subsequently enlarge this sense of JFK as the leader of a dynasty. But in 1946 the idea that he was a symbol of the family, as well as a sex symbol, gave his candidacy a distinctive appeal.[59]

If that was not enough to seduce the voters of the Eleventh Congressional District, there was the important factor of Kennedy's status as a war hero. That he was also a published, bestselling author was of less significance to his campaign. The Kennedy team did not emphasize his literary credentials, which probably had little influence apart from with the denizens of Harvard and MIT. But with the Second World War ending only months earlier and many returning veterans in the district, and JFK's credentials as a decorated naval officer, Kennedy and his advisers made the sensible decision to highlight his military heroics. Although modest in private about his wartime service, at campaign stops he would remind audiences that he was a combat veteran. In the days before the Democratic primary 100,000 copies of John Hersey's *Reader's Digest* article on Kennedy's wartime service were mailed to Massachusetts voters. Veterans' enthusiasm for their fellow veteran was strong anyway in 1946, but that mass mailing bolstered support for Kennedy just as voters were about to go to the polls.[60]

All of these factors contributed to Kennedy's triumph in the primary in June 1946. He received almost 11,000 votes more than his closest challenger, Michael J. Neville. His victory in the November election against his Republican opponent Lester Bowen was a foregone conclusion: he won by a margin of 43,000 votes. Still, it was a commendable performance in an election in which the GOP reclaimed control of Congress. Kennedy had applied himself with impressive energy and skill. He was a superb campaigner, with the drive of Lyndon Johnson, the charm of Franklin Roosevelt and the political acumen of both. His compelling image, already emerging before 1946, helped him win; and, in turn, the campaign enabled him to bring his multifaceted image as war hero, sex symbol, symbol of the family and (to a lesser extent at this point) man of letters into sharper focus.[61]

On the night of his decisive primary victory his campaign workers joined JFK's parents and the rest of the Kennedy clan at the Bellevue Hotel in downtown Boston. For a man who rarely showed his feelings, JFK was uncharacteristically emotional. He even shed a tear. He was touched by the support he had received from his staff and his family, including his proud father. But his state of mind must have been due mainly to his emotional and physical exhaustion. He had, heroically, forced his always-frail body through months of a gruelling campaign, and had applied all of the political acumen and strategy he could bring to bear. He was justified in taking pride in his victory. More than Joe Kennedy's influence or money, the accomplishment was due to JFK's own ability and dazzling image.[62]

Arriving on Capitol Hill at the start of 1947, Kennedy had to define his approach to a range of policy issues. Since the assassination in Dallas, an idea of JFK as a liberal leader has taken root. After all, he saved the peace during the Cuban missile crisis, slowed the arms race with the Nuclear Test Ban Treaty, improved America's image overseas with the Peace Corps and fought alongside Martin Luther King for the noble cause of civil rights. After Dallas he was invariably portrayed as a liberal-hero president in the tradition of Woodrow Wilson and Franklin Roosevelt. Articles and magazine covers after 1963 often bracketed him with other liberal icons, such as King and Robert Kennedy. There is a partial logic to this portrayal of JFK as he did shift towards a more progressive politics in the final year of his life.[63]

For most of his political career, and particularly during his early years in Congress, however, he did not embrace New Deal liberalism and took a hard-line stance on the Cold War that shared much with the Republican critique of the Roosevelt–Truman foreign policy. Essentially he was a centrist Democrat. For those many politicians attracted to liberal causes at home and a less militantly anti-communist policy overseas, FDR – with his record of New Deal reform to create a more just society and cooperation with the Russians in order to defeat Hitler – was a hero. But, oddly, Kennedy was not a fan. 'There just wasn't anything about President Roosevelt that stirred . . . Kennedy emotionally,' said Charles Spalding. Even though the New Deal excited so many students when he was an undergraduate, Kennedy maintained a cool detachment, declining to join the Liberal Union or the Young Democratic Club at Harvard.[64]

The complex relationship between Roosevelt and Joe Kennedy was a major reason for JFK's frostiness towards FDR. Despite appointing him to various positions in the New Deal, Roosevelt had kept Joe at arm's length, withholding the cabinet position he so coveted. When he did award him a prestigious post, the ambassadorship in London, Joe Kennedy's pro-appeasement, pro-isolationist stance put him at odds with FDR. The claim he made in a press interview in November 1940 that democracy was finished in Britain and perhaps America too incurred FDR's wrath, compelled his resignation as ambassador, and signalled the end of his political career. Observing how his father had struggled to find his place at the court of Roosevelt before being destroyed, in a political sense, by his stint as FDR's man in London, Kennedy felt no loyalty to the legacy of the New Deal. That made him amenable as a congressman to the more outrageous claims by Joe McCarthy and other Republicans that Roosevelt had failed to defend American interests against a predatory Stalin.[65]

Scepticism towards FDR and the New Deal was not the only factor shaping Kennedy's thinking during his early years in Congress. His refusal to identify with liberals and their causes was also a matter of political calculation. He believed that if Democrats were to be successful at the ballot box and effective in government, they needed to occupy the centre ground in politics. His view, as an aide once said, was that 'the balance of feeling in the electorate lay with a "moderate, decent, conservative margin," which a Democratic candidate had to reach. It was, therefore, impossible to build a victorious base on the left-wing of the Democratic Party'. There is a parallel here between Kennedy's calculations and Bill Clinton's a few decades later. Clinton fashioned a 'Third Way' ideology partly because he was convinced that a centrist approach rather than a 1930s- or 1960s-style liberalism was required if the Democratic Party were to recapture the presidency. Whilst JFK did not develop a precisely formulated ideology in the way Clinton did in presenting himself as a New Democrat, he shared with the Arkansan the idea that the centre, and not the Left, was the place to be. As the 1950s unfolded, the landslide defeats of quintessential liberal Adlai Stevenson at the hands of Dwight Eisenhower in the 1952 and 1956 presidential elections reinforced that conviction.[66]

Sensibility, as well as strategy, influenced Kennedy's disdain for liberals like Stevenson and Eleanor Roosevelt. Their belief in their own moral superiority and their preference for lofty sentiment over sensible pragmatism was distasteful to him. If there was one thing Kennedy loathed it was sanctimony. That was a key reason why he did not identify with liberals, declaring in 1953: 'I'm not a liberal at all. I never joined the Americans for Democratic Action or the American Veterans Committee. I'm not comfortable with those people.' That was reflected in his vote to cut funds for the iconic New Deal programme, the Tennessee Valley Authority, and his criticisms of Social Security in 1953. He did back public housing and other liberal policies, not surprising for a congressman whose constituency was urban and industrialized. But his record on domestic issues during his early years in Congress was not that of an ardent liberal. His response to McCarthyism in the early 1950s would be the most infamous case in point.[67]

The gap between Kennedy and the liberals was also evident in his hard-line views on foreign policy. Most Democrats came to believe in the importance of meeting the communist challenge as the Cold War intensified, and so backed Truman's containment programme. Unlike liberals loyal to Truman, however, Kennedy developed a harsh critique of not only his foreign policy but Roosevelt's as well.

Kennedy was elected to the House of Representatives in the very same year, 1946, that Truman concluded Stalin could not be trusted and hence he needed to confront the Soviet dictator. The young congressman took his seat in the House of Representatives the following year just as Truman was about to unveil the two key initiatives in his policy of containment: the Truman Doctrine and the Marshall Plan. Formulating his response to the communist threat and Truman's reaction to it was the most pressing challenge of Kennedy's early congressional career. In defining that response, he drew on his earlier analysis of the failures of appeasement in handling Hitler. *Why England Slept* had highlighted the need for democratic leaders with the steel to stand up to aggressive dictators, not least by bolstering the nation's defences regardless of whether such a policy found favour with public opinion. Congressman Kennedy therefore backed Truman's proposal in March 1947 to support the Greek and Turkish governments with $400 million worth of aid against the communist threat, and the president's general pledge – the Truman Doctrine – to oppose communist expansion anywhere. In a speech delivered at the University of North Carolina at Chapel Hill, Kennedy argued that Truman's aid bill for Greece and Turkey was 'essential to the security of our country' as it would help prevent the 'red tide' from flowing 'across the face of Europe and through Asia with new power and vigor'. Deterring Soviet domination of Europe and Asia had become 'the central theme of our American foreign policy', he said, and given the geo-strategic importance of Greece and Turkey, aid to those nations was imperative. Kennedy also supported the Marshall Plan for a huge infusion of aid to Western Europe in order to rejuvenate it economically and to prevent it from succumbing to communism. (Indigenous communist parties were popular in Italy and France.)[68]

Despite backing the Truman Doctrine and Marshall Plan, Kennedy soon emerged as a critic of Truman's foreign policy. He came to believe it was not robust enough in confronting communism, and in that he was a bedfellow of those Republicans who railed against Truman and the legacy of FDR. It was at a dinner in Salem, Massachusetts, at the end of January 1949 that he gave a speech notable for the kind of alarmist, accusatory language that would soon be used by Joe McCarthy. As China was falling to the communists, said JFK, 'it is of the utmost importance that we search out and spotlight those who must bear the responsibility for our present predicament.' He proceeded to do just that, tarnishing the reputation of the great liberal hero of the age in the process: 'At the Yalta conference in 1945 a sick Roosevelt, with the advice of General Marshall and other Chiefs of Staff, gave the Kurile Islands as well as the control of various strategic Chinese ports, such as Port Arthur and Darien, to the Soviet Union.' He accused the Truman administration of failing to deliver military equipment to the Nationalist government in China out of a misguided belief that this would compel Chiang Kai-shek to enter into a coalition with the communists. 'This is the tragic story of China whose freedom we once fought to preserve,' Kennedy angrily concluded. 'What our young men had saved, our diplomats and our President have frittered away.'[69]

Kennedy's hard-line views on foreign policy were apparent not only from these attacks on Truman and FDR, but from his insistence that levels of US military spending were inadequate. 'The most serious deficiency in our military strength is our weakness in the air,' he asserted in the House of Representatives in April 1952. 'We started late and even with a maximum effort at the present time it will be 1955 before we overtake the lead the Soviets developed during the "Locust Years" of 1946 to 1950.' Due to his belief that American and North Atlantic Treaty Organization (NATO) defences were weak, Kennedy often thought that the Russians might well take advantage of this state of affairs by invading Western Europe. He said so in August 1951 and repeated the prediction a year later.[70]

Kennedy's ideas as a congressman on the incompetence of Truman and Roosevelt, the government's naivety on national security and Russian intentions to invade Western Europe will seem surprising to those whose impression of JFK is of an enlightened and progressive leader. There is here a troubling overlap between Kennedy's views and those of Joe McCarthy. This was a factor behind Kennedy's subsequent refusal to take a stand against the anti-communist crusader.

A quality displayed by Kennedy throughout his public life, however, was an ability to learn and grow; this was a political asset but also a character strength. It is a reasonable assumption that we are all affected by our experiences, and this must (or at least should) be the case with politicians too. In the 1950s Kennedy refined his views on foreign policy. They became more nuanced and sophisticated. In part this was due to political calculation. He wanted to be president. If he were ever to win the Democratic presidential nomination, he needed to increase his support from liberals sceptical of this Cold Warrior son of Joe Kennedy, who used kid gloves and not an iron fist with the appalling Joe McCarthy. As the decade unfolded, Kennedy sought to improve his image with liberals, and he expressed sympathy for some of the innovative ideas championed by their standard bearer Stevenson, including a nuclear test ban treaty.[71]

Experience, as well as political calculation, altered JFK's thinking. In particular his seven-week trip to the Middle and Far East in the autumn of 1951 influenced him. Accompanied by Bobby Kennedy and his sister Patricia, he visited numerous countries, including Indochina. As a result of this first-hand observation, which included meetings with local officials and leaders such as Indian prime minister Jawaharlal Nehru, JFK came to appreciate the force of nationalism in old colonial areas. A deep-rooted desire for independence, and not meddling by Moscow, was often – he now understood – the root cause of instability in developing countries. In a November 1951 radio report on his trip, Kennedy explained to his listeners that, 'It is a troubled area of the world I saw. It is an area in which poverty and sickness and disease are rampant, in which injustice and inequality are old and ingrained, and in which the fires of nationalism so long dormant have been kindled and are now ablaze.' He went on to criticize US policy in Indochina as 'we have allied ourselves to the desperate effort of a French regime to hang on to the remnants of empire,' and called on France to work for Vietnamese independence. 'To the rising tide of nationalism,' lamented Kennedy, 'we have unfortunately become a friend of its enemy and as such its enemy and not its friend.' Experience and observation had thus furnished Kennedy with a more subtle understanding of global politics.[72]

While that reflected a greater maturity on Kennedy's part, shocking developments in the Cold War in 1957 would return his priorities to what they had been when writing *Why England Slept*, namely the paramount importance of military power and hard-nosed leadership in confronting a totalitarian aggressor state. A landmark Russian technological breakthrough, *Sputnik*, the world's first man-made satellite, sent shockwaves through America. The belief that Soviet technological superiority meant Moscow was winning the arms race, and hence a 'missile gap' had emerged, became widespread. For Kennedy, his thesis in *Why England Slept* was directly applicable to America's post-Sputnik situation: increasing US military might was vital.[73]

In a speech in the Senate on 14 August 1958, Kennedy claimed that the Russians were acquiring a dangerous military superiority and that, 'The most critical years of the gap would appear to be 1960-1964' – which, as things turned out, coincided with Kennedy's time in the White House. He chided Eisenhower for being more interested in balancing the budget than ensuring that the military was fit for purpose. He did briefly say that liberals like Hubert Humphrey were right to work for nuclear disarmament. But he argued that the United States needed to take steps to close the 'missile gap' should no sort of disarmament be achieved. These steps included a rapid military build-up. Kennedy concluded by quoting the Cassandra of the 1930s, Winston Churchill: 'Come then – let us to the task, to the battle and the toil – each to our part, each to our station.'[74]

It was to his credit that Kennedy refined his thinking on American foreign policy in the 1950s, factoring nationalism more fully into his thinking on developing nations, and defining disarmament as a worthwhile goal of national policy. But as a matter of *emphasis*, by the end of the 1950s, as he prepared to run for the presidency, JFK again stressed toughness and military power in dealing with the Russians.

Kennedy's analysis of US foreign policy was important not only for the way it established the framework of ideas that would shape his policies as president, but also for how it influenced his image. Implicit in *Why England Slept*, his 1956 book *Profiles in Courage* and his speeches on the Cold War was the idea of the hero in politics. The United States, he suggested, needed a leader with the courage, independence, strength and wisdom to stand up to dictators and shore up the nation's defences. The man with the brains to write a bestseller at twenty-three and win a Pulitzer Prize thereafter, the valour to fight the Japanese and save his crew in the Pacific, and with the sober understanding of the Russian threat which his record in Congress demonstrated, might just be the hero America needed at this time of crisis in the Cold War. That notion was a political and electoral asset for JFK throughout the 1950s.

Chapter 2

RISE TO POWER

The 1952 Senate campaign in Massachusetts was a crucial milestone on the road to the presidency for John Kennedy. It moved him from the House of Representatives to the Senate. It provided him with a famous victory over a distinguished Republican incumbent, Henry Cabot Lodge, and that in an election season when the GOP recaptured the presidency with their war-hero candidate Dwight Eisenhower trouncing Democrat Adlai Stevenson. JFK's victory in 1952 raised his profile, making a future presidential bid feasible.

That 1952 campaign raises a variety of issues, including the extent of Joe Kennedy's influence and how the campaign provided a dramatic setting for the crystallization of JFK's compelling image. But it also illustrates the significance of character to an understanding of Kennedy's rise to power. Despite his flaws, it was Kennedy's character strengths which were to the fore and which help explain his successful public life.

Confidence and courage in a political sense were important elements in Kennedy's triumph in 1952. Lodge was a formidable opponent. Hailing from a famous family in Massachusetts – his grandfather had led the fight in the Senate against Woodrow Wilson's campaign for US membership of the League of Nations – he had given up his Senate seat in 1942 to fight in the army, was decorated for his military service, and was elected again to the Senate in 1946 against the redoubtable Democrat David I. Walsh. Lodge was handsome, committed to public service, an eloquent speaker, respected in the Senate, and his exploits on the battlefield would presumably neutralize JFK's heroics with *PT 109*. Hardly anyone thought Kennedy could win. As one of his campaign staff put it, 'everybody…thought that Kennedy never had a chance, that Lodge was popular.' Yet as early as 1950 Kennedy had told friend Thomas Broderick that he was planning to challenge Lodge, even though the odds of victory seemed insurmountable. 'Well, you can leave me home anytime,' said Broderick. 'Well, Tommie, why do you say that?' 'Oh, you can't beat him, Jack.' 'I think we can,' responded JFK. That confidence that he could defy political logic by defeating Lodge, and the courage to take on the challenge despite the odds being so stacked against him, were prerequisites for Kennedy's victory in 1952. A good many politicians would not even have run in the first place against this very popular incumbent.[1]

In taking on Lodge, Kennedy was assisted by a slick campaign run with enormous energy by his brother Bobby. Modern advertising techniques were again utilized, including the use of television. But as he had in the 1946 campaign, Joe Kennedy played an important role. He spent lavishly. One estimate puts it at a half-million dollars, but it may have been more. He gave a $500,000 loan to the cash-strapped conservative *Boston Post*, which endorsed JFK, but the paper's owner may have done so anyway, impressed, as he was, by the Democrat's robust views on the Cold War. Joe Kennedy may well have given money to Senator Joe McCarthy's re-election campaign in Wisconsin. While McCarthy did not campaign for his fellow Republican Lodge in a state where he was popular with Irish Catholics in another possible quid pro quo, it seems that the main reason McCarthy did not campaign for Lodge was the latter's refusal to ask in public for the Wisconsinite to come and campaign for him, as McCarthy had demanded. Joe Kennedy also dealt with the minutiae of the campaign. John T. Burke, who worked for an advertising agency recruited by the Kennedy campaign in 1952, recalled how he often met with not only the candidate but his father as well. At the same time, however, JFK made clear to his father that though he welcomed his input and, of course, his financial support, he reserved for himself the role as the campaign's key strategist.[2]

Despite his dad's influence, the most important factor in Kennedy's victory in 1952 was his own exceptional strength as a candidate. John Burke's observations of JFK's drive and appeal as a campaigner are telling: 'I never met a person who would work as hard as that man morning, noon and night. He was a human dynamo.' In this campaign, that hard work started early – months, even years before its formal launch – so that he could raise his profile and increase his contacts throughout Massachusetts. That preparatory work, which Logevall judges to be vital to his victory in 1952, saw him make speeches in 'every one of the [state's] 39 cities,' as one aide recalled, by December 1951. Kennedy's diligence contrasted sharply with the approach of Lodge who, tardily, began campaigning in earnest only in early September 1952.[3]

Burke also noticed Kennedy's extraordinary attraction to women voters: 'I never knew a man who had this electric quality.' Others too observed Kennedy's magnetic appeal on the campaign trail. That special charisma, that sense of connection with the voters he met – these were John Kennedy's impressive gifts, not Joe's.[4]

What was doubly impressive was that JFK displayed such dynamism in the campaign while continuing to suffer from illness and pain. Robert Dallek has totted up the maladies afflicting Kennedy in 1952, and the treatments they required:

> headaches, upper respiratory infections, stomachaches, urinary-tract discomfort, and nearly unceasing back pain. He consulted an ear, nose, and throat specialist about his headaches; took anti-spasmodics and applied heat fifteen minutes a day to ease his stomach troubles; consulted urologists about his bladder and prostate discomfort; had DOCA pellets implanted and took daily oral doses of cortisone to control his Addison's disease; and struggled unsuccessfully to find relief from his back miseries.

The pain was such that he had to grit his teeth to get through campaign events. After them, he needed to use crutches to get from his car back to his hotel room. That Kennedy overcame all of that pain and what must have been great worry over his health to campaign so indefatigably in 1952 was remarkable. Once again, it showed character.⁵

Also important to JFK's victory over Lodge was his seductive image as war hero, sex symbol, literary figure and symbol of the family. Of course, Joe had promoted his son. But, fundamentally, those core elements of his image were due to JFK's own achievements and natural endowments. The key ideas in *Why England Slept* had been his own and, significantly, at variance with Joe's isolationist, pro-appeasement stance. Mightily successful with women, he may have been, but Joe never had his son's allure. JFK was an authentic war hero; Joe was not. Who he was and what he had done provided the bedrock of JFK's political persona. Joe's money helped propagate that image but it was largely created by JFK himself.

The relationship between Kennedy's image and the 1952 Senate campaign was twofold: his image helped him win the election, and at the same time the way he was presented in this high-profile campaign made his image even more vivid. His sex appeal was indeed an important feature of the campaign, as it would be eight years later when running for the White House. 'The women especially seemed to be particularly interested in this young man,' observed an aide. 'They all wanted to make his acquaintance.' Photographs of him looking at his most handsome were selected for campaign posters. The staff at the advertising agency, which he hired in 1952, concluded that his good looks meant that he could not be overexposed and that his impact on the visual medium of television was immense.⁶

Part of the effort to court the women's vote was the holding of teas by Rose Kennedy and her daughters. This is the most famous part of the 1952 campaign. It has been estimated that 70,000 women attended these teas, which turned out to be JFK's margin of victory. Rose and her daughters were tireless campaigners for Jack. In Fall River, one Kennedy supporter observed Patricia and Eunice knocking on door after door. But it was not only the Kennedy women who were to the fore. As JFK's campaign manager, Bobby attracted much attention. The most striking example of the familial dimension of the campaign was the airing in October of a 30-minute TV special, *Coffee with the Kennedys*, with matriarch Rose as the key figure but appearances made by JFK and his sisters. Even though the controversial Joe Kennedy kept a low profile as he invariably did when Jack was running for office, the sense conveyed to the voters was of JFK as part of an extensive and fascinating family that included an ambassador, a mayor's daughter and the manager of a major political campaign. The 1952 Senate race showcased JFK as a symbol of the family and a representative of a political dynasty. This set him apart from other politicians and, in time, created the idea of the Kennedys as America's royal family.⁷

JFK's campaign highlighted his heroics in battle. Campaign literature emphasized his record as a decorated war hero, and more than a million copies of the John Hersey *Reader's Digest* article on *PT 109* were circulated. With his exciting sex-symbol status and his resonance as a family symbol also prominent during the campaign, it all made for an intoxicating image that many voters found irresistible in 1952.⁸

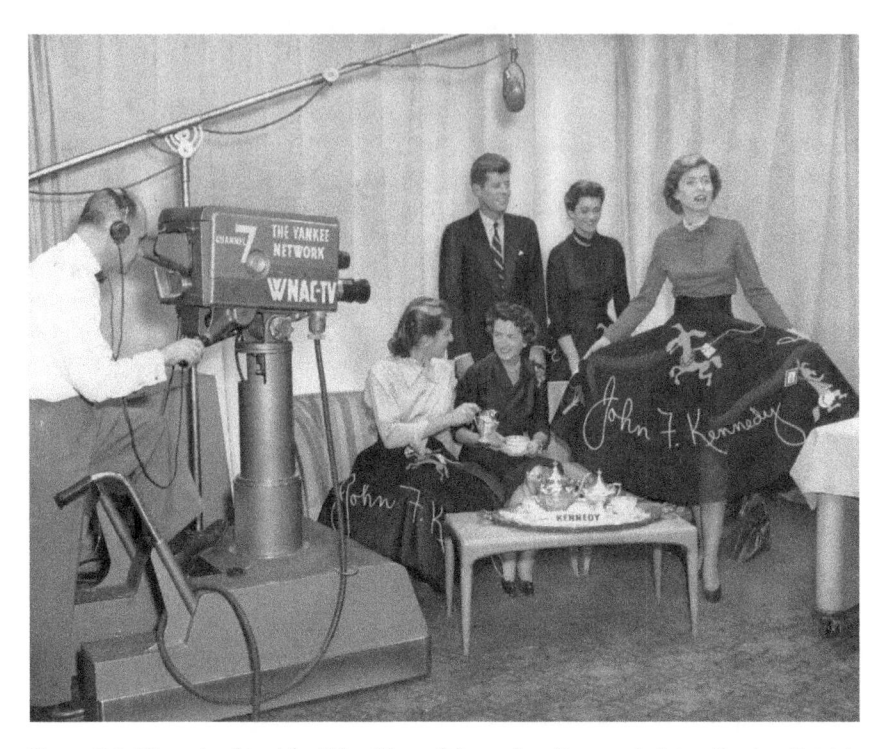

Figure 2.1 The role played by John Kennedy's mother Rose and sisters Eunice, Patricia and Jean was a significant factor in his successful bid for the US Senate in 1952. Here they join the candidate for a TV appearance during the campaign. (Wikimedia, public domain, Search media – Wikimedia Commons.)

A force of nature on the campaign trail with a striking image, Kennedy also prevailed against Lodge because of sensible strategy. Reflecting the hard-line views on foreign policy he had expressed in the House of Representatives, JFK came across to many voters as tougher on the communists than did Lodge. Kennedy realized, though, that many in Massachusetts were moved more by bread-and-butter domestic issues. Accordingly, his campaign dwelt on the inadequacies of Lodge's record on worker's rights, price controls and the economy generally. He succeeded in convincing many voters that, more than Lodge, he would improve their basic standard of living. In this way, the 1952 campaign can be seen as an early stage in the process by which Kennedy increased his appeal to liberals whose support he would need when running for the presidency.[9]

On Election Day on 4 November, Kennedy won 51.35 per cent of the vote, while Lodge received 48.35 per cent. His victory over Lodge was an impressive achievement. Given that the Republicans recaptured the presidency and both houses of Congress in 1952 with a popular five-star general at the top of the ticket, Kennedy's triumph was all the more remarkable. It was testimony, above anything else, to his own gifts as a politician. One other factor came into play: Kennedy's religion, for Lodge's share of the Catholic vote plummeted in comparison to his election to the Senate in 1946. JFK's Catholicism would prove a major issue once again when running for the White House in 1960. But in the context of a national campaign, his Catholic faith would be more of an obstacle to his success.[10]

Election to the Senate was followed by marriage. On the morning of 12 September 1953 Kennedy's bacchanalian bachelorhood came to an end at St. Mary's Catholic Church in Newport, Rhode Island, when he wed Jacqueline Bouvier. Prior to the mass, a special blessing from Pope Pius XII was read out. Family friend Richard Cardinal Cushing married the couple. Jackie wore a dress of ivory silk taffeta and pearls. Outside the church 3,000 members of the public, as well as photographers and reporters, greeted the newlyweds. Splashed over the front page of the following day's *New York Times*, it was *the* social event of 1953. The glamour of the wedding of Jack and Jackie was not a one-off for throughout their decade-long marriage her elegance would, by association, enhance his own allure.[11]

For those familiar with JFK's social life, his marriage to Jackie was surprising. Sleeping with as many women as possible, rather than pledging his troth to one, had been his priority. As Lem Billings recalled, 'He was [always] interested in having a lot of fun. . . . He was interested, very interested in girls.' Yet with few exceptions, notably Inga Arvad, he was not interested in developing meaningful friendships with women, just bedding them. 'Until he married Jackie Bouvier,' said Billings, 'he never really gave any serious consideration to marrying any particular girl.' Part of the reason for his disinterest in walking down the aisle was political in the sense that he was focused in the late 1940s on building his career in Congress. But it was also the case that he was loath to do anything that might complicate his playboy lifestyle.[12]

It was journalist and friend Charles Bartlett who introduced Jack to Jackie at a dinner party in his Georgetown home in spring 1951. When Bartlett walked out with her to the car, an intrigued JFK followed and said shyly to her, 'Shall we go someplace and have a drink?' But a young man, stockbroker John G. W. Husted Jr., had been waiting on the street and gotten into the backseat of her car; so she had to decline Kennedy's offer. But they soon started dating. That was interrupted when Jackie took a long trip to Europe and JFK started his campaign for the Senate. 'He hurt me terribly when he was campaigning and never called for weeks,' she told a friend. She looked elsewhere and became engaged to Husted, but the engagement did not last long. Prompted by Bartlett's wife, Jackie invited the newly elected senator to a dinner. Their courtship resumed, and in June 1953, their engagement was announced. Three months later they married.[13]

For Jackie, it was love, as she told her confidant, the Irish priest Fr. Joseph Leonard. She said of JFK: 'I think he was as much in love with me as he could be with anyone.' Political considerations also influenced his decision to marry her. A senator and presidential aspirant needed a wife. Jackie thought that conviction shaped his thinking. His friends thought so too. JFK himself acknowledged as much. But there was more to it than that. Her elegant Social Register background and demeanour, and her Catholicism, made her suitable to him. She had an allure,

Figure 2.2 Kennedy with his bride Jacqueline Bouvier at their wedding in Rhode Island in September 1953. Over time, her glamour, role as wife and mother, and extensive cultural interests bolstered JFK's image. (*Source*: Wikimedia, public domain, Search media – Wikimedia Commons.)

a mystery, a style that intrigued him. Her intelligence and deep cultural interests, honed by her Vassar-Sorbonne-George Washington education, and evident in her Francophilia and polyglot talents, made her stimulating company. Truth be told, she was as smart as he was and far more cultured. So he could not patronize her. In time, her passion for the arts would be a political asset for Kennedy. The way she used the White House as First Lady to showcase the arts made his presidential leadership appear sophisticated. The potential political benefits of her good taste may have occurred to him in 1953. His marriage, however, was not just a matter of calculation. As Jackie said, he *was* in love with her. Not as much as he had been with the impossibly charming Inga Arvad in the winter of 1941–42, but more in love than he had been with anyone since. His aide Priscilla Johnson McMillan recalled a party at which Kennedy told her the only reason he married was to prevent rumours circulating that, as a single man, he was gay. But as he made that cynical remark, he could not take his eyes off her as she moved around the room. With Kennedy's marriage, calculation did not preclude a strong attraction and genuine affection.[14]

Another important element in his marriage was her acceptance of his philandering, and his anticipation of her tolerance. For Jackie, his waywardness was simply typical male behaviour, which she was used to as the daughter of the hard-drinking, womanizing stockbroker, John Vernou Bouvier, who had left her mother when Jackie was only seven. 'He's like my father in a way,' said Jackie in a letter to Fr Leonard written nine months *before* her wedding, 'loves the chase and is bored with the conquest – and once married needs proof he's still attractive, so flirts with other women and resents you. I saw how that nearly killed Mummy.' For her own piece of mind as Kennedy's wife, she knew she had to cultivate a functional nonchalance in turning a blind eye to his affairs. It was probably the case that on a purely carnal level Kennedy's womanizing was not only acceptable to her but increased her attraction for him. Deep down she was drawn to dangerous men, as well as wealthy ones, as her subsequent marriage to Aristotle Onassis indicated. She had a father fixation, an inveterate desire to be with a man who reminded her of John Bouvier. Kennedy identified this dynamic in his relationship with Jackie, and even discussed it with his friends. To Kennedy's chums, the father obsession she had was obvious and yet she seemed oblivious to it. What it meant was that she was unlikely to divorce Jack, despite his affairs, and that was important. No divorcee had ever been elected president. With Adlai Stevenson, his divorce was viewed as a political liability.[15]

The private reality of Kennedy's marriage to Jackie co-existed with its appearance to the public and its significance for his political career. That private reality was at times an ordeal for even the broad-minded Jackie. The demands on his time as senator meant she was often alone. Marriage did not alter his compulsive womanizing one jot. He had affairs as often as he could.

One of these was with the Swedish aristocrat Gunilla von Post. Their relationship began on the French Riviera only weeks before his wedding to Jackie. They kissed under the Mediterranean stars. 'I fell in love with you tonight,' he told her. He claimed it had happened only once before: 'Five years ago [so before she was a movie star], I fell in love with Grace Kelly, the moment I saw her.' What followed between Kennedy and von Post was a frequent correspondence and phone conversations. His acute spinal problems in 1954 thwarted their plan to get together a year after their meeting and his marriage. But they did get together in southwestern Sweden in the summer of 1955. Within minutes of their reunion, he took her into their hotel bedroom and they made love. Years later, in her memoir of their affair, she remembered the encounter with immense fondness. 'Gunilla, we've waited two years for this,' he said to her. 'It seems almost too good to be true, and I want to make you happy.' 'I knew I must be gentle and careful, too,' she recalled. 'His back trouble was always a critical factor. Jack made love with his hands, with his marvelous, healthy Irish skin, with his mouth – with everything.' 'We were wonderfully *sensual*,' she added. During their time together, he again said he loved her and that he would talk to his father in order to discuss divorcing Jackie, so as to end an unhappy marriage, enabling him to marry von Post. He later reported to her that when he raised the matter, Joe Sr. flew into a rage. 'It wasn't a very pleasant conversation,' he said. Joe argued that a divorce would damage his son's political career.[16]

It is a fair assumption that von Post recalled all of this accurately. It may well have been the case, though, that JFK was dissembling – that while he was strongly attracted to von Post and enjoyed the affair with her, he never had any serious intentions of divorcing Jackie. A lot of the honeyed words he used with her can be interpreted as part of his seductive technique to get her in bed and then to sustain the affair. Her memoir is revealing, however, not least in conveying a sense of his astonishing charm. She recalled a dinner with her kith and kin in which,

> Jack made a point of conversing with everybody, and found something personal to say to them all. He positively radiated warmth, pulling everyone into his aura like a bright lantern attracts the creatures of the night. Jack was seductive; he rarely missed a chance to flirt with all the women, our mothers included. But he cast a spell on people that I've never quite seen before or since.[17]

JFK's most infamous extramarital conduct in this period came in August 1956 when Jackie was pregnant having suffered a miscarriage early in their marriage. The news came through that Jackie had given birth to a stillborn child after an emergency cesarean. Kennedy was not there as he was enjoying a cruise on the Mediterranean with Florida senator George Smathers and other friends. Young women boarded the boat at various ports of call. It was a veritable orgy, with JFK particularly enamoured of the charms of a sexy blonde called 'Pooh'. It seems that Kennedy returned to his wife only after Smathers insisted he return home in order to prevent serious damage to his political career. In other words, a divorce would end his presidential ambitions. So callous had Kennedy's conduct been that Jackie may have contemplated divorce. The rumour has long circulated that Joe Kennedy offered or actually paid her a million dollars to stay in the marriage after JFK blotted his copybook in the summer of 1956. Jack did love Jackie, but his womanizing hurt her, even though she had anticipated that it would be part of their married life.[18]

The American people remained blissfully unaware of Kennedy's libertine ways. What they saw was a golden couple: beautiful, charming, intelligent and happy. JFK's partnership with Jackie was not like those between Franklin and Eleanor Roosevelt, and Bill and Hillary Clinton. The Roosevelts and the Clintons developed political partnerships. Apart from her husband's success, Jackie was not interested in politics. She found it vulgar and resented the press intrusion into her life that accompanied her marriage to a senator, then a president. She would have no programme like the National Youth Administration, as Eleanor

Roosevelt did, or the healthcare reform championed by Hillary Clinton. Yet Jackie did influence Jack's political career by bolstering two core elements of his image – that he was a glamorous sex symbol and at the same time a symbol of family life. Jackie was young, elegant and immaculately dressed. Her own glamour had the effect of increasing Jack's by association. No longer viewed as a feature of his fun bachelorhood, his glamour was now presented – by both the Kennedys and the media – as part of his marriage to the chic Jackie.

It is easy to assume that the iconic status of the Jack–Jackie marriage was achieved during the White House years, but a perusal of the covers of major magazines in the 1950s reveals that the presentation of Jack and Jackie Kennedy as a couple with Hollywood allure *preceded* his presidency. *Life* magazine, in particular, showcased the photogenic couple. In their debut appearance in *Life* in July 1953, two months before their wedding, they were photographed in a glamorous setting, on a sailing boat. The caption read: 'Senator Kennedy Goes A-Courting.' The image conjured up a world of ease and affluent pleasure. It could be a scene out of Hitchcock's *To Catch a Thief*, with Jack and Jackie substituting for Cary Grant and Grace Kelly. A sense of indulgence, implicitly sensual indulgence, was conveyed by the picture. In August 1959 they again graced the cover of *Life*, with JFK sitting behind his wife who looked composed and stylish in pearls and an incarnadine dress. The caption read: 'Jackie Kennedy: A Front Runner's Appealing Wife.' The spatial arrangement of the picture, with Jackie more prominent than her husband, reflected her importance to his image.[19]

Marriage to Jackie also deepened Jack's resonance as a symbol of the family. With prominent parents and numerous siblings, Kennedy had already been able to present himself, notably in his 1946 and 1952 campaigns, as an emblem of family life. By marrying a glamorous wife who sparked the media's attention, and becoming a father in 1957 with the birth of his daughter Caroline, Jack was portrayed in a family setting more completely. The cover of *Life* magazine on 21 April 1958 showed Jack and Jackie in their baby's bedroom with a doting father holding Caroline. It was an image of such undiluted familial bliss, of the perfect American family, that it could be the handiwork of Norman Rockwell, who two years later would paint JFK for the *Saturday Evening Post*. The key point is that Americans looked at Kennedy and, more than any other politician, thought of sex. They looked at Kennedy and, again more than any other politician, thought of family. Those were crucial elements in JFK's appeal. His marriage to Jacqueline Bouvier bolstered them.[20]

As Kennedy's marriage to Jackie boosted his image and political career in the early 1950s, his association with Joseph McCarthy damaged it. On 9 February 1950 McCarthy delivered a speech in Wheeling, West Virginia, alleging that President Truman's State Department was riddled with communists. This extraordinary claim by the Republican senator from Wisconsin intensified the Red Scare that had emerged in American political life after the Second World War. He soon became the leading figure in this anti-communist backlash. McCarthy would remain a dominant figure in American politics for almost half a decade, until he was 'condemned' for unethical conduct by his Senate colleagues on 2 December

1954. The vote was 67–22 in support of the measure. Hospitalized following a major back operation, Kennedy did not cast a vote. Nor did he 'pair' on the record in favour of the vote against McCarthy, or express regret for this thereafter.[21]

That failure to take a stand against a right-wing demagogue who, in the eyes of many Americans and certainly liberals, had trampled over civil liberties with wanton disregard would haunt Kennedy for years to come. It aggravated his relationship with liberal luminaries, not least the grand dame of the New Deal, Eleanor Roosevelt. It put the spotlight on his character, his sense of morality, or lack thereof, decades before Thomas Reeves highlighted the issue. It even compromised his bid for the presidency. More than any other political issue before he reached the White House, McCarthyism damaged him.

That came as no surprise to Kennedy, for he immediately grasped his vulnerability on McCarthy. As he waited in his hospital room in late 1954, he tapped his tooth and said to his pal Chuck Spalding:

> You know, when I get downstairs I know exactly what's going to happen. Those reporters are going to lean over my stretcher. There's going to be about ninety-five faces bent over me with great concern, and everyone of those guys is going to say…, 'Now, senator, what about McCarthy?' Do you know what I'm going to do? I'm going to reach back for my back and I'm going to yell, 'Oow,' and then I'm going to pull the sheet over my head and hope we can get out of there.

Kennedy knew that in future he would be forced to defend himself from accusations of cowardice over McCarthyism.[22]

The liberal wing of the Democratic Party, as well as the press, fixated on JFK's failure to take a stand against McCarthy. For liberals, McCarthy was such an abominable threat to democratic values and traditions in America that it became a litmus test of a politician's moral fibre, one that Kennedy failed. If he could not be trusted on McCarthy, then perhaps he could not be trusted at all. Certainly that was the view taken by Eleanor Roosevelt. When JFK challenged Tennessee senator Estes Kefauver for the vice-presidential nomination at the 1956 Democratic National Convention, he sought the former First Lady's endorsement. She refused to give it, telling him she could not back someone who had failed to oppose McCarthy. She understood that he had been too ill to vote in December 1954 but was perturbed by his refusal to say how he would have voted and what he felt about McCarthyism when asked later by reporters. To Kennedy's friend who came on his behalf to ask for her support, she said: 'I think McCarthyism is a question on which public officials must stand up and be counted. I still have not heard Senator Kennedy express his convictions.' Two years later Eleanor Roosevelt recalled this episode for the readers of her newspaper column. Her criticism was serious for Kennedy not only due to her stature within the Democratic Party but also because of the nub of her argument: she was questioning his political courage and thus his character.[23]

Anticipating that the McCarthy issue would hurt his upcoming presidential campaign, Kennedy tried in 1959 to reframe the public debate on his record. His

Senate office released the statement he had drafted on McCarthy in 1954, even though its criticism of the Wisconsin senator was lukewarm and confined largely to the role of his aide Roy Cohn. It also released a list of individuals such as Charles Bohlen and James Conant whose appointments Kennedy had voted to confirm (or not) in opposition to McCarthy's wishes. In June that year Kennedy wrote a review for *The Washington Post* of Richard Rovere's critical biography *Senator Joe McCarthy*, in which he latched onto Robert Taft's role in nurturing the Red Scare. Given his praise for Taft in his 1956 book *Profiles in Courage*, this could be viewed as a dubious attempt to use the Republican senator who was now dead and so unable to defend himself in order to deflect attention from his own unimpressive role. This effort to neutralize the McCarthy issue before the 1960 campaign got underway was unsuccessful, as liberals continued to challenge him on it during the Democratic primaries.[24]

It was not until Election Day on 8 November 1960 when those persistent concerns over his refusal to denounce McCarthy had manifestly failed to prevent him from reaching the White House that the Kennedy–McCarthy controversy faded away. But for much of the 1950s this had been a major issue for Kennedy. It was one with several facets, including the ideological tension between JFK and the liberal wing of the Democratic Party, and the influence of his family – especially his father – on his political career. Most importantly, it sheds light on the matter that so concerned Eleanor Roosevelt: Kennedy's character.

JFK's reluctance to distance himself from McCarthy, even as the Senate moved against him in 1954, was due in part to the friendship that had developed between the Wisconsinite and the Kennedy clan. Both Irish Catholic, both elected to Congress in 1946, it was no surprise that JFK and McCarthy would get along; even less of a surprise given their mutual interest in an active social life. Kennedy did not share McCarthy's fondness for the bottle, but he had the same penchant for chasing women. A British friend, Alastair Forbes, recalled going around to Kennedy's house, long before McCarthy was famous, and asking him, 'What are you doing tonight?' 'I thought Joe McCarthy's coming around for a drink,' replied JFK, 'and we might take out a couple of girls from the Senate typing pool.' McCarthy sometimes visited Kennedy at Hyannisport. They were once spotted playing croquet against the backdrop of the Atlantic. It was clear, as George Smathers recalled on the basis of many conversations with him about the Red-baiter, that 'Jack liked McCarthy.… he was friendly to McCarthy all the way through'. He saw McCarthy as flawed but as talented and likeable.[25]

McCarthy became a friend of not only JFK but his family too. Joe Kennedy, in particular, was a fan. 'I liked Joe McCarthy,' he recalled. 'I always liked him.' They spent time together in Washington, Palm Beach and Cape Cod. 'I thought he'd be a sensation,' said Joe. 'He was smart. But he went off the deep end.' There is a sense of Joe Kennedy deriving pleasure from the way McCarthy took pot shots at Establishment figures, those sorts of WASP snobs who had snubbed him, even as he became one of the richest men in America. Bobby Kennedy too became part of McCarthy's circle, going to work as counsel for the senator's investigations subcommittee. He would quit after falling out with Roy Cohn, but testimony to his enduring affection for McCarthy was his attendance at his funeral in 1957. JFK's sisters Eunice and Patricia even 'went out' with McCarthy. These family ties to McCarthy would make Kennedy uncomfortable about coming out against him, even as the tide of opinion turned against his heavy-handed tactics. As he said later, 'How the hell could I get up there and denounce Joe McCarthy when my own brother was working for him.' And for JFK in this case, family loyalty trumped political principle.[26]

It was not just McCarthy's intimacy with clan Kennedy that induced JFK's caution as the sands started to run out for the senator. There was also an ideological compatibility between McCarthy, who insisted that a group of corrupt, incompetent officials in government were selling out American interests in the battle against communism, and JFK's own hard-line views on foreign policy. As discussed earlier, he believed that the Roosevelt and Truman administrations had been weak in dealing with the Soviet Union and the communists in China. His determination to resist the communists was also evident in his decision in 1950 to vote for the McCarran Internal Security Act, which required the official registration of all communist groups in America and made the laws against espionage and subversion stricter. This accounts for his comment in 1950 that he 'knew Joe pretty well, and he may have something', and his furious response at a Harvard dinner two years later when someone said how pleased he was that their college had produced neither convicted spy Alger Hiss nor Joe McCarthy: 'How dare you couple the name of a great American patriot with that of a traitor!' Kennedy would come to suspect that McCarthy had overstated his case and his theatricality was at odds with Kennedy's more measured political style. Still, he sympathized with a good deal of what McCarthy had to say on the severity of the communist threat. That shaped his response to the move to censure McCarthy in 1954.[27]

Kennedy's Senate race in 1952 highlighted another factor in his attitude to McCarthy: his popularity in Massachusetts, especially with Irish Catholics in Boston. In his battle with Henry Cabot Lodge, Kennedy knew that he would be damned if he did attack McCarthy and damned if he did not. On the one hand there were liberal groups, including the Harvard community, which would take umbrage if he spoke, as he had in private, of his belief that McCarthy had raised some important issues. On the other, there were many Irish Catholics who revered McCarthy. As Massachusetts politician Paul Dever put it, 'Joe McCarthy is the only man I know who could beat Archbishop Cushing in a two-man election fight in South Boston.' (Cushing had been born in South Boston.) Another element in the political equation in Kennedy's home state was the press. In particular, the *Boston Post* was unwavering in its support for McCarthy's anti-communist crusade, so much so that the paper would later chide Kennedy for not backing the campaign to rid the government of communists wholeheartedly enough.[28]

Active behind the scenes in his son's Senate campaign, Joe Kennedy reinforced his son's inclination to keep quiet on McCarthy, and certainly not to attack him. When one adviser urged JFK to issue a statement that included a condemnation of McCarthy, Joe Kennedy exploded and that statement was never released. On the McCarthy issue, therefore, Joe Kennedy played an influential role in the 1952 campaign. But its effect was to endorse an approach that had been adopted by JFK since 1950, which was generally to avoid taking a public stance on McCarthy, and that included eschewing the sort of outraged assault on him made by many liberals.[29]

Small wonder that Kennedy once said of the McCarthy issue, 'What was I supposed to do, commit hara-kiri?' As a politician seeking elective office, it was reasonable for Kennedy to dwell on such realities as McCarthy's popularity in his home state, and to factor that in to the public stance he took on this issue. These sorts of compromises and fudges are commonplace in politics, and it would have been naïve of him to think he could lambaste McCarthy in Massachusetts without compromising his campaign for the Senate. But the chronological limits to that argument are clear: after November 1952 Kennedy was not up for re-election for six years, giving him ample time to develop a public position on McCarthy more reflective of his dangerous excesses.[30]

Following his victory over Lodge, Kennedy joined McCarthy in the Senate. The independently minded fellow that he was, he did not always do McCarthy's bidding. As well as voting differently to the Wisconsinite on the confirmation of various officials, he was unhappy with Bobby Kennedy – at their father's behest – going to work for McCarthy on his investigations subcommittee. His overall approach, though, was to continue to avoid taking a stance on McCarthy. Asked by a journalist what he thought of McCarthy, he replied, 'Not very much. But I get along with him. When I was in the House, I used to get along with [socialist Vito] Marcantonio and [racist John] Rankin. As long as they don't step in my way, I don't want to get into personal fights.' But as McCarthy careened towards self-destruction by attacking the army for harbouring communists, which culminated in the Senate's televised Army–McCarthy hearings in the spring of 1954, Kennedy's studied neutrality on McCarthyism was no longer so free of political consequences. This was especially the case for a Democrat like Kennedy, with his sights already set on the White House, who needed to court the goodwill of his party in order to realize those ambitions. And in 1954 the Democratic Party was coming to the conclusion that it needed to move decisively against McCarthy to end his reign of terror.[31]

The initiative for taking down McCarthy actually came from a Republican, Vermont senator Ralph Flanders, who introduced a resolution on 30 July calling for the censure of McCarthy. It seemed that Kennedy was finally going to have to formulate a public response to the McCarthy issue. He instructed his aide Ted Sorensen to draft a statement, which JFK edited. But Senate Republicans contrived to postpone any action against McCarthy until after the congressional elections in November. Kennedy shelved the statement.[32]

The statement which Kennedy had been prepared to release was a fudge. Discerning the decisive loss of credibility on McCarthy's part caused by his attack on the army, and the greater determination on Capitol Hill to clip McCarthy's wings, Kennedy's statement supported the censure of McCarthy. Yet it did so merely on the narrow grounds of misconduct on the part of McCarthy's aides Roy Cohn and G. David Schine. The statement questioned neither the goals nor methods of McCarthy's anti-communist campaign. It made clear JFK's previous support for McCarthy, the voting of funds for his Senate committee and for his amendment to curtail aid to countries trading with the communist bloc. Kennedy refuted the idea that McCarthy should be censured for damaging America's reputation overseas or dividing the American people. Given his and his family's friendly relations with McCarthy, his sympathy for the senator's claim that the foreign policy Establishment had been asleep at the wheel at the outset of the Cold War, and his recognition of McCarthy's popularity with many of his constituents in Massachusetts, JFK decided against presenting a wide-ranging critique of McCarthy's crusade.[33]

As the Senate moved after the congressional elections to censure McCarthy, Kennedy was in the midst of a personal crisis: his failing health had left him at death's door. His bad back had deteriorated. He was in intense pain. Aides Kenneth O'Donnell and Dave Powers noticed how he needed to use crutches constantly. In the end Kennedy agreed that major spinal surgery was unavoidable. On 21 October 1954 that complex, three-hour surgery was carried out. The surgery was particularly dangerous given JFK's Addison's disease. But, as Rose Kennedy recalled, 'Jack was determined to have the operation. He told his father that even if the risks were fifty-fifty, he would rather be dead than spend the rest of his life hobbling on crutches and paralyzed by pain.' Three days after the operation a urinary-tract infection left Kennedy in a coma. With death seemingly imminent his family was summoned. He was read the last rites of the church. Then he rallied. There is evidence that he deteriorated again to such an extent that he was read the last rites for a second time. On 10 February 1955 he returned to hospital for another operation as he had an open, infected draining wound that would not heal. After a long convalescence, Kennedy finally returned to the Senate in May 1955 – seven months after entering hospital for the original surgery.[34]

The explanation given by Kennedy and his supporters for his failure to vote or 'pair' in favour of the Senate's condemnation of McCarthy in December 1954 was the devastating impact of the surgery. This defence of Kennedy's record on McCarthy should not be dismissed out of hand. Close to death, his medical situation could hardly have been more serious. Understandably his focus and of those close to him was on his survival and not any political issues, even one as explosive as McCarthyism. Jean McGonigle Mannix, who worked in Kennedy's Senate office, said that in late 1954, 'I never heard anything, any discussion in the office about it [the vote to condemn McCarthy] because frankly, at that time we were so concerned about his operation and whether he would live.' Even basic communication between Kennedy and his Senate staff was curtailed. As a practical matter, it was not feasible for Kennedy to have voted for McCarthy's condemnation. As Jack Bell of the Associated Press observed, 'he probably would have had to fly to Washington…on a hospital stretcher to vote'.[35]

Kennedy, however, could have declared his support for the Senate's condemnation of McCarthy by 'pairing' in favour of it. That would have required only a brief phone call from Kennedy to Sorensen, who years later told historian Herbert Parmet that he had been waiting by his phone for Kennedy's call. It never came. Yet JFK could have made the call. Despite his painful convalescence, he was not comatose. In January 1955, between his back operations, Kennedy paired with another senator when he sought to exclude a US commitment to defend the islands of Quemoy and Matsu from the Formosa Resolution. Clearly he could have paired on the Senate condemnation of McCarthy as well, and saved himself from the dubious distinction of being the only Democratic senator neither to vote nor pair in favour of McCarthy's censure.[36]

Kennedy's failure to do so represents the most disappointing feature of his early political career. It was a moral as well as a political failure. The Red Scare had profound and devastating human consequences. Kennedy was aware of this. He knew of the case of the Hollywood Ten who would go to prison. University faculty lost their livelihoods due to the witch hunt, as did others. There were a number of suicides. But JFK was either unable or unwilling to consider McCarthy in a broader context, the extent to which his methods were inconsistent with democratic values and even basic standards of propriety. JFK's friend Alastair Forbes noticed how Kennedy 'didn't see in what direction McCarthy was running – totally counter not just [to] liberal American tradition but to a basic American tradition'.[37]

A combination of misplaced loyalty to McCarthy borne out of his family's friendship with the senator, the staunch anti-communism and critique of Truman and FDR that he shared with McCarthy, his concerns about the Wisconsinite's popularity in Massachusetts and this inability to ponder the fundamental damage done by McCarthy to civil liberties in America account for Kennedy's failure to provide moral leadership on McCarthyism. A decade later, as president, he would be faced with the second great moral challenge of his political career: civil rights. This time he would meet that challenge with greater resolve and courage.

The issue of courage, so lacking in Kennedy's response to McCarthyism, was paradoxically the central theme of his second book, *Profiles in Courage*, published in 1956 by Harper and Brothers. A study of senators such as John Quincy Adams, Daniel Webster and Sam Houston who had displayed a courageous independence in going against the will of their party or constituents, *Profiles in Courage* was a spectacular success. Sales were substantial. Reviews waxed lyrical. Newspaper serializations promoted both the book and the author. *Kraft Theater* bought the television rights. Beyond all of this success and praise, there was one accomplishment that magnified the book's significance: in May 1957 it was announced that the Pulitzer Prize for best biography had been awarded to JFK.[38]

Profiles in Courage represented an important milestone for Kennedy on the road to the White House. As a Pulitzer Prize-winning author, his reputation as a man of letters – established by the writing of *Why England Slept* – was enhanced. Those literary credentials set Kennedy apart from other politicians. It made him appear more sophisticated, well-rounded and wise. It furthered the construction of Kennedy's alluring image that would be so important to his future political success. To be a Pulitzer Prize winner as well as a war hero, a sex symbol and an emblem of the family endowed Kennedy's image with an astonishing power.

Profiles in Courage made his image yet more irresistible by associating him more closely with a heroic brand of leadership. A major theme of *Why England*

Slept had been the need for leaders like Churchill who had the courage to stand up to Hitler and the wisdom to bolster the nation's defences. Valiant leadership was a key theme in *Profiles in Courage* too. Here Kennedy praised those politicians who had resisted party and constituent pressure to do what they thought was in the national interest – men such as Massachusetts senator Daniel Webster who backed the Compromise of 1850 in order to save the Union despite strong opposition from his own constituents, and Texas senator Sam Houston who opposed the Kansas–Nebraska bill against the wishes of other Southern Democrats in Congress as well as his constituents. In JFK's opinion, sensible compromise – rather than dogmatism – was often a key ingredient of the political courage he explored in this work.[39]

As well as entrenching his image as man of letters and advancing his narrative on heroic leadership, *Profiles in Courage* revealed Kennedy's further thoughts on the relationship between the public and the ruling elite. In *Why England Slept* he had stressed the need for leaders able to ignore public opposition to a military build-up that was essential in countering the Nazi threat. In his Pulitzer Prize-winning follow-up, he again emphasized the importance of independent leadership prepared to ignore public opinion in doing what was in the national interest. This scepticism over the public's influence on policymaking would remain an important element in Kennedy's thinking as he moved on to the White House, attracting him to covert solutions to foreign policy problems.

It has sometimes been believed that Kennedy's decision to write a book about political courage was linked to a wish to expiate his guilt over his refusal to take a stand against McCarthy, or his reflection on the theme of courage in light of his life-threatening back problems. But his original decision to write on courage in American politics preceded both his equivocation on McCarthy and his spinal surgery in 1954. As the controversy over his failure to vote for the censure of McCarthy deepened, he may well have realized that a study linking him to political bravery would be useful in obscuring his lack of resolve over McCarthyism. Originally planning an article on courage in politics, Kennedy decided instead to write a book on the subject. Harper and Brothers agreed to publish it. The next thing was to identify the politicians who best exemplified political courage. He sought advice from Sorensen, journalists such as Arthur Krock, and academics – including James MacGregor Burns – as to which historical figures to examine.[40]

The writing of *Profiles in Courage*, shortly after publication and ever since, has been controversial as JFK's authorship has been contested. It was journalist Drew Pearson who asserted before a national television audience what had been whispered behind closed doors: Kennedy had not written *Profiles in Courage*. In December 1957 he made that claim on Mike Wallace's show, and it was a shocking one as six months earlier Kennedy had been awarded the Pulitzer.[41]

This was an occasion when the Kennedys' power and money were of decisive importance, for JFK hired savvy lawyer Clark M. Clifford. He explained to Clifford how seriously he regarded Pearson's claim that *Profiles in Courage* had been ghost-written. An enraged Joe Kennedy intervened, calling Clifford to tell him that he planned to sue ABC and Pearson. Clifford urged a different strategy, which was to press ABC for a retraction. Examining some of JFK's written notes for the book, the lawyer concluded that although others had helped with the research, 'the book was his'. Clifford presented this evidence over a two-day conference with ABC officials, after which they accepted that Kennedy was the author of the Pulitzer Prize-winning book. According to Clifford, ABC became concerned that their refusal to back down might result in a 'dangerous' law suit from JFK for libel.[42]

When he hired Clifford, Kennedy told him that Pearson's comment was so troubling as it called into question 'his character and integrity and veracity'. Despite Kennedy's protestations, Pearson had been justified in querying the senator's literary credentials. For all intents and purposes, Kennedy had *not* written *Profiles in Courage*. After publication Ted Sorensen visited Williams College where he spoke to students. After lunch with James MacGregor Burns, who taught there, the academic said, 'That was a very good book, *Profiles in Courage*. Who really wrote it?' It was windy, but Burns thought he heard Sorensen say, 'I did.'[43]

Burns had probably heard Sorensen correctly, for the Kennedy aide had indeed penned a substantial portion of the book, writing, inter alia, the chapters on John Quincy Adams, Edmund Ross and Thomas Hart Benton. He also edited the entire manuscript to give it a stylistic coherence. Georgetown University's Jules Davids, who had taught an American history course audited by Jackie Kennedy, made a major contribution too, writing sections of various chapters. His role was the most important, apart from Sorensen's. Joe Kennedy pal James Landis drafted the chapter on Robert Taft. Distinguished academics, including Arthur Schlesinger Jr. and Allan Nevins, also had an input. The documentary record on which Kennedy rested his authorial claims was slight. At the Kennedy Library, files of JFK's handwritten notes show that he did have an involvement, but for the most part they were notes from secondary sources, particularly on John Quincy Adams, together with some of his own observations. This was also the case with tapes that recorded Kennedy's dictation. 'There is no evidence,' as Herbert Parmet writes, 'of a Kennedy draft for the overwhelming bulk of the book; and there is evidence for concluding that much of what he did draft was simply not included in the final version.' Kennedy shaped *Profiles in Courage* by deciding at the outset on its content and approving the final draft. But, for the most part, he did not write it.[44]

To some degree that was understandable. Kennedy was recuperating from back surgery and hospitalized for periods during the research and writing of the book; and when not incapacitated in this way, his responsibilities as a diligent senator were onerous and time-consuming. Moreover, it is not a rare thing for busy politicians to use ghost-writers. Ronald Reagan's autobiography *An American Life* is a case in point. But it is one thing for a politician to have a book published which they did not compose, and another to do that and then accept a prestigious literary prize like the Pulitzer for such a work. That Kennedy did so does not reflect well on his scruples. He had failed to be candid with not only the Pulitzer Advisory Board, but the American people as well. This episode had no obvious bearing on his effectiveness as a senator or later as a presidential policymaker. But, in retrospect, it exposed his vanity and unwillingness to turn down an accolade so beneficial to his image and reputation.[45]

And boost his reputation it did. It was part of a process in 1956–7 that converted Kennedy from a recently elected senator to a strong presidential contender. At the Democratic National Convention in Chicago in August 1956 he made a major impression on a national television audience. He narrated a campaign film, gave the nominating speech for the party's presidential candidate Adlai Stevenson, and – most importantly – almost won the Democratic vice-presidential nomination, losing narrowly to Tennessee senator Estes Kefauver. That, together with the Pulitzer, the dazzling image crafted over the previous decade and a half, and his re-election as Massachusetts senator in 1958 in a record landslide, made JFK a frontrunner for the Democratic presidential nomination in 1960. Kennedy busied himself in 1958–9 by travelling throughout the nation, speaking to enthusiastic audiences and taking strong positions on national security. In this way he sustained, indeed raised his profile yet further. He did so knowing that he would run for president in 1960, having made that decision as early as Thanksgiving in 1956.[46]

When Jack declared his candidacy for the presidency on 2 January 1960, he had already decided on a clear strategy for winning the Democratic presidential nomination: he would enter a number of primaries and win them all both to establish his leadership credentials and to line up delegate support before the Democratic National Convention in Los Angeles in July. What he could not do was duplicate Senate Majority Leader Lyndon Johnson's tactic of staying out of the race until only just before the Convention, remaining in Washington and appearing above the fray up until that point, while surreptitiously securing delegate support for the Convention behind the scenes. He simply did not exert the sort of influence within the Democratic Party that Johnson did which would have made that approach feasible. As well as Johnson, JFK worried about another luminary waiting in the wings – the darling of the liberal set, Stevenson. Although Eisenhower had trounced him in 1952 and 1956 and he professed to have no presidential aspirations in 1960, the Illinoisan did secretly pine for the Democratic nomination yet again. A grassroots draft-Stevenson movement took off throughout the country, gathering momentum as the Democratic Convention approached; the Illinoisan did nothing to stop it. Like LBJ, he hoped the Convention would turn to him.[47]

Nothing caused Kennedy more consternation in the spring and summer of 1960 than the possibility that Stevenson would take the nomination away from him at the last moment. That fear was due in part to Kennedy's recognition of the distrust which existed between himself and the liberal wing of the party over his failure to take a stand against McCarthy. The contrast between Eleanor Roosevelt's admiration for Stevenson and her scepticism of JFK was one sign of that enduring tension. In 1960 the liberal infatuation with Stevenson was not over, and that troubled JFK. He tried to eradicate any possibility of Stevenson winning the nomination by persuading him to support the Kennedy campaign. Stevenson refused, provoking JFK's wrath.[48]

With Stevenson and LBJ biding their time, it was the Democrat from Minnesota Hubert Humphrey – much respected senator, fine orator, impeccable liberal credentials – who threw his hat into the ring for the primaries. Wisconsin was the first major contest for JFK and Humphrey, followed by West Virginia. Humphrey found himself up against a formidable political machine: well funded, managed with relentless zeal by Bobby Kennedy, with a modern-PR slickness and a candidate with star appeal. As JFK's Republican rival Richard Nixon would discover in the autumn, Humphrey found it almost impossible to compete with Kennedy in terms of image. The core elements of JFK's image as it had developed over the previous two decades remained evident in the 1960 campaign. A TV documentary broadcast during the West Virginia primary, for example, started with a shot of a PT boat before showing Kennedy with the Pulitzer Prize. This candidate, voters were reminded, was both war hero and literary luminary. His status as a familial symbol was very much to the fore. In Wisconsin his wife, brothers, sisters and mother campaigned energetically on his behalf. Sex featured in a presidential campaign like never before. If Paul Newman, Elvis Presley or Marlon Brando had been the candidate, the effect would have been similar – but no contemporary politician could compete with Kennedy when it came to glamour, aesthetics and sex appeal. Accounts of the campaign make clear the extent to which JFK's sex-symbol status influenced voters. 'Oh, Jack I love yuh, Jack, I love yuh, Jack – Jack, Jack, I love yuh,' one woman was heard muttering to herself. The mass swooning for candidate Kennedy increased markedly after the first Kennedy–Nixon TV debate on 26 September, and his adoring female fans even acquired their own typology: 'jumpers', 'screamers', 'touchers' and 'leapers'.[49]

Another facet of Kennedy's image emerged in the campaign: the idea of him as a man of faith. That might seem paradoxical given his hedonistic private life (which continued unabated during the campaign as he embarked on an affair with Californian socialite Judith Campbell), but rather like Bill Clinton three decades later JFK was a presidential candidate who combined a playboy lifestyle with genuine religious faith. His faith became part of his image in 1960 because it was a prominent issue in the campaign. Indeed, more than any policy issue during the Wisconsin and West Virginia primaries Kennedy grappled with the question of how to defend himself against the accusation that as a Catholic he would owe his allegiance to Rome rather than the American Constitution. Privately, Kennedy told Judy Campbell he saw it, fundamentally, as an issue of prejudice and that his role therefore would be to educate Americans. Initially, however, he preferred not to dwell on the matter in public. He knew how tricky it was for him; no Catholic had ever been elected president, and when a major party had nominated one – Democrat Al Smith in 1928 – he had lost heavily. But after failing to win in Protestant-dominated districts in Wisconsin, despite winning in Catholic districts and the primary itself, he decided that he had to confront the issue, especially as the next primary was in the largely Protestant West Virginia. From this point on, Kennedy made a series of cogent arguments to refute the idea that his Catholic faith should be viewed as a reasonable bar to his candidacy: No one cared about their faith when he fought and his elder brother died in the Second World War, he pointed out. Had his chance to become president been taken away the day he was baptized? Should not his affirmation of his belief in the strict separation between church and state be enough to assuage the fears of those concerned? His speech on the religious issue and his response to questions at the Greater Houston Ministerial Association on 12 September became his definitive rebuttal of the attacks on his candidacy on the basis of his faith. His handling of the issue was adroit and manifestly effective: concerns over his Catholicism did not prevent him from becoming president. However, the focus on this issue in 1960 added a new element to his image as man of faith, as the premise of the discussion of his Catholicism was that his religious faith was genuine, as indeed it was. This served to bolster Kennedy's traditionalist credentials as a symbol of family and military service – and now, also, religious faith. This, alongside the cutting-edge appeal provided by his youth (he would be the youngest elected president in US history) and sex-symbol status, gave his image an extraordinary dualistic appeal.[50]

Kennedy continued the theme of the need for heroic leadership in a time of crisis, introduced in *Why England Slept* and continued in *Profiles in Courage*, by adopting a forthright stance in the campaign on America's position in the Cold War. The Eisenhower–Nixon administration, he argued, had been asleep at the wheel, allowing a 'missile gap' to emerge in Moscow's favour that Khrushchev would exploit in the early 1960s in order to expand Russian influence. It was a fear that had been articulated by many of Ike's critics ever since the Soviets succeeded in 1957 in sending *Sputnik* into orbit. To develop further his argument on the Eisenhower–Nixon laxness on the Cold War, Kennedy highlighted the issue of Cuba, as only the year before the left-wing revolutionary Fidel Castro had come to power, a mere ninety miles from the coast of Florida. The day before the second Kennedy–Nixon TV debate JFK said the advent of Castro to power represented 'the most glaring failure of American foreign policy'; and the day before the fourth and final debate Kennedy released a statement blaming Nixon explicitly for Cuba going communist and promising to support anti-Castro Cubans in exile who could bring about the overthrow of Castro – in other words, essentially the plan that Kennedy would carry out three months into his presidency at the Bay of Pigs. What JFK was promising was the steely brand of leadership required in dealing with the threat posed by communism in general and Castro in particular.[51]

That Kennedy was able to attack Nixon so effectively on national security, thereby undermining any attempt by the Republican to portray him as another 'soft' liberal, was one factor behind his narrow victory in November – 34,226,731 votes (49.7 per cent) to 34,108,157 (49.5 per cent); a more comfortable 303 to 219 votes in the Electoral College. But a range of factors accounted for his triumph in the election of 1960. These included the slick organisation, vast financial resources and vigorous management (in the form of Robert Kennedy) of the campaign; the recession of 1960; the tactical mistakes of Nixon in pledging to campaign in every state of the Union, a number of which had few Electoral College votes or/ and were not competitive; JFK's ability to win the Black vote, aided by his widely publicised decision to intervene when Martin Luther King was imprisoned (for taking part in a 'sit-in' protest at a restaurant) by phoning King's pregnant wife Coretta to offer support and by having Bobby call the judge in Georgia to persuade him to release the civil rights leader; his shrewd decision in July at the Democratic

National Convention in Los Angeles, where he won the nomination on the first ballot ahead of his nearest rival Lyndon Johnson, to select the formidable Texan Senate Majority Leader as his vice-presidential running-mate, as this helped carry the South; and his effective handling of the controversy over his Catholic faith.[52]

The analytical challenge is in gauging the relative significance of the various factors underpinning JFK's victory in 1960; and it is the argument here that the most important was Kennedy's dazzling image. As argued earlier, he succeeded during the campaign in sustaining and developing further the mesmerizing image he had constructed in the two decades prior to his presidential bid in 1960. In a televisual era, which made American politics so different to what it had been in say 1948, this was no trivial matter. Most important, in terms of the impact of image on the campaign, were the four Kennedy–Nixon television debates, in particular the first one in Chicago on 26 September 1960, which has become one of the most iconic episodes in American political folklore. Read the transcript of that debate, and it is apparent that Kennedy performed well and that Nixon was too passive and defensive. But it was the visuals that really mattered. Kennedy looked film-star handsome and (paradoxically given the Addison's disease and ongoing spinal problems) a picture of health, with a Cary Grant suntan. Nixon was ill and looked it, having lost five pounds of weight after damaging his knee, and then knocking it again on his way into the studio for the debate. Kennedy was more attuned than Nixon to the significance of the sartorial: his dark suit contrasted sharply with the studio backdrop, whereas Nixon's light grey suit blended into it. When told by a producer about the glare of his white shirt under television lights, Kennedy rectified the problem by dispatching an aide to collect a blue shirt. JFK wore make-up; Nixon did not, instead using 'Lazy Shave' which streaked in the heat of the studio. While those Americans who listened to the debate on radio believed that the candidates performed with roughly equal skill, the vast majority of those who watched on television thought Kennedy had been so much more impressive than his Republican rival. The impact of the visual was thus profound. American politics would never be the same again.[53]

There is one key fact in the 1960 presidential campaign: prior to that first debate, Kennedy was behind in the polls; after the debate he moved ahead of Nixon – and stayed ahead. A Gallup poll released before the debate had Nixon on 47 per cent and Kennedy on 46 per cent. In the first Gallup poll taken after the debate, Kennedy was on 49 per cent and Nixon 46 per cent. The great chronicler of the 1960 campaign, Theodore White, observed how after that debate the crowds attending Kennedy campaign events increased substantially and the atmosphere was more febrile. It was 'as if', wrote White, 'the sight of him in their [Americans'] homes on the video box, had given him a "star quality" reserved only for television and movie idols'. That increased momentum and enhanced star status carried John Kennedy to victory on Election Day on Tuesday, 8 November. And then through the transition, onto an unforgettable inauguration as president of the United States on 20 January 1961.[54]

On John Kennedy's journey to the White House, Joseph Kennedy had played a notable role, providing encouragement, connections and financial support. But

Figure 2.3 Kennedy's performance in his first TV debate with Richard Nixon, including his superior visual impact, was crucial to his victory in the 1960 presidential election. (Wikimedia, public domain, Search media – Wikimedia Commons.)

JFK's own role had been much more important. As he himself said – in reference to the 1960 campaign – 'I'm getting awfully tired of reading how my father bought me the election. I think of all the things I did – I was the one out there.'[55]

On his rise to power, he had shown himself to be a gifted politician. But he had not been an outstanding legislator in Congress, as Lyndon Johnson had. He knew a lot about foreign relations, but his track record on policy issues was not more impressive than that of say Hubert Humphrey. Where he was far superior to any politician of his generation – and I think the argument can be cogently made, more than any politician in US history – was in his ability to create an image that dazzled the American people. He understood how the aesthetic considerations of Hollywood could be used in shaping his own political image. He grasped how television was changing politics. He realized how such elemental factors as family and sexual attraction could be used to strengthen the sense of connection between himself and the voting public. When it came to creating a powerful and seductive image, he was simply brilliant. This constitutes the most important factor in his rise to presidential power.

Another influential factor was his character. This is the point at which the argument made by his detractors needs to be inverted. Often his character has been portrayed as a terrible weakness. As a young man, he could at times be immature. On one key political issue, McCarthyism, his moral compass was askew. He allowed his family connections to the controversial senator and his concerns over McCarthy's popularity in Massachusetts to supersede his concerns about the Wisconsinite's impact on civil liberties in America. But his character comprised numerous traits, including many positive ones. He possessed a strong sense of independence, physical courage and a genuine commitment to public service. Had he not had the independence of mind to chart a different course to his domineering father in his response to Hitler – his brother Joe didn't – then *Why England Slept* would have been a defeatist, isolationist work that would have severely damaged his political aspirations. Had he not shown such commendable courage and ingenuity in leading his *PT 109* crew to safety, he not only would have been unable to make use of his wartime heroism as a political asset on the campaign trail, as he did after the Second World War, he would not have been around anyway to run for office. If he had not shown immense resilience in dealing with life-threatening illness, he would have succumbed to the temptation to leave political life for a quieter, less stressful one. His strength of character, therefore, was also an important factor in the journey to 1600 Pennsylvania Avenue.

Chapter 3

A YEAR OF CRISIS

At 12.52 pm on Friday, 20 January 1961, the youngest elected president in American history, with friends and dignitaries behind him on the steps of the Capitol Building and a crowd in front almost a million strong despite the sub-zero temperatures, began to deliver his inaugural address. Projecting an aura of youthful vitality despite the freezing cold, he sought to provide a rhetorical compass for the policy direction his administration would take, to inspire the American people, and to convince them he was the heroic leader the nation needed.[1]

With input from various associates but written by his most gifted wordsmith Ted Sorensen, JFK's inaugural proved to be the great success he had sought. Its rhetorical flourishes and Kennedy's impassioned delivery of the speech *did* inspire many Americans. He portrayed the Sixties as a time of crisis – especially because of the Cold War – emphasized his own fearlessness in meeting that challenge, and urged the American people to join him in this quest to protect America. 'In the long history of the world,' he declared, 'only a few generations have been granted the role of defending freedom in its hour of maximum danger. I do not shrink from this responsibility – I welcome it. I do not believe that any of us would exchange places with any other people or any other generation.' 'And so, my fellow Americans, ask not what your country can do for you – ask what you can do for your country.'[2]

Reflecting that emphasis on the dangers of the Cold War, as well as his greater long-standing interest in foreign affairs, Kennedy said little on domestic policy. He would soon unveil an ambitious programme of reform in areas such as education and healthcare, but he did not dwell on this in his inaugural. The only domestic issue he did touch on was civil rights when he stated that Americans were 'unwilling to witness or permit the slow undoing of those human rights to which this nation has always been committed, and to which we are committed today *at home* and around the world'.[3]

It was America's role on the international stage that was the main issue explored by the new president. On this he offered words of comfort and promise to liberals like Adlai Stevenson who had called for a less gung-ho American foreign policy, one based instead on patient diplomacy. Speaking of the dangers of nuclear weaponry, Kennedy urged the superpowers 'to begin anew'. 'Let us never negotiate out of fear,' he said. 'But let us never fear to negotiate.'[4]

On the other hand, much of JFK's inaugural was reminiscent of what the twenty-three-year-old Kennedy had said in *Why England Slept*: 'Let every nation know, whether it wishes us well or ill, that we shall pay any price, bear any burden, meet any hardship, support any friend, oppose any foe to assure the survival and the success of liberty.' Backing up that steely resolution would be immense military power: 'We dare not tempt them [enemies] with weakness. For only when our arms are sufficient beyond doubt can we be certain beyond doubt that they will never be employed.' This indicated that Kennedy would in general carry out a hard-line foreign policy.[5]

That is precisely what happened in the first year of the Kennedy presidency. In 1961 Kennedy began what would become (up to that time) the largest peacetime increase in US military spending. He sought to overthrow Fidel Castro, authorizing the Bay of Pigs invasion, assassination attempts and Operation Mongoose. He faced down the Russians in Berlin during the tense crisis that dominated the summer with strong rhetoric and a further military build-up that indicated a readiness for war, though his handling of the crisis was more nuanced than this suggests, given the policy options presented to him by his more bellicose advisers. He escalated US involvement in Vietnam. To be sure, there were other elements in Kennedy's early foreign policy that seemed more progressive: the Peace Corps, the Alliance for Progress aid programme for Latin America and a negotiated settlement in the Cold War hotspot of Laos. But the main thrust of JFK's foreign policy in 1961 was towards a tough, militarized approach to Cold War adversaries. The consequences of that were profound and troubling: a spiralling arms race in the Sixties, for the Russians would respond to Kennedy's military build-up with one of their own; another milestone on the road to full US involvement in the disastrous Vietnam War; and a Soviet decision to back Moscow's ally in Cuba, threatened as Fidel Castro was by Kennedy's policies, with nuclear missiles.[6]

The story of JFK's record as presidential policymaker, however, is one of change. Like anyone, a president is (or at least should be) influenced by their experiences in life, including their time in the White House. This was certainly the case with Kennedy, and to his credit he learned from his presidential experiences so as to redefine his policies in ways that served the national interest. The two most profound experiences for Kennedy would be the Cuban missile crisis of October 1962 and the civil rights crisis in Birmingham, Alabama, the following spring. The missile crisis impressed on Kennedy the dangers of the nuclear age and the importance therefore of reducing Cold War tensions. The Birmingham crisis increased Kennedy's determination to fight for racial equality. The Bay of Pigs disaster and the Berlin crisis also altered his thinking in constructive ways. The Kennedy who died in Dallas was, in a political sense, a very different man to the one who delivered his inaugural address on that cold January afternoon. He was more experienced and mature. He was more courageous. He was more progressive in outlook. Change and growth, then, were the commendable hallmarks of Kennedy's political record in the White House.

Kennedy's determination as he entered the White House to use an iron fist and not a velvet glove in handling communist adversaries was to some degree understandable. He was right to be concerned by Khrushchev and Castro. Khrushchev was dangerously unpredictable. He might speak of 'peaceful coexistence' with the West but that conciliatory rhetoric did not prevent him from threatening other nations with nuclear annihilation. Brinkmanship is a foreign policy strategy associated with Eisenhower's secretary of state, John Foster Dulles, but Khrushchev practised it with reckless abandon. 'One bomb is sufficient to destroy Bonn and Ruhr and that is all of Germany,' he had told US diplomat W. Averell Harriman in 1959. Khrushchev's insistence on forcing a change to the status of West Berlin *was* a threat to the security of the West as well as the freedom of West Berliners. It was understandable too that JFK was sobered by Khrushchev's speech on 6 January 1961 in which he proclaimed his support for wars of national liberation, in which countries like Cuba sought to throw off the shackles of imperial domination. Delivered just a fortnight before JFK replaced Ike, Khrushchev's address seemed to portend troubling times ahead in which the Russians expanded their influence throughout the developing world. Moreover, Kennedy was justified in his concern over Castro's rule in Cuba for it meant Moscow had an ally just ninety miles off the coast of Florida.[7]

A general resolve to meet the communist challenge, then, was appropriate. Kennedy's initial approach was flawed nonetheless. For one thing, he was too deferential to the generals and the CIA. He tended to assume their wisdom when it came to the use of force. That deference for his military and intelligence chiefs would be eroded by the bruising experiences of his presidency, not least the Bay of Pigs. But in January 1961 he viewed the military top brass as more reliable in their judgements than naïve liberals like Stevenson, and the intelligence chiefs as James Bond geniuses who had succeeded in covertly overthrowing undesirable governments in Iran and Guatemala in the 1950s.

That wariness towards leading liberals, both personally and in terms of their ideas, was another shortcoming in Kennedy's outlook at the start of his presidency. The tension between Kennedy and the liberal wing of his party was rooted in the contempt of Eleanor Roosevelt and other prominent liberals for JFK's failure to take a stand against McCarthy. For Kennedy's part, Stevenson's quixotic presidential campaigns in 1952 and 1956 exposed the failings of liberals: they were more interested in articulating lofty sentiments than gaining power. Relations between Kennedy and liberals in general and Stevenson in particular had been further strained by the battle for the 1960 Democratic presidential nomination. Stevenson's consistent refusal to endorse his candidacy irked JFK, and he was troubled and enraged by Stevenson's last-ditch attempt to steal the nomination at the Democratic Convention despite having not entered the primaries. Kennedy's comment to Stevenson in May 1960 on the Illinoian's refusal to support him said everything about the contempt he had come to feel for the liberal standard bearer in America: 'Look, I have the votes for the nomination and if you don't give me your support, I'll have to shit all over you.'[8]

The tension between Kennedy and senior liberals was evident after Election Day in the appointments he made to his administration, especially in national security positions. Stevenson yearned to be secretary of state; all he got from Kennedy was the largely ceremonial post of United Nations ambassador. Other liberals were appointed to the second tier. Mennen 'Soapy' Williams, for instance, became assistant secretary of state for African Affairs. Chester Bowles, who had worked for Kennedy in the 1960 campaign as a foreign policy adviser, was the liberal awarded the most senior post: undersecretary of state, and so the no. 2 man at the State Department, working under Dean Rusk.

Striking for what it said about Kennedy's belief that liberals were naïve about the communist threat and so not to be trusted when it came to the defence of America was not only this paucity of liberals in key positions but also the fact that a good many advisers were Republicans, holdovers from the Eisenhower administration, or had at least voted for Ike in 1956. Kennedy retained the services of Eisenhower's CIA director, Allen Dulles, and when it came to replacing him in 1961 he turned to the ferociously anti-communist Republican, John McCone, who believed Moscow was bent on world domination and had clashed with Stevenson during the 1956 presidential campaign over the feasibility of a nuclear test ban treaty with the Russians. JFK appointed Republican McGeorge Bundy as his national security adviser. He selected Eisenhower adviser C. Douglas Dillon as secretary of the treasury, and consulted him during the Cuban missile crisis. His formidable secretary of defense, Robert McNamara, was known to be a GOP supporter in the 1950s. Bobby Kennedy, disillusioned by Stevenson after working briefly on his presidential campaign, voted for Eisenhower in 1956. The lack of liberals and numerous Republicans in major foreign policy positions in his administration said much about the direction – tough and unyielding, buttressed by military power – he planned to take on the world stage.[9]

Liberals like Stevenson and Bowles were not all-knowing oracles. They were not better informed than JFK on world affairs. But where their views did merit attention was the emphasis they placed on exploring any possible diplomatic avenues for reducing Cold War tensions. That idea was important as the alternative was to accept as inevitable dangerous confrontation and an escalating arms race. The trick, from an American point of view, was to be resolute in dealing with the communist threat while at the same time taking advantage of any opportunities to improve relations with the communist bloc. It was a question of emphasis. JFK was not totally averse in 1961 to negotiating with adversaries, as shown by his meeting with Khrushchev in Vienna in June, but he did not come to prioritize diplomacy, as Stevenson and Bowles did, until later in his presidency.[10]

That was unfortunate because Khrushchev and Castro hoped for better relations with Kennedy than had been the case with Eisenhower, and did so for the sincerest of reasons: self-interest. Khrushchev had embarked on a major reform programme in Russia, slashing the military in order to boost spending on the civilian economy. As part of that policy he had announced in January 1960 further defence cuts, reducing troop numbers by more than a million. Khrushchev knew that this reform, controversial with the generals and Kremlin hard-liners, would only appear credible, domestically, if Cold War tensions and the perceived threat from America diminished. Hence he hoped Kennedy's foreign policy would prove more conciliatory than Ike's. Khrushchev not only thought that, he said it after JFK's election in correspondence with Harriman and Stevenson. In a phone conversation with Kennedy a week before his inauguration, Stevenson urged him to send a special envoy to Moscow for early talks with Khrushchev;

and shortly after the inauguration Harriman advised JFK to authorise talks with Russian officials to gauge the extent of Khrushchev's interest in better relations with Washington. In effect, Stevenson and Harriman were telling Kennedy to take Khrushchev's overtures seriously.[11]

Castro too wanted a warmer relationship with Washington. He knew about the planning in the final days of the Eisenhower administration for an invasion of Cuba – what would become the Bay of Pigs operation. That was why in November 1960 he mobilized some of his rural militia (which totalled 200,000) in readiness for an attack. That mobilization meant, however, that there were less people to help with the harvest, which in turn made it difficult to supply the Soviets with the amount of sugar that had been agreed. Fearful that a US invasion would oust him from power and that the current situation was damaging the Cuban economy, Castro was interested in a reconciliation with the United States. He too made sure that Kennedy was aware of this, authorizing his advisers to make this clear in speeches and interviews in January and February 1961.[12]

JFK missed the opportunity to change the tone and perhaps the substance of Cold War politics. Influenced by the relatively hard-line beliefs about foreign policy that he had developed before running for president and by the promises he had made on the campaign trail in 1960 to confront Khrushchev and topple Castro, Kennedy was more disposed to the big stick than gentle diplomatic language as he took hold of the reins of power. In his State of the Union address on 30 January, he portrayed the early Sixties as a time of crisis in world affairs, emphasized the need to regain the initiative in the Cold War and promised a vast military build-up. Khrushchev's hopes for a new chapter in the Cold War were dashed. From Kennedy's perspective, responding to Khrushchev's talk of harmonious superpower relations was not straightforward. For one thing, Khrushchev had made clear his determination to force a change in the status of West Berlin. Surely that rendered his talk of a new Soviet–American understanding redundant. Still, Kennedy could have at least explored in the transition between administrations and the early days of his presidency the possibility of greater superpower harmony, created by Khrushchev's enthusiastic response to JFK's election. He did not do so.[13]

That was also the case with his response to the Cuban overtures of early 1961. JFK was not of a mind to parley with Castro for various reasons. He viewed the Cuban leader as Moscow's puppet and the promoter of revolution in Latin America. He wished to make good on his campaign promise to overthrow Castro. He had faith in the CIA to implement its plan to oust a left-wing government in Cuba as they had done so in Guatemala seven years earlier. The outgoing president strengthened Kennedy's conviction that he could not live with a communist government in Havana. The day before he left office Ike met with JFK at the White House. His advice was clear: he told Kennedy to increase US support for the anti-Castro guerrilla force being trained in Guatemala. 'President Eisenhower stated in the long run,' according to Robert McNamara who attended the meeting, 'the United States cannot allow the Castro government to continue to exist in Cuba.'[14]

There is now a widespread belief among historians that Eisenhower was an outstanding president. He is usually portrayed as wise, deft and restrained in his handling of foreign policy. In surveys of academic opinion, he is invariably rated as a better president than Kennedy. It is the contention of this book that this consensus is misguided. Kennedy was a superior president to Eisenhower as their respective handling of the morally transcendent issue of civil rights indicated. Ike's abilities have been overrated. His hawkish and imprudent advice to Kennedy on 19 January is a case in point.[15]

Kennedy had been aware of the CIA plan to use anti-Castro Cuban exiles in an invasion of Cuba since July 1960 when Allen Dulles briefed the Democratic presidential candidate on national security. It was in late January 1961 that JFK began to focus on the scheme. At a meeting with his foreign policy advisers on the 28th Dulles portrayed Castro's Cuba as a menace and said a decision had to be made soon on how to use the Cuban exiles being trained by the CIA in Guatemala, as they could not stay there indefinitely. Kennedy responded to Dulles's dire warnings by ordering an intensification of the CIA's anti-Castro efforts, and a Pentagon review of Langley's plan to use exiles in an invasion of Cuba. He also disregarded the concerns of State Department officials about the impact of a US-backed invasion of Cuba on America's reputation in the Western Hemisphere. This was a sign of things to come in how Kennedy handled the planning for the Bay of Pigs: unwisely, he disregarded the dissent in his administration over the invasion.[16]

The idea that there was very little opposition to the Bay of Pigs, articulated by Camelot defenders of JFK, including brother-protector Bobby, is a fallacy. In fact a good many advisers objected to the CIA plan. Rusk, the quiet man of the administration but secretary of state nonetheless, told other officials on 8 February that an invasion would damage the US position in Latin America. He reiterated his objections in a meeting on 4 April attended by Kennedy. In a substantial memorandum written for Rusk at the end of March, Bowles presented an impassioned argument against the Bay of Pigs invasion. It would contravene America's international treaty organizations, he asserted, was unlikely to succeed, and would tarnish the new administration's reputation throughout the world. Rusk conveyed Bowles's concerns to Kennedy.[17]

That the top two men in the State Department were sceptical should have given Kennedy pause for thought. It was not just Rusk and Bowles, however. The man regarded by many as the doyen of Democrats on matters of diplomacy, Dean Acheson, dismissed the idea out of hand. 'It was [not] necessary to call Price Waterhouse,' he told JFK, 'to discover that 1500 Cubans weren't as good as 25 000 Cubans.' Adlai Stevenson, though not fully briefed, had a negative view of the plan. Others who were opposed included covert operations whizz Edward Lansdale, Vice President Lyndon Johnson, Edward Murrow, Charles Bohlen, Richard Goodwin, Arthur Schlesinger, Roger Hilsman and – from outside the administration – Senator J. William Fulbright.[18]

Kennedy should have listened carefully to these dissenting opinions. Their advice was manifestly sound, for the Bay of Pigs turned out to be a catastrophe. A factor behind his failure to do so was his belief that liberals lacked the mettle needed to confront Cold War adversaries. Many of the dissenters, such as Bowles,

Goodwin, Schlesinger and Stevenson, were archetypal liberals. There is a sense of JFK, at the start of his presidency, thinking that liberals lacked the machismo needed in the rough-and-tumble world of the Cold War.

Excessive deference for the Joint Chiefs and the CIA co-existed with this distrust of liberal views on foreign policy. When the CIA made its case for the plan to invade Cuba, he did not view it with the critical eye brought to bear by the likes of Schlesinger and Bowles. He should have done so as some of the claims made by the boys from Langley were palpably false. In the meeting on 28 January, Dulles made his case for invasion by asserting that there was 'a great increase ... in popular opposition' to Castro. In other words, many Cubans were ready to rise up in support of an invading exile army in order to overthrow a despot. But since the closure of the US embassy in the final days of the Eisenhower administration, the United States was more dependent on intelligence from the British about what was happening on the ground in Cuba; and what the British told the new administration was that no uprising would accompany a Cuban émigré invasion. That squared with other sources of information made available to Kennedy. For example, in late March Schlesinger passed on to JFK the report of a US journalist, who had just visited Cuba, that there remained 'an impressive amount of intense enthusiasm for and faith in Castro'. Kennedy should have factored this sort of information into his thinking on the Bay of Pigs as an assumption of the plan was that the invasion would spark a widespread anti-Castro uprising. If this key assumption was flawed then the plan itself should have been jettisoned.[19]

Kennedy made yet another mistake in his handling of the Bay of Pigs: in a quest to conceal US involvement in the plan, he ordered alterations to it that made the operation even less likely to succeed. He was keen to topple Castro but at the same time wished to preserve the new administration's reputation as an exciting new progressive force in world politics by hiding the fact that the United States was behind the invasion. On 8 February he informed his advisers that he wanted them to develop 'alternatives to a full-fledged "invasion"'. A month later he again told the CIA that 'he could not endorse a plan that put us in so openly, in view of the world situation'. At Kennedy's insistence, the CIA changed the plan so that the invasion would take place not at Trinidad on Cuba's southern coast but at the more sparsely populated Bay of Pigs. Kennedy compelled the CIA to make further changes: the landing would take place not at dawn but night-time, and the ships involved in the operation should have left the invasion area by first light.[20]

This represented a failure of Kennedy to take on board the advice he received, as well as the operation's own logic. The plan was based on the idea that the invasion would result in an anti-Castro uprising, but by insisting that the landing take place at a less conspicuous, less populated location, he reduced the chances that such an insurgency would occur. In reporting that the CIA's plan had a fair chance of succeeding, the Joint Chiefs made clear that their uprising assessment was dependent upon 'political factors; i.e., a sizeable popular or substantial follow-on forces'. By reducing the chances of an uprising in moving the invasion to the Bay of Pigs and by emphasizing his determination to keep the overt involvement of the US military to a minimum, Kennedy failed to heed his generals' assessment of the military viability of the CIA's plan. In short, his handling of the planning for the Bay of Pigs was a catalogue of errors.[21]

The execution of the invasion in mid-April was also bungled. The initial air strike on Castro's main airfields by B-26 bombers taking off from Nicaragua destroyed some T-33 jet trainers, but many survived to be used by Castro against the invading exile force on 17 April after it had reached the Bay of Pigs. Having mobilized his 200,000-strong militia on the 16th, Castro was able to send a large force to the beachhead. He also rounded up 100,000 Cubans suspected of being opposed to his rule. This meant that Kennedy's hope that the Bay of Pigs invasion would trigger an anti-Castro uprising was dashed. JFK's decision to cancel air strikes on Cuban airfields, on 17 April due to concern that US involvement was becoming apparent and the following day because of hazy weather, meant the chances of success at the Bay of Pigs were further reduced. On 19 April the Cuban exile force started to surrender. Around 1,200 were taken prisoners and about 100 were killed during the invasion. The Bay of Pigs was over. It was the greatest disaster of Kennedy's presidency, indeed his entire life in politics. Complete failure. Utter humiliation.[22]

Failure: it was not something to which he was accustomed. It was no surprise, then, that Kennedy's emotional response to the disaster was one of despair and uncharacteristic self-pity. 'Let me tell you something,' he told veteran Democrat Clark Clifford, 'I have had two full days of hell – I haven't slept – this has been the most excruciating period of my life. I doubt my Presidency could survive another catastrophe like this.' In Moscow Khrushchev wasted no time in entering the fray: he dispatched a letter to Kennedy vowing to defend Castro with Russian military power. The only thing to buoy Kennedy's spirits in the days following the Bay of Pigs was the support of the American people. A Gallup poll revealed that four times as many Americans approved as disapproved of his handling of Cuba, and a remarkable 83 per cent of Americans approved of his overall presidential leadership.[23]

The key question for Kennedy after the Bay of Pigs was what to do next about Castro. In the longer term he would learn valuable lessons from this debacle, particularly the importance of viewing the invariably hawkish ideas of his generals and intelligence chiefs with a more critical eye. That would ultimately help shift his foreign policy in a more promising direction. In the short term, however, a humiliated Kennedy yearned for revenge. So rather than consider a more patient approach towards Castro, he decided to continue to work for Castro's overthrow. In that, he was egged on by Bobby Kennedy, who absorbed all of his brother's pain and anger over the Bay of Pigs. In the aftermath of this disaster, JFK decided to bring in Bobby as a key adviser on international affairs, especially Cuba, despite his position as attorney general. The consequences of that would turn out to be both positive (during the missile crisis) and negative (in Operation Mongoose). In the days after the Bay of Pigs, Bobby tore into any adviser who argued that the United States would just have to accept that Castro would remain as the leader of Cuba. When Bowles made precisely that argument, Bobby responded with rage: 'That's the most meaningless, worthless thing I've ever heard. You people are so anxious to protect your own asses that you're afraid to do anything. All you want to do is dump the whole thing on the president.' What Bobby wanted was an invasion of Cuba to topple Castro.[24]

JFK shared many of his brother's belligerent sentiments in late April. In a speech given in Washington to the American Society of Newspaper Editors only a day after the Bay of Pigs invasion had fizzled out, he listed the lessons he had learned from this failure. Rather than showing contrition, he argued that what the Bay of Pigs demonstrated was that 'the forces of communism are not to be underestimated', and that the United States and other nations 'must take an ever closer and more realistic look at the menace of external Communist [in other words, Russian] intervention and domination in Cuba'. He predicted that communists would try to promote revolution through subversion and infiltration, and argued that the United States would need to respond covertly to what was essentially a covert threat. Any thought of solving the Castro problem by simply invading Cuba was rejected by Kennedy out of concern over how his Soviet counterpart would react. As he explained in a private meeting with Richard Nixon, 'there is a good chance that, if we move on Cuba, Khrushchev will move on Berlin.'[25]

In deciding to work energetically for Castro's overthrow (but not with an invasion) JFK again turned a deaf ear to the counsels of restraint from his liberal advisers. This was a serious error. Had he heeded their warnings and not sought the overthrow of Castro after the Bay of Pigs, Khrushchev may not have decided a year later that his Cuban ally needed to be protected by Russian nuclear weapons – in which case, there would have been no missile crisis in October 1962.

In the days following the Bay of Pigs, JFK's adviser Richard Goodwin urged him to focus on the successful implementation of his aid programme for Latin America, the Alliance for Progress. That, he said, was the best way to reduce Castro's influence in the Western Hemisphere. Chester Bowles also encouraged Kennedy to adopt a calmer approach. Diplomacy via the Organization of American States should be the focus of US efforts against Castro, he argued.[26]

Adlai Stevenson, in particular, made a concerted effort to persuade the president to plump for a more patient policy. In a memorandum on 23 April 1961, he told Kennedy that the United States should not overreact every time another country went communist. 'We are not going to be destroyed in our beds,' he said, 'even if Castro does continue to mismanage Cuba for another decade.' 'Of one thing we may be sure,' he added, 'the 19th century system of gunboat diplomacy or landing the Marines is highly unpopular.' Instead, economic aid for Latin America was the most effective way to handle Castro and reduce his influence in the long term.[27]

Kennedy, though, was not interested in the long term. He wanted to change the perception rapidly that Castro had bested him at the Bay of Pigs. Accordingly, he decided to embark on a multifaceted policy to oust Castro, one that would culminate in November 1961 in Mongoose, a James Bond–type covert operation designed to do away with the dastardly despot in Havana. It was at a National Security Council (NSC) meeting on 5 May that Kennedy defined his post–Bay of Pigs policy towards Cuba. The aim was clear: 'U.S. policy toward Cuba should aim at the downfall of Castro.' The United States 'should not undertake military intervention in Cuba', with how the Russians would retaliate in Berlin a concern, but 'nothing [was to be done] that would foreclose the possibility of military intervention in the future'. The anti-Castro initiatives to be taken for the time being included the dissemination of anti-Castro propaganda in Latin America, and the identification of 'possible weaknesses and vulnerabilities in the elements which exert control in Cuba today'. The path mapped out by Kennedy on 5 May defined his policy towards Cuba right up until the missile crisis.[28]

It would not be until the Cuban missile crisis that Kennedy considered a major reappraisal of the relatively hard-line approach to foreign policy that he had favoured since his critique of British appeasement in *Why England Slept*. In the meantime, he got to develop his skills as a crisis manager, which would serve him well in the missile crisis, during the confrontation over Berlin that dominated the summer of 1961. The Berlin crisis would also serve to impress upon him the dangers of the Cold War, a lesson he would learn again in October 1962 in even more dramatic fashion.

Tensions over Berlin derived from the ending of World War II. Unable to agree on how to unify Germany, the Allied powers fashioned their respective zones within the country so as to mirror their own political systems. The result was two Germanies, east and west, with the Russians imposing communism on the former and the United States, Britain and France shaping the latter along capitalist and democratic lines. Within eastern Germany, a Berlin divided between the victorious Allies – with a Western enclave deep within the communist bloc – created a source of superpower tension that would explode into crisis in 1948–9 and 1958–9 when first Stalin, then Khrushchev, tried to eject the Western powers from Berlin. The famous airlift in the Truman years and Eisenhower's patient resolve a decade later resulted in a Russian failure to incorporate West Berlin into communist East Germany.

That failure did not convince Khrushchev that he should accept the status quo in Berlin. He continued to talk about making West Berlin a demilitarized free city and signing a peace treaty with East Germany so as to end Allied occupation rights in the city, and said he would raise the issue of Berlin again once a new president was installed in the White House. That made it inevitable that Berlin would become one of the key international issues of Kennedy's presidency.[29]

Why Khrushchev felt he had to pressure JFK on Berlin was clear. For one thing, the city was a propaganda embarrassment for communism. While West Berlin boomed, the economy of East Berlin was sluggish in comparison. For another, the United States used West Berlin as an intelligence outpost to acquire information on what was happening behind the 'iron curtain'. The relentless exodus of East German refugees to the West, around 250,000 a year, drained the East German economy and offered further proof of the shortcomings of the communist system. The emergence of a strong, rearmed, NATO-aligned West Germany, headed by the flinty Konrad Adenauer, also troubled Khrushchev for whom painful memories of the German invasion of Russia in the Second World War remained fresh. 'What concerns Khrushchev most of all,' wrote Stevenson in a private letter in July, 'is a re-armed Germany – and I don't blame him.' Furthermore, Chinese criticism of what they construed as Moscow's timidity in promoting world revolution and pressure from East German leader Walter Ulbricht to do something about West Berlin increased Khrushchev's determination to act decisively on the matter.[30]

For Kennedy's part, he was not opposed to the idea early in his presidency of some sort of modus vivendi over Berlin – an arrangement that would somehow normalize the situation there while maintaining the basic US commitment to West Berlin. Any such progress would depend on a conciliatory Khrushchev. Kennedy convened a meeting on 11 February in the Cabinet Room with the pantheon of America's experts on Russia: George Kennan, Averell Harriman, Charles Bohlen and the current US ambassador in Moscow Llewellyn 'Tommy' Thompson. These experts informed JFK that Khrushchev 'is now eager … for an early meeting with the President'. Their view was that while Kennedy should avoid the sort of 'serious negotiations' that a formal summit implied, 'a meeting in due course, for an exchange of courtesies and the opportunity of becoming personally acquainted, might be useful'. These Russian experts advised the young president that Khrushchev was genuinely interested in negotiations on disarmament, and while he remained intent on causing trouble in Berlin, he was 'not likely to bring this situation to a boil'. Thus assured that an early face-to-face meeting with the Soviet premier was a good idea and that the tension in Berlin was unlikely to escalate out of control, Kennedy wrote eleven days later to Khrushchev, saying: 'I hope it will be possible, before too long, for us to meet personally for an informal exchange of views.' The Bay of Pigs controversy in April, however, seemed to make the prospects for such a meeting remote.[31]

As Kennedy pondered the Berlin situation, he consulted Dean Acheson, the most prominent hardliner in the Democratic Party's foreign policy establishment, on NATO issues and Berlin. The thrust of Acheson's thinking was expressed at a White House meeting he attended on 5 April with senior British and American officials, including Prime Minister Harold Macmillan and JFK. With characteristic candour, Acheson declared that there was no compromise solution to the Berlin problem that would not damage Western interests, and predicted that 'the Soviets would press the Berlin issue this year'. This was dangerous, he argued, because, 'If the West funks Germany will become unhooked from the Alliance'. As a political or economic reaction from the West would be inadequate, 'There has got to be some sort of military response.' Acheson advocated a ground operation in which a division of troops was sent down the Autobahn to West Berlin. Not surprisingly, British officials were sobered by Acheson's comments. Kennedy revealed that 'he had not come to a conclusion over what to do'.[32]

The rest of April was dominated by the planning for, the failed execution of and the fallout from the Bay of Pigs invasion. Troubled by perceptions that the Bay of Pigs made him look weak, Kennedy emerged from that humiliation deeply depressed but determined to show his mettle not only in Cuba but elsewhere, including Berlin. He could not have two foreign policy disasters in one year and retain credibility as a leader on the world stage. On Berlin he could not and would not buckle.

Despite the Bay of Pigs embarrassment, Kennedy remained interested in a summit meeting with his counterpart in the Kremlin – and conveyed that interest to Khrushchev via an unusual backchannel, namely clandestine contacts between Georgi Bolshakov, who worked for Soviet military intelligence, and Bobby Kennedy. JFK viewed a summit meeting as an opportunity not only to take the measure of his counterpart in the Kremlin, but also to reach a sensible understanding on how to prevent superpower conflict in the years to come – basically by urging Khrushchev to resist any temptation to expand Soviet influence. He may have been confident, over-confident in fact, in his ability to charm and persuade the temperamental Khrushchev. As his trip to Europe approached, Kennedy's mood was not helped by an accident in mid-May during his trip to Canada which aggravated his back so badly that he turned to the services of Max Jacobson, the eccentric doctor who treated him – as he had done since first seeing him during the 1960 presidential campaign – with injections of speed (amphetamines) and steroids. After a few days in Paris, where the Kennedys and especially Jackie charmed the French, Kennedy arrived in Vienna for what turned out to be his one and only meeting with Khrushchev during his presidency.[33]

There is a traditional view of the Vienna summit which perhaps still holds sway over the popular imagination, and that is the idea that a more experienced and aggressive Russian leader intimidated and got the better of the young American president. The declassified records from the summit, however, indicate that JFK's performance was not only better than traditionally assumed, but was in fact very impressive. His main objective, in seeking a sensible understanding with Khrushchev that would prevent superpower conflict, was a commendable one. Where he could, he made progress with the Soviet premier, as he did on Laos. It was hardly Kennedy's fault if Khrushchev, with his penchant for bluster, tried to intimidate him. If he needed to stand up to Khrushchev when the Russian resorted to such tactics, JFK did so with a clearly expressed resolve. He demonstrated that steeliness when Khrushchev threatened him over Berlin. In a sense, this approach was consistent with the views he had expressed in *Why England Slept*: always stand up to aggressive dictators. But in this case that approach was entirely warranted as Berlin was so strategically and symbolically important, and in addition Kennedy needed to show his mettle in the wake of the Bay of Pigs disaster. The crisis over Berlin in the summer of 1961 would show one of the great strengths of the Kennedy presidency: he was very good at crisis management. He had the ability to stay cool under immense pressure. He was effective at conveying to an adversary that he was prepared to use force if necessary without escalating to the point where that was unavoidable. His handling of the Berlin crisis was excellent but that excellence was evident not only after the Vienna summit, which triggered the crisis, but during it as well.

Early in his first meeting with Khrushchev in Vienna, in the early afternoon of 3 June at the US embassy, Kennedy articulated his aim for the summit: to discuss 'how it would be possible for the[ir] two countries ... to find during his Presidency ways and means of not permitting situations where the two countries would be committed to actions involving their security or endangering peace, to secure which is our basic objective'. When Khrushchev said Russia was committed to peace and harmony, and complained about John Foster Dulles's policy aimed at liquidating communism where it already existed, Kennedy demurred: 'His own interpretation of the situation was . . . that the Soviet Union was seeking to eliminate free systems in areas that are associated with us. . . . This is a matter of very serious concern to us.' Khrushchev argued that the attractiveness of communist ideology meant that even though a peaceful Russia would not interfere in the internal affairs of other countries, communism would inevitably take root elsewhere. Kennedy interjected that 'Mao Tse Tung had said that power was at the end of the rifle'. He was making clear that he understood Khrushchev's argument was pure sophistry, which it certainly was given how Soviet military power had installed and sustained communist governments throughout Eastern Europe.[34]

In pursuit of his worthy objective of using the Vienna talks to reduce the chances of Soviet–American conflict, JFK emphasized the necessity for both Khrushchev and himself to avoid miscalculation in reading the other's intentions. After Khrushchev scoffed at his concern with the danger of miscalculation, Kennedy replied that recent history showed the importance of not misjudging what other nations would do next. As a student of and indeed published author on war in the twentieth century, Kennedy's argument derived from his careful consideration of the matter. It has sometimes been said that a crafty Khrushchev bested Kennedy at this opening meeting at Vienna by luring him into an ideological discussion and then tying the American president in knots. The declassified transcripts show no such thing.[35]

After lunch on 3 June, Kennedy resumed talks with Khrushchev in the American embassy. They continued their disagreement on 'miscalculation'. Again, Kennedy said he wanted to maintain the current balance of power between America and Russia and prevent a direct clash between them, whereas Khrushchev emphasized the inevitability of revolutionary change. Kennedy acknowledged his mistakes in his recent handling of Cuba but put his Russian counterpart on the back foot by asking 'what the USSR's reaction would be if a government associated with the West were established in Poland'. That elicited from Khrushchev the nonsense that communist Poland was more democratic than the United States. Kennedy also gave the lie to Khrushchev's constant portrayal of Russia as a paragon of peace by highlighting Khrushchev's support for wars of national liberation. Progress was made on the issue of Laos, with both agreeing to work for a ceasefire and then the establishment of a neutral and independent government. But it was a sign of the acrimony that would follow at Vienna when the meeting ended with Khrushchev vowing to force a change in Berlin, come what may.[36]

The following morning, 4 June, talks resumed at the Soviet embassy. It was on this day that the Berlin crisis of 1961, one of the most dangerous confrontations of the entire Cold War era, erupted. After further talks on Laos and a fruitless discussion on nuclear testing, Khrushchev turned to Berlin. Citing West Germany's rearmament and its affiliation with NATO, he stressed his determination to sign a peace treaty with East Germany terminating the Western rights in Berlin that derived from the Second World War. West Berlin, he explained, would become a 'free city'. Kennedy's response was resolute:

This matter is of greatest concern to the US. We are in Berlin not because of someone's sufferance. We fought our way there. . . . We are in Berlin not by agreement of East Germans but by contractual rights. This is an area in which every President of the US since World War II has been committed by treaty and other contractual rights and where every President has reaffirmed his faithfulness to his obligations. If we were expelled from that area and if we accepted the loss of our rights no one would have any confidence in US commitments and pledges. US national security is involved in this matter because if we were to accept the Soviet proposal US commitments would be regarded as a mere scrap of paper. West Berlin is vital to our national security.

The tone and content of Kennedy's response to Khrushchev's threats on Berlin were well judged. Without being needlessly provocative, he left Khrushchev in no doubt as to his determination to preserve the US position in the city. When the Russian premier sarcastically said perhaps Kennedy also wanted to go to Moscow as that too was in the interests of American national security, JFK retorted that 'the US was not asking to go anywhere… What we are talking about is that we are in Berlin and have been there for 15 years. We suggest that we stay there'.[37]

Kennedy proceeded to make the case that Khrushchev's attempt to force the United States out of Berlin was unacceptable as Russia 'should not seek to change our position and thus disturb the balance of power'. That was a neat, well-thought-out assertion which showed the purpose behind his line of argument the previous day. On the opening day of the summit Kennedy had spoken in general terms of the need to preserve the balance of power between Moscow and Washington. Once the discussion turned to Berlin on 4 June, he was able to build on that argument in saying why Khrushchev's demands on Berlin were intolerable. There was a logical sequence to Kennedy's comments over the course of the summit that added weight to his argument.[38]

In the rest of the meeting, Kennedy continued to fight his corner with skill and vigour. He said again that as the forcible ejection of the United States from Berlin would destroy American credibility on the world stage, Khrushchev's demands were unacceptable. He pointed out that West Berliners were strongly supportive of a continuing American presence in their city. Sensing that Khrushchev believed he could intimidate him because of his youth, he also commented: 'Mr. Khrushchev has said that the President was a young man, but … he had not assumed office to accept arrangements totally inimical to US interests.' Kennedy remained firm as Khrushchev recklessly talked about war and claimed that if Kennedy did not bow to Soviet pressure on Berlin, he would be responsible for the conflagration that would follow.[39]

Over lunch a lighter tone prevailed. When Khrushchev bemoaned the costs of space exploration, Kennedy proposed a joint Soviet–American mission to the moon. Khrushchev said that despite his earlier demands on Berlin, he wanted peace. Pointing out the horror of war in a nuclear age, Kennedy suggested that Khrushchev act in a way that acknowledged America's vital interests in Berlin.[40]

After lunch the final conversation between Kennedy and Khrushchev revealed no meeting of minds and ensured that a superpower crisis lay ahead that summer. Alone with their interpreters, Kennedy and Khrushchev restated their irreconcilable positions on the divided city. JFK said that US access rights to Berlin were inviolable, and expressed the hope that direct Soviet–American conflict could be prevented. Khrushchev said that if the United States violated East German territory once the peace treaty had been signed, Russia would use force.[41]

Unflinchingly, Kennedy remarked that 'either Mr. Khrushchev did not believe that the US was serious or the situation in that area was so unsatisfactory to the Soviet Union that it had to take drastic action'. He was off to see Harold Macmillan after Vienna and would have to tell the British prime minister that 'he had gained the impression that the USSR was presenting him with the alternative of accepting the Soviet act on Berlin or having a face-to-face confrontation. He had come here to prevent a confrontation between our two countries and he regretted to leave Vienna with this impression'. Khrushchev insisted that access to Berlin would be controlled by East Germany, adding, 'It is not the USSR that threatens with war, it is the US.' 'It was the Chairman, not he, who wanted to force a change,' countered Kennedy.[42]

The summit ended chillingly, for Khrushchev kept talking – with apparent nonchalance – about war: 'It is up to the US to decide whether there will be war or peace.' For that reason, the famous metaphor used by Kennedy to end the conversation was apt: 'it would be a cold winter.' 'I felt doubly sorry,' Khrushchev said later, 'because what happened did not create favorable conditions for improving relations. On the contrary, it aggravated the Cold War.' Interestingly, his impression of Kennedy, despite their acrimonious exchanges, was that he was 'more intelligent than any of the Presidents before him'.[43]

Kennedy's performance at Vienna was almost flawless. He countered the impression acquired by Khrushchev, from his age and his humiliation at the Bay of Pigs, that he could be intimidated. Every time Khrushchev threatened him over Berlin, he stood his ground. His arguments were clear and cogent: the necessity of avoiding direct superpower conflict in the nuclear age; doing nothing that would drastically alter the balance of power between Moscow and Washington; the connection between the preservation of America's rights in the strategically important city of Berlin and its credibility on the world stage. At the same time Kennedy stated his case without resorting to the immature and bellicose language employed by Khrushchev. JFK maintained a statesmanlike deportment; the same cannot be said for his Soviet counterpart. As State Department official Foy Kohler, who accompanied Kennedy on this trip, said, JFK had conducted himself at Vienna 'with dignity, frankness, determination, but yet with admirable statesmanlike restraint in the face of considerable provocation.' Moreover, it should have been apparent to Khrushchev, not least because of the precedent of how previous presidents had responded to similar Russian threats in 1948 and 1958, that no American leader – due to considerations of credibility – could defer to his demands over Berlin. Kennedy made that very point to Khrushchev time and again at Vienna. Khrushchev should have recognized that reality. So the tension and crisis triggered by the Vienna summit were due to Khrushchev's recklessness. But it meant that Kennedy's first summer in the White House would be devoted to meeting Khrushchev's challenge in Berlin.[44]

Although Kennedy had performed so admirably at Vienna, he was taken aback by the way Khrushchev had behaved like a bully. This was his most important diplomatic outing as president. Kennedy found the experience distressing. He said so to others. It was 'like dealing with Dad', he told Bobby. 'All give and no take.' James Reston of *The New York Times*, who interviewed JFK in Vienna, judged the president to be 'shaken and angry' by Khrushchev's antics. Kennedy was 'much concerned and even surprised by the almost brutal frankness and confidence of the Soviet leader', noted Macmillan in his diary when meeting with JFK shortly after the Vienna summit. Small wonder that Kennedy had been sobered by the demands made by Khrushchev in Vienna. It was not just his aggressive manner that troubled JFK; it was also because, as McGeorge Bundy later wrote, fundamentally those demands constituted a 'nuclear threat. While many other [Soviet] pressures and incentives were deployed during this long crisis, the underlying threat was that the only escape from unendurable nuclear risk was for the West to accept change in West Berlin'.[45]

Figure 3.1 Kennedy's acrimonious encounter with Soviet leader Nikita Khrushchev in Vienna in June 1961 triggered the Berlin crisis that dominated his first summer in the White House. (*Source*: Wikimedia, public domain, Search media – Wikimedia Commons.)

It is easy to extrapolate backwards in assuming Kennedy's bruised feelings after the Vienna summit were proof of a spineless performance during it. That had not been the case at all. Furthermore, JFK wasted no time in conveying to the American people the same resolve he had shown to Khrushchev. In a television address delivered on his return to the United States, he said: 'I wanted to make certain Mr. Khrushchev . . . understood our strength and our determination,' as well as America's desire for peace. On Berlin,

> I made it clear to Mr. Khrushchev that the security of Western Europe and therefore our own security are deeply involved in our presence and our access rights to West Berlin, that those rights are based on law and not on sufferance, and that we are determined to maintain those rights at any risk, and thus meet our obligation to the people of West Berlin, and their right to choose their own future.

By saying, 'Generally, Mr. Khrushchev did not talk in terms of war,' Kennedy revealed that on occasion he had. The American people were left in no doubt therefore as to the severity of the situation. This report on Vienna made clear in the immediate aftermath of the summit that on Berlin Kennedy would brook no Russian objections to America's continuing presence in the city.[46]

Any hopes that the Berlin crisis would quickly fade away were dashed on 10 June when *Pravda* published the aide-memoire given by Khrushchev to Kennedy in Vienna, which set a deadline of December for US acquiescence in Russia's demands. Now the crisis had an ominous time frame, and the public knew that the stakes were frighteningly high: the implication was that Khrushchev was prepared to take drastic action if his demands were not met by the end of the year. War seemed a distinct possibility.[47]

On the same day that the Russians published their aide-memoire, National Security Advisor McGeorge Bundy provided JFK with a memorandum that anticipated the sort of debate on Berlin that would emerge in the Kennedy administration that summer. Read through the key documents in June and July 1961 and one is struck by how little Kennedy has to say. It is not like the Cuban missile crisis in 1962 when he often did play a leading role in administration discussions, particularly towards the end of that confrontation. That was a sign of his increasing assurance as his presidency unfolded. Berlin 1961 was at an earlier stage in his presidential learning curve. It was more a case of Kennedy listening, sifting advice carefully and coming gradually to his own conclusion on how best to respond to Khrushchev's threats – although his basic objective had been established before Vienna and articulated during it, namely the maintenance of an American presence in and access rights to West Berlin. On Berlin, Kennedy conducted himself like Oliver Cromwell – absorbing, listening, but giving little away. Bundy's 10 June memorandum was part of the process by which Kennedy enhanced his sense of the range of US policy options on Berlin and inched towards the approach that he would present to America and the world in his television address on 25 July.[48]

In his memo Bundy conveyed to JFK the basic range of options by passing on to him messages from two journalists, Joe Alsop and Walter Lippmann, with contrasting views. Hard-liner Alsop, explained Bundy, was for 'a strong and essentially unyielding position, carried all the way to war if necessary'. Lippmann, however, wanted 'a negotiated solution' that would include 'the genuine neutralization of West Berlin', entailing a Russian presence in that sector of the city. Bundy warned that most of JFK's advisers would view that as an intolerable concession, one that would damage 'the whole position of the West'. Bundy himself was attracted to a combination of the Alsop and Lippmann positions, 'making serious military preparations' while devising a meaningful diplomatic strategy. The national security advisor said he agreed with these two distinguished journalists that on Berlin JFK would have to 'master and manage' the crisis 'under your own personal leadership and authority'. A week after Vienna Bundy had spelled out the key issue for Kennedy: whether force or diplomacy should take precedence in the US response to Khrushchev's threats.[49]

Intensifying the spotlight on this issue was the man who made the running in the administration debate on Berlin in June: Dean Acheson. His views would have attracted attention anyway. For one thing, JFK had requested a report from Acheson on Berlin, and as the month drew to a close he was putting the final touches to it. For another, Acheson's personality and style – domineering, self-confident, quick and incisive in debate – demanded respect, and at times engendered even awe. That was also the case due to his status as one of the principal architects of US national security policy after the Second World War. As he mulled over the crisis in Berlin, Acheson was troubled by what he was convinced was a series of hostile Soviet objectives that included the absorption of West Berlin into East Germany, the fracturing of NATO and the erosion of US credibility. What was needed, he believed, was a president prepared to make clear to the Russians that he was prepared to go to war, even nuclear war, in order to prevail. Acheson's private correspondence with Harry Truman added to his sense that he must guide and bolster the resolve of the callow new president. 'The performance of our Chief Executive worries me,' Truman told him in early July. To a large extent, Kennedy's handling of the Berlin crisis would be determined by how he responded to Acheson's bellicose advice. In this way, the Berlin crisis foreshadowed the Cuban missile crisis when Kennedy had to confront the hawks in his administration, who once again included Acheson in their ranks.[50]

JFK had sensibly established a Berlin task force, headed by State Department officials Foy Kohler and Martin Hillenbrand, to guide his administration's deliberations that summer. As the task force became bogged down in drafting a reply to Khrushchev's aide-memoire, Acheson took the lead in charting a course for Kennedy. When Acheson joined the task force on 16 June, he told the other officials that Kennedy needed to take up the cudgels. Berlin, he argued, was vital to US credibility, even its survival. What Khrushchev had presented Kennedy with was a test of wills. To pass that test, the key thing was 'to increase the belief [in Moscow] that we would use nuclear weapons to oppose Russian advances'. To that end, Acheson liaised with the Joint Chiefs, requesting three studies from them on the Berlin question. The Joint Chiefs forwarded their conclusions to McNamara to pass on to the White House. Agreeing with Acheson, they argued that 'the basic consideration remains the need for re-establishing the credibility of the [US] nuclear deterrent'. The impetus in the administration debate over Berlin, therefore, was with the hawks.[51]

Kennedy used his press conference on 28 June to assure the American people, as he had after the Vienna summit, of his determination to stand firm in Berlin. Reminding Americans of how the Soviets had 'illegally blockaded' Berlin in 1948 and threatened the city again in 1958, he asserted that Khrushchev's demands over the city would mean that 'the rights of the citizens of West Berlin' were 'gradually but relentlessly extinguished'. He went on to warn that the Russians 'would make a grave mistake if they supposed that Allied unity and determination can be undermined by threats or fresh aggressive acts'. He also dismissed Khrushchev's claim that Russia would soon out-produce America. US economic growth far surpassed Russia's, he said, implying that in the Berlin crisis it would be Washington, not Moscow, that would be operating from a position of strength.[52]

On the same day that Kennedy took this strong public stance, Acheson completed his long memo on Berlin. His key point was that this was not a localized dispute over a specific city but, rather, a crucial contest for global influence between the superpowers. Khrushchev was deliberately testing Kennedy's will to withstand Soviet pressure in Berlin. Should JFK fail to resist, American credibility on the world stage would be irreparably damaged. Negotiating with Khrushchev at the outset of the crisis was pointless as the United States could not give up its vital interests in Berlin, including access to the Western sector. Khrushchev had provoked the crisis as his fear that America would risk nuclear war had diminished. What Kennedy needed to do was to disabuse the Soviet dictator of that notion by carrying out a major build-up of nuclear as well as conventional forces. If the communists cut off US access to West Berlin, Kennedy must respond with an airlift and then, if required, a ground probe of Allied troops. Hopefully this would convince Khrushchev that Kennedy was ready to risk nuclear war and that he must therefore back down. But it might not do so, in which case nuclear war would be unavoidable. Acheson did discuss facing-saving concessions that could be made by Kennedy should Khrushchev back down, but the emphasis in his memorandum was on a militaristic approach to the crisis that countenanced, with troubling equanimity, a nuclear confrontation. News of Acheson's belligerence did filter out to the press. Columnist Drew Pearson wrote in his diary that, according to another journalist, Acheson was 'trying to take Kennedy into a war in order to vindicate his own past policies'.[53]

When the National Security Council discussed Acheson's proposals the next day, Kennedy kept his cards close to his chest. Rather than revealing whether he agreed with Acheson's hard-line stance, he asked the veteran Democrat and other officials a series of questions. Should the US continue to call for German unification? How might a reciprocal Soviet-American military build-up over Berlin play out? What should his response be if Khrushchev called for a summit meeting? Kennedy was not yet at the point where he had decided on his precise response to Russian threats over Berlin. He was carefully mulling over the options, including Acheson's truculent proposals. That was a commendably prudent approach and was reflected in the minutes for the meeting: 'It was decided not to make substantive decisions on the basis of this first discussion.'[54]

Saturday, 8 July, was an important day in the development of JFK's thinking on Berlin as Khrushchev announced the cancellation of his plan to cut the Red Army by 1.2 million men. Instead, he would increase the Russian military budget by a third. It was a sign that Khrushchev was upping the ante in Berlin. It strengthened Kennedy's conviction that he would need to stand firm in order to prevail in the crisis.[55]

8 July was also the day, however, when Kennedy's concerns over the immoderate Acheson plan deepened. Combining business with pleasure that weekend back home at Hyannisport, he took a cruise on the *Marlin* with Jackie and some friends. He also brought along McNamara, Rusk and his top military adviser Maxwell Taylor to talk about Berlin. Influencing JFK's approach to these discussions were memos he had received that served to question US military planning for Berlin. A missive from Mac Bundy warned that current military planning was too rigid, pushing the president towards a nuclear strike on Russia. For that reason, he advised JFK to ask McNamara to revise US military plans for Berlin.[56]

White House aide Arthur Schlesinger had been troubled by how the administration's consideration of Berlin, not least by the formidable Acheson, resembled the planning for the Bay of Pigs – an excessive and unquestioning emphasis on a military approach coupled with a neglect of the political dimension of the crisis. Schlesinger said as much in a memo he handed to Kennedy, who read it immediately. 'Agreeing that Acheson's plan was far too narrowly directed to military problems', recalled Schlesinger, JFK 'said with emphasis that Berlin planning had to be brought back into balance'. He ordered the historian to produce a memo he could use in his Hyannisport talks. As Kennedy was to leave for Massachusetts in only a few hours, Schlesinger worked with State Department official Abram Chayes and National Security Council consultant Henry Kissinger in writing the memo at great speed. In it, they asked: 'What political moves do we make until the crisis develops? If we are silent, or confine ourselves to rebutting Soviet contentions . . ., we permit Khrushchev to establish the framework of discussion.' In other words diplomacy, not just military preparations, mattered. Acheson was asking Kennedy to contemplate nuclear war, but the Pentagon had not spelled out in detail what this would mean for the United States. 'The Pentagon should be required [therefore] to make an analysis of the possible levels and implications of nuclear warfare and the possible gradations of our own nuclear response.' The Schlesinger-Kissinger-Chayes message concluded by urging Kennedy to instruct the State Department to develop a negotiating strategy, and Acheson to consider the political aspects of the situation.[57]

This advice impressed Kennedy. At Hyannisport he told Rusk that the State Department should quickly formulate a plan for negotiations over Berlin. He instructed McNamara to produce a plan for a military, but non-nuclear, Western resistance to Communist pressure in the city. That resistance should be sufficient to demonstrate US resolve and prevent a quick takeover of West Berlin but at the same time provide a window of opportunity for diplomacy that could settle the crisis without resorting to nuclear war.[58]

By this point Kennedy was showing signs of moving towards the policy that would result in an acceptable resolution of the Berlin crisis. He understood that the key was the balance to be struck between the implicit willingness to use force and the readiness to embrace a political settlement. The former was required to stop Khrushchev from thinking he could simply take West Berlin. The latter was needed to reduce the likelihood of a devastating nuclear exchange. Kennedy was also beginning to learn the importance of standing up to the hawks in his administration. He knew they had let him down at the Bay of Pigs. That made him wary when Acheson and his supporters promoted such a pugnacious policy over Berlin.

At the NSC meeting on 13 July discussion again centred on the merits of Acheson's confrontational approach. Once more Kennedy listened carefully, asking pertinent questions, but did not disclose his hand. The advantage of that was it facilitated an uninhibited discussion in which officials felt at liberty to speak their mind. Less of the unhelpful 'group think' that at times characterized the Bay of Pigs discussions was evident in the deliberations over Berlin.[59]

Acheson was nothing if not consistent. He told NSC officials that it was important to initiate military preparations sooner rather than later in order to influence Khrushchev's thinking in the crisis. JFK, he added, should 'support a full program of decisive action', including a declaration of national emergency which, as Schlesinger observed, 'became the symbol of the drastic [Achesonian] reaction to the crisis'. Maxwell Taylor backed the idea of a declaration of national emergency. McNamara and Rusk did not, recommending instead all military preparations that did not require such a declaration. Lyndon Johnson was closer to Acheson's position in supporting a substantial bolstering of US military forces as rapidly as possible.[60]

As the minutes to this NSC meeting indicate, 'The President did not make a choice.' But he did disclose his definition of America's vital interests in the crisis: 'there are two things which matter: our presence in Berlin, and our access to Berlin.' On these matters Kennedy would cede no ground to Khrushchev. But by implication he was saying that he did not define what Khrushchev did in East Berlin, including the prevention of East German refugees fleeing to the West, as a vital US interest. Here Kennedy hinted at the pragmatic, Realpolitik approach that he would come to adopt in handling the Berlin crisis. He had not yet formulated his policy over Berlin with precision, but he was moving incrementally towards doing so.[61]

Kennedy knew that conveying to Khrushchev his determination to prevail in the crisis was imperative. He knew that he needed to correct an impression of presidential weakness gained by Khrushchev due to his bungling over the Bay of Pigs. He was increasingly convinced that Acheson's proposals, in pursuit of that objective, went too far and were too dangerous. Nonetheless he wanted to relay to Khrushchev his unwillingness to buckle over Berlin. Accordingly, he dispatched brother Bobby to the Soviet ambassador in Washington, Mikhail Menshikov. Robert Kennedy told Menshikov that he and his brother would choose death over surrender on this matter. The Kennedy administration would never abandon the city, he insisted, and Menshikov should pass that information onto Khrushchev without editing. Here JFK was using secret diplomacy to strengthen Moscow's impression of his tenacity in protecting America's key interests in Berlin.[62]

At the same time JFK was moving decisively against the symbolic fulcrum of the hard-line Acheson policy, the declaration of a national emergency. In a meeting of senior officials on 17 July, the influential McNamara told him that this declaration would not be required until the fall. In a memo sent to JFK that same day, Sorensen too argued against a declaration of national emergency and other hard-line options, warning that Kennedy should not 'engage Khrushchev's prestige to a point where he could not back down from a showdown'. At a meeting of the Interdepartmental Coordinating Group on Germany and Berlin the following day, officials discussed the 'apparent desire of the President and the Secretary [Rusk] to avoid [a] declaration of a national emergency at this time'. That same day JFK told the Joint Chiefs of Staff, 'it would be wise to postpone the declaration of such an emergency until it was required as a foundation for the mobilization of our reserve forces.' The generals indicated their acceptance of Kennedy's restraint on this point.[63]

It was on 19 July, after this period of careful consideration, that JFK and his advisers reached a final position on how best to respond to Khrushchev's threats over Berlin. At an NSC meeting in the Cabinet Room Kennedy's view that a declaration of national emergency would be premature was confirmed in a tense exchange in which McNamara bested Acheson who called for a prompt declaration of national emergency and the calling up of reserves no later than September. The secretary of defense argued that these steps would be hasty – they should be taken only 'when the situation required.' McNamara explained that military preparations would create a force in the United States of eight Army and Marine divisions, a number of which could be deployed in Europe, should the crisis intensify, and replaced with reserve divisions. Acheson backed down, indicating that he would go along with that. There was also general agreement that this build-up of US conventional forces would be sufficient to enlarge the credibility of America's nuclear deterrent in the crisis. When Secretary of the Treasury Dillon said that US military preparations over Berlin should be regarded as providing 'a capability, and not a present decision to deploy troops to Europe on a large scale', Kennedy 'strongly agreed' with the distinction made by Dillon. So no declaration of national emergency, but a build-up of conventional forces that would be authorized to let Khrushchev know that Kennedy was not willing to give up West Berlin to the Soviet bloc. What must have confirmed for JFK the soundness of his rejection of the more extreme policy options was a Gallup poll released just a few days earlier indicating that almost 60 per cent of Americans now feared that nuclear war would break out.[64]

In the days following this NSC meeting Ted Sorensen burned the midnight oil drafting the address on Berlin that JFK would deliver to the nation on 25 July.

In this period a paper prepared by Harvard Professor Thomas C. Schelling, the pioneer of game theory and an expert on strategic behaviour, made what Bundy described as a 'deep impression' on Kennedy. Sent to Kennedy at Hyannisport on the weekend of 21 July, Schelling's memo addressed the issue of 'Nuclear Strategy in the Berlin Crisis'. The use of nuclear weapons should not be considered at the start of the crisis, argued Schelling, and their role 'should not be to win a grand nuclear campaign, but to pose a higher level of risk to the enemy'. The main purpose of a 'limited nuclear war' in Europe from America's point of view would be to convince the Kremlin of the risks of a general war. Written with an impressive intellectual rigour, Schelling's paper was nonetheless, and perhaps inadvertently, chilling. He discussed, for instance, the selection of targets, including within Russia, for a US nuclear strike, making the case that they should be chosen not for their 'tactical contribution to the European battlefield' but for their impact on 'what the Soviet leadership perceives about the character of the war and about our intent'.[65]

When Bundy scribbled on Schelling's memo that it profoundly affected JFK, this must have referred not to the precise guidance it offered the president on how to approach nuclear conflict with Khrushchev over Berlin but rather the ominous and apocalyptic sense it conjured up as to what might lay ahead for America and the world in the summer of 1961. The Cuban missile crisis was crucial in developing in Kennedy a profound fear of nuclear war. But this was a two-stage process, with Berlin making clear to the young president the actual, not just the theoretical, dangers of the nuclear age.

Kennedy's address to the nation was set for 10:00 pm on the evening of Tuesday, 25 July. It was his most important presidential address since his inauguration. Along with his speeches during the missile crisis on 22 October 1962 and at American University on 10 June 1963, it would be one of the three most important foreign policy addresses of his entire presidency. Kennedy had long emphasized the dangers of the Cold War struggle. He had talked for even longer, beginning with *Why England Slept*, of the need for strong political leadership in America. In the 1960 presidential campaign he had promised the American people new, courageous and successful leadership in the White House. As he started his speech on the 25th, he now had to prove his mettle in one of the most dangerous crises of the Cold War and to convince the American people that he was up to the task.

'Seven weeks ago tonight I returned from Europe to report on my meeting with Premier Khrushchev and the others,' Kennedy began. He reminded Americans of Khrushchev's recent threats to end US rights in and commitments to West Berlin. 'That we cannot permit,' he declared. To that end, Kennedy said he wished 'to talk frankly with you tonight about the first steps that we shall take.'[66]

In defining the core US interests at stake, JFK spoke of the rights not of Berliners in general, such as freedom of movement for those in East Berlin, but specifically of West Berliners and America's protection of them: 'So long as the Communists insist that they are preparing to end by themselves unilaterally our rights in West Berlin and our commitments to its people, we must be prepared to defend those rights and those commitments. We will at all times be ready to talk, if talk will help. But we must also be ready to resist with force, if force is used upon us.'[67]

Kennedy proceeded to list the military measures he would take in readying America for a showdown with Russia over West Berlin: an additional $3.25 billion of spending on defence (on top of the increases in military spending he had already requested from Congress); an increase in the army's strength from 875,000 to about 1 million men; increases of 29,000 men in the navy and 63,000 in airforce personnel; the doubling and tripling of draft calls, putting reservists on active duty and prolonging tours of duty; retaining the use of ships and planes scheduled for deactivation; and spending $1.8 billion on 'non-nuclear weapons', ammunition and other military equipment.[68]

With all of this, Kennedy was telling Khrushchev that he would not back down over Berlin. If Khrushchev was seriously considering military action to eject the Western powers from the city, he now knew that Kennedy would respond with a force enlarged by these measures. It was a tactic right out of the *Why England Slept* playbook: stand up to aggressive dictators and back up that resolution with military power. In the context of the Bay of Pigs setback and Khrushchev's explosive behaviour at Vienna, Kennedy's approach was justified. It was vital that the Soviet dictator be under no illusion as to JFK's willingness to take up the cudgels should Russia try to force the United States and its allies out of Berlin.

At the same time Kennedy avoided the sort of dangerous hyperbole favoured by Acheson. There was no declaration of national emergency. He explained that the increase in US military spending would be on 'non-nuclear weapons'. As Dillon had argued at the 19 July NSC meeting, Kennedy said that the military steps he had authorized were designed to increase America's capability to act effectively in the crisis, not to presage imminent US military action in Berlin. 'Our primary purpose,' he said, 'is neither propaganda nor provocation – but preparation.' Kennedy also devoted a portion of his speech to 'our diplomatic posture' in the crisis. The freedom of West Berlin was non-negotiable, but he would listen to constructive proposals, as opposed to demands, from Moscow. His response to Khrushchev's threats over Berlin would not be solely militaristic, for 'we do not intend to leave it to others to choose and monopolize the forum and the framework of discussion. We do not intend to abandon our duty to mankind to seek a peaceful solution'. Noting legitimate Russian security concerns in Central and Eastern Europe given the catalogue of invasions it had endured through history, he indicated that some adjustments, which did not compromise the freedom of West Berliners, might be feasible in meeting those concerns. These sentiments, even if in part diplomatic posturing, were quite different from what Acheson and the hard-liners had in mind.[69]

Towards the end of his speech, Kennedy returned to its central theme: the commitment of America and the Atlantic Community to the freedom and defence of West Berlin. 'The solemn vow each of us gave to West Berlin in time of peace will not be broken in time of danger,' he insisted. 'To sum it all up: we seek peace – but we shall not surrender. That is the central meaning of this crisis, and the meaning of your government's policy.'[70]

Personalizing the crisis, Kennedy revealed that when he ran for president, he knew that grave challenges lay ahead but did not fully appreciate 'how heavy and constant would be those burdens'. He discussed the world wars and the Korean War that had drawn America and Europe into conflict during his own lifetime. If this were to happen again in the nuclear age as a result of misjudgement in either Moscow or Washington, the result could be 'more devastation in several hours than has been wrought in all the wars of human history'. 'Therefore I, as President and Commander-in-Chief, and all of us as Americans, are moving through serious days,' he said. He would 'bear this responsibility' for the rest of his presidency but 'I am sure that we all, regardless of our occupations, will do our very best for our country, and for our cause. For all of us want to see our children grow up in a country at peace, and in a world where freedom endures'.[71]

Part of Kennedy's political genius was his ability to make Americans feel that they were part of a shared national mission that was noble in purpose. With most leaders, this sort of rhetoric would appear to be nothing but vacuous cant. But with JFK it *felt* sincere. Put another way, Kennedy was able to inspire, to create a sense of national purpose. FDR could do that; Reagan to some extent. But it was a rare gift, and Kennedy had it. That served him well in the Berlin crisis, not least with his 25 July address.

Kennedy, though, was sobered by the gravity of the situation. When he uttered the final words of his speech, he neither smiled nor said a word to those assembled in the Oval Office. Instead he walked to the family residence alone, deep in thought. Like everyone else, he did not know how the Berlin crisis would play out, and also knew that in the nuclear age the worst-case scenario was profound and terrible.[72]

His 25 July speech, however, which defined his response to Khrushchev's Vienna threats over Berlin, increased the chances of an acceptable settlement of the crisis. He had struck the right balance between a willingness to use force to defend West Berlin, implicit in the military measures that he announced, so as to deter Khrushchev from aggressive action, and an emphasis on a peaceful, negotiated ending to the crisis in order to lessen the likelihood that it would spiral out of control. But Kennedy had also paved the way for a pragmatic, Realpolitik settlement. By emphasizing his commitment to West Berlin, but not his concern for the rights and freedoms of East Berliners, he signalled in his speech that he could live with a decision by Khrushchev to close the border to end the flow of refugees to the West that so drained the East German economy. As the number of East Germans fleeing to the West in July exceeded 30,000 in that month alone, such a development seemed likely.[73]

In the weeks that followed, Kennedy continued to handle the Berlin crisis with calmness and skill. He responded with composure when Khrushchev reacted to his 25 July speech with the same rashness he had displayed at Vienna. In a conversation with veteran US diplomat John McCloy at the Soviet leader's country retreat, Khrushchev claimed that Kennedy's speech was a declaration of preliminary war on Russia. If war started, he warned, JFK would become the last American president. In early August, Kennedy read an account of Kremlin discussions in which Khrushchev had told Italian prime minister Amintore Fanfani 'about twelve times' that any war over Berlin would be nuclear from the beginning. But coolness under pressure was one of Kennedy's strengths, and Khrushchev's bluster made no impact on his calm determination and basic strategic calculations during the crisis.[74]

As he had indicated in his 25 July address, JFK continued to consider diplomacy alongside the military preparations he had ordered. He instructed aides to work on a negotiating strategy. They considered a meeting of Western foreign ministers as a way of agreeing a coherent diplomatic approach. In early August Rusk met in Paris with the British, West German and French foreign ministers in the hope of finding enough common ground to make feasible the invitation of Russia to a conference. The British were keen and the West Germans somewhat amenable, but the French were strongly opposed. Negotiating with the Russians, warned de Gaulle, would be interpreted as the beginning of the abandonment of Berlin by the West. Not surprisingly, these Paris talks made little progress. Kennedy's attempt to fashion a meaningful diplomatic strategy proved to be of little consequence.[75]

At the same time, he continued to view the sealing of the border between West and East Berlin as a sensible, practical way of ending the crisis. In a television interview on 30 July, Senator William Fulbright said, 'The truth of the matter is... the Russians have the power to close it [the border] in any case. I mean, you are not giving up very much because ... next week, if they chose to close their borders, they could, without violating any treaty. I don't understand why the East Germans don't close their border because I think they have a right to close it.' It could have been the case that Kennedy secretly prompted Fulbright's statement as a signal to the Kremlin about what he was prepared to accept, though McGeorge Bundy later wrote that such collusion between president and senator was implausible. But when asked at a 10 August press conference about Fulbright's suggestion that the border in Berlin could be closed, Kennedy did not express any opposition to the idea.[76]

What was the case was that privately Kennedy felt the same way as did Fulbright. Chatting with his aide Walt Rostow in early August, he said the situation had become 'unbearable' for Khrushchev: 'The entire East bloc is in danger. He has to do something to stop this. Perhaps a wall. And there's not a damn thing I can do about it.' Kennedy succeeded here in anticipating how events in the Berlin crisis were likely to play out, given the Russian interests at stake. Hence, the dramatic events of 13 August did not come as a surprise to him.[77]

In Moscow, Khrushchev was under continual pressure from East German leader Walter Ulbricht to close the border between East and West Berlin to stop the flow of refugees. He urged Khrushchev at a Kremlin meeting on 5 August to permit this. Khrushchev relented: Ulbricht could seal the border with barbed wire. If the West did not retaliate with force, the barbed wire should be replaced by a wall. This was to be done at the border, warned Khrushchev, but the new barrier must not occupy any Western territory. 'Not one millimeter further,' he told Ulbricht.[78]

As Saturday, 12 August, turned into Sunday, the 13th, trucks and troop carriers approached the border with West Berlin. East German troops and police took guard at border crossing points. Cement road blocks were put up. A barbed-wire barrier between East and West Berlin was erected. 'We kidded among ourselves,' recalled Khrushchev, 'that in the West the thirteenth is supposed to be an unlucky day. I joked that for us and for the whole socialist camp it would be a very lucky day indeed.' Movement between the two sectors of the city was still feasible. It was not until 17 August that the building of the concrete Berlin Wall began. The CIA had failed to advise Kennedy of the possibility or likelihood that the Wall would go up, ignoring evidence that indicated it might well happen.[79]

The question for JFK was how to react to the Wall. That weekend Kennedy was home at Hyannisport. Due to the elephantine pace of communications in 1961, the State Department Operations Center in Washington did not hear about these monumental developments in Berlin for six hours. It was not until much later – early afternoon, Sunday, East Coast time – that the border closing was reported to Kennedy. Given the news in person by General Chester Clifton, Kennedy remarked: 'How come we didn't know anything about this.' Foy Kohler recalled that JFK was 'clearly disappointed by the lack of firm prior intelligence' on the closing of the border.[80]

On 13 August and the days which followed Kennedy grasped that the barrier being built between East and West Berlin represented a potential solution to the Berlin problem, as his earlier comments to Walt Rostow indicated. So he did not overreact and encouraged others to do likewise. When Rusk told him on the 13th that he had intended to watch a baseball game, Kennedy advised: 'Go to the ball game as you had planned. I am going sailing.' The point, as he told Rusk, was to do nothing that might inflame the situation. He never considered the option of attempting to bring down the Wall, morally objectionable as that edifice was, as such an act would be provocative and run the risk of war with the Russians.[81]

His response to the Wall, however, was not one of indifference. While he adopted a calm public posture, in private he gave much thought to how the Wall could be used by the United States in the Cold War battle for 'hearts and minds'. 'What steps will we take this week to exploit politically propagandawise the Soviet-East German cut-off of the border?' he asked Rusk in a memo on the 14th. In this, he received strong encouragement from Bobby Kennedy, who told his brother: 'We have been handed a propaganda victory of tremendous dimensions on a silver platter and we are just not taking advantage of it.' In addition to the public-relations dimension of the crisis, JFK attended to the ongoing US military preparations. On the 14th he wrote to McNamara to ask his views 'as to the maximum military strength that can be generated from the resources we have requested of the Congress'. It seemed prudent to remain vigilant in case the crisis in Berlin still somehow spiralled out of control.[82]

In the following days and weeks Kennedy's Berlin Task Force monitored the situation closely. A formal letter of protest, saying, 'The United States Government expects the Soviet Government to put an end to these illegal measures,' was drafted but not delivered in Moscow for several days. Kennedy's pragmatic outlook in this period was summed up in comments he made to his aides: 'Why would Khrushchev put up a wall if he really intended to seize West Berlin? There wouldn't be any need of a wall if he occupied the whole city. This is his way out of his predicament. It's not a very nice solution, but a wall is a hell of a lot better than a war.' West Berlin remained safe. War had been avoided. For Kennedy, that was an acceptable settlement to the crisis.[83]

On 16 August West Berlin mayor Willy Brandt wrote to Kennedy condemning what he perceived to be a weak Western response to the closing of the border by the communists, and demanding more vigorous action. Kennedy replied by pointing out that only war could force the Russians to reverse their decision on the border closing, and no one believed that 'we should go to war on this point'. Still Brandt's complaints highlighted the need for Kennedy to demonstrate America's enduring commitment to West Berlin in order to shore up morale in that sector of the city. He proceeded to do just that. He sent Lyndon Johnson to West Berlin to reassure the people there and also to urge Brandt to tone down his criticisms of US policy. The vice president delivered a stirring speech before the Berlin House of Representatives. Johnson received 'a wonderful reception' from West Berliners who viewed his visit as 'a sign of encouragement', recalled Brandt. To demonstrate that access rights to West Berlin remained unimpeded, Kennedy dispatched a 1,500-strong battle group from West Germany through the Autobahn in East Germany to West Berlin. Johnson greeted the troops at the Berlin Gate. As a precaution Kennedy had put US air and ground forces based in Europe on alert. But neither Russian nor East German forces troubled the battle group. On 30 August Kennedy appointed General Lucius Clay, hero of the 1948–9 Berlin Airlift, as his personal representative in West Berlin. Hence, his strong commitment to West Berlin was emphasized in these ways in the late summer of 1961. That contributed to the high level of public support he received over Berlin: in a 6 September poll, 66 per cent of Americans were satisfied with his handling of the situation while only one in five was dissatisfied. Two years later he would bask in the gratitude of West Berliners as they reacted euphorically to his 'Ich bin ein Berliner' speech.[84]

In a private conversation with Drew Pearson at the end of his first summer in the White House, JFK explained the extent to which his view – that West Berlin was an essential US commitment in the Cold War that could not be compromised – had shaped his handling of the crisis over the German city. 'We'll give him Laos,' he said of Khrushchev. 'He's got British Guiana. He's more or less got Cuba, but we'll not give him Berlin.'[85]

The Berlin crisis showed one of Kennedy's great strengths as leader: his skilful crisis management. He handled pressure well. He was able to navigate a path out of a crisis that entailed no surrender of key American interests. His adroit crisis management was particularly important given that the Kennedy years would be punctuated by crisis, both at home and abroad.

His leadership during the Berlin crisis also demonstrated his capacity to learn and grow. The Bay of Pigs disaster taught him the importance of viewing 'expert' advice with a more sceptical eye. In particular, he became wary of hard-liners, whether the generals or an adviser such as Acheson, who advocated dangerous militaristic policies that paid little or no heed to the dangers of the nuclear age. This steeliness in standing up to the hard-liners would be apparent again in October 1962 when dealing with the missiles in Cuba.[86]

The drama of the early Kennedy presidency centred on international affairs, not least the Berlin crisis. Nevertheless JFK spent a good deal of time, as presidents always do, mulling over domestic matters. Since the writing of *Why England Slept*, foreign policy had been his overriding passion in public affairs. But as congressman, then senator for fourteen years he had dwelt on domestic policies. As a candidate for president in 1960, he had been compelled to define his position on a variety of domestic-policy issues.

Prior to the presidency, Kennedy had not identified with the liberal wing of the Democratic Party. His father's relationship with Franklin Roosevelt had been difficult, and FDR had been no hero to him, as he had been for millions of Americans. His failure to take a stand against Joe McCarthy had damaged his relationship with liberals, including Eleanor Roosevelt. In his quest for the Democratic presidential nomination, however, Kennedy had needed to secure the backing and votes of liberals, and expressed his support for many liberal positions accordingly.

Domestic policy has not generally been perceived as one of the strong suits of the Kennedy presidency. But there has been a range of interpretation on this. In his 1991 study *Promises Kept*, Irving Bernstein made the case that Kennedy's domestic policies had been impressive. As with biographer James Giglio, he pointed to the mathematical reality of his legislative record. In 1961 33 of his 53 major proposals were enacted in Congress; 40 out of 54 in 1962; 35 of 58 in 1963. Compared to other modern presidents, that represents a fine performance.[87]

That does not tell the whole story. The relative importance of bills passed and those which did not should be considered. FDR secured passage of his landmark Social Security Act, as did Lyndon Johnson with the Civil Rights Act and the Voting Rights Act. Barack Obama succeeded in getting passed in Congress the Patient Protection and Affordable Care Act ('Obamacare'), which had a transformative effect on the US healthcare system. But JFK's ability to get his most important bills passed was more questionable.

Take, for instance, what Kennedy himself described as his five 'must' bills in 1961. Of these the two most important potentially were his school-assistance bill, an attempt to bolster American education by investing $2.3 billion on the building and operation of public schools and on teachers' salaries, and Medicare, hospital insurance for the elderly. Congress rejected both initiatives. Kennedy did enjoy success with the passage of his aid-to-depressed areas bill, inspired by the time he spent in poverty-stricken West Virginia in the 1960 campaign, which allocated $394 million over a four-year period to areas suffering high unemployment. His housing bill, which appropriated $5 billion on various housing, transportation and urban development programmes, passed in June 1961. With his plan to raise the minimum wage, Kennedy's record was mixed. In the end Congress approved an increase in the minimum wage but as part of a compromise deal laundry workers (mainly Black women) and 350,000 other poorly paid workers – those in greatest need of a salary increase – were excluded. With his five 'must' bills, therefore, Kennedy's record was a curate's egg, and his two most important reforms were rejected.[88]

How to interpret that performance? It was not the case that Kennedy's New Frontier reforms suffered from a lack of presidential attention or prioritization. Despite the dramatic foreign policy events of his presidency, Kennedy devoted a good deal of time to domestic policy. Yet he could have made greater use of Lyndon Johnson's expertise in dealing with Congress. Lawrence F. O'Brien, his special assistant for congressional relations, could have done a better job in dealing with key legislators on Capitol Hill.

An important issue in evaluating Kennedy's New Frontier is *context*. As with Franklin Roosevelt in the late 1930s, he had to deal with a political reality that meant no matter how much skill he could bring to bear as a legislative leader, Congress would inevitably block important parts of his domestic programme: an informal alliance of Republicans and Southern conservative Democrats would oppose liberal change. Despite the Democratic majority in both houses of Congress, the subtler reality was that 108 Democrats in the House and 21 in the Senate hailed from the conservative South. Kennedy could use the power and patronage of the presidency to try to cajole recalcitrant Southern legislators to do his bidding. Still, the limits of his legislative achievement need to be understood in the context of the entrenched conservative opposition, spanning both political parties, to his progressive legislative ambitions.

Kennedy's economic policies also need to be factored into an assessment of his domestic record. It is manifestly the case that the American people attach importance to economic matters in reaching an overall judgement on a president. When experiencing hard times, they have consistently turfed the offending party out of the Oval Office. By contrast, when the perception is that the economy is doing well or has at least improved, presidents have been re-elected.

As the American people have viewed economic success as an important element in a successful domestic presidency, it should be noted that in this area Kennedy's record was exceptional. Compare the growth rates of the Kennedy years to those of other modern presidencies, and a convincing case can be made that JFK was the most successful or at least one of the most successful stewards of the economic life of the country. The recession which Kennedy inherited from Eisenhower ended in February 1961, and the economy grew robustly thereafter. Well-conceived policies contributed to this growth. The 1962 Manpower Development and Training Act retrained workers whose skills were inadequate for the job market. The same year the Trade Expansion Act gave the president the authority to negotiate a 50 per cent reduction in tariff duties, to remove them altogether on certain products and to take retaliatory steps against nations carrying out hostile trade policies. This constituted the most important trade bill since the 1930s. Considering carefully the views and proposals of his economic advisers, he came by 1962 to support a tax cut, promoted in particular by arch-Keynesian and Chairman of the Council of Economic Advisers, Walter Heller. He unveiled the tax bill in January 1963. James Giglio has described it as one of Kennedy's 'most innovative and enduring initiatives. No other president had dared to impose a tax cut on top of a significant deficit or to ask for deficits to avert a possible recession'. The tax bill passed in the House of Representatives in September 1963 and would probably have been approved by the Senate at the start of 1964 had Kennedy lived, as it did with Lyndon Johnson in the White House.[89]

Three further points on Kennedy's leadership on domestic matters should be made. First, as with foreign policy he proved to be a skilled crisis manager, remaining cool under pressure and ending confrontations while achieving his key objectives. This was apparent from his handling of the steel industry crisis in April 1962, which erupted when U.S. Steel brazenly ignored Kennedy and increased steel prices beyond the administration's guidelines. Other companies followed suit. 'Are we supposed to sit there and take a cold, deliberate fucking?' JFK asked his journalist friend Ben Bradlee. He and his advisers did not exhibit such passivity. Kennedy condemned the U.S. Steel price hike at a press conference as selfish and unpatriotic, and used Robert Kennedy's Justice Department behind the scenes to put pressure on steel industry executives, even looking into their expense accounts. Other steel companies backed down, deciding against the price hike. Within three days the crisis was over. Kennedy's handling of it had been masterful.[90]

Second, some of Kennedy's efforts lay the groundwork for the achievements of Johnson's Great Society. In late 1962 he asked Heller to study the extent of poverty in America. Some of the anti-poverty planning in the final year of the Kennedy presidency would influence LBJ's War on Poverty, and some of the key policymakers in the War on Poverty cut their teeth on the poverty issue in the Kennedy White House.[91]

Third, JFK – to his credit – made significant progress in the area of women's rights. The feminist movement was not as intense as it would become later in the 1960s, but Betty Friedan's classic work *The Feminine Mystique* was published during the final year of the Kennedy presidency. His appointment of women to Cabinet-level posts left a lot to be desired: he did not make any. FDR, it will be recalled, had made Frances Perkins his Secretary of Labor three decades earlier. But three Kennedy initiatives were important. He established the President's Commission on the Status of Women, with Eleanor Roosevelt as chair, to make recommendations on reducing discrimination. He ordered the prohibiting of gender discrimination in the hiring of federal employees. In addition, he signed the Equal Pay Act of 1963, an administration bill guaranteeing equal pay for women (for the same work undertaken as men). On the fiftieth anniversary of JFK's assassination, a posting on the National Organization for Women's website argued that 'The cause of equality for women is an important part of John F. Kennedy's legacy'.[92]

Of all the domestic issues handled by JFK during his presidency, the most prominent was civil rights. It was the most important in that it related to the very nature of democracy and equality in American life. For those civil rights activists who had high hopes for what a Kennedy presidency would do for equal rights in America, the early months of Camelot were a disappointment, starting with the inauguration itself. Despite its eloquence and powerful message on America's role on the world stage, JFK's inaugural address said nothing on civil rights apart from a brief pledge to support human rights at home and overseas. The 1960 campaign promise to end segregation in federal housing at the stroke of a pen remained unfulfilled as the weeks and months went by. As for the new president's legislative programme, his five 'must bills' – on such policy matters as education and housing – did not include one on civil rights. Cautious, concerned about alienating Southern Congressmen who could then block his overall legislative programme, and unmotivated by the moral urgency that would characterize his later stance, Kennedy defined no clear strategy on civil rights, except a commitment to increasing Black voter registration and, of course, an obligation to manage and defuse any racial crises that broke out.[93]

Small wonder, then, that Roy Wilkins of the National Association for the Advancement of Colored People (NAACP) told Ted Sorensen that young activists in the Civil Rights Movement were becoming frustrated by JFK's unwillingness to introduce civil rights legislation. James Farmer, director of the Congress of Racial Equality (CORE), felt the same way. It was not just the lack of legislative leadership that vexed the Civil Rights Movement; it was the lack of even basic contact and communication with JFK. When Martin Luther King said he wanted to meet Kennedy, presidential aide Ken O'Donnell fobbed him off, claiming that the demands of the international situation meant it was not feasible. The president's view that civil rights was less important than foreign affairs at this point in his presidency was apparent from his private comments two weeks after the inauguration: 'I may have to send the Alabama National Guard to Berlin tomorrow and I don't want to have to do it in the middle of a revolution at home.' But JFK's Black political adviser Louis E. Martin thought it imperative that senior administration officials demonstrate a willingness to meet with the most prominent civil rights leader in the country, namely King. Robert Kennedy concurred but insisted that any such meeting be clandestine so as not to antagonize Southern Democrats. The meeting with Robert Kennedy, head of the Justice Department's Civil Rights Division Burke Marshall, Special Assistant on Civil Rights Harris Wofford and three other JFK advisers took place on 22 April at the Mayflower Hotel. At the meeting Marshall told King that there were limits to what the federal government could do on such issues as police brutality and school desegregation, but that Black voter registration was the area where most progress could be made. At the end of the meeting Wofford walked with King to the White House for an informal chat. On learning that King was in the White House, JFK decided to drop by. 'It's good to see you,' said JFK, adding that as attorney general, Robert Kennedy was keeping him informed of King's actions. He let King know that he would back any efforts at Southern voter registration. But JFK appeared distracted, not surprising given that this meeting was taking place in the immediate aftermath of the Bay of Pigs disaster. When King asked how he was enjoying life in the White House, a candid Kennedy said that it had become more difficult due to the Bay of Pigs. This meeting between two of the most iconic leaders in twentieth-century US history had lasted a mere five minutes. This did not indicate that the new administration would be fully engaged by and collaborative with the Civil Rights Movement.[94]

As would be the dynamic throughout the 1960s, however, the Movement would elicit presidential action in the spring of 1961 in what would be the most notable civil rights protest of the year: the Freedom Rides. CORE's James Farmer was the prime mover in instigating the Freedom Rides, which started in Washington on 4 May with seven Black and six White protestors travelling by bus through Virginia and then the South, arriving in New Orleans on 17 May, significantly the seventh anniversary of the Supreme Court's *Brown v. Board of Education* ruling against segregation in schools. Farmer's purpose was twofold: one specific, one general. The specific goal was to challenge segregation at interstate bus terminals, which had been outlawed by the Supreme Court's 1960 ruling in the case of *Boynton v. Virginia*. The broader motive, as Farmer later explained, was to compel the new president to move on civil rights, 'to keep up enough pressure on the Administration … so that a crisis which was intolerable would be created and the government would have no choice but to act'. The failure of JFK, as well as Bobby Kennedy, to respond to a letter sent by Farmer giving them advance warning as well as the itinerary of the Freedom Rides must have left the CORE director with the uneasy feeling that such intervention from the Kennedy administration might not be forthcoming.[95]

The Freedom Rides proceeded smoothly through Virginia. But there was some trouble in South Carolina, and then on 14 May in Anniston, Alabama, the first major domestic crisis of the Kennedy years exploded when a mob bombed the Greyhound bus and attacked the Riders with iron bars and clubs. The police did not lift a finger. The Riders who moved on to Birmingham were assaulted on arrival with chains and baseball bats, an outrage facilitated by thuggish police commissioner 'Bull' Connor's promise to the KKK that they could have at least ten minutes to beat up the Riders before his officers would intercede. Several Riders were hospitalized. FBI agents learned of this attack in advance, but J. Edgar Hoover neither informed the Kennedys not instructed his agents to intervene to help protect the Riders.[96]

Such brutal attacks on American citizens protesting peacefully and hoping only for the implementation of the law raised important issues for JFK and his advisers. As Assistant Attorney General Nicholas deB. Katzenbach later put it, if local law enforcement officers 'would look the other way and tolerate the violent acts of segregationists . . . when was federal intervention justified? . . . And how would intervention and its timing be managed?' Nor would it just be a matter of introspective analysis, for the Fourth Estate put the public spotlight on the sort of leadership JFK would provide in this time of crisis. 'If the confusion in the Southern mind is genuine and not willful,' asserted Howard K. Smith of CBS News, 'laws of the land and purposes of the nation badly need a basic restatement, perhaps by the one American assured of an intent mass hearing at any time, the President.'[97]

The following morning, 15 May, JFK read a detailed account of these shocking events in *The New York Times*. Sobered as he must have been, he was not sufficiently stirred to intervene boldly in the Freedom-Rides crisis. Rather, he remained focused at this juncture, sandwiched as it was between the Bay of Pigs calamity and the upcoming encounter with Khrushchev at the Vienna summit, on international matters. That prioritization of policy, foreign affairs taking precedence over civil rights, helps explain his view of the Freedom Riders, as Katzenbach recalled, as a 'pain in the ass'. Moreover, Kennedy sought to resolve this civil rights dispute not by assisting them in the accomplishment of their perfectly reasonable goals but by getting them to give up. That was the gist of his comments when, in an uncharacteristically angry mood, he phoned Wofford. 'Tell them to call it off!' he said. 'Stop them!' 'I don't think anybody's going to stop them right now,' warned Wofford. JFK made no statement on the crisis, which could have offered a sense of national leadership on this difficult issue. He did not authorize the federal protection of the Freedom Riders. He delegated the management of the crisis to Bobby Kennedy.[98]

To exhibit presidential concern and to provide some assistance to the Riders, however, Bobby sent his Executive Assistant John Seigenthaler to Birmingham, where he accompanied a group of bruised and battered Riders to the airport so they could fly on to New Orleans. If the Kennedys thought the crisis was now winding down, they were mistaken as another group of impassioned Riders headed to Montgomery. Alabama governor John Patterson, a strong supporter of JFK in the 1960 campaign, promised the Kennedys to provide state protection to these Riders. But as they approached Montgomery the state patrol cars drove away, leaving the Riders exposed at the Montgomery bus terminal to the fury of a White mob. Sticks, pipes and clubs were used as weapons to attack the Riders. Crucially, this outrage became personalized for Bobby Kennedy when Seigenthaler, who was a friend as well as Justice Department aide, was smashed over the head with a lead pipe when he arrived at the scene and tried to help a Black girl who was being attacked by several men. This assault rendered Seigenthaler unconscious. He lay on the sidewalk for almost half an hour before being taken to hospital.[99]

Bobby Kennedy was enraged, a fury undiminished when phoning Patterson only to be told the governor was unavailable. For Bobby, as one authority put it, 'this was the final straw. No governor could be allowed to thumb his nose at the federal government while countenancing the wanton disruption of civil order'. Bobby did not make a statement condemning the attack and behind the scenes urged Southern segregationists in Congress to respond temperately to events in return for his commitment not to lend any overt support to the Freedom Riders apart from providing them with 'the protection of the law'. Nevertheless, it was at this juncture that he acted more decisively. He and JFK were very reluctant to dispatch troops to bring order, with all the connotations of Reconstruction that would bring, but a plan had been developed to deploy marshals; and Bobby now decided to carry out that plan. A group of around 500 marshals, under the leadership of Deputy Attorney General Byron White, was sent to the scene. Fifty of them arrived in time to escort Martin Luther King from the airport to the First Baptist Church, where he was to speak to a large audience. Soon a large, frightening mob of 3,000 Whites gathered outside the church. One hundred federal marshals, carrying weapons and teargas, formed a barrier of protection outside the church. As the mob grew ever more threatening after dark, White sent in more marshals who managed to repel the Whites surging towards the church. Worried that a massacre would ensue, Bobby asked his brother permission to mobilize troops.

But the president withheld it, worried that this would only intensify the crisis. 'Even as the mob was on the verge of overrunning the church, with almost certain loss of life,' writes historian Nick Bryant, '[John] Kennedy remained disinclined to authorize the use of federal force.' Fortunately, Governor Patterson then decided to declare martial law, sending Alabama National Guardsmen to the church. The rioters began to leave. King was finally able to deliver his sermon, which included a stern warning for JFK: 'Unless the Federal government acts forthrightly in the South to assure every citizen his constitutional rights, we will be plunged into a dark abyss of chaos. The federal government must not stand by while bloodthirsty mobs beat non-violent students with impunity.'[100]

JFK's leadership during the Montgomery phase of the Freedom Rides was underwhelming. He had allowed Bobby to make the running in shaping the administration's response. As for the 'bully pulpit' aspect of presidential leadership, his contribution was slight and morally neutral. On 20 May he did release his first public statement on the crisis. A mere six sentences long, it expressed concern over the situation, said (somewhat nebulously) that he had 'instructed the Justice Department to take all necessary steps', urged Alabama government officials to try to prevent further violence and added: 'I would also hope that any persons, whether a citizen of Alabama or a visitor there, would refrain from any action which would in any way tend to provoke further outbreaks.' Not only did this statement seek to discourage the Freedom Riders from interstate travel, as was their legal right, but it made no moral distinction between the Riders and the mobs that had attacked them. The only crumb of comfort to civil rights activists provided by the statement was its ending: 'I hope that state and local officials in Alabama will meet their responsibilities. The United States Government intends to meet its.' The main way in which his administration had done so – and for this JFK deserves credit – was to use marshals to protect the Riders.[101]

Two days after that statement, Kennedy showed a revealing defensiveness over his record on the Freedom Rides. At a Cabinet meeting of the Peace Corps' National Advisory Council, singer Harry Belafonte said, 'Mr. President, I know how much you're doing in civil rights. I deeply respect your leadership in civil rights. . . . But perhaps you could say something a little more about the Freedom Riders.' Dean of the Yale Law School Eugene Rostow spoke too, very respectfully towards JFK, but emphasizing the importance of moral leadership on issues of equal rights. Kennedy responded by asking them if they had read his 20 May statement. They had not. He said it would satisfy them. On reading the statement after the meeting, they were, recalled Wofford, 'still dissatisfied – it was limited to a plea for law and order'. As Wofford chatted to Belafonte, Rostow et al. after the meeting, a guard came over to say the president wished to see him in the Oval Office. 'Who the hell was that man with Harry Belafonte?' asked Kennedy. Wofford explained it was Gene Rostow, the brother of his foreign policy adviser Walt. 'Well, what in the world does he think I should do?' complained Kennedy. 'Doesn't he know I've done more for civil rights than any President in American history? How could any man have done more than I've done?' Wofford was struck by 'how sensitive he was to criticism about his moral leadership'. It indicated that, deep down, Kennedy knew his handling of the first major civil rights crisis of his presidency had been neither as bold nor as inspiring as it might have been.[102]

As the Riders moved on smoothly and with state protection from Alabama to Mississippi, the Kennedys hoped an end to the Freedom Rides really was in sight. In releasing his first official statement on the crisis, welcoming the more peaceful progress of the Riders, Bobby revealed the way he and his brother continued to view the issue through the prism of foreign policy. 'I think we should all bear in mind that the President is about to embark on a mission [to Europe, including the Vienna summit] of great importance,' said Bobby. 'What we do in the United States at this time, which brings or causes discredit on our country, can be harmful to his mission.' The 'causes discredit' part of that statement seemed to refer to the Freedom Riders, and the argument clearly was that civil rights activists should place the Cold War concerns of the nation ahead of their (disruptive) quest for equal rights. When a second wave of Riders set off for Jackson, Mississippi, Bobby issued another statement, calling for a 'cooling off period' – in other words, a halt to any additional rides. This provoked James Farmer's famous rejoinder: 'We had been cooling off for 100 years. If we got any cooler we'd be in a deep freeze.'[103]

As for JFK, the way in which the Freedom Rides had not brought about any fundamental reappraisal of the urgency of his commitment to civil rights was apparent from his 'Second State of the Union' message on 25 May on 'Urgent National Needs'. The key objectives for the nation and thus his presidency, he argued, were bolstering national defence, promoting economic growth, enlarging foreign aid and putting a man on the moon – not, even in the context of that spring's febrile Freedom Rides crisis, civil rights. Not only civil rights activists, but some of Kennedy's own advisers, notably Harris Wofford, were disappointed. When Wofford implored Kennedy to include a 'few stout words' about civil rights in his television address to the nation on his return from Vienna, Kennedy refused.[104]

JFK's reluctance to use his oratorical gifts to provide national leadership on the Freedom Rides was striking. Apart from his brief and perfunctory statement on 20 May, the only other public comment he made came at a news conference on 19 July when asked by a journalist for his views on the Rides. On this occasion he said little beyond affirming that everyone had the legal right 'to move freely in interstate commerce', even if some Americans did not like that reality.[105]

Despite this rhetorical tentativeness, JFK's Justice Department did take decisive steps to shore up the legal rights of interstate travellers. A lawyer in Katzenbach's office, Robert Saloschin, came up with the idea of petitioning the Interstate Commerce Commission (ICC) to make the desegregation of buses and bus terminals a requirement. Both John and Robert Kennedy liked the idea, and on 29 May the Justice Department submitted a document to the ICC requesting the abolition of segregation in interstate travel. On 22 September the ICC did the Kennedy administration's bidding, issuing just such an order. The first major civil rights crisis of the Kennedy years was over.[106]

The positive steps taken by JFK and his advisers, particularly Bobby Kennedy, should be acknowledged. The Kennedys were genuinely concerned about the physical safety of the Freedom Riders. Deploying marshals in Montgomery was an important and effective decision. Petitioning the ICC was successful, though the order outlawing segregation in interstate travel took two years to carry out throughout the South. It is worth noting that the key figure in the Freedom Rides, James Farmer, said that he and his associates were 'pleased' by the administration's decision to use marshals and regarded the ICC ruling as 'a partial victory.'[107]

JFK's handling of the Freedom Rides, though, left much to be desired. The Cold War image of America figured too prominently in his attitude towards the Riders. He did not impose himself with sufficient vigour on the situation. Robert Kennedy was highly competent and, as attorney general, inevitably a key figure in the administration's handling of this crisis, but nonetheless JFK should have provided more substantial leadership. His unwillingness to use his oratorical gifts to shape the nation's perspective on the Freedom Rides was disappointing. In particular, the lack of moral urgency he displayed throughout the Freedom Rides was not only disappointing but inappropriate for what was, at root, a moral issue. After the Bay of Pigs, Kennedy's adroit handling of the Berlin crisis boded well for his future stewardship of US foreign policy. His management of the Freedom Rides, however, was less promising for his subsequent leadership on civil rights. Kennedy's record on the Freedom Rides represents an important benchmark in gauging the shift in his approach to civil rights over the course of his presidency, particularly in the wake of the Birmingham crisis in 1963.

Chapter 4

MICHAEL CARTER AND THE MISSILE CRISIS

In late August 1961 presidential aide Richard Goodwin strolled into the Oval Office carrying a box of Cuban cigars. He handed them to John Kennedy. Goodwin had just returned from Uruguay where at a party following the Inter-American conference Castro's confidant Che Guevara had presented him with the cigars. Kennedy asked Goodwin if the cigars were good. 'They're the best,' he replied. The president took one from the box, lit it and smoked. Then he looked worried. 'You should have smoked the first one,' he told Goodwin.[1]

How to explain Kennedy's sudden concern? Since 1960 the CIA had planned the assassination of Castro, and one of these plots sought to kill the Cuban leader with a poisoned cigar. If Kennedy knew of this plot it may well have occurred to him that the Cubans might be attempting to do to him what the CIA was trying to do to Castro. That would explain JFK's comment that Goodwin should have smoked the cigar first, rather like a servant in the days of ancient Rome testing the food before the emperor ate it to check if it had been poisoned.[2]

Assassination remains the murkiest and most controversial of Kennedy's efforts after the Bay of Pigs to remove Castro from power. The relevant documentation is sparse because of the CIA practice of 'plausible deniability', which means that even if a president is briefed about assassination plots against foreign leaders, it is not written down so that the president's knowledge of this is plausibly deniable at a later point. However, a 1975 Senate investigation provided some important information and other evidence exists too.[3]

What that 1975 Senate investigation showed is that beginning in 1960 the CIA used an ex-FBI agent to hire mobster John Rosselli to kill Castro. Rosselli soon recruited underworld associates Sam Giancana and Santos Trafficante to assist with this operation. It is an extraordinary, but wholly accurate, observation that in this instance the government was relying on the mob to carry out US foreign policy. At least one, perhaps two attempts were made by this CIA–Mafia alliance before the Bay of Pigs to assassinate Castro with poison pills prepared by the CIA's Technical Services Division. In spring 1962 CIA official William Harvey supplied Rosselli with four more poison pills during a meeting in Miami. Rosselli told Harvey they would be utilized to kill not only the Cuban leader but Raúl Castro and Che Guevara as well. By the end of June Rosselli reported to Harvey that a three-man team had been dispatched to Cuba to use the poison pills to assassinate Castro.[4]

The Senate committee leading the 1975 investigation considered whether Kennedy knew about and endorsed these plots to kill Castro. The smoking gun in that report was the record of a conversation in late 1961 between JFK and Tad Szulc of *The New York Times*. In his notes on that conversation, written at the time, Szulc said that Kennedy had revealed 'he was under terrific pressure from advisers (think he said intelligence people, but not positive) to okay a Castro murder'. Szulc claimed that he told JFK he could not condone the assassination of the Cuban leader, and that Kennedy then said he felt the same way. This mirrored Kennedy's conversation earlier in the year with Florida senator George Smathers: when he asked his good friend for his views on killing Castro, Smathers said he was opposed and JFK said he was too.[5]

It is clear, therefore, that Kennedy was briefed about the assassination plotting and that he had mulled over its value as a policy option – or why else raise such a delicate matter with a journalist and a senator. Once he heard the reservations of Szulc and of Smathers to the idea of killing Castro, he may well have thought it diplomatic to dissemble by expressing his own disapproval of such an ethically questionable instrument of foreign policy as assassination. Kennedy's associates told the Senate committee in 1975 that his personal sense of morality meant he would never have sanctioned the murder of a foreign leader. But in fact Kennedy was intrigued rather than repelled by the world of espionage and the moral compromises it entailed. His penchant for the James Bond stories reflected his fascination for the clandestine. As discussed earlier, at a Washington party during the 1960 presidential campaign he had even asked Fleming's advice on how to handle Castro. The author came up with a series of schemes fantastical even by his standards. When informed that William Harvey was the American James Bond, an enthralled Kennedy insisted on meeting the man described by one Kennedy aide as 'a pistol-carrying, martini-drinking adventurer'.[6]

A 5 October 1961 memorandum written by Thomas Parrott, assistant to JFK's military adviser Maxwell Taylor, substantiates the idea that Kennedy was not only aware of but also actively interested in the plotting to kill Castro. In this memorandum produced for the record, Parrott said he had conveyed to Assistant Secretary of State Robert Woodward instructions from Taylor about preparing a contingency plan. As Woodward was heading out of town, he assigned the task to his deputy Wymberley Coerr. When he met Coerr, Parrott explained that 'what was wanted was a plan against the contingency that Castro would in some way or other be removed from the Cuban scene'. This planning, he added, should consider the positions of Raúl Castro and Che Guevara, be supervised by the State Department but with input from the Pentagon and the CIA, and should proceed with 'reasonable speed'.[7]

The crucial passage of the memorandum was Parrott's disclosure that he had told Woodward of 'the President's interest in this matter, before General Taylor had told me he preferred this not be done. Therefore, I felt it necessary to tell Mr Coerr, on the assumption that Mr Woodward would have already told him. I asked that this aspect be kept completely out of the picture'. Coerr said he understood and offered to present this assignment as originating from his office. Parrott said that was up to him, but it would be fine to attribute it to Taylor.[8]

As Taylor was close to Kennedy, it is sensible to conclude that the president would have been aware of his military representative's instructions. Decoded, 'the contingency that Castro would in some way or other be removed from the Cuban scene' refers to assassination. Unless Taylor was in possession of specific intelligence indicating that an internal coup was imminent – and there is no evidence to suggest he was – then why would he even pose the question about Castro suddenly being removed unless he was aware of the ongoing CIA plans to kill Castro. The revelation of JFK's 'interest in this matter' of contingency planning for Castro's removal represents a partial failure to adhere to the practice of plausible deniability. It is worth noting that the initiation of this contingency planning was around the same time as Kennedy's conversation with Tad Szulc about assassinating the Cuban leader.

Assassination was but one strand in the tapestry of Kennedy's drive after the Bay of Pigs to remove Castro from power. Another thread was the application of covert pressure such as sabotage, which culminated in November 1961 in the establishment of Operation Mongoose. At a 5 May NSC meeting, a fortnight after the failure of the Bay of Pigs invasion, Kennedy had defined his future policy towards Cuba: he would do everything short of a direct attack to oust Castro, but 'military intervention in the future' would be retained as a policy option.[9]

If Kennedy wanted Castro out of power, dead or alive, but believed a US attack on Cuba was out of the question following the Bay of Pigs embarrassment, then the focus of his anti-Castro efforts would have to be on the clandestine. Shortly after the Bay of Pigs he established the Cuban Task Force, comprising senior administration officials, to devise ways to limit Castro's influence in Latin America and ultimately to overthrow the Cuban leader. By August 1961 Kennedy had authorized a six-month CIA programme, with a budget in excess of $5 million, to carry out anti-Castro covert actions that would include sabotage and propaganda.[10]

As Kennedy reflected on his rivalry with the Cuban revolutionary in the autumn of 1961, his frustration boiled over. Licking his wounds after the Bay of Pigs, resentful towards the military and intelligence leaders who had misled him over that affair, absorbing Bobby Kennedy's rage over these matters, this was one of the rare instances in his presidency when raw emotion, rather than cool calculation, characterized his decision-making. It was at this time that he and Bobby berated CIA deputy director Richard Bissell for 'sitting on his ass and not doing anything about getting rid of Castro and the Castro regime'. It was also in this period that JFK discussed the assassination of Castro with Szulc.[11]

Out of this general sense of frustration came a specific plan of action: Operation Mongoose. Launched by JFK on 30 November 1961, with the instruction to his advisers that 'We will use our available assets to go ahead with the discussed project in order to help Cuba overthrow the communist regime', Mongoose became the centrepiece of his effort before the missile crisis to overthrow Castro. To head up the operation, Kennedy turned to the American who most resembled James Bond, Edward Lansdale. A covert operations specialist who had inspired Graham Greene's novel *The Quiet American*, Lansdale was to work alongside Bobby Kennedy in driving Mongoose forward. As 1961 turned into 1962, Lansdale and Bobby could have been in no doubt as to the president's determination to oust Castro. In his notes for an 18 January 1962 NSC meeting, JFK said that 'the elimination of Castro communism remains a clear purpose of this Administration'. The next day Bobby conveyed that presidential resolve to military and intelligence officials by telling them that solving the Castro problem was 'The top priority in the United States Government – all else is secondary – no time, money, effort, or manpower is to be spared'.[12]

From the start of Mongoose until spring 1962, Lansdale brainstormed about the actions to be taken to discredit Castro and bring him down – and he encouraged colleagues to do likewise. In early February 1962, Pentagon official William Craig supplied Lansdale with a range of fantastical schemes that could easily have flowed from the pen of JFK's favourite author, Ian Fleming. Craig recommended the distribution in Cuba of a fake photo, 'such as an obese Castro with two beauties in any situation desired, ostensibly within a room in the Castro residence, lavishly furnished, and a table briming [sic] over with the most delectable Cuban food with an underlying caption (appropriately Cuban) such as "My ration is different"'. This, Craig claimed, 'should put even a Commie Dictator in the proper perspective with the underprivileged masses'.[13]

This period of brainstorming ended on 14 March 1962 when Maxwell Taylor issued the guidelines for the first phase of Mongoose. These made clear that the US government would use Cuban exiles and anti-Castro Cubans still on the island in working for Castro's overthrow. It was recognized that 'final success will require decisive U.S. military intervention'. However, the initial focus of the operation was modest: gathering intelligence. Any other actions taken were not to be so dramatic as to spark a rebellion that would necessitate armed US intervention.[14]

Although it is easy to view Kennedy's early Cuban policies as overzealous, it was more complicated than that. In endorsing these guidelines for Mongoose, he told his advisers that 'in so far as can now be foreseen [he doubted] circumstances will arise that would justify and make desirable the use of American forces for overt military action. It was clearly understood no decision was expressed or implied approving the use of such forces although contingency planning would proceed'. Those caveats reflected Kennedy's scepticism after the Bay of Pigs towards his own military, and anticipated the greater caution he showed on the Cold War during the final year of his life.[15]

That being said, he used various methods to undermine Castro in early 1962. He applied diplomatic pressure by engineering Cuba's expulsion from the Organization of American States. Also in February, a complete economic embargo on trade with Cuba was imposed, apart from the export to the island of vital medical supplies and foodstuffs. Before Mongoose Kennedy had ordered his top brass to update contingency plans for an attack on Cuba. Once Mongoose began, this military contingency planning became linked to the operation, which envisaged US armed intervention as the endgame to Mongoose.[16]

The US military did more than just put plans on paper; it tested their feasibility by carrying out large-scale practice operations, such as Lantphibex-1-62, which in April ended with the landing of an 11,000-strong force on an island near Puerto Rico. Keen to keep tabs on the preparations of his military for action in the Caribbean, Kennedy watched the exercise in person. His presence during an exercise that was clearly a dry run for an invasion of Cuba was reported in the American press.[17]

A few weeks later Nikita Khrushchev walked along the Black Sea coast with Rodion Malinovsky. His defence minister pointed out that just across the water in Turkey were American Jupiter missiles that could strike Soviet cities in a matter of minutes. Put missiles in Cuba, Khrushchev responded, and the United States would have to deal with the same sort of threat. The daring, dangerous Russian plan to dispatch nuclear weapons to Cuba, so close to American soil, had been hatched.[18]

What would surprise many readers is that some historians have blamed Kennedy for playing a major role in causing the Cuban missile crisis. For many years it had been assumed there was no debate to be had about the origins of the missile crisis: it occurred because of Khrushchev's reckless decision to send missiles to Cuba. What various historians in the late 1980s and 1990s argued was that it was Kennedy's attempt to intimidate and oust Castro through the Bay of Pigs, Operation Mongoose (known to Cuban and Soviet officials, if not by name), economic and diplomatic sanctions, military manoeuvres in the Caribbean and even assassination attempts (about which the Cubans complained in the United Nations General Assembly in autumn 1961) – as well as the general US military build-up he authorized – that prompted Khrushchev's missile gambit in Cuba. It was a sequential matter. Khrushchev ordered missiles to be dispatched to Cuba only *after* Kennedy's escalation of the arms race and his multifaceted campaign to overthrow Castro, a Russian ally by this point. In other words, had JFK charted a different course on Cuba and the arms race, Khrushchev would probably not have put nuclear weapons in Cuba, and hence there would have been no missile crisis.[19]

The allegation could not be more serious: in essence, it attributes a good deal of the blame for the most dangerous crisis in the Cold War – in human history in terms of its potential for apocalyptic devastation – to Kennedy. So this is one of the most important questions concerning his presidency. Khrushchev always insisted that the main reason he sent missiles to Cuba was to prevent a US invasion of the island that seemed inevitable given Kennedy's hostility to Castro in 1961–2, notably with the Bay of Pigs operation. Anatoly Gribkov, a military adviser to Khrushchev, later revealed the intelligence data received by Moscow in spring 1962 indicating that a US attack on Cuba was imminent. This must have related to the US military exercises taking place in the Caribbean, such as Lantphibex. When Mikhail Gorbachev introduced his glasnost policy of greater openness in the Soviet Union in the 1980s, Khrushchev's former advisers were able to express their views, and in doing so confirmed what Khrushchev, who died in 1971, had said – that defending Cuba from invasion was the main motive behind the missile deployment in Cuba.[20]

The other Soviet aim was to redress the nuclear imbalance between the superpowers. Kennedy had inherited a vast lead in nuclear weapons over the Russians, one he had sought to extend by increasing US defence spending. Unlike Eisenhower, his administration had boasted publicly about their nuclear advantage. In a remarkably imprudent March 1962 interview, Kennedy seemed to agree with those military thinkers who in *Dr. Strangelove* fashion were saying this nuclear lead meant a US first strike on the Soviet Union was possible because the Russian missiles aimed at America would be destroyed before they could be fired in retaliation. Shortly after JFK's provocative declaration, the Soviet military went on a special alert.[21]

Khrushchev's missile gamble may have been a complex ploy influenced by a wider variety of considerations, including a desire to undercut Chinese criticism that he was not doing enough to bolster communist movements throughout the world, and to acquire another card he could play to extract concessions from Kennedy on Berlin. But historians generally agree that defending Cuba and changing the nuclear equation were Khrushchev's chief concerns. It would seem reasonable to argue that it was Kennedy who created those concerns. Had he not approved the Bay of Pigs, Operation Mongoose, diplomatic sanctions, an economic embargo, assassination attempts and threatening military manoeuvres in the Caribbean, Khrushchev's fears of a likely American attack on Cuba would have been far less acute; and hence he probably would not have felt compelled to dispatch missiles to defend Cuba. If Kennedy had not authorized a US military build-up, despite inheriting a sizeable nuclear lead over the Soviets, Khrushchev's concerns about the arms race would have been less profound; and the need to send to the Caribbean missiles that could not strike American territory from Russia, but which could from Cuba, would have seemed less pressing. By this account Kennedy was largely culpable for causing the missile crisis.

It is not that straightforward, however. Khrushchev did not need to send nuclear weapons to Cuba to deter a US attack. Russian troops and conventional weapons, which he did deploy on the island in 1962 along with the missiles, would have sufficed. Kennedy would have known attacking Cuba would have meant engaging Soviet troops. That would have meant the Third World War. In those circumstances Kennedy would never have invaded Cuba. Khrushchev could also have achieved his objective of changing the nuclear balance by simply authorizing a substantial build-up of missiles based on Russian soil, which is precisely what the Soviets did later in the 1960s. The nuclear gap with the United States would have been closed without the provocative deployment of missiles close to Florida.

Put another way, Kennedy's Cuban and defence policies did *not* force Khrushchev to dispatch missiles to the Caribbean. The Soviet leader therefore bears the greater responsibility for triggering the missile crisis. An important factor here is Khrushchev's leadership style, which reflected his personality. He was impulsive, unpredictable, a risk-taker. This was the man who threatened not only war over Berlin in 1958 and 1961, but other nations with nuclear devastation. Installing missiles in Cuba was of a piece with that sort of bellicosity. It is something the more draconian, but less impetuous, Joseph Stalin would probably not have done.

The extent to which Kennedy deviated from the policies of his predecessor also needs to be considered. The impression given by some accounts of American foreign policy in this era is of Kennedy the Cold Warrior succeeding the commendably wise and restrained Dwight Eisenhower. It is seldom observed that the planning for what became the Bay of Pigs invasion, economic sanctions against Castro, diplomatic pressure (diplomatic relations with Cuba were severed shortly before JFK's inauguration), contingency planning for a military strike on Cuba and assassination plots all began not in the Kennedy years but during the Eisenhower presidency. Hence, the missile crisis cannot be viewed as the product of a foreign policy on Kennedy's part that was exceptionally aggressive; it was in fact in line with the approach of his predecessor who since the 1980s has been the recipient of extravagant praise from historians.[22]

That, however, does not cast JFK's handling of Castro in a wholly positive light. On the contrary, it exposes a shortcoming of his presidency, particularly during the early part of it: an inability to anticipate consistently the long-term consequences of his policies. Even if his policies towards Cuba did not necessitate Khrushchev's missile ploy, he should have considered the impact of his anti-Castro initiatives and military build-up on Moscow and the likely Russian response. This myopia would be evident elsewhere, including Kennedy's escalation in Vietnam, deepening US involvement there without reflecting sufficiently on how that would make any subsequent US withdrawal more difficult.

After securing Castro's approval for a missile deployment, the top-secret Operation Anadyr got underway in July 1962 to transport nuclear missiles, conventional weapons and troops from Russia to Cuba. The lengths to which Russian military planners went to preserve the operation's secrecy were extraordinary. The captains of the ships involved left the Soviet Union ignorant that their destination was Cuba. They were given only a set of coordinates in the Atlantic Ocean. On reaching that location they were to open an envelope with the instruction that they were to head for Cuba. Personnel on board were supplied with parkas and skis to create the illusion that the final destination was arctic rather than tropical. As Kennedy seduced yet another member of his White House staff, intern Mimi Beardsley, on those indulgent, languid evenings that summer, he could not have anticipated the impending storm.[23]

Operation Anadyr did not remain secret for long. American intelligence detected the Russian build-up in Cuba. The US press reported it. Republicans criticized Kennedy for being asleep at the wheel as Soviet military power established itself close to the shores of America. New York senator Kenneth Keating featured in this GOP assault on JFK as he claimed to enjoy access to secret sources that indicated Kennedy was underestimating the scale of the Russian build-up. But it was not just Keating who denounced JFK. Senator Barry Goldwater and Richard Nixon urged Kennedy to blockade Cuba, while Indiana senator Homer Capehart called for an invasion. All of this was to do with foreign policy; but it was to do with partisan politics too as the congressional elections were just around the corner, and Republicans understood that events in Cuba made Kennedy politically vulnerable.[24]

The question for JFK in the fall of 1962 was how to react to the Russian build-up in Cuba and the Republican attacks. His belief that this build-up did not include nuclear weapons shaped his response. For one thing, the Kremlin had never deployed nuclear missiles beyond Soviet territory before. For another, Russian officials assured their American counterparts behind the scenes that no missiles would be dispatched to Cuba. Although CIA director John McCone believed nuclear weapons would be sent, the agency itself found no evidence of missiles in Cuba. Indeed it was not until 8 September when the freighter the *Omsk* reached the island that the arrival of equipment for the installation of nuclear weapons began.[25]

Kennedy felt he could use the apparent fact that there were no missiles in Cuba to drive a wedge through the Republican critique of his leadership. The reason why GOP claims that developments in Cuba constituted a dire threat to US national security were fanciful, he would tell the American people, was that no Russian missiles that could actually strike the United States had been installed. Accordingly he released a statement via Press Secretary Pierre Salinger on 4 September that said there was no evidence in Cuba of 'offensive ground-to-ground missiles; or of other significant offensive capability either in Cuban hands or under Soviet direction and guidance. Were it to be otherwise, the gravest issues would arise.' At a press conference nine days later Kennedy reiterated the point.[26]

The apparent absence of missiles in Cuba was, then, a convenient hook for Kennedy to hang the argument that Republicans were exploiting the current situation for shameless partisan reasons as there was no clear and present danger to the United States. Adopting that position, however, would have implications for the missile crisis. By arguing that the lack of missiles meant the US was not threatened, Kennedy was acknowledging that nuclear weapons in Cuba *would* constitute a severe threat requiring a vigorous American response. What this meant was that when the missile crisis began, simply tolerating nuclear weapons in Cuba (as the Russians had had to do with American Jupiter missiles in Turkey) would not be an option. The question would be not whether to act but how to act.

While in public JFK urged restraint, in private he cut a very different figure, intensifying Operation Mongoose, demanding updated contingency plans for a US attack on Cuba and permitting new military exercises in the Caribbean. The first phase of Operation Mongoose, with its focus on intelligence collection, ended in the summer of 1962, with Lansdale pressing for a more assertive second phase. In the proposed guidelines for that second phase, sent by Taylor to JFK on 17 August, Mongoose planners proposed 'a somewhat more aggressive program than the one carried on in Phase I, wherein we continue to press for intelligence, attempt to hurt the local regime as much as possible on the economic front and work further to discredit the regime locally and abroad'. Kennedy endorsed these guidelines three days later. As the Russian build-up in Cuba continued apace that autumn, he injected a sense of urgency into Operation Mongoose. On 4 October Bobby Kennedy reported to Mongoose officials on his 'discussions with the President on Cuba; dissatisfied with lack of action in the sabotage field'. When McCone claimed that 'hesitancy' in the upper echelons of the administration accounted for Mongoose's slow progress, Bobby disabused him of that notion in no uncertain terms. 'There followed a sharp exchange,' McCone's minutes of the meeting revealed, 'which finally was clarifying inasmuch as it resulted in a reaffirmation of a determination to move forward'.[27]

As in March 1962 when JFK approved the guidelines for the first phase of Mongoose, the switch to phase two was not a case of a president permitting a policy towards Cuba of unrestricted aggression. Those August guidelines, which Kennedy backed, made clear that although the overthrow of Castro was the operation's ultimate objective 'a revolt [against the Cuban leader] is not sought at this time'.[28]

Kennedy and his advisers thought it prudent, nonetheless, to advance the contingency planning for a US attack on Cuba in case a rebellion did take place or if other circumstances arose that necessitated military intervention, especially given the context of a Russian build-up on the island. Hence, the plans for an invasion or blockade of Cuba, and an air strike on the island, were advanced. Kennedy took an active interest in this planning. On 21 September he sent a memorandum to McNamara about a US air strike on a Soviet surface-to-air missile in Cuba. 'Would it be useful to build a model of such a site for exercises to be observed by an objective and disinterested party?' he asked his secretary of defense. 'Would you assure that contingency plans with relation to Cuba are kept up-to-date,' Kennedy added, 'taking into account the additions to their armaments resulting from the continuous influx of Soviet equipment and technicians.'[29]

On 11 October JFK mulled over the situation in Cuba with McCone. His CIA director showed him intelligence photographs of the Russian build-up there. A sobered Kennedy declared: 'we'll have to do something drastic about Cuba.' This was five days before he learned that there were nuclear missiles on the island. It raises the issue, explored by historian James Hershberg in a brilliant 1990 article, of whether Kennedy had decided to attack Cuba before the missile crisis began. It is an important matter because if Kennedy was so inclined then this could be viewed as justification for Khrushchev's belief that he needed to bolster Cuba's defences in order to deter an imminent US attack. On the other hand, the readying of American military power in the autumn of 1962 for action against Cuba could be regarded as sensible given the Russian build-up on the island. There is no evidence to indicate that Kennedy had decided to attack Cuba. His statement to McCone on the need to do something 'drastic about Cuba' should be interpreted circumspectly. The adroit politician he was, Kennedy – like Harry Truman – knew how to tailor his comments to please his advisers; and he was well aware of McCone's hard-line views. With the Soviet military escalation in Cuba, Kennedy judged it sensible to be prepared for the use of force. It was an option he requested. He wanted to be able to carry it out on short notice if necessary. But he had not given the go-ahead for a military strike on Cuba. Given the evident Russian military presence on the island and the hullabaloo over it in Congress and the media, one wonders if any other president would have handled the situation differently.[30]

From the perspective of Moscow and Havana, however, US military preparations must have appeared ominous. When a practice operation was announced for 15 October, in which the Caribbean island of Vieques would be stormed, the Pentagon mischievously informed the press that the purpose of the exercise was to free the island from a fictional tyrant called Ortsac. Read that name backwards and the true target of American military planning that autumn becomes apparent. Ian Fleming would have enjoyed the ruse.[31]

The morning of Tuesday, 16 October 1962, the White House: a relaxed Kennedy was lying in bed in his dressing gown, reading the morning papers. Just before 9 a.m. McGeorge Bundy entered the bedroom and informed Kennedy that photographic evidence from a U-2 flight two days earlier proved that the Russians had put nuclear weapons in Cuba. Khrushchev 'can't do this to me,' was the thrust of Kennedy's reaction to the terrible news, Bundy recalled. The Cuban missile crisis, the gravest crisis of the Cold War, the greatest challenge of Kennedy's presidency, had begun.[32]

To meet that challenge, JFK established a group of senior officials to advise him on the management of the missile crisis. It was called the Executive Committee of the National Security Council (or ExComm). In that conversation with Bundy, Kennedy listed the officials he wanted to attend the ExComm meetings.

One of Kennedy's great virtues was his ice-in-the-veins reaction to moments of intense pressure. It derived in part from a certain innate confidence, a belief that he could always handle things, but it also related to his life experiences. Whether it was being rammed by a Japanese destroyer in the Pacific or being read the last rites following back surgery, knowing what it was like to be at death's door meant Kennedy was familiar with extraordinary, potentially fatal pressure.

The history of John Kennedy and the missile crisis is a story about change and growth. It's a political but also a family story of two brothers working together, relying on each other. It's also a story about the importance of remaining open-minded. Kennedy's successful stewardship of the missile crisis depended on his capacity to avoid the perils of dogmatism. In the context of his time in the White House, the missile crisis was the turning point: the start of a shift towards a more progressive sort of politics that he would champion until his fateful trip to Dallas a year later.

With a switch under the desk to activate a taping system in the Cabinet Room, Kennedy has provided historians with an excellent record of ExComm's deliberations. In the two ExComm meetings held on the opening day of the missile crisis, his reaction was the same as most of his advisers: he believed that the United States had to respond by taking decisive military action. 'We're certainly going to do number one,' JFK told his advisers, 'we're going to take out these missiles . . . the questions will be whether . . . [we go for] what I would describe as number two, which would be a general air strike. . . . The third is the general invasion.' In the second ExComm session he reiterated that the three options were an air strike on the Russian missile sites in Cuba; a more general strike on those sites but also targets such as surface-to-air missile sites and airfields; and a full-scale invasion. Of those alternatives, his preference was for the general strike. Although during the missile crisis Kennedy displayed an admirable coolness in general, the discovery that Khrushchev had deceived him by sending missiles to Cuba disturbed his equanimity on 16 October. Several US officials have recalled his vexation that day. His state of mind may have influenced his initial inclination towards a military response to the missiles in Cuba.[33]

The paradox of Kennedy's position was that he made clear in ExComm his belief that Khrushchev would never fire the missiles in Cuba at the United States, presumably because he knew America would launch a retaliatory strike on Russia. He was also sympathetic to McNamara's argument that missiles in Cuba were strategically irrelevant as Khrushchev could already attack the United States with missiles based in the Soviet Union. Furthermore, JFK was not sure as to why Khrushchev had sent missiles to Cuba, though he speculated that he might use the threat posed by these weapons to pressure West Berlin. Yet despite his uncertainty as to Khrushchev's motives, his certainty Khrushchev would not use the missiles in Cuba to attack the United States and his belief that the missiles were strategically irrelevant, he was convinced that a US attack on Cuba was essential. The explanation of this apparent contradiction lies in his 4 and 13 September statements in which he had vowed to take robust action should Khrushchev ever send nuclear weapons to Cuba. He had attached his own credibility to the upholding of that pledge in a clear and decisive manner. Nothing would be more decisive than a military strike on Cuba. A secondary factor was the extensive contingency planning undertaken by the American military for an attack on Cuba. Kennedy understood that this meant the United States was well prepared for war in the Caribbean. He raised both the issue of the September pledges and military contingency planning on 16 October.[34]

The conclusion which must be reached is that it was a good thing that JFK did not believe he needed to make a snap decision at the start of the missile crisis. The evidence suggests he would have plumped for an air strike on Cuba, to which Khrushchev would have felt obliged to respond somehow, somewhere – and so the outcome could well have been the Third World War. In a sense, Kennedy's initial belligerence was of a piece with his hard-line approach towards Cuba before the missile crisis: the Bay of Pigs, Operation Mongoose, assassination plots.

While most of Kennedy's advisers agreed on 16 October with his support for military action, a few explored other options. Secretary of State Dean Rusk discussed a diplomatic approach that would have included a message to Castro. But it was McNamara who made the most important contribution that day, for he was the official who introduced the idea of a naval blockade around Cuba, independent of any military action against the island. The Kennedy administration, he said, could issue a statement that 'we would immediately impose a blockade against offensive weapons entering Cuba'. This was a crucial moment in ExComm for it converted a discussion over the merits of various military options to a debate over the likely effectiveness of military action in comparison to a blockade. A villain on the Vietnam War, McNamara was a hero in the missile crisis.[35]

State Department official George Ball, as well as McNamara, influenced the thinking of JFK, Bobby Kennedy and other senior officials. It was the CIA's deputy director Marshall Carter who in the evening ExComm meeting on 16 October introduced a powerful metaphor for an American air attack on Cuba: 'This coming in there, on a Pearl Harbor [type of surprise strike], just frightens the hell out of me as to what goes beyond.' But it was Ball who would dwell on the metaphor in a way that struck his colleagues. In an ExComm discussion on the morning of

Thursday, 18 October, he argued that a US strike on Cuba, without warning, would be 'like Pearl Harbor. It's the kind of conduct that one might expect of the Soviet Union. It is not conduct that one expects of the United States'. An impressed Bobby Kennedy, who on the first day of the missile crisis was for an invasion of Cuba, told his brother: 'I think George Ball has a hell of a good point.'[36]

From 17 to 20 October JFK kept to his planned schedule of campaign trips across the country on behalf of Democrats running in the November congressional elections. To have cancelled those campaign commitments, he calculated, would have alerted the press to the fact that an extraordinary event was underway. During the early days of the crisis he attended the ExComm meetings permitted by that schedule. But Bobby Kennedy kept him abreast of how the ExComm debate was proceeding in his absence.[37]

John Kennedy's important contribution in this period to saving the peace was simply to keep an open mind. The Bay of Pigs had taught him that, as well as other vital lessons – not least the capacity of the military and the CIA to give sloppy advice. JFK's flexibility at this juncture should not be taken for granted. It was an example of mature presidential leadership in a time of crisis that contrasts with that provided by George W. Bush in 2003 when deciding whether to fight in Iraq.

Step by step, absorbing the ideas emerging in ExComm against military action – its moral equivalence to Pearl Harbor, the danger it would trigger Soviet military reprisals, the window of opportunity that the blockade would provide for negotiations that could end the crisis – JFK abandoned his initial support for an air strike on Cuba and instead championed the blockade against the hawks in his administration, which meant not only the Joint Chiefs and the leaders at Langley but also the formidable Dean Acheson.

By 18 October JFK was showing signs of shifting his position. In a lunchtime ExComm session he told his advisers that there might be merit in promising to remove US Jupiter missiles in Turkey in return for the withdrawal of Russian missiles from Cuba. He also explored the blockade with his colleagues, and expressed his concerns about preserving NATO solidarity and preventing a Russian move on Berlin and nuclear war itself.[38]

That afternoon a private White House meeting with Acheson revealed the direction of Kennedy's thinking. The president used the Pearl Harbor precedent to question the wisdom of a military strike on Cuba. The acerbic Acheson made no attempt to conceal his contempt for that comparison. As the meeting drew to a close a reflective Kennedy gazed out at the Rose Garden. 'I guess I better earn my salary this week,' he said. 'I'm afraid you have to,' agreed the veteran Democrat. Earning his salary that day included deciding against disclosing his knowledge of the missiles in Cuba in a meeting arranged before the crisis with Soviet Foreign Minister Andrei Gromyko.[39]

As Kennedy began to back the blockade, he had to confront the hawks, particularly the Joint Chiefs. In a morning meeting with them on Friday, 19 October, Taylor told JFK that the Joint Chiefs were for an air strike on Cuba, to be carried out with no prior warning. A patient, resolute Kennedy refused to buckle under considerable pressure from his top brass. He told them that the problem with attacking Cuba was the likelihood that Khrushchev would retaliate in Berlin. 'We would be regarded as the trigger-happy Americans who lost Berlin,' he argued. 'We would have no support among our allies.' That stereotype of a gung-ho general Curtis E. LeMay thundered that a blockade would be akin to appeasement. In the face of such provocation – and, truth be told, an appalling lack of respect for JFK's integrity – Kennedy persisted with his wholly valid argument that the Joint Chiefs needed to view the crisis in a broader Cold War context, to dwell on the likely consequences of an American air strike, especially in Berlin. Kennedy also made clear to his military advisers his ultimate concern: 'The argument for the blockade was that what we want to do is to avoid, if we can, nuclear war by escalation or imbalance.' If keeping an open mind was one reason for Kennedy's successful management of the missile crisis, his backbone in standing up to his own generals was another.[40]

After his confrontation with the Joint Chiefs JFK headed to Ohio and Illinois for the congressional campaign, but not before instructing Bobby to forge a consensus in ExComm in support of the blockade. 'I'll make my own decision anyway,' he told his brother, if that consensus proved elusive. In his absence, Bobby locked horns with the hawks in ExComm, telling them that 'the memory of Pearl Harbor and … all the implications this would have for us in whatever world there would be afterward' meant an air strike on Cuba was unthinkable. By the end of that ExComm session the hawks had not been silenced, but their case had been weakened.[41]

Bobby passed all of this on to JFK on his return from Chicago the following day, Saturday, 20 October. In the ExComm meeting that afternoon the president told his colleagues that he was 'ready to go ahead with the blockade'. But his United Nations ambassador Adlai Stevenson dashed the hopes Kennedy must have had for a clear-cut resolution to the debate in ExComm, for he raised the difficult issue of the endgame: How exactly would a blockade, which Stevenson supported, lead to a diplomatic settlement? Mutual concessions was Stevenson's answer. Specifically, Kennedy should pledge to remove the US Jupiter missiles from Turkey and to quit the base at Guantanamo so as to persuade the Russians to withdraw their missiles from Cuba.[42]

As discussed earlier, Kennedy did not care for Stevenson, and that animus probably influenced the tone of Kennedy's forthright response to his proposals, for he 'sharply rejected the thought of surrendering our base at Guantanamo,' and 'felt that such action would convey to the world that we had been frightened into abandoning our position'. He went on to say he did not object to negotiations over the withdrawal of the Jupiters from Turkey but insisted such a concession could be made only at a later point.[43]

Kennedy's rebuke hurt Stevenson, so much so that he told a Kennedy aide at a Washington party that evening that he knew JFK and other ExComm officials would now regard him as a coward. But, he added, 'perhaps we need a coward in the room when we are talking about a nuclear war'. However, the differences between Kennedy and his leading liberal adviser should not be overstated. Both backed the blockade. Both countenanced trading the Jupiters. The only difference on that was one of timing. Kennedy did not want to initiate discussions with Moscow by volunteering to give up the missiles in Turkey; he wanted the pressure from the blockade to build so as to make Khrushchev more conciliatory, before bartering over the Jupiters. On the issue of Guantanamo Kennedy was right: to cede that base would have looked like appeasement, undermining the administration's credibility at home and abroad. But later in the crisis Kennedy moved closer to Stevenson's position, which essentially emphasized the importance of diplomacy in ending the crisis peacefully. That would turn out to be part of a broader theme in Kennedy's foreign policy during the final year of his life: a greater determination to ease Cold War tensions. This highlights another important aspect of the Cuban missile crisis: it was a vital part of the political education of John Kennedy. It taught him a lesson based not on theory but on the raw, frightening, first-hand experience of the missile crisis: the risk of nuclear war was real, and it was thus a vital obligation of a president to do all he could to reduce the chances of that apocalyptic scenario.[44]

By 20 October, therefore, Kennedy had placed his chips on a US naval blockade around Cuba. The concerns he had developed over an air strike increased the next day when Commander-in-Chief of the Tactical Air Command General Walter Sweeney and Maxwell Taylor told him even a perfectly executed air strike would destroy no more than 90 per cent of the known missiles, which probably constituted no more than 60 per cent of all the nuclear weapons in Cuba. To be precise, the best-case scenario with an air strike was that 54 per cent of all the missiles in Cuba would be destroyed, meaning plenty would remain to launch a retaliatory strike on the United States. This point had been made to Kennedy earlier in the crisis, but this was the most precise and authoritative presentation of the issue that he had heard. It undermined the position of the hawks whose central argument had been that the chief shortcoming of the blockade was that it did not deal directly with the problem at hand; that is, it did not destroy or remove the missiles already in Cuba – unlike an air strike. Now JFK knew that the Russians' ability to retaliate with a nuclear attack on the United States in response to an air strike on Cuba would be considerable, as it would following a blockade.[45]

On Monday, 22 October, Kennedy's stewardship of the missile crisis moved from clandestine meetings to the world stage, for at 7 pm he delivered from the Oval Office the most important foreign policy address of his presidency, informing the American people and the international community that Khrushchev had sent missiles to Cuba and that he would respond by establishing a naval blockade around the island to prevent the further delivery of nuclear weapons. Earlier that day he had summed up for his ExComm colleagues the reasons why he had chosen the blockade instead of an air strike: a strike would not destroy all of the missiles in Cuba, was reminiscent of Pearl Harbor and would make nuclear war more likely. Two hours before his speech to the nation he met with the congressional leadership, from whom he hoped to receive bipartisan support. He would be disappointed, with senators Richard Russell and William Fulbright particularly strident in their criticism of the blockade.[46]

That evening Rusk handed the Soviet ambassador in Washington, Anatoly Dobrynin, a letter from Kennedy to Khrushchev that triggered a frenetic correspondence between the superpower leaders for the remainder of the crisis. In his message, Kennedy said that in their earlier dealings he had been concerned that Khrushchev underestimated US resolve, and reminded him that at the Vienna summit he had emphasized that he could not tolerate any Russian attempt to disrupt the international balance of power. Kennedy added that the blockade constituted only the minimum action necessary to bring about the removal of the missiles from Cuba, and he urged Khrushchev to do nothing to intensify the crisis.[47]

From the Oval Office Kennedy delivered his sobering and, no doubt to millions of Americans, shocking television and radio address. 'This Government, as promised,' he began, 'has maintained the closest surveillance of the Soviet military build-up on the island of Cuba. Within the past week, unmistakable evidence has established the fact that a series of offensive missile sites is now in preparation on that imprisoned island. The purpose of these bases can be none other than to provide a nuclear strike capability against the Western Hemisphere.'[48]

In building a case for the unacceptable provocation of the Russian missile deployment in Cuba and hence a justification for the blockade, Kennedy argued that it defied not only the Rio Pact and UN Charter, but his own public warnings on 4 and 13 September. But in developing a rationale for the blockade, his most striking argument derived from the same concerns he had expressed two decades earlier in *Why England Slept*. 'The 1930's,' he asserted, 'taught us a clear lesson: aggressive conduct, if allowed to go unchecked and unchallenged, ultimately leads to war. This nation is opposed to war. We are also true to our word. Our unswerving objective, therefore, must be to prevent the use of these missiles against this or any other country, and to secure their withdrawal or elimination from the Western Hemisphere.' Appeasement had failed in the 1930s, Kennedy was saying, and a determination to avoid those mistakes must shape US policy in the missile crisis. Hence, Pearl Harbor was not the only historical precedent to influence Kennedy's thinking in October 1962.[49]

The least impressive aspect of JFK's speech was the often-overlooked part in which he called upon Cubans to rebel and oust Castro: 'Many times in the past, the Cuban people have risen to throw out tyrants who destroyed their liberty. And I have no doubt that most Cubans today look forward to the time when they will be truly free.' As with a number of his colleagues, JFK believed the optimal outcome of the missile crisis would be the removal of Castro as well as the nuclear weapons from Cuba. That squared with his pre-missile crisis hostility towards Cuba and would mean Castro could not again be the recipient of Russian missiles in the future. It was flawed thinking, as the withdrawal of the missiles to end the crisis should have been his exclusive concern. Manifestly, though, this enduring wish to overthrow Castro did not prevent JFK from engaging in the sort of diplomacy required to save the peace in October 1962.[50]

The impact of Kennedy's speech on the American people was profound. Fear suffused the nation. A man in Illinois, for instance, charted a course for Canada. And Mimi Beardsley noticed young women holding hands as she watched her lover's speech on television in her college dorm.[51]

JFK's address on the missile crisis coincided with the release overseas of the first James Bond movie. A fortnight before the speech *Dr. No*, starring Sean Connery, opened in Britain. This meant that many British moviegoers saw this film about a missile crisis in the Caribbean at the same time that an actual missile crisis in the Caribbean was taking place. As one critic put it, *Dr. No* was 'surely the most timely [of all Bond movies] in its concern with a malevolent island despot and secret missile base in the Caribbean'.[52]

After Kennedy told *Life* magazine in spring 1961 about his penchant for James Bond, the media frequently commented on the connection between JFK and the fictional British spy. When the *Dr. No* movie was released in the UK, *Time* magazine mused:

> It is almost a certainty. One evening . . . the President of the United States will enter a small room. For two hours a machine will play with his emotions. He may groan, but he will not be physically hurt. If he is disappointed when he leaves, he will at least emerge into a world where his job seems relatively tame, for he will have seen *Doctor No*, the first attempt to approximate on film the cosmic bravery, stupefying virility, six-acre brain, and deathproof nonchalance of Secret Agent James Bond – the President's favourite fictional hero – and Writer Ian Fleming's generous gift to literature.

Kennedy's association with Bond became an important part of his alpha-male image created by his valour in the Pacific during the Second World War, sex-symbol status and the reports of all those games of touch football on the White House lawn. When *Dr. No* was released in the United States in the spring of 1963, therefore, Americans were reminded of the real Caribbean crisis a few months earlier which their president – the nation's most famous James Bond fan – had handled with great skill. Kennedy's link to Bond accentuated the glamour, virility and heroism intrinsic to his own image.[53]

Caution, as well as an open-mind and a steel to stand up to his generals and other hawks, explains the effective crisis management of America's own James Bond in October 1962. On the 22nd Kennedy had insisted on issuing fresh orders to the military that his commanders in Turkey could fire the Jupiter missiles only after securing presidential approval, despite being told by the Joint Chiefs and other ExComm officials that such instructions were already in place and hence superfluous. Given the dangers of the situation, his prudence on this was appropriate.[54]

The next day, Tuesday, 23 October, Kennedy continued to display this commendable caution. He arranged for US planes in Florida to be checked to ensure they were not wingtip to wingtip and thus a vulnerable target for a Russian air strike, and ordered their dispersal once it was reported they had been so positioned.[55]

Later Kennedy revealed, in a conversation with Bobby, speechwriter Ted Sorensen and close aide Ken O'Donnell, his determination not only to protect US security interests but also to prevent war. Having read Barbara Tuchman's book

The Guns of August, JFK was much preoccupied with 1914, as well as 1939, and how the great powers had stumbled into war on those occasions. He expressed a resolve to avoid the sorts of misjudgements and provocative acts that had resulted in war earlier in the century. So 1914, the late 1930s and December 1941 were the historical precedents influencing JFK's thinking in the missile crisis; and *The Guns of August* and *Why England Slept* were the key texts.[56]

In the evening JFK responded to the indignant message sent by Khrushchev earlier in the day. He insisted that the secret installation of missiles in Cuba was the root cause of the crisis. But he also urged restraint: 'I am concerned that we both show prudence and do nothing to allow events to make the situation more difficult to control than it already is.' Elsewhere others were less circumspect that evening. A Russian press officer at the United Nations, Mikhail Polonik, reportedly told a US official: 'This could well be our last conversation. . . . New York will be blown up tomorrow by Soviet nuclear weapons.'[57]

Nerves became even more frayed the following morning, Wednesday, 24 October, as the superpowers teetered on the brink of a war on the seas around Cuba. It was the most frightening day of Kennedy's presidency and the most profound test of his presidential leadership. The previous evening Kennedy had signed the proclamation authorizing the initiation of the blockade on the 24th. That Wednesday morning the US Strategic Air Command for the first time moved to DEFCON 2, a mere step from war (DEFCON 1). Disturbing JFK's composure further was a meeting on the evening of 23 October that he had asked Bobby to arrange with Dobrynin. When his brother asked the Russian ambassador whether the Soviet ships were still under instructions to head to Cuba, despite the blockade, Dobrynin indicated that this was the case.[58]

On the morning of the 24th JFK, Bobby and other ExComm officials waited with bated breath in the White House for updated reports as two Soviet ships and a submarine approached the blockade line. Robert Kennedy recorded the moment: 'I think these few minutes were the time of gravest concern for the President. Was the world on the brink of a holocaust? Was it our error? A mistake? Was there something further that should have been done? Or not done? His hand went up to his face and covered his mouth. He opened and closed his fist. His face seemed drawn, his eyes pained, almost gray.'[59]

Then an official handed a report to McCone. To the relief of all, the CIA director revealed that Soviet ships had suddenly stopped. This was the moment for Rusk to say to Bundy the immortal words: 'We're eyeball to eyeball, and I think the other fellow just blinked.' Other good news arrived: some Soviet ships were motionless, others were heading back to Russia. In his response, Kennedy continued to show caution. He barred the navy from intercepting Soviet vessels for at least an hour. That way Russian ships would have time to turn around and head home. He also refused when advisers urged him to stop a Soviet tanker, the *Bucharest*, as it most likely had no military equipment on board.[60]

What developments on the seas around Cuba on 24 October indicated was that Khrushchev, contrary to what his message to Kennedy that day suggested, would respect the blockade. No more Russian missiles would reach Cuba. But for

Kennedy that still left the problem of how to remove the nuclear weapons already there. On Thursday, 25 October, with the blockade successfully established, he began to focus on this issue. That morning he instructed ExComm officials to prepare three alternatives: a diplomatic settlement, an air strike on Cuba and an intensification of the blockade so as to intercept petroleum, oil and lubricants (POL) as well as Russian military equipment. Secretary of the Treasury Douglas Dillon led a group of officials who drafted the air-strike scenario. The thinking behind the extension of the blockade to include POL was that it would increase the pressure on Khrushchev and Castro by bringing the Cuban economy to a standstill; and since announcing the blockade JFK had expressed interest in this tactic as a feasible next step. The diplomatic approach built on a discussion of the role the Jupiter missiles might play in a negotiated settlement that had been intermittent but ongoing since the early days of the crisis, a discussion in which Kennedy had been a vocal participant. The two main ideas on the Jupiters in Turkey were, first, their withdrawal in return for the removal of Russian missiles from Cuba; and, second, the deployment of UN inspection teams at the missile sites in Cuba and Turkey so as to reduce the chances of a Russian strike on Turkey and a US strike on Cuba, and as an intermediate step to a withdrawal of the missiles from both Cuba and Turkey. Back on 22 October Kennedy had told his ExComm advisers to regard the UN inspection team idea as a sensible first step to take, which could lead to a diplomatic settlement centring on the Jupiters.[61]

There is evidence that by 25 October Kennedy was moving in this direction of using the Jupiters to facilitate a diplomatic settlement of the crisis. That afternoon a British official at the UN sent a telegram to the Foreign Office in London reporting that 'a most reliable source' had conveyed to him comments from Andrew Cordier of Columbia University that 'if a United Nations Commission could be introduced to keep a watch on Russian bases in Cuba under satisfactory guarantees, the United States might be prepared to consider allowing a similar United Nations Commission to look at some bases elsewhere, e.g. the United States bases in Turkey'. In this way, Kennedy displayed another leadership trait vital to saving the peace: a willingness to compromise.[62]

Despite the unaccommodating message he sent to Khrushchev that day, asserting that the crisis had been caused by the Kremlin's aggressive and duplicitous deployment of nuclear weapons in Cuba, behind the scenes Kennedy was weighing up the diplomatic options. He also continued to be prudent, allowing the *Volker Freundschaft*, an East German passenger ship, through the blockade line. Particularly gratifying to JFK that afternoon was Stevenson's stellar performance in the United Nations Security Council. In a televised duel with his Russian counterpart, Valerian Zorin, it was the American who landed the most telling blows. He asked Zorin directly whether the Russians were placing missiles in Cuba, said he was 'in the courtroom of world opinion', and – when Zorin declined to respond to his question – told him, in what became the most famous words uttered in the missile crisis, 'I am prepared to wait for my answer until hell freezes over, if that's your decision. And I am also prepared to present the evidence in this room'. The battle for 'world opinion' was an important part of the missile crisis, and here Kennedy's old rival had helped him win that battle.[63]

Friday, 26 October, started well for Kennedy and ended even better when he received a heartfelt letter from Khrushchev proposing a settlement. In the early morning the United States Navy boarded a ship, the *Marucla*, making absolutely clear that the blockade had been successfully enforced. Kennedy and his advisers grappled in the morning ExComm meeting with the issue of how to remove the missiles already in Cuba. As he had earlier in the crisis, Kennedy had to contend with the hawks. Dillon urged an air strike on the missile sites rather than an extension of the blockade to POL, an option which Kennedy and other officials considered at the meeting. When his more aggressive advisers spoke out against any settlement to the crisis that would allow Castro to stay in power, he stated that his own position was the only thing that mattered now was getting the missiles out of Cuba.[64]

The clearest indication of how JFK had become a consistent force for moderation in his administration's debate on the missile crisis was the way he responded to Stevenson's controversial intervention in that morning's ExComm meeting. As in the ExComm discussion on 20 October, Stevenson urged his colleagues to focus on diplomacy, predicting (correctly for the most part) that Khrushchev would soon demand the withdrawal of the Jupiter missiles from Turkey and Italy, and a US assurance that it would never invade Cuba. As on the 20th, Stevenson's detractors assailed him. McCone, in particular, mocked Stevenson's parallel between the missiles in Turkey and in Cuba. But when JFK entered the fray he did so in at least partial defence of his beleaguered UN ambassador. In discussing a diplomatic trade, he said, Stevenson had identified one of only two approaches that could actually get the missiles out of Cuba. 'We've only got two ways of removing the weapons,' Kennedy told McCone. 'One is to negotiate them out . . . the other is to go over and just take them out.' Given how JFK had been viewing the Jupiter missiles as a key element in any settlement, he was not unsympathetic to Stevenson's opinions, though he did express concern about the idea of promising not to invade Cuba. Kennedy's argument indicated that he viewed the intensification of the blockade as only an intermediate step to increase pressure on Khrushchev, not a tactic that could in itself end the crisis.[65]

A heartfelt message from Khrushchev to Kennedy changed the dynamics of the missile crisis that evening. In it, he dwelt on the horrors of warfare: 'I have taken part in two wars, and I know that war ends only when it has rolled through cities and villages, sowing death and destruction everywhere.' Fearful that another war could be triggered at any moment, Khrushchev outlined a settlement: JFK should pledge never to attack Cuba, discourage other nations from doing so and end the blockade; and for his part Khrushchev would withdraw the missiles from Cuba. What strengthened Kennedy's belief that this offer was sincere was that the same terms of settlement were discussed over a lunch arranged in Washington that day by KGB officer Aleksandr Feklisov with ABC reporter John Scali (who passed on details of their conversation to the State Department). The assumption in the Kennedy administration was that the Kremlin had coordinated a two-pronged manoeuvre: Khrushchev's message reinforced by Feklisov's discussion with Scali. In fact it was a coincidence. Feklisov had been acting on his own initiative, not at the behest of the Kremlin. Still, Kennedy must have slept more easily that night. The blockade had been based on the belief that it would provide a window of opportunity in which a negotiated settlement could be reached, and would apply pressure on Khrushchev to make him amenable to that. It seemed that this belief had been sound.[66]

As was so often the case with the mercurial Khrushchev, things were not that straightforward. At 9 am on Saturday, 27 October, Radio Moscow broadcast a message from the Soviet leader to JFK. Sent only hours after Kennedy had received Khrushchev's letter the evening before, this new message was delivered not privately but in the public sphere, was far more formal in tone that Khrushchev's earlier, emotional letter, and – most importantly – demanded an extra concession from Kennedy. In return for the withdrawal of missiles from Cuba, said Khrushchev, Kennedy would not only have to promise never to invade the island but would also have to remove the Jupiters from Turkey.[67]

It is unclear why Khrushchev sent within a matter of hours two different messages containing two different offers before Kennedy had replied to his first letter. Had hard-liners in the Kremlin insisted on the second, less accommodating, message? Had Soviet intelligence played a role in the second message, informing Khrushchev that a US attack on Cuba was not as imminent as previously thought? Scholars Fursenko and Naftali argue that by the 27th Khrushchev no longer thought that JFK was likely to attack Cuba, and this could have influenced his thinking on the proposals made in the letter he sent that day to Kennedy. Or did the sudden change in the proposal now made by Khrushchev merely reflect his impulsive personality?[68]

Whatever the answer, it presented a dilemma to Kennedy when he met at the White House at 10 am with his ExComm colleagues. Those crucial ExComm meetings on the 27th took place against an ominous sense that events were spiralling out of control. A few minutes after the ExComm meeting began an American U-2 plane accidentally entered Russian airspace over Chukotski Peninsula. Soviet planes took off in pursuit. A superpower clash in the skies seemed close at hand. Before shots were fired, however, the U-2 managed to make it out of Russian airspace. Shortly afterwards, a Soviet surface-to-air missile shot down a U-2 flying over Cuba, and the American pilot Major Rudolf Anderson was killed. He would be the only casualty of the missile crisis, but it seemed that the Russians were upping the ante. Kennedy and his colleagues would have been even more alarmed had they been privy to the astonishing letter composed by Castro to Khrushchev in the early hours of the 27th. Kennedy was about to order an attack on Cuba, predicted Castro, probably an air strike but possibly a full-scale invasion. If the latter, he added, 'that would be the moment to eliminate such danger forever through an act of clear legitimate defence, however harsh and terrible the solution would be, for there is no other.' In other words, if Kennedy invaded Cuba, Castro wanted Khrushchev to launch a nuclear attack on the United States.[69]

Enlarging the sense in ExComm on the 27th that the approach of war was irresistible was the fact that the generals were chomping at the bit. The Joint Chiefs, announced Taylor, insisted a 'big strike' be carried out on Cuba unless the Russians started to dismantle the missiles there. Lyndon Johnson scribbled down notes that indicated how the hawks were thinking: 'regarding the peace in the Caribbean – By strike no later than Mon a.m. Invasion'. As he had earlier in the crisis, a resilient president stood up to the generals. 'I'm not convinced yet of an invasion,' he declared.[70]

When it came to the perplexing matter of how to react to Khrushchev's two different proposals, Kennedy took on board the advice of ExComm officials. There is a traditional explanation of this which claims Robert Kennedy hatched the plan to ignore Khrushchev's message of 27 October but to accept his proposals of the 26th. The United States would promise not to invade Cuba in return for the removal of Russian missiles from the island. The Jupiters in Turkey would not be part of the formal settlement to the crisis.[71]

Perhaps historians should have been sceptical of the claim that Bobby Kennedy was the mastermind behind the plan that ended the missile crisis and so prevented the Third World War as it was Bobby himself (with the editorial assistance of Ted Sorensen) who made this self-serving claim in his posthumous memoir of the missile crisis, *Thirteen Days*. What the records of this ExComm meeting show is that it was not Bobby Kennedy who devised the plan. A number of other advisers said they were for it – notably Defense Department official Paul Nitze, McGeorge Bundy and Ted Sorensen – before Robert Kennedy endorsed this approach. Bundy, for example, told JFK to 'answer back saying that "I would prefer to deal . . . with your interesting proposals of last night"'. The president, sensibly, accepted that advice.[72]

JFK also impressed in the ExComm meeting on the 27th with his vigorous support for diplomacy in ending the crisis, and linked to that his willingness to compromise. This was especially evident in his discussion of the Jupiter issue raised by Khrushchev in his public message that morning. Kennedy understood how this would play with world opinion, how to many people trading the withdrawal of missiles in Cuba close to America for missiles in Turkey on the Soviet border would appear eminently sensible. He also felt that a refusal to compromise on the Jupiters was too flimsy a reason to go to war: 'We all know how quickly everybody's courage goes when the blood starts to flow. . . . Let's not kid ourselves. . . . Today it sounds great to reject it [Khrushchev's proposal on the Jupiters], but it's not going to, after we do something [militarily]'.[73]

The only reservation Kennedy had about a Jupiter trade was that Khrushchev had demanded this concession in public via his 27 October message. To agree to the Jupiter trade in the public domain would appear to be a case of America buckling under pressure from the Kremlin. That was an impression he wished to avoid, and that determination shaped his crisis management. He would send a message to Khrushchev accepting the terms offered in his 26 October message, so promising never to invade Cuba in exchange for the withdrawal of the Russian missiles there. The Jupiters in Turkey would not be part of the formal settlement to the crisis. But Robert Kennedy invited Ambassador Dobrynin to a 7.45 pm meeting at the Justice Department and informed him that a few months down the road the Jupiters in Turkey would be dismantled. JFK was prepared to make that concession to end the crisis. Bobby impressed upon Dobrynin that this had to remain a secret component of the settlement. If the Russians leaked this part of the pact, the deal would be off. At 8.05 pm JFK sent a letter to Khrushchev and released it to the press. In it, he agreed to a settlement 'along the lines suggested in your letter of October 26'.[74]

An important issue is how Kennedy would have responded if Khrushchev had replied that he was happy to accept the settlement defined by JFK's letter and Bobby Kennedy's meeting with Dobrynin but that the deal on the Jupiters had to be public knowledge. The evidence indicates that JFK would then have sought to arrange a public deal on the Jupiters that appeared to have been initiated by others. That way his Jupiter concession would have appeared less like the United States caving in to Soviet pressure and more a statesmanlike response to the urgings of the international community. Accordingly, he asked Turkey and other NATO powers to request the Jupiter trade themselves if Khrushchev refused to accept a private deal on the Jupiters. If Dean Rusk's recollections in 1987 were accurate, Kennedy instructed him to phone Andrew Cordier of Columbia University to ask him to be ready to give UN secretary general U Thant a statement for him to make calling for the withdrawal of nuclear weapons from Cuba and Turkey. This would have been a reworking of the Cordier ploy he originally devised two days earlier. It is a question of hypotheticals here, ultimately unprovable, but the weight of evidence suggests that had Khrushchev insisted on a public deal on the Jupiters, Kennedy would have arranged it. That reflects his resolution, at the climax of the missile crisis, to end this superpower confrontation by diplomacy and not by the use of force urged by his generals that might well have resulted in the Third World War.[75]

On 27 October Kennedy lived with the very real prospect not only of war but of a nuclear conflict. We all understand nuclear war as an abstract concept, but people throughout the world in October 1962 actually had to brace themselves for the apocalyptic. But for Kennedy the pressure was greater still, for he – along with one other man in Moscow – was chiefly responsible for whether there would be war or peace. Even for someone like Kennedy who had the ability to remain cool under pressure, the strain must have been immense.

There are stories that by the end of the crisis Khrushchev was sleeping in his Kremlin office and even that he was imbibing vodka with inadvisable regularity. For Kennedy, the antidote to such pressure was not alcoholic but sensual – his habitual distraction. At one point he noticed a good-looking new secretary. 'Bob, I want her name and number,' he told McNamara. 'We may avert war here tonight.' He also asked aide Dave Powers to phone Mimi Beardsley on 26 October. 'Come to Washington,' Kennedy's aide told her. 'Mrs. Kennedy is going to Glen Ora. I'll send a car.'[76]

When Beardsley returned to college in the early autumn Kennedy, as he had promised, stayed in touch. In mid-September she was in her dormitory when someone yelled that there was a call for her from Michael Carter. He phoned regularly thereafter, always using his pseudonym. Beardsley was struck by how he never seemed at all worried that his cover would be blown. As was often the case in his personal affairs, he relished risk – the antithesis of the caution he showed in his handling of public affairs.[77]

As Kennedy led the tense ExComm deliberations at the White House that Saturday, 27 October, Mimi Beardsley waited for him in the residence living room with Powers. When Kennedy joined them, his mind, recalled Beardsley, 'was clearly elsewhere. His expression was grave.... Even his quips had a halfhearted, funereal tone'. After leaving the room to take a phone call he returned shaking his head and remarked: 'I'd rather my children be red than dead.' The comment showed his concern for the familial implications of a failure to end the missile crisis, and his resolve to do all he could to avoid a military clash.[78]

As he was so preoccupied that evening, Kennedy suggested that Beardsley and Powers go ahead without him and eat the roast chicken supper that had been prepared for them. That the missile crisis was an extraordinary event was reflected in the fact that this turned out to be a rare, sexless encounter with Beardsley. 'Our get-togethers were always quite sexually charged,' she said, but 'it wasn't to be on this occasion'. She stayed up until 11 p.m., as he dealt with the crisis, then went to bed. By the time Kennedy came back to the second floor of the White House she was asleep. To unwind, he opted for cinematic pleasures: he watched *Roman Holiday* with Powers. It would be the charms of Audrey Hepburn, rather than Mimi Beardsley, who would provide Kennedy with respite from the stress of the missile crisis as Saturday turned into Sunday, 28 October. Various historians have criticized JFK's sexual shenanigans in the White House. In the missile crisis, however, it was clearly the case that his affair with Beardsley had no bearing on the quality of his leadership.[79]

When Beardsley opened her eyes the following morning, Kennedy was already sitting up in bed, speaking on the phone, continuing to deal with the Cuban crisis. She waved goodbye shortly before 8 a.m. An hour later Radio Moscow started to broadcast a new message from Khrushchev to JFK. The downing of the U-2 plane over Cuba, which he had not ordered, Soviet intelligence reports that a US attack on the island was being readied and the shocking letter from Castro contemplating nuclear war had convinced the Soviet leader that events were spiralling out of control and that, consequently, it was essential the confrontation over Cuba be brought to a close. At a meeting of his top advisers at the Kremlin Khrushchev declared that there was no alternative but to accept Kennedy's offer. Many of his colleagues remained silent, 'as if hinting to Khrushchev', as one participant put it, 'that since he had made his bed he could sleep on it'. Khrushchev dictated a message for Radio Moscow to broadcast. He also wrote to Castro, urging him to stay calm and to recognize that the settlement included an American promise not to invade Cuba, thereby safeguarding his security.[80]

In his message to Kennedy, Khrushchev revealed that he had 'issued a new order on the dismantling of the weapons which you describe as "offensive," and their crating and return to the Soviet Union'. He also said that he respected 'your statement in your message of October 27, 1962 that no attack will be made on Cuba'. Khrushchev made no mention of the Jupiters in Turkey, thus adhering to Bobby Kennedy's stipulation that the plan to remove them must remain a secret part of the agreement. At a meeting later that morning between Bobby and Dobrynin, the Soviet ambassador confirmed that Khrushchev had agreed to the settlement proposed by JFK the previous day. Bobby said again that the Jupiter deal must not be mentioned in public.[81]

At the ExComm meeting, which began at 11 a.m., a feeling of both relief and elation suffused the discussion. JFK himself, recalled an adviser, was 'in great form.... He was smiling and he was full of humor and he, too, had obviously felt a great burden lift'.[82]

Following his meeting with Dobrynin, Bobby Kennedy went to the White House to see the president. The two brothers had been through so much together, from political campaigns to family tragedies. But they had never had to endure anything so monumental. There was no one – not Jackie, not Ethel – with whom they would rather share this moment, at the end of the most dangerous crisis since the Second World War.[83]

'This is the night I should go to the theater,' said John Kennedy, thinking of Abraham Lincoln.

'If you go,' said his brother, 'I want to go with you.'[84]

Figure 4.1 Kennedy with his secretary of defense, Robert McNamara, in an ExComm meeting as the Cuban missile crisis drew to a close. Defusing the most dangerous crisis in the Cold War era represented a key achievement of the Kennedy presidency. (*Source*: Wikimedia, public domain, Search media – Wikimedia Commons.)

For John Kennedy, the Cuban missile crisis did indeed represent a familial as well as a political triumph. His and Bobby's mettle had been severely tested – and they had prevailed. Through a combination of open-mindedness, caution, strength in standing up to his own generals and his willingness to compromise – and with the assistance of his Camelot courtiers, including his brother – JFK had succeeded in ending the most dangerous crisis of his presidency and the entire Cold War era. That he did so reflected well on his character as well as his political skill.

This success in October 1962 added lustre to Kennedy's dazzling image. Throughout his public life, he had developed a narrative on how America was living through a time of crisis that required brave and brilliant leadership. Back in 1940 he had argued in *Why England Slept* that America needed a president with the determination to bolster the nation's military power so that it could stand up to the threat posed by Hitler. During his time in Congress in the late 1940s and 1950s, he claimed that Harry Truman had failed to match Russia's military build-up and that Dwight Eisenhower had allowed a dangerous 'missile gap' to emerge that meant the Soviets were winning the arms race. As a result, Senator Kennedy contended, the early 1960s would be a perilous period in the Cold War for the next president. In his Pulitzer Prize–winning second book *Profiles in Courage*, he had again highlighted the need for exceptional and independently minded leadership in the political life of the nation. In his inaugural address on 20 January 1961, Kennedy emphasized that freedom and democracy were living through a time of maximum peril. It was a challenge, he assured the American people, that he welcomed. At the start of his presidency, then, he promised America a brand of heroic leadership that for two decades, in his view, the United States had needed but lacked.

With his success in ending the most dangerous nuclear crisis in the Cold War, Kennedy stood as the embodiment of the exceptional leadership that he had been calling for since 1940. His image had long exhibited a tremendous allure. After the Cuban missile crisis he appeared even more remarkable: the ultimate hero as the man with the courage to face down the Russians and the skill and wisdom to prevent the Third World War.

Chapter 5

ENDGAME

After the Cuban missile crisis John Kennedy changed. He became a more progressive leader and a better one. The roots of that change preceded October 1962. The Bay of Pigs made him sceptical of the belligerent advice he would often continue to receive from the generals, intelligence chiefs and others. His handling of the Berlin crisis had increased his sense of the dangers of the Cold War in the summer of 1961. The Freedom Rides and also the 1962 University of Mississippi desegregation crisis had enlarged his concerns about the inequalities in American society. But it was the two volcanic events of the last year or so of his life and presidency – not only the missile crisis but also the racial conflict in spring 1963 in Birmingham, Alabama – that made JFK a leader intent on mitigating Cold War tensions and pressing for fundamental change in civil rights. The leader gunned down in Dallas was a very different one to the man inaugurated as president roughly a thousand days earlier.

The implications of this for an overall assessment of the Kennedy presidency are considerable, for they cast a favourable light on JFK in a number of important respects. It is clear that Kennedy kept a commendably open mind on key issues, and was able to change his perspective and commitments when informed by his presidential experiences. He was prepared to take political risks on behalf of the national interest; the stance he took on civil rights in the summer of 1963 would cost him the support of many white Southerners as his 1964 presidential re-election campaign approached. This courageous commitment to civil rights also reflected well on his character, his moral compass in the area that mattered most – policy, in the public domain, that affected the lives of millions. All of this serves to discredit the revisionist, counter-Camelot critique of Kennedy that took root in historical writing in the 1980s and 1990s and centred on the idea that Kennedy was a belligerent Cold Warrior with an appalling character.

This chapter will consider these matters by examining the three salient issues of the final year of the Kennedy presidency: the negotiations with the Soviets that led to the historic Nuclear Test Ban Treaty; the crisis in Birmingham that culminated in JFK's introduction of the civil rights bill to end segregation in American life; and his response to the deteriorating situation in South Vietnam as the US-backed Diem government staggered from one crisis to another. It was his record in Vietnam that would become the most ambiguous part of his presidential legacy.

There was no achievement in which Kennedy took greater pride than the Test Ban Treaty. Part of the reason he could do so with some justification is that efforts to reach such an agreement had failed to bear fruit for so long. Those efforts had begun in Geneva in 1958, following a proposal by Khrushchev on a nuclear test moratorium which Eisenhower and Macmillan accepted. A test ban treaty seemed within reach by spring 1960, but the shooting down of Gary Powers's U-2 reconnaissance plane over the Soviet Union damaged superpower relations, thus thwarting Ike's ambitions for a legacy-defining accord on nuclear testing at the end of his presidency. Divisions within his administration and his unwillingness to lead on the issue also contributed to Eisenhower's failure to achieve a test ban, according to one authority. For JFK, the 1961 Berlin crisis did not help the ongoing test ban discussions, as Khrushchev responded to it by resuming nuclear testing. Kennedy felt obliged to follow suit with underground testing in mid-September and then with atmospheric testing in spring 1962. As Kennedy and Khrushchev reflected on how close to the nuclear brink they had got in the Cuban missile crisis, however, a greater urgency was injected into test ban discussions. For Kennedy's part, he was troubled by the way the superpowers had almost stumbled into the Third World War. 'You know it's absolutely crazy,' he said to Richard Goodwin, 'the two men sitting on opposite sides of the world have the power to destroy all of Western civilization.' This was one issue where he began to connect the political with the personal. UK ambassador and Kennedy friend David Ormsby-Gore observed: 'he finally realized that the decision for a nuclear holocaust was his. And he saw it in terms of children – his children and everybody else's children. And then that's where his passion came in, that's when his emotions came in.'[1]

Nor were these fears articulated only in private. In a television interview with the major networks a week before Christmas 1962, he outlined starkly the nuclear scenario: 'Once he [Khrushchev] fires his missiles, it is all over anyway, because we are going to have sufficient resources to fire back at him to destroy the Soviet Union. When that day comes and there is a massive exchange, then that is the end, because you are talking about Western Europe, the Soviet Union, the United States, of 150 million fatalities in the first 18 hours.' As 1962 turned into 1963, then, JFK dwelt on the profound dangers of the nuclear age, which the recent superpower confrontation over Cuba had made only too clear.[2]

The result of those reflections, in 1963, was a greater determination to achieve whatever sort of agreement with Khrushchev was possible in limiting nuclear testing. As McGeorge Bundy recalled, 'the more he [JFK] measured the situation after [the] Cuba[n missile crisis] the clearer he was that a kind of corner had been turned [in the Cold War] and that it was certainly part of his job to keep that corner turned and to move along.' And a nuclear test ban agreement was the most feasible way to move things along in 1963. The culmination of this shift in thinking would be Kennedy's remarkable speech in June at American University in which he called on the American people to change their attitude towards the Russian people. Objections can and have been articulated against the notion that Kennedy became less of a Cold Warrior as his presidency unfolded. After all, what about the hostility his administration continued to display at times in its covert policies towards Castro's Cuba? What about his controversial handling of the communist challenge in Vietnam in 1963? Those objections are unpersuasive. To be sure, JFK did not stop believing in the seriousness of the communist threat and the importance therefore of continuing to wage the Cold War. He did not become a Henry Wallace–type figure sanguine about Soviet intentions. But it was a case of Kennedy's views changing not absolutely but by a significant degree. Despite continuing to craft his policies in the context of an ongoing Cold War, he was more determined than before the missile crisis to do what he reasonably could to reduce superpower tensions. That was a noteworthy and commendable development.[3]

Despite Kennedy's greater resolve after the missile crisis to ameliorate relations with Moscow, test ban discussions had hit a cul-de-sac by the early weeks of 1963. Khrushchev and Kennedy exchanged a number of messages on this between 19 December and 7 January which showed that the Soviet premier believed the Americans had reneged on the key issue of on-site inspections. Concerned that these inspections might be used as a ruse for espionage on Russian soil, Khrushchev had said he could permit three inspections, but no more. The US position was that between eight and ten inspections would be needed to ensure that no agreement was contravened. However, discussions between Soviet and American officials in New York had left Khrushchev with the erroneous impression that the United States had agreed to between two and four inspections a year. In a meeting with JFK on 9 January, Soviet First Deputy Foreign Minister Vasiliy Kuznetsov confirmed that Moscow's position was that no more than three annual on-site inspections would be permitted. A month later Kennedy, privately, informed senior aides that he might be able to agree to six inspections as 'the rock-bottom [US] position', and on another occasion he told an adviser he could accept five, but that still left a significant gap between his view on this and Khrushchev's.[4]

In the early months of 1963 Kennedy was compelled to define in public his position on Soviet–American nuclear testing as he was quizzed periodically on this at press conferences. With candour, he explained that he was not optimistic about the prospects for reaching an agreement, citing the gap between Khrushchev and himself on the number of on-site inspections required to monitor underground testing. But at the same time he expressed his determination to press ahead with negotiations on this issue, emphasizing the importance of preventing the proliferation of nuclear powers, which would make the world much more dangerous. At his news conference on 21 March he revealed that 'personally I am haunted by the feeling that by 1970, unless we are successful, there may be 10 nuclear powers instead of four, and by 1975, 15 or 20'. (The four were the United States, Russia, Britain and France.) Of those new nuclear powers, a belligerent China was uppermost in his mind. He continued:

> With all of the history of war, and the human race's history, unfortunately has been a good deal more war than peace, with nuclear weapons distributed all through the world, and available, and the strong reluctance of any people to accept defeat, I see the possibility in the 1970's of the President of the United States having to face a world in which 15 or 20 or 25 nations may have these weapons. I regard that as the greatest possible danger and hazard.

Now, I am not even talking about the contamination of the atmosphere which would come when all of these nations begin testing, but as you know, every test does affect [future] generations. . . . We have come this far [in negotiations on this issue], and I think that we ought to stay at it.

There was a strong sense here of the moral urgency that Kennedy would bring to bear with still greater fervour and eloquence a few months later at American University. The concern he articulated in public over nuclear proliferation reflected not only his personal convictions on the matter but also the advice he received from senior aides; a month earlier McNamara had sent him a memo estimating the number of nations that might soon develop nuclear weapons.[5]

In the spring, though, things remained unpromising. On 3 April Soviet ambassador Dobrynin delivered in person to Bobby Kennedy a message from Khrushchev, covering the test ban issue, inter alia, which the attorney general regarded as 'so insulting' that he refused to pass it on to JFK. But then editor of the *Saturday Review* and nuclear disarmament campaigner Norman Cousins, who had co-founded the Committee for a SANE Nuclear Policy in 1957, visited the White House in early April to discuss with JFK a trip he was about to make to visit Khrushchev at his Black Sea dacha. 'I have no doubt that Mr Khrushchev is sincere in his belief that the U.S. reneged on its offer of three inspections,' Kennedy told Cousins in a follow-up phone call the next day. 'But he's wrong. . . . I believe there's been an honest misunderstanding. . . . See if you can't get the Premier to accept the fact of an honest misunderstanding. There need be no question of veracity or honor and the way can be cleared for a fresh start.' Kennedy was trying to move beyond the impasse in the effort to agree on a test ban treaty.[6]

What Kennedy's discussion with Cousins also revealed was the increasing sense of empathy he felt for his Soviet counterpart: 'Khrushchev and I occupy approximately the same political positions in our governments. He would like to prevent a nuclear war but is under severe pressure from his hard-line critics who interpret every move in that direction as appeasement. I've got similar problems. The hard-liners in the Soviet Union and the United States feed on each other.' In Kennedy's mind, his hard-line critics included his own generals, and their poor advice on the feasibility of the Bay of Pigs and their hawkish zeal in the missile crisis had deepened his scepticism towards their ideas about the Cold War. Beyond the Kremlin, Khrushchev's hard-line critics included communist China. JFK himself was troubled by Chinese belligerence. He had told Kuznetsov as much in their meeting back on 9 January. Hence, an important motivation behind Kennedy's interest in a test ban treaty, which co-existed with his genuine desire to reduce Cold War tensions, was to do what he could to lessen the chances of China becoming a nuclear power. He said so in a meeting with senior aides in early February. Khrushchev shared that objective. Kennedy also believed that a test ban would reduce the likelihood that other states such as Germany and Israel would develop the bomb, thereby preventing dissemination of nuclear weapons and making the world safer.[7]

On 12 April Cousins handed a message from Kennedy to Khrushchev at his Black Sea dacha. As he was prone to do, the Soviet leader spoke at length and in an accusatory fashion. 'Frankly, we feel we were misled' on the issue of inspections, he told Cousins. But he went on to say: 'You want me to set all misunderstandings aside and make a fresh start? All right, I agree to make a fresh start.' 'The next step', he added, was up to JFK.[8]

Kennedy in fact was already in the process of taking that next step. With Harold Macmillan, who was strongly committed to securing a ban on nuclear explosions, he had been corresponding on the idea of a joint letter to Khrushchev proposing the resumption of test ban negotiations. Exchanging drafts, they were essentially of one mind in wanting to urge Khrushchev to agree to further talks. JFK insisted, though, on downplaying the likelihood of a Kennedy-Khrushchev-Macmillan summit meeting. Memories of Khrushchev's belligerence at Vienna in June 1961 probably influenced his outlook on this. What Jack and Mac did say in their message of 15 April to the Soviet leader was that they 'would be ready to send in due course very senior representatives who would be empowered to speak for us and talk in Moscow directly with you'. The emollience of this message had been evident too in one sent four days earlier by JFK to the Soviet leader in which he attributed the hitherto stalled negotiations on the test ban to 'an honest misunderstanding between us', emphasized his (and Macmillan's) genuine commitment to an agreement on nuclear testing and closed by saying:

> These are difficult and dangerous times in which we live, and both you and I have grave responsibilities to our families and to all of mankind. The pressures from those who have a less patient and peaceful outlook [a reference no doubt to their respective militaries and China] are very great – but I assure you of my own determination to work at all times to strengthen world peace.

That conciliatory message could have only helped in persuading Khrushchev to accept the Kennedy–Macmillan proposal for test ban talks in Moscow. His reply on 8 May, though abrasive in tone and accusatory in argument, indicated that he was open to this proposal for direct talks. He did so again in a message to JFK a month later.[9]

As Kennedy awaited this response from Khrushchev to the Anglo-American proposal for Moscow talks, he made certain his advisers were left in no doubt as to his sincere determination to reduce nuclear testing and forge a broader détente. In a 6 May National Security Action Memorandum, he informed them: 'I have in no way changed my views of the desirability of a test ban treaty or the value of our proposals on general and complete disarmament. Further, the events of the last two years have increased my concern for the consequences of an un-checked continuation of the arms race between ourselves and the Soviet Bloc.' Evidently, the Cuban missile crisis and Berlin crisis had left their mark on the man.[10]

At the end of April Cousins had again stiffened Kennedy's resolve by urging him to give 'the most important speech of your Presidency', which should include 'breathtaking proposals for genuine peace' and display a 'tone of friendliness for the Soviet people' and an 'understanding of their ordeal during the last war'. This was the spark for Kennedy's great American University address. It says much about the shift in his attitude towards the Cold War that he was willing to be so influenced by a prominent peace campaigner like Cousins.[11]

It also says much about JFK's resolve to make a bold speech, uncompromised by the sorts of bureaucratic opposition he anticipated, that he circumvented the Defense and State departments and instead confined the preparation of the address to Sorensen with input from Bundy and a few other White House advisers, including Schlesinger. Remarkably for a speech that had such clear implications for the future direction of US national security, Kennedy did not divulge the contents of the address to Rusk, McNamara or Chairman of the Joint Chiefs Maxwell Taylor until only two days before he was scheduled to give the speech on 10 June and only after he had left for a trip out West – from which he would return shortly before he was to deliver his American University address. The heads of the State and Defense departments and of the Joint Chiefs were given no opportunity to pressure the president in person to modify his audacious address.[12]

It was Sorensen, his most gifted wordsmith, who was chiefly responsible for drafting the speech. He flew to San Francisco to meet up with JFK, show him the latest draft of the American University address and accompany him on the flight back to Washington – during which Kennedy edited the text. His plane landed around 9 am, less than two hours before he was due to speak.[13]

Before the faculty and graduating class at American University on 10 June, Kennedy delivered an address unlike any other presidential speech during the Cold War up to that point. Historian Michael Beschloss judged it to be 'easily the best speech of Kennedy's life'. To compare it to say his hard-line address to the American Society of Newspaper Editors on 20 April 1961, following the Bay of Pigs debacle, is instructive: the speeches are so unlike in both tone and substance, and that difference said much about the maturation of his approach to foreign policy.[14]

Kennedy signposted the progressive thrust of his speech right from the start by citing Woodrow Wilson. Wilson, he noted, had opened American University as president in 1914. He proceeded to quote Wilson on how university graduates should be public-spirited. When he went on to discuss his commitment to disarmament and the international organization that was the successor to the League of Nations, namely the United Nations, it was clear that Kennedy was laying claim to the Wilsonian tradition in American foreign policy – collective rather than unilateral in approach, committed to the restraint rather than the enlargement of military power, intent on reducing international tensions.[15]

The central theme of Kennedy's speech, as he explained to his audience, was 'the most important topic on earth: world peace'.

> What kind of peace do I mean? What kind of peace do we seek? Not a Pax Americana enforced on the world by American weapons of war. Not the peace of the grave or the security of the slave. I am talking about genuine peace, the kind of peace that makes life on earth worth living, the kind that enables men

and nations to grow and to hope and to build a better life for their children – not merely peace for Americans but peace for all men and women – not merely peace in our time but peace for all time.

Peace was essential, he proceeded to point out, given the colossal damage that a nuclear conflict would inflict on mankind.[16]

There was a balance evident in Kennedy's speech that was rare in presidential rhetoric on the Russian challenge during the Cold War. It was no use, he said, to argue that aggressive Soviet attitudes meant that for Americans to aspire to world peace or disarmament was misguided, as 'we must reexamine our own attitude … for our attitude is as essential as theirs'. Accordingly, he asserted that Americans needed to reconsider their attitude towards peace, the Soviet Union, the Cold War and social justice in the United States.[17]

Rather than harbouring naïve fantasies about world peace, he encouraged his audience to think more practically about 'concrete actions and effective agreements' that make the goal of world peace seem more achievable and 'less remote'. Despite Moscow's outlandish propaganda about US intentions to start war and enslave other peoples, argued Kennedy, 'No government or social system is so evil that its people must be considered as lacking in virtue,' Soviet achievements in such areas as space and science should be commended, and their heroic sacrifices in the Second World War must likewise be acknowledged. The United States and the Soviet Union, in fact, had much in common: they would be the 'primary targets' in a nuclear war, and the astronomical costs of the arms race meant that they were both spending enormous sums on weapons of mass destruction that could and should be spent on 'combating ignorance, poverty, and disease'. With compelling eloquence, Kennedy reflected on how Americans and Russians had a shared humanity: 'in the final analysis, our most basic common link is that we all inhabit this small planet. We all breathe the same air. We all cherish our children's future. And we are all mortal.' He also urged Americans to reconsider their attitude towards the Cold War. Rather than apportioning blame for the superpower confrontation, the US should seek 'a relaxation of tensions without relaxing our guard'.[18]

Kennedy linked the quest for peace overseas to the pursuit of social justice at home. 'The quality and spirit of our own society must justify and support our efforts abroad,' he said, adding that, 'In too many of our cities today, the peace is not secure because freedom is incomplete.' Kennedy was talking about civil rights, the battle for equality in American life that had been brought into recent focus by the brutally suppressed protests against segregation in Birmingham, Alabama, and the efforts to desegregate the University of Alabama. He would confront these issues more directly the following day when he spoke to the nation on race in America, but at American University he did indicate that the more progressive thrust of his presidency in 1963 would include the pursuit of equality at home as well as world peace. It is instructive to compare the way Kennedy had sought to avoid a public stance on the Freedom Rides in 1961 out of concern that it might compromise his and the nation's image on the international stage, with his public linkage of US policy on the Cold War and on civil rights two years later.[19]

As Kennedy spoke, the fundamental rationale for his address became apparent: it was to pave the way for a test ban treaty later that summer. His talk of 'concrete actions and effective agreements' on the road to peace had alluded to that goal, but he went on to say explicitly that the 'one major area' of superpower negotiations 'where the end is in sight . . . is in a treaty to outlaw nuclear tests'. This, he asserted, would prevent the arms race from spiralling out of control, reduce the likelihood that other nations would become nuclear powers, enhance US security and decrease the chances of war. JFK revealed that Khrushchev, Macmillan and himself had agreed to begin high-level talks in Moscow on reaching an agreement on a test ban treaty. As an act of good faith as those talks approached, he announced that the United States would not carry out any nuclear tests in the atmosphere providing other nations did not do so.[20]

Kennedy's discussion in his American University speech of the need for Americans to reconsider their attitudes towards peace, the Soviet Union and the Cold War were all part of his effort to build public support for a test ban treaty and, more broadly, for the sort of détente that this specific policy objective represented. This public-relations campaign was linked to a political objective: to put pressure on Congress as a test ban treaty would require the approval of the Senate to secure its ratification. To influence the American people and Capitol Hill in this way was no easy matter. The political discourse in Washington since the onset of the Cold War had so assailed the Soviet Union – albeit understandably so at times – that to make the case that it was in fact a nation with people of virtue, with a shared humanity with Americans, with whom the United States could negotiate in good faith was a considerable rhetorical challenge. With his American University speech, Kennedy met that challenge with aplomb. It was eloquent, persuasive, even inspirational. Indeed the belief of a good many Americans following this address that an end to the Cold War was now in sight was testimony to the power of Kennedy's rhetoric that day.[21]

Kennedy ended his address by affirming that the United States would play its part in building 'a world of peace'. 'Confident and unafraid,' he declared, 'we labor on – not toward a strategy of annihilation but toward a strategy of peace.' Despite the complexities of the Cold War, not least a deteriorating situation in South Vietnam, that strategy became the major motif of Kennedy's foreign policy during the final months of his life.[22]

A fitting postscript to the sentiments expressed in the American University speech came ten days later when a Soviet–American accord on the establishment of a 'hot line' between the White House and the Kremlin was reached. Mindful of how the elephantine transmission of messages to and from Khrushchev during the missile crisis had made that nuclear standoff even more dangerous than it would otherwise have been, Kennedy proposed a more direct form of superpower communication. Khrushchev finally agreed to this, and on 20 June 1963, the setting up of a wire-telegraph-teleprinter circuit, which would ensure rapid coded messaging during any future crisis, was announced. It was another step that summer towards a safer world.[23]

Kennedy, meanwhile, continued to impress upon his aides the importance he attached to the upcoming talks in Moscow. Four days after the American University address, Rusk told a group of senior administration officials that 'The President feels the mission should be made because this may be our last chance to avoid a larger and more difficult arms race. In 10 or 20 years it will be important that the U.S. made as great an effort as possible to achieve a test ban'. That conviction was fortified a fortnight later by a CIA National Intelligence Estimate which informed the president that 'eight countries, in addition to France, have the physical and financial resources to develop an operational nuclear capability (weapons and means of delivery) over the next decade'. As well as taking the general view that the arms race should be curbed, Kennedy continued to be influenced by a more specific consideration: how to clip the wings of communist China. How the test ban negotiations might be used to achieve that end was an issue raised by JFK with his advisers at a meeting a week later.[24]

To secure an agreement with Khrushchev on the Test Ban Treaty, Kennedy turned to W. Averell Harriman (after first approaching Chase Manhattan Bank chief John McCloy). As US ambassador in Moscow in the Second World War, Harriman was a throwback to the days of Soviet–American cooperation. Hence, his appointment as envoy was a decision that indicated to the Kremlin that Kennedy's interest in reaching an accord was sincere, especially as he told Khrushchev explicitly in a letter handed over personally by Harriman at the start of the Moscow talks that he had chosen the veteran diplomat 'because of his clear record of sympathetic understanding of the Russian people and his service to our common cause in the critical days of World War 2'. This reinforced the favourable impression made on not only Khrushchev but also the Soviet people by his American University address. The text of the speech was printed in the Soviet press. Some Russians tore out copies of the speech and kept them in their purses or wallets. Khrushchev would tell Harriman that it was 'the greatest speech by any American President since Roosevelt'. A 11 June CIA report, based on information from a Russian diplomat, confirmed that Kennedy's American University speech had been well received in Moscow.[25]

A fortnight prior to Harriman's arrival in Moscow Khrushchev indicated in a speech on 2 July in East Berlin that he was ready to reach an agreement not on underground testing (which would raise the thorny issue of on-site verification), but on a limited ban, prohibiting tests in the atmosphere, under water and in outer space. He also called for a non-aggression pact between NATO and Warsaw Pact countries which, he said, would be 'another major step toward easing of international tensions'. JFK regarded this speech as a good sign. The prospects for the Moscow talks now looked promising.[26]

Kennedy was not averse to exploring the idea of a non-aggression pact if it were to facilitate an agreement on nuclear testing. But as the German government was opposed, fearing it would militate against the future reunification of Germany, and the French as well, Kennedy concluded that it would be best for the United States to take the position in the Moscow talks that securing agreement on a test ban and a non-aggression pact should not be linked – advice he included in the instructions given to Harriman before setting out on his diplomatic mission. Also included in that guidance for Harriman was the stipulation that while reaching agreement on a comprehensive test ban treaty would be optimal, the more realistic objective was a limited test ban outlawing testing in the atmosphere, under water and outer space. On this, Harriman was told, 'You are authorized to carry such negotiations as far as you can.' This reflected Kennedy's (and many of his advisers') immediate reaction to Khrushchev's speech in East Berlin on 2 July, which was that it was highly promising. Khrushchev's proposal for a limited test ban, he thought, was an eminently sensible way to proceed.[27]

Striving for some sort of test ban accord with the Russians entailed, as it so often did for Kennedy at key junctures in his presidency, locking horns with hard-liners, and in particular his own generals. At an NSC meeting on 9 July Taylor insisted that a test ban was 'not in the national interest', and so called for a formal government review of the Test Ban Treaty, which would include a (no doubt hostile) review by the Joint Chiefs of Staff. Kennedy refused, telling Taylor that he was concerned a Joint Chiefs review might leak and lead to media speculation about differences of opinion within his administration. In an Oval Office discussion with Taylor (and McNamara and Rusk) following this NSC meeting, Kennedy assured Taylor that the Joint Chiefs would have their 'full day in court before the Senate if and when a formal treaty proposal' had been agreed and was being considered by the Senate for ratification. At the same time, he warned Taylor that the Joint Chiefs should 'avoid doing anything capable of affecting adversely the Harriman discussions'.[28]

To help shape and give impetus to the Moscow talks, Kennedy wrote a letter for Harriman, whose talks with Khrushchev and British delegate Lord Hailsham were set to begin on 15 July, to hand to the Soviet premier. In this message, Kennedy said, 'I share the view which you have put forward in your important statement in Berlin that it is sensible to reach agreement where agreement is now possible, in the area of testing in the atmosphere, under water, and in outer space. Governor Harriman will explain that we continue to be in favor of such a more limited agreement and that we are encouraged by your statement in Berlin to believe that it is now possible.' Here Kennedy was, sensibly, using flattery to grease the diplomatic wheels, implying an agreement in Moscow would be a success founded on Khrushchev's sagacious speech in East Berlin.[29]

In addition to corresponding with Khrushchev, Kennedy monitored the Moscow talks on the test ban very closely. He remained in contact with Harriman, sometimes three or four times a day. 'Spending hours in the cramped White House Situation Room,' historian Richard Reeves has written, 'Kennedy personally edited the U.S. position, as if he were at the table himself.'[30]

At the start of the Moscow talks Khrushchev made clear that he still viewed inspections (on Russian soil) as akin to espionage. That ruled out any possibility of a comprehensive test ban treaty. Harriman confined himself therefore to pursuing a limited ban. Khrushchev, as he had prior to Harriman's visit, argued that a non-aggression pact between NATO and Warsaw Pact countries should accompany a test ban. Harriman countered persuasively that the latter should not be made dependent on the former as such a pact would require a lengthy consultation with allies, whereas a test ban treaty could be completed quickly. He presented the Kennedy administration's proposal for a non-proliferation treaty, prohibiting nuclear weapons from being supplied by one country to another, but Khrushchev demurred. Difficult technical issues remained, such as the language to be used in the preamble to the treaty and the terms on which nations might withdraw from the treaty, but with diplomatic dexterity Harriman helped resolved these. He did raise the issue of US concern over Chinese belligerence and nuclear aspirations, as Kennedy had instructed, but, as Lawrence Freedman has cogently argued, this did not represent a specific proposal for a US or joint Soviet–American strike on China to destroy its nuclear capability – rather, it was 'a generalized anxiety [on JFK's part] about the impact of a more militant China on international affairs'. Anyway when Harriman raised concerns over China, Khrushchev dismissed them, telling him in their opening session, 'If you want to talk about China, go to China. You can't talk about China here.' Off-the-record, though, the Soviets would indicate, perhaps inadvertently, that dealing with Chinese nuclear ambitions had influenced their own thinking. At a Polish embassy reception the wife of Soviet foreign minister Andrei A. Gromyko, Lydia, told US ambassador Foy Kohler that the test ban agreement was a way 'to call them [Peking] to account' when it carried out its first nuclear explosion.[31]

Kennedy endorsed the final terms of the treaty agreed by Harriman and his Soviet and British counterparts. When a worried Macmillan phoned the White House, JFK said, 'Don't worry. David [Ormsby-Gore] is right here. It's been worked out, and I've told them to go ahead.' By 26 July a test ban treaty had been achieved. The importance JFK attached to this was revealed by his comment to Sorensen that he would happily lose the 1964 election if the sixty-seven votes required to ensure Senate ratification of the treaty could be secured.[32]

On his return to the United States, Harriman headed for Hyannisport. 'Well this is a good job,' Kennedy commended him. The president's jubilation was genuine. As Rusk recalled, 'news of Harriman's achievement excited us all [in Washington], especially John Kennedy.' And not just in the nation's capital. 'My goodness life,' exclaimed Harry Truman when JFK phoned the former president in his hometown of Independence, Missouri, 'maybe we can save a total war with it.'[33]

Not only was JFK emotionally invested in a test ban, he was politically invested too. In particular, his American University speech had tied presidential credibility to treaty success. That audacious address was partly responsible for the test ban agreement as it influenced the public and political mood, demonstrated the extent of Kennedy's commitment to a successful outcome and helped persuade Khrushchev that business with the United States could be done on this matter. His handling of the test ban issue that summer had been brave and manifestly successful.

There still remained the challenge of securing Senate ratification of the treaty. This would be difficult due to the inevitable opposition of not only hard-line Cold Warriors in the upper chamber but also some Southerners – such as Richard Russell of Georgia – enraged by the stance taken by JFK on civil rights. For

Kennedy, treaty ratification required winning over the public and his own military advisers, as well as US senators. He applied himself to that task immediately. Shortly after the treaty had been initialled in Moscow he spoke to the nation from the Oval Office. 'Yesterday,' he told the American people, 'a shaft of light cut into the darkness,' after years of Cold War tensions. He did not oversell the test ban – 'It will not reduce nuclear stockpiles; it will not halt the production of nuclear weapons' – but did say that 'it is an important first step – a step towards peace – a step towards reason – a step away from war'. Listing the benefits of the treaty, he argued that it could reduce international tensions and pave the way for other constructive agreements; reduce radioactive pollution of the atmosphere; decrease the likelihood of other nations developing nuclear weapons and 'limit the nuclear arms race' and thus bolster US security. The journey to world peace, concluded Kennedy, might be 'a thousand miles, or even more', but 'let history record that we, in this land, at this time, took the first step'. As well as bringing his oratorical skills to bear, he encouraged the formation of a Citizens' Committee for a Nuclear Test Ban, led by Cousins, and advised its officials on how best to wage its campaign. Winning over public opinion – a 1 September Gallup poll revealed that almost four times as many Americans backed the treaty as opposed it – put pressure on senators in favour of ratification.[34]

Of crucial importance to that vote in the Senate was the attitude of the Joint Chiefs. Had they come out to a man against the treaty, the Senate would never have ratified it. In a way, Kennedy's dealings with the military on the test ban are further evidence of his wariness towards the generals following the Bay of Pigs and even more so after the missile crisis.

As of spring 1963, the Joint Chiefs were the staunchest opponents of a test ban among Kennedy's advisers, believing that it would not safeguard against secret Soviet testing and development of nuclear missiles. Then just before Harriman left for Moscow, as explained earlier, the Joint Chiefs sought to impede negotiations by requesting a review of a test ban treaty to assess whether it was in the national interest; Kennedy had barred such a review. JFK's strategy for securing a test ban agreement, therefore, entailed the outmanoeuvring of his own generals.[35]

Once a conclusion to the Harriman talks in Moscow was close, JFK told the Joint Chiefs that most of his administration supported the test ban. He spoke to each of them individually and instructed other senior officials such as Rusk and McCone to do likewise so as to convince them of the treaty's merits. The Joint Chiefs came to acknowledge the political benefits of the test ban, and Taylor played an important role in persuading them to back the treaty. They did so only after requesting from Kennedy four safeguards that he was willing to provide: the continuation of an extensive underground testing programme; the readiness to resume atmospheric testing if suddenly required; improvement in the capacity to detect any treaty violations and the retention of nuclear laboratories. Thus secured, the support of the Joint Chiefs was vital in winning Senate ratification.[36]

Kennedy also used good old-fashioned, Lyndon Johnson–style, behind-the-scenes wheeling and dealing to gain the important support of Dwight Eisenhower and Republican Minority Leader in the Senate Everett Dirksen. On 12 August he met at the White House with Dirksen, who, like Eisenhower, had been wary and critical in public of the test ban negotiations. At that meeting JFK reminded Dirksen that 'Ike said I had coin in his bank, and you say I have coin in yours. Ev, I must write a check on you and Ike'. What Kennedy was referring to was a conversation with Dirksen in late 1961 when the GOP Senate Leader conveyed a request from Eisenhower that he order Bobby Kennedy's Justice Department to cancel an imminent indictment of Ike's former Chief of Staff Sherman Adams for tax fraud. In return, Eisenhower promised Kennedy 'a blank check in my bank if he will grant me this favor' – in other words, future public support on an important issue when requested. In August 1963, on the matter of the Test Ban Treaty, Kennedy was now requesting it. Dirksen acknowledged that they 'owed him one'. 'Ev,' said Kennedy, 'I want you to reverse yourself and come out for the treaty. I also want Ike's public endorsement of the treaty before the Senate votes. We'll call it square on that other matter.' 'Mr President,' said Dirksen, 'you're a hell of a horse trader. But I'll honor my commitment, and I'm sure that General Eisenhower will.' That proved to be the case. Pragmatic political skill combined with crusading idealism on this issue in enabling JFK to build support for the Test Ban Treaty.[37]

As well as influencing public opinion and bringing the Joint Chiefs on board, and cajoling Dirksen and Ike to back the treaty, Kennedy courted goodwill on Capitol Hill by arranging for a delegation of senators, Republicans as well as Democrats, to accompany Rusk to Moscow for the signing ceremony. The invitation to GOP senators was not pure altruism; it was also canny politics. It was useful to have Republican participation in the signing of a treaty that some hard-liners regarded as too conciliatory to Moscow (which was why some GOP senators declined the offer.) Kennedy's indefatigable efforts paid off: on 24 September the Senate voted by a margin of 80–19 to ratify the Test Ban Treaty. The achievement here is not to be underestimated. In a meeting with advisers on 7 August, JFK had said, 'If there was a vote now, we would not get close to the two-thirds [of Senate votes] we need.' By adroit political leadership and taking steps to influence the grassroots public debate so as to pressure US senators, Kennedy had – seven weeks later – secured the votes required.[38]

Given the striking superpower rapprochement of the later Cold War, especially during the Gorbachev years, it would be easy to understate the significance of the Limited Test Ban Treaty. It was the case too that the treaty did not slow the arms race in the remainder of the 1960s and the 1970s. But, in 1963, it was of historic importance, unprecedented in the Cold War and evidently something beyond Eisenhower's reach; and in retrospect it can be viewed as a foundation on which future superpower accommodation and arms agreements could be built. In addition, it was an accomplishment that responded meaningfully to the profound fears that had developed in society during the previous decade over the public-health dangers of radioactive fallout. Not surprisingly, Kennedy regarded the test ban as the greatest achievement of his presidency.[39]

In terms of Kennedy's journey as a statesman over the course of his presidency, it is worth noting the response of Adlai Stevenson to the treaty when replying to a letter from the great writer John Steinbeck who recalled that it was Stevenson in

1956 who had originally proposed a nuclear test ban and been savagely attacked for doing so. 'As you surmise,' Stevenson said to Steinbeck, 'my heart and head have been full of poignant and persistent recollections for the past several weeks, and I am comforted that someone hasn't forgotten, now that the bandwagon is so crowded! I guess seven years is too far to be ahead of history!' For much of the previous decade, Kennedy had viewed Stevenson as the personification of liberal ineffectuality. But by the summer of 1963, his outlook and Stevenson's on international affairs were closer than they had been hitherto; and in the final months of his life he considered other ways of reducing Cold War tensions, including some sort of accommodation with Castro and a joint-moon project with the Soviets.[40]

As Kennedy moved US foreign policy onto a different plane in the summer of 1963, he did likewise in domestic policy with civil rights. For much of his presidency, his approach to civil rights had been reactive. He was broadly supportive of the advancement of equal rights for Black Americans. Underpinning that view was some empathy on Kennedy's part given the prejudice endured by Irish Americans earlier in the twentieth century which remained apparent even as recently as his own 1960 presidential campaign. His friend Senator George Smathers recalled that JFK supported civil rights as 'he felt that as an Irishman somewhere along the line he had been discriminated against'. Kennedy was also conscious of the importance of the Black vote to his own victory in 1960, and the way his stirring rhetoric in that campaign had encouraged African Americans to redouble their efforts to achieve equal rights. On the other hand, the pragmatic side of JFK recognized that the Democratic Party included a Southern conservative as well as a Northern liberal wing, and that this made the prospects for any civil rights legislation he might introduce unpromising. In the first two years of his presidency, he had used his skills at crisis management over the Freedom Rides in 1961 and also the desegregation of the University of Mississippi in 1962 to defuse those situations with settlements that achieved the objectives of the Civil Rights Movement. But he had failed to use the Freedom Rides to make a rhetorical case to the American people for equal rights. He had procrastinated for almost two years before making good on his 1960 campaign promise to end segregation in federally funded housing by executive order. To civil rights leaders, his Southern judicial appointments had been disappointing. He deferred excessively to Southern senators in these matters, and this sometimes resulted in reactionary appointments, such as William Harold Cox whose descriptions of Black Americans were appalling. Most importantly, JFK had not introduced civil rights legislation, which is clearly what was required to end segregation in the South. State governments in Dixie were not going to do this on their own accord.[41]

On 28 February 1963, however, Kennedy sent a special message to Congress saying he planned to introduce a civil rights bill that would enact various changes, including the bolstering of voting rights by ending the widespread practice among Southern registrars of denying voting rights to Blacks who could not interpret every article of the Constitution. Literacy tests would be abolished in federal elections, with a sixth-grade education being sufficient for voter registration. 'The most helpful thing' about this, recalled Roy Wilkins, 'was that it finally signaled that the administration recognized the necessity and efficacy of legislation.' But Kennedy's bill, introduced at the start of April, made no progress in Congress, and he did not bestir himself to win support for this legislation in the way he would a few months later for his subsequent civil rights bill. Indeed, a group of liberal Republican senators introduced their own, somewhat bolder bill, highlighting what they regarded as the inadequacies of JFK's civil rights efforts. Beyond Capitol Hill, liberal Republican New York governor Nelson Rockefeller was relentless in his attacks on Kennedy for what he regarded as the disappointing pace of his reforms on behalf of equality. This partisan criticism increased the pressure on the president to act more decisively on civil rights. Kennedy was also under pressure from the liberals in his own party. He took umbrage when Hubert Humphrey called for more comprehensive civil rights legislation. As liberal Republicans like Jacob Javits and Kenneth Keating were demanding fundamental change on civil rights, argued Humphrey, Democrats needed to be forthright on this issue too. 'When I feel that there's necessity for a congressional action with a chance of getting that congressional action,' Kennedy told Humphrey and others, 'then I will recommend it to the Congress.'[42]

That disclosed one key criterion for JFK if he were to introduce sweeping legislation: the feasibility of securing passage of such a bill on Capitol Hill. The second would be a shift in the public mood in favour of civil rights, which would pressure Congress, and the third – though Kennedy would not have acknowledged this at the start of 1963 – a greater sense of moral compulsion on his part to act boldly on equal rights.

It was the crisis in the spring in Birmingham, Alabama, described by Martin Luther King as the most rigidly segregated city in America, that wrought all of those necessary changes in Kennedy's moral commitment, the public mood and the feasibility of major legislation. To dramatize the issue of segregation in the South and compel JFK to act, King's Southern Christian Leadership Conference and Fred Shuttlesworth's Alabama Christian Movement for Human Rights had begun in mid-January to plan a series of protests in Birmingham. Sit-ins at lunch counters, marches towards City Hall and the boycotting of downtown stores would not only highlight the nefarious Southern practice of segregation, they would also put economic pressure on the city's merchants during what was usually their busy Easter shopping season. King encouraged those participating in the protests, which began in early April, to take the moral high ground by practising nonviolence. Soon the range of protests widened to include a library sit-in and kneel-ins at churches.[43]

In response the city government sought and on 10 April won a court injunction barring further protests. When Martin Luther King continued to protest, despite that injunction, he was arrested. After a week's incarceration bail money secured King's release but not before he had penned his historic 'Letter from Birmingham Jail' in which he made an eloquent, impassioned case against segregation and those local clergymen who had castigated the protestors for pushing for change too quickly.[44]

It was the next phase of the Birmingham protests that intensified the crisis, put the national spotlight on the city and increased the pressure on Kennedy to act. The children's crusade was the idea of King adviser James Bevel. To recruit large numbers of young children – to put them in harm's way – seemed reckless. At first King hesitated in agreeing to it. But it proved to be inspired. As *The Washington Post* later put it, 'History shows that kids, with their innocence, honesty and moral urgency, can shame adults into discovering their conscience.' The children's crusade commenced on 2 May when around 800 children skipped school and dashed to the Sixteenth Street Baptist Church, from where they began their march, carrying placards with slogans such as 'Segregation is a sin'. Their youth was of no concern to local police commissioner Bull Connor, whose men wasted no time in putting hundreds of children behind bars. The children's crusade escalated over the next few days, and the police's response to that was infamously draconian. They used dogs and high-powered water cannon to attack the protestors. Newspaper photographers and television cameras captured these egregious events for a nationwide (and international) audience. No image was more shocking than that of a policeman holding a student as his dog lunged open-mouthed at the boy's abdomen. These images, JFK disclosed to a delegation from the Americans for Democratic Action, made him feel disgusted, suggesting his emotional involvement in the issue of racial equality had deepened. 'We have not done enough for a situation so desperate,' he acknowledged, adding: 'if I was a Negro I'd be sore.' These shocking images also influenced the thinking of many Americans. Before the police atrocities in Birmingham, only 4 per cent of Americans regarded civil rights as the most pressing issue in the country. After Birmingham, the figure rose to 52 per cent.[45]

As the Birmingham crisis raged, the question for Kennedy was how to react to it. Initially his response largely mirrored his earlier presidential efforts on civil rights: crisis management. He phoned Coretta Scott King, when her husband was behind bars, to offer support. Brother Bobby sent aides, including Burke Marshall, to Birmingham to ameliorate the situation. He elicited from King and other civil rights leaders their specific demands: the desegregation of lunch counters and greater employment opportunities for Blacks. Marshall then negotiated with business leaders in Birmingham, whose economic interests had been damaged by the slump caused by the protests in the city. But it was a multipronged effort by the administration as not only Cabinet officials but JFK himself devoted much time to phoning business leaders to persuade them to make the necessary concessions to the Black community. As always at these moments of acute tension in his presidency, whether in Berlin in 1961 or with the missiles in Cuba in 1962, Kennedy's coolness under pressure assisted his crisis management in Birmingham, as Marshall observed.[46]

As was so often the case during his presidency, Kennedy's crisis management worked. A settlement was announced, which included the desegregation of lunch counters and the promotion of Blacks from menial positions. At a press conference on 8 May a relieved JFK reported that business leaders in Birmingham had promised to take steps that would 'begin to meet the justifiable needs of the Negro community'. Hence Black leaders had halted their demonstrations. What the Birmingham crisis showed, said Kennedy, was 'how urgent it is that all bars to equal opportunity and treatment be removed as promptly as possible'. He emphasized the damage to America's reputation by the upheaval in Birmingham, and argued that 'the best way to prevent that kind of damage ... is to, in time, take steps to provide equal treatment to all of our citizens'. The 'in time' qualification indicated that an element of caution, as noted by columnist Drew Pearson when watching the press conference, remained in Kennedy's thinking on civil rights. Despite the relief expressed by JFK on 8 May, the Birmingham crisis was not yet over. King and his associate Ralph Abernathy were incarcerated. The street protests resumed. King called for the release of the hundreds of children still imprisoned in Birmingham, but the authorities demanded an astronomical sum for the bond money in return. Robert Kennedy helped raise the money, after which a truce was announced on 10 May. But the following evening, as Pearson recorded in his diary on the 12th, 'all hell had broken out in Birmingham last night. The Ku Klux Klan had met just outside Birmingham. The Negro motel, where Dr Martin Luther King had his headquarters, was bombed, together with King's brother's home. My prediction that trouble will continue in Birmingham looks all too true'. That was indeed the case. In response to those bombings, a crowd of 2,500 young Blacks came out onto the streets. For several hours, they vented their fury – setting fire to an apartment, wrecking police vehicles and destroying six stores. It took 250 state troopers to restore order the following morning. At an Oval Office meeting on 13 May JFK had to consider military contingency plans for Birmingham should the violence return. In his comments, Bobby revealed his concern with Black violence on the streets, and the possibility that many Blacks would turn from the ideas of King to those of the Black Muslims – concerns he reiterated in an off-the-record White House meeting with Alabama newspaper editors.[47]

In shifting to a bolder approach in seeking to resolve the issues in Birmingham, Robert Kennedy was a major influence. From a limited engagement with civil rights prior to the 1960 election, his responsibilities as head of the Justice Department – including the Freedom Rides and the Birmingham protests – had compelled him to dwell on the issue of racial inequality, and in the process his commitment to equal rights had increased. On 13 May he took note when Louis Martin, White House adviser on civil rights, told him that 'the accelerated tempo of Negro restiveness and the rivalry of some leaders for top billing coupled with the resistance of segregationists may soon create the most critical state of race relations since the Civil War'. What happened at the Kennedys' New York City apartment on 24 May heightened Bobby's concerns. In a meeting there with writer James Baldwin, other prominent Black artists and Jerome Smith, a CORE field worker brutalized by his experiences in the South, Robert Kennedy was presented with an unvarnished picture, over a three-hour period, of what it meant to be Black in the United States in 1963. Smith, in particular, did nothing to conceal his rage at his experiences. He even told Bobby Kennedy that he felt sick to be in the same room as him. For Bobby, it was an excruciating experience. He left the meeting feeling angry and disturbed. But as historian James Giglio put it, the meeting 'had alerted him to the intensity of the blacks' frustration and to the need for government to do more'.[48]

The crisis over the desegregation of the University of Alabama in June intensified the focus of John and Robert Kennedy on civil rights. Pledged to oppose desegregation, recently elected governor George Wallace took umbrage when two Black students – James Hood and Vivian Malone – sought to enrol at the University of Alabama at Tuscaloosa, the only state university still segregated, after a federal court had ruled in their favour. Quizzed about this issue at a press conference on 8 May and then again a fortnight later, JFK said that while he hoped the local authorities would settle the matter according to the law and so permit Hood and Malone to enrol, his administration would act – by sending federal marshals to Alabama if necessary – to ensure that the law was respected. Kennedy held several White House meetings with advisers on how best to handle the tense situation. As with Birmingham, his team liaised with local business and other community leaders who urged Wallace to settle the issue promptly. But on 2 June Wallace stated on national television that he would block the two students so they could not enrol. Two days later, however, the Justice Department won a federal injunction against the governor. In planning for worst-case scenarios, the Kennedy team selected an escape route for Malone and Hood should violence break out on campus. On 11 June Robert Kennedy aide Nicholas Katzenbach confronted Wallace on campus. The governor stood in front of the registration building and refused to budge. This, however, was pre-arranged theatre. As Sorensen recalled, the Kennedys had reached 'an advance agreement with the governor that he would have his few minutes in the doorway, in the limelight and on national television before stepping aside when informed by . . . Katzenbach that the Alabama National Guard had been federalized by presidential order and that [the] two qualified Negro students were entering to register by court order'. So it was essentially a futile gesture on Wallace's part. JFK did indeed federalize the Alabama National Guard and a general ordered Wallace to leave the campus quietly. Marshalls escorted Malone and Hood to the dormitories. JFK had outmanoeuvred Wallace. Not surprisingly, he was pleased with the outcome. Another civil rights crisis had been managed and defused.[49]

It confirmed for the president, however, the conclusion he had begun to reach in recent weeks that an ad hoc approach to civil rights would no longer suffice and that major legislation needed to be considered 'to get to the heart of the problem', as Robert Kennedy later put it. Birmingham had been a seminal experience for JFK. It stirred his moral conscience but also convinced him that the passage of a civil rights bill in Congress was now possible given the impact of the shocking events in Birmingham on the national mood. As Bobby explained, 'What he realized in Birmingham in 1963 ... was that – then – you could obtain the passage of certain legislation which could never have been obtained prior to that time.' As well as the moralistic and political arguments in favour of equal rights, JFK was probably influenced by the concern articulated by Bobby that an administration failure to act boldly could result in greater Black extremism and violence. The fact that the protests in Birmingham had been followed by demonstrations in many other towns and cities in both North and South deepened that concern, creating a sense that things were spiralling out of control. There is evidence in both his public and private statements in May that JFK was moving towards a more wholehearted commitment to equal rights. At news conferences he said that he would consider making a nationwide address on civil rights if he thought it helpful, there was an 'important moral issue involved of equality for all of our citizens' in recent events in Birmingham, and notably – on 22 May – that he was contemplating the introduction in Congress of civil rights legislation. That 22 May statement followed Oval Office discussions two days earlier with advisers such as Robert Kennedy and Marshall in which JFK concluded, in the wake of Birmingham, that sweeping civil rights legislation outlawing segregation in public accommodations must be introduced. Accordingly, Bobby Kennedy's Justice Department advisers worked away on drafting such a bill. When his secretary of commerce urged JFK to frame his prospective address on civil rights in terms of law and order, rather than anything more sweeping or moralistic, the president said: 'There comes a time when a man has to take a stand.'[50]

Bobby backed his brother when he thus decided to give a televised address to the nation only hours after the resolution of the University of Alabama crisis. He did so despite opposition from several key advisers. Lyndon Johnson thought the introduction of a bill to end segregation premature as insufficient preparations had been made for its passage in Congress. Ted Sorensen and Ken O'Donnell feared the speech would damage JFK's prospects in the 1964 election. Key domestic adviser Lawrence O'Brien also opposed the making of the speech. Given that lack of enthusiasm from JFK's aides, Bobby's backing was undoubtedly an important factor in convincing his brother of the need for a major address. In the 1963 documentary *Crisis: Behind a Presidential Commitment*, in which director Robert Drew was given unprecedented access to White House discussions, Bobby is seen taking the lead in a meeting of senior officials, insisting: 'I don't think you can get by now without … having an address on television at least during this period of time giving some direction and having it in the hands of the president.' He added that a rough draft of a civil rights address, with some strong sentences, had already been written in the Justice Department, which speechwriter Sorensen could use. What should be emphasized here is JFK's political courage in delivering this address. He decided to take this stand knowing it would cost him the support of many white Southerners and hence damage his prospects for re-election in 1964. One cannot assume any other president of that era would have acted in the same way. It is the view of this author that Eisenhower, the paeans of praise from revisionist scholars in recent decades notwithstanding, would have failed this moral challenge. The fact that Ike told Kennedy in a phone conversation the day after the speech that he was opposed to passing a 'whole bunch of [civil rights] laws' suggests this was the case.[51]

Sorensen completed the text of the speech in a matter of hours. Uncertain that he would have it ready in time, JFK discussed with Bobby ideas for the address, including what he ended up using for his closing remarks. Marshall recalled JFK, only a few minutes before he was due to start speaking, 'making notes in longhand on a scratch pad'. Marshall himself and Louis Martin also had an input. Due to the moral urgency it conveyed and as it was unprecedented in the history of the presidency in the twentieth century for its commitment to racial change, this was *the* great speech of the Kennedy presidency, not his inaugural address.[52]

JFK began by reviewing the desegregation of the University of Alabama, asking all Americans to 'stop and examine his conscience about this and other related incidents', and reminding them that the United States was 'founded on the principle that all men are created equal, and that the rights of every man are diminished when the rights of one man are threatened'. Echoing the point which he had made in the 1960 presidential campaign in response to the anti-Catholic prejudice he encountered, he argued that Black Americans sent to defend the freedom of people in Vietnam or West Berlin should be able to attend a university they choose, be served at a hotel or restaurant, and vote. He presented the statistical realities of inequality. A Black baby had only half as much chance of finishing high school as a white baby, was twice as likely to become unemployed and had a life expectancy that was seven years shorter.[53]

Then Kennedy moved to the emotional core of his address:

> We are confronted primarily with a moral issue. It is as old as the scriptures and is as clear as the American Constitution.
>
> The heart of the question is whether all Americans are to be afforded equal rights and equal opportunities, whether we are going to treat our fellow Americans as we want to be treated.[54]

Kennedy proceeded to argue against those who said racial change should happen only gradually, aligning himself with the views expressed by Martin Luther King in his letter from Birmingham City Jail. He observed that the work of Abraham Lincoln remained incomplete as a century after emancipation the slaves' descendants were not yet fully free. He cited the impact of the Birmingham crisis, how it had 'increased the cries for equality'. Throughout, a profound moral urgency infused his address: 'We face, therefore, a moral crisis as a country and as a people. It cannot be met by repressive police action. . . . Those who do nothing are inviting shame as well as violence.' Having made such an impassioned case for equal rights, Kennedy announced the introduction of a major civil rights bill to end segregation. Impressively, JFK looked up from his text and spoke extemporaneously for the last four minutes of his speech, and did so with fluency. Coming the day after his American University speech, this address confirmed the progressive, indeed moral tilt of the Kennedy presidency, in its third year. Some observers described his 11 June civil rights address and bill as 'the Second Emancipation Proclamation'. Kennedy did not object to the appellation. From Atlanta, Martin Luther King characterized the speech as 'one of the most eloquent, profound and unequivocal pleas for justice and freedom by any President'.[55]

Kennedy not only gave a powerful speech and introduced legislation of historic significance, he worked diligently in order to create a consensus for his civil rights bill, which in particular would guarantee Blacks equal access to public accommodations such as restaurants and hotels. He did so by meeting congressional leaders but also, as Marshall recalled, 'lawyers, business groups, church groups, women's groups, labor, educators, most of the governors' – urging them all to support his efforts on behalf of equal rights. Kennedy proved persuasive on these occasions.[56]

Despite that, JFK had a problem with a group which had long provoked his suspicions: liberals. He believed that they were often more interested in lofty ideals than practical success. That view was shared by Robert Kennedy. What happened to the civil rights bill in Congress confirmed their suspicions for in Congressman Emanuel Celler's (Dem-New York) House Judiciary Committee, which was dominated by liberals, clauses were added to extend its provisions on matters like school desegregation and equal access to public accommodations. The corollary, though, was that some Republicans became less sympathetic than they had been to the bill in its original form. Consequently, the Kennedy team worked on Celler and with House Minority Leader Charles Halleck and William M. McCulloch, the senior Republican sitting on the Judiciary Committee, to help deliver GOP votes. In his memoir, Katzenbach describes the adroit and painstaking work undertaken by the Kennedy administration in advancing the bill on Capitol Hill prior to the tragic events in Dallas. JFK's own leadership on this issue was important. Marshall has cited 'the crucial, personal involvement of President Kennedy' in persuading a number of liberal Democrats to vote for the compromise bill. This work ultimately bore fruit: in October 1963 Celler passed out of his committee a bill broader in scope than JFK's original legislation but less sweeping than what had been envisaged by the liberals on the Judiciary Committee. Had Kennedy lived, the next requirement would have been to navigate the bill out of the House Rules Committee, but it seems likely that in the end the House of Representatives would have approved the civil rights bill. Next would have been the battle for passage in the Senate.[57]

In the effort to secure passage of his civil rights bill, Kennedy was concerned about the potentially deleterious impact of a major public event scheduled for 28 August: the March on Washington. A massive civil rights demonstration in the nation's capital might, worried Kennedy, result in criticisms of his policies from the speakers and cause some on Capitol Hill to vote against his bill out of resentment that they were being coerced by the protestors. When at a meeting with civil rights leaders, A. Philip Randolph told him, 'The black masses are restless, and we're going to march on Washington,' Kennedy turned and twisted uneasily in his chair before saying, 'Mr. Randolph, if you bring a lot of people to Washington, won't there be a crisis, disorder, chaos? And we would never be able to get a civil rights bill through the Congress.' But Randolph assured him that the protest would be 'orderly, peaceful, nonviolent', and Kennedy soon accepted the inevitability and possible helpfulness of the event. (There was even behind-the-scenes discussion as to whether JFK should himself make a speech at the March on

Washington.) As early as 17 July he told journalists that he supported the march, which (he was confident) would be 'a peaceful assembly calling for a redress of grievances' and 'in the great [American] tradition' of democratic expression. Some of those who railed against the march, he added, 'never talk about the problem of redressing [the] grievances' that had inspired the march in the first place. Kennedy therefore instructed administration officials to work with the organisers of the march. Bobby encouraged unions and churches to participate so that the event was interracial rather than having the appearance of Black versus White; and the administration liaised with the police chief to ensure that the police were welcoming to everyone attending the march. After the stirring events of the day, including King's magnificent 'I have a dream' speech, he met with King and other leaders of the march at the White House. 'I have a dream,' Kennedy told them.[58]

Borrowing from King's lexicon, JFK had indeed moved closer in 1963 to King's position on civil rights – taking bold legislative action on behalf of equality, using inspiring oratory to advance the cause, and arguing that the achievement of equal rights was a moral imperative. Kennedy's commitment was evident from the political realities he was ready to discount and the political price he was willing to pay for the strong commitment to civil rights that he had made in June 1963. Those realities, as shown by public opinion data, included the fact that in a 10 July Gallup poll 82 per cent of Southern Whites opposed the legislation outlawing segregation proposed by JFK, while only 12 per cent supported it; and even in the country as a whole opinion was fairly evenly split, with 42 per cent opposed and 49 per cent in favour. In a poll released four days later, 77 per cent of Southern Whites thought Kennedy's administration was pushing racial integration too quickly, while only 4 per cent thought it was not fast enough, and just 10 per cent judged it to be about right.[59]

A consequence of these attitudinal realities and Kennedy's stance on civil rights in the summer of 1963 was that his popularity in the South fell rapidly. It had been 70 per cent in a 1 March Gallup poll. By September it had plummeted to 44 per cent. As JFK's re-election campaign was just around the corner, the implications of that drop in popularity were severe. This was why JFK wondered whether his civil rights speech of 11 June and subsequent legislation might prove 'to be his political swan song', as Bobby Kennedy recalled his brother's articulated fears. It did him credit in what turned out to be the final months of his life that he did the right thing on civil rights despite the political consequences for himself. That is important in casting doubt over the claim that as president, Kennedy lacked character.[60]

In the summer and autumn of 1963, Vietnam came to dominate Kennedy's thinking on foreign policy. It had been a significant element in his approach to international affairs since his inauguration, as he had inherited from Eisenhower a commitment to defend South Vietnam, led since the mid-1950s by Ngo Dinh Diem. Diem's position had become increasingly precarious, with Ho Chi Minh and his communist supporters ensconced in the North as well as an increasingly assertive communist resistance, the Viet Cong, in the South. In essence, Kennedy showed a determination to defend Diem and deter the communists in South

Vietnam – over the course of his presidency the US military personnel there increased from 685 to 16,700 – but without making the fateful decision that Lyndon Johnson would in 1965 to deploy large numbers of US combat troops in the South. This greater American presence had the deleterious effect of making Diem seem less of a credible nationalist. Not mere advisory bystanders, many of these US officials accompanied South Vietnamese forces on their combat missions. As with the French before them, American officials and their Vietnamese allies struggled even to locate their communist adversaries in the forests and paddies. Kennedy's much-vaunted strategic hamlet program, aimed at separating the communists from the South Vietnamese people by moving peasants from the villages in an area into militarily protected hamlets, was ineffectual. Moreover, some of the more unsavoury features of the subsequent US war in Vietnam, such as the use of napalm and defoliants, also began during the Kennedy years. Despite his concerns over these sorts of problems, Vietnam had been less central to JFK's thinking on the Cold War during the first two years of his presidency than Cuba, Berlin and, of course, relations with Russia. Contributing to that prioritization of policy was a media interest in Vietnam that was less substantial than it would become by late 1963. As Robert Dallek notes perceptively, at JFK's twice-monthly press conferences he was asked not a single question on Vietnam after April 1962 for the rest of the year.[61]

With Kennedy and Vietnam, there are two key issues. The first, considered here, is his record as policymaker, particularly during the critical period of summer and fall 1963. The second is the hypothetical question of what he would have done in Vietnam had he lived. In particular, would he have gone to war, as Lyndon Johnson did, with the same catastrophic consequences? This hypothetical issue is discussed in Chapter 8.

Early in his presidency Kennedy had been compelled at times to confront the complex situation in South Vietnam. In May 1961, when he was determined to show his steel in meeting the communist challenge after the Bay of Pigs, JFK sent 500 Special Forces along with other military advisers to bolster the Diem regime. On the other hand, he rejected advice from Maxwell Taylor and NSC official Walt Rostow in the autumn, following their mission to Saigon, to deploy 8,000 US combat troops in South Vietnam, even though Diem's position appeared particularly precarious in that period as communist insurgency had intensified. A cluster of factors influenced the thinking of Kennedy and most of his advisers on their commitment to maintaining a non-communist government in South Vietnam: fear of falling dominoes in Southeast Asia should the Saigon regime lose to the communists; the belief that South Vietnam going communist would strengthen the hand of Moscow and Peking in the Cold War; the lessons of the 1930s in confronting aggressive dictators (which was how they viewed Ho Chi Minh); the perceived need to uphold previous presidential commitments, by Truman and Eisenhower, to counter the communist threat in Vietnam; and, as Dean Rusk always emphasized, the paramount importance to US credibility as *the* guarantor of collective security to its many allies, including South Vietnam via the SEATO Treaty, that meant walking away from the struggle there was either unthinkable or highly problematic. On the other hand, the prospect of getting dragged into a land war in Asia only a decade after Korea could not be viewed with equanimity.[62]

While this range of factors influenced JFK's outlook, his precise thinking on Vietnam in 1961–2 is hard to fathom. But the possibility has to be considered that his personal views were at variance from those of his more hawkish advisers. First, there were those times when he resisted pressure from aides to send troops to South Vietnam, as with the Taylor–Rostow recommendations in the fall of 1961. In rejecting these recommendations, he told his advisers that there was a big difference between the naked aggression in Korea in 1950 that had prompted US military intervention and the situation they were faced with in Vietnam. He was also concerned that a modest US troop deployment would soon lead to a more substantial commitment. 'The troops will march in; the bands will play; the crowds will cheer,' he told an aide, 'and in four days everyone will have forgotten. Then we will be told we have to send in more troops. It's like taking a drink. The effect wears off, and you have to take another.' When back in spring 1961 a task force headed by Deputy Secretary of Defense Roswell Gilpatric urged him to deploy 3,600 US combat troops in South Vietnam, he refused to do so, sending instead the 500 Special Forces and military advisers. When McNamara forwarded (without his endorsement) in January 1962 a memo from the Joint Chiefs advising him to send US troops to South Vietnam, Kennedy again refused. In the spring of 1962 JFK discussed with his ambassador to India John Kenneth Galbraith a plan (not in the end carried out) to contact North Vietnam via Indian officials in order to propose a modus vivendi: de-escalation of US activity in Vietnam in return for cessation of Northern guerrilla actions in the South. There may also have been significance in JFK's decision at the start of 1963 to try to reduce press reports of visits by US officials to South Vietnam that could be interpreted as signifying a deepening American commitment to the struggle there. Moreover, some officials recall Kennedy's cautious comments on Vietnam. 'Kennedy did not want to insert the United States in the middle of a civil war in a country whose history and culture were little known to American decision makers,' said Sorensen. 'He was constantly asking one advisor or outside expert after another: How can we ever get out? On more than one occasion, he asked whether Vietnam was the right place for the United States to fight and take a stand.'[63]

Indicative of the wariness on Kennedy's part about his inheritance in Vietnam, even at an early stage in his presidency, was his response to the analysis offered by General Douglas MacArthur when the two men met in the iconic general's suite at New York's Waldorf Astoria Hotel in late April 1961. On the issue of US involvement in Indochina, MacArthur asserted that 'Anyone wanting to commit ground troops to Asia should have his head examined'. Instead, he argued, the US should establish a defensive perimeter around Japan, Formosa and the Philippines. When the generals or any other adviser urged him to take military action in Indochina, Kennedy would invariably respond by saying, 'Well now, you gentlemen, you go back and convince General MacArthur, then I'll be convinced.'[64]

Kennedy's outlook became influenced by his heightened scepticism towards his gung-ho generals and intelligence chiefs after they had let him down by advising him to authorize the Bay of Pigs invasion, and then again by urging him to bomb Cuba during the missile crisis. His trip to Vietnam in 1951, when he observed how large numbers of tough and experienced French soldiers were unable to defeat the communists, shaped his thinking and was a factor behind his rejection of the Taylor–Rostow recommendation to send in US troops. Having approached the nuclear precipice in Cuba in October 1962, his resolve to reduce Cold War tensions had increased thereafter, with the Test Ban Treaty the most striking example of that resolve. To some degree, Kennedy viewed Vietnam through this new prism of Cold War rapprochement.[65]

The Democrat who had replaced Lyndon Johnson as Senate majority leader, Mike Mansfield of Montana, also influenced JFK's thinking. Mansfield was an expert on Asian history and had taught the subject at college. After visiting Southeast Asia at Kennedy's request, Mansfield spoke to the president at Palm Beach in December 1962. There he urged Kennedy to resist any US escalation in Vietnam and instead to withdraw before the United States became a major combatant in a Vietnamese civil war, damaging its reputation in the process. 'I got angry with Mike for disagreeing with our policy so completely,' Kennedy later told an aide, 'and I got angry with myself because I found myself agreeing with him.' In spring 1963 Mansfield again assailed the administration's military involvement in Vietnam in a White House meeting between Kennedy and the Congressional Leadership. According to close aides O'Donnell and Powers, Kennedy then told Mansfield in a private discussion that 'he had been having serious second thoughts about Mansfield's argument and that he now agreed with the senator's thinking on the need for a complete military withdrawal from Vietnam'. He could not carry this out though until 1965, after he had been re-elected as president. O'Donnell and Powers, writing at a time when the Vietnam War had become a disaster, might have been indulging in wishful recollection here so as to protect the reputation of their beloved friend and boss when it came to Vietnam. But on the other hand their memory of this discussion may have been accurate.[66]

In the summer of 1963, the situation in South Vietnam deteriorated. It was the policy of Diem, a Catholic, of religious repression against the Buddhists, who constituted the majority of the South Vietnamese population, that made clear that in backing Diem the United States was hardly supporting an enlightened, progressive, democratic leader. In particular, the shocking self-immolation of Buddhist monk Thich Quang Duc on 11 June 1963, major news throughout the world, exposed Diem's draconian rule. Anti-Diem protests, not least among disaffected students, proliferated.

Yet it remained the case in the summer of 1963 that for Kennedy Vietnam was a definite, but not a dominant, concern. He delivered no major set-piece speech on Vietnam, as he had previously on Cuba and Berlin. At the eight press conferences which he gave between 3 April and 20 August, he made no opening statements on the situation in Vietnam, as he sometimes did on important issues. Gallup polls were conducted on a wide range of policy matters in this period but none on Vietnam, judged by Gallup to be insufficiently significant to merit a public opinion survey. Adding to that sense for JFK that Vietnam was of less concern to the nation than, say, relations with Russia, on which the negotiations for the Test Ban Treaty focused attention, or with Cuba, about which he was peppered with questions by journalists at news conferences, was the fact that at press conferences on 3 and 24 April, 24 June, 1 and 20 August he was asked not a single question on Vietnam.[67]

All of this suggests that Kennedy had by the summer of 1963 given less thought to Vietnam than he had to Cuba, Berlin and the Soviet Union. He was still in the process of defining his precise ideas on the issue. But what he did say to the Fourth Estate can be viewed as indicating, as had many of his earlier decisions and his response to MacArthur's caveats, that he was wary about escalating US involvement. While on 17 July he said the United States would continue to back the Diem government, in late May – when asked about the recent comments by Diem's brother Ngo Dinh Nhu that there were too many American troops in Vietnam – he had stated that 'we would withdraw troops . . . any time the government of South Vietnam would suggest it', adding that 'we are hopeful that the situation . . . would permit some withdrawal in any case by the end of the year'. Kennedy may have been preparing American public opinion for a gradual reduction in US military personnel in South Vietnam, and this statement should be considered in conjunction with his policy directive NSAM-263 five months later authorizing a 1,000-man withdrawal. NSAM-263 was the culmination of a process of deliberation in McNamara's Defense Department about the feasibility of training the South Vietnamese so that they could defend themselves, thereby facilitating a US withdrawal. It was based on overly optimistic assessments of the effectiveness of the ongoing military campaign against the Viet Cong. Nevertheless, by 1962 McNamara – at Kennedy's behest – had ordered, as he later put it, 'long-range planning for a phased withdrawal of U.S. advisers based on the assumption that it would take three years to subdue the Vietcong'. By late spring 1963 he had instructed the military to initiate this plan by preparing for the withdrawal of 1,000 US military officials by the end of the year.[68]

An indication of Kennedy's thinking on Vietnam in mid-August was given in an Oval Office meeting with Henry Cabot Lodge, the Republican he had recently appointed as the new US ambassador in Saigon in part to share the blame for any future woes in South Vietnam with the GOP and in part to put pressure on Diem, of whom Lodge was decidedly sceptical. As well as showing his prurient side by asking Lodge whether Diem's sister-in-law Madame Nhu was a lesbian, he raised the issue of whether the removal of Diem would soon be necessary: 'The time may come . . . we've gotta just have to try to do something about Diem, and I think that's going to be an awfully critical period.' Given that a South Vietnamese general had informed a CIA operative back in early July that plans were afoot for a military coup against Diem, Kennedy here was simply dealing with the reality of the situation. However, he did not at this point give to Lodge his unequivocal support for a coup, saying that it was not clear if the United States could find a new leader who would be any better; Diem had shown considerable resilience over many years in combatting the French and then the communists; and that the United States should be wary about being pushed into precipitous action by overzealous journalists, fiercely critical of Diem and America's role in backing him, such as David Halberstam of *The New York Times*. (All of this undermines the idea that at this meeting JFK instructed Lodge to work for the overthrow of Diem, as has sometimes been claimed.) Beyond the issue of whether Diem should stay or go, Kennedy did not discuss with his new ambassador any long-term plans he harboured for US policy in Vietnam.[69]

Diem's policy of religious repression resumed on 21 August when Nhu launched attacks throughout the country on Buddhist pagodas. This was the day before Henry Cabot Lodge arrived in Saigon. Lodge was no friend of Diem, convinced his ouster was essential if South Vietnam were ever to have a government capable of defeating the communists. Given the turmoil in South Vietnam that summer, it was not surprising that misgivings over Diem's rule within the Kennedy administration had increased. State Department officials George Ball, Roger Hilsman, Averell Harriman and Deputy National Security Adviser Michael Forrestal were among those troubled by developments in Saigon. Ball, for instance, had become ever more certain that 'we had tied our nation's fortunes to a weak, third-rate bigot with little support in the countryside and not much even in Saigon'. By late August the issue being considered was whether Kennedy should jettison Diem in a coup so as to bring about a government more capable of winning the support of the South Vietnamese people, thereby reducing the appeal of the communists. As Robert Kennedy said, it meant JFK was on the horns of a dilemma: it would be better not to have the corrupt Diem as leader, but, on the other hand, the United States did not want to be seen to be instigating coups.[70]

This issue came to the fore in late August when Kennedy was out of town, as were McNamara, Rusk and McCone. Summer holidays thus furnished an opportunity for those officials now convinced that Diem had to go. When Lodge reported that some South Vietnamese generals were plotting a coup, Hilsman drafted a cable to Lodge saying that unless Diem removed Nhu 'and his coterie' (including, no doubt, his controversial wife) – who were regarded by US officials as responsible for the more nefarious aspects of Diem's rule, including the repression of the Buddhists – 'we must face the possibility that Diem himself cannot be preserved'. In other words, if Diem did not part ways with Nhu, then the coup plotters should be given the green light. 'You may tell appropriate [South Vietnamese] military commanders we will give them direct support in any interim period of breakdown [of] central government mechanism,' the State Department cable briefed Lodge, who was also instructed to discuss with other US officials in Saigon 'all possible alternative leadership' to Diem. Harriman approved the cable. With Rusk out of town, Harriman and Hilsman located Ball as the number two man in the State Department on a golf course to update him on the situation in South Vietnam and the proposed cable to Lodge. Ball would not send it without JFK's clearance, and so he phoned the president, who was grieving at Cape Cod that weekend following the death of his third child Patrick after only a few days of life. Kennedy told Ball of his concern that a coup would result in a leader no better than Diem, but indicated that he would approve the cable as long as other senior officials, notably Rusk and Deputy Secretary of Defense Roswell Gilpatric, did likewise. Rusk later revealed that when Ball called him, his false impression from their conversation was that Kennedy's endorsement of the cable, and implicitly a coup to topple Diem (should he not disown Nhu), had been unequivocal; so Rusk too approved it. Gilpatric endorsed the cable on McNamara's behalf. In an interview conducted just a few months later, Robert Kennedy said JFK had approved the cable only because 'He thought that it had been approved by McNamara and Maxwell Taylor and everybody else. It had not'. Hence, the cable to Lodge was sent.[71]

When the principals – JFK, Rusk, McNamara, McCone, Mac Bundy and Taylor – convened in Washington at noon on Monday, 26 August, there was a distinct feeling that it might well have been unwise to send a cable that in effect encouraged a coup. Taylor expressed doubts 'as to whether we could get along without Diem,' and would later claim that 'The anti-Diem group centered in [the] State [Department] had taken advantage of the absence of the principal officials to get out instructions which would never have been approved as written under normal circumstances'. Kennedy thought too that his administration, in its agitation over Diem, was being unduly influenced by the reporting of Halberstam of *The New York Times*, whom he described as 'a 28-year old kid'. He was also concerned about whether the coup was likely to succeed. The administration discussions that followed in the next few days – described by JFK as 'EXCOM' talks, and so akin to the missile crisis meetings in October 1962, revealing his view of the importance of this historical moment – were acrimonious, with officials dividing into camps supporting and opposing the coup. 'The government split in two,' recalled Robert Kennedy. 'It was the only time, really, in three years that the government was broken in two in a very disturbing way.' State Department officials, particularly Harriman, Hilsman and Ball, were vociferous in their support for the coup. But Frederick Nolting, Lodge's predecessor as US ambassador in Saigon, was strongly opposed; and others, including McNamara and Dillon, expressed reservations. From Saigon, Lodge was adamant that the overthrow of Diem was a prerequisite if ever credible leadership against the communists in South Vietnam was to be established. The CIA told Kennedy the same thing. Lodge got the local CIA station to liaise with the coup plotters.[72]

JFK came to back the coup but only if it were likely to succeed. At an NSC meeting on the 28th he said they should 'ask Lodge & [General Paul D.] Harkins how to build up coup forces' as 'at present [it] does not look like coup forces can win'. He also reserved the right to rescind his approval of the coup until the last moment. Lodge warned him that should the plotters decide to go ahead with the coup, regardless of presidential opinion, the United States might not be able to prevent it. By 30 August, however, it was apparent that the coup plotters were beginning to have second thoughts. The following day the CIA station in Saigon sent a report stating: 'this particular coup is finished.' The aborted coup, nonetheless, signified that time was running out for Diem.[73]

In hindsight, it might well appear that Kennedy's support for the coup, albeit tentative and equivocating, was misguided, even egregious. A president arrogantly deciding the fate of a nation. It should be remembered, though, that the fundamental impulse behind his consideration of support for the coup was to rid the country of a corrupt, repressive regime and to replace it with a better government, one more capable of winning the support of the South Vietnamese people; and that would make a full US military intervention in the form of ground troops unnecessary. On the other hand, compared to his handling of the Berlin crisis and the Cuban missile crisis, his leadership on Vietnam at this juncture was less impressive. Some of the caution evident in his outlook on Vietnam up to that point was again apparent. Knowing Nolting's strong support for Diem, Kennedy must have anticipated his opposition to the coup and that by inviting him to these ExComm 2 meetings in late August he would ensure an administration discussion that included consideration of the potential pitfalls in proceeding with a coup. At the end of the White House meeting on 27 August, dominated by Nolting's enumeration of the problems with the planned coup, JFK said that he now 'wondered whether we should not take another look at the situation'. He also believed (as did McNamara) that US officials should be wary about proceeding with the coup merely because 'we have gone so far already' in contemplating it. Yet at these ExComm 2 meetings he was often quiet and did not provide his advisers with a clear steer. The fact that his key adviser on the ground, Lodge, favoured the coup seems to have influenced JFK's thinking, as did the brief comments by Bobby Kennedy in ExComm 2 in support of Diem's overthrow. But it is not entirely clear why he decided to go along with the coup (providing its chances of success seemed good) beyond a vague feeling that the momentum behind it was irresistible, as well as the more commendable conviction that Diem's ouster might usher in a better government in Saigon.[74]

The complexity of the conflict in Vietnam and in JFK's basic view of it, wanting to prevent a communist takeover but without the deployment of US troops, was apparent from two media interviews he gave in early September. In an interview with revered news anchor Walter Cronkite broadcast on 2 September, he criticized Diem's repression of the Buddhists, accused his government of being 'out of touch with the people', warned the war would most likely be lost unless Diem changed policy and personnel, and said that ultimately it was not the responsibility of the United States to defeat communism there: 'I don't think that unless a greater effort is made by the [Saigon] Government to win popular support that the war can be won out there. In the final analysis, it is their war. They are the ones who have to win it or lose it. We can help them . . . but they have to win it, the people of Viet-Nam, against the Communists.' At the same time, though, he said it would be 'a great mistake' for the United States to withdraw from Vietnam as 'this is a very important struggle even though it is far away'. A week later, in an interview for NBC's 'Huntley-Brinkley Report', he said he did not intend to reduce US aid to South Vietnam, believed in the domino theory and again argued against withdrawal. In these interviews, Kennedy gave contrary signals to the American people.[75]

Contrary signals were given to Kennedy himself. In the reports submitted on 10 September on their visits to Vietnam, General Victor Krulak and State

Department official Joseph Mendenhall painted very different pictures, positive in the case of the former, pessimistic with the latter. 'The two of you did visit the same country, didn't you?' asked an exasperated Kennedy. It was to provide a clearer picture that Kennedy sent two senior officials, McNamara and Taylor, on another fact-finding mission to South Vietnam so that he could receive 'the best possible on-the-spot appraisal of the military and paramilitary effort to defeat the Viet Cong'. It was a commendable feature of Kennedy's leadership on Vietnam that he constantly sought updated information on the situation there from trusted aides. An indication that JFK was not unequivocally committed to a coup against Diem came in the cable he sent to Lodge in mid-September informing him of the McNamara-Taylor mission. 'We see no good opportunity for action to remove present government in immediate future,' he said, adding that Diem should be encouraged to carry out reforms such as releasing imprisoned students and Buddhists and permitting a free press. On 2 October McNamara and Taylor, after a ten-day trip that included a lengthy meeting with Diem, sent their report to JFK.[76]

That report was a melange of positive and pessimistic perceptions of the campaign against the communists. Considerable progress in the battle against the Viet Cong was being made but 'political tensions in Saigon' were acute. They discussed the possibility of a coup against Diem and the potential effectiveness of pressuring him to carry out much-needed reforms by cutting US aid to his government, with those cuts being made in October. McNamara and Taylor made a specific policy proposal, which JFK would authorize nine days later in National Security Action Memorandum No. 263, to withdraw (as planned earlier in 1963) 1,000 US military personnel from South Vietnam by the end of the year. This was to be viewed as prologue to a full withdrawal by the end of 1965. To facilitate that, the United States should expedite the training of the South Vietnamese military. At a 2 October NSC meeting attended by McNamara and Taylor on their return, JFK expressed concern that a public announcement of the 1,000-man withdrawal by the end of 1963 might leave his administration open to the criticism that they had been overly optimistic should prevailing conditions at the end of the year necessitate the suspension of the 1,000-man departure. But he proceeded with NSAM-263 in part as a way of signalling that the United States did not plan to remain in Vietnam indefinitely, and also to pressure Diem into providing better government to the South Vietnamese people by making clear that continuous US assistance for Saigon should not be assumed. He wanted NSAM-263 to be a low-key, discreet policy, which could be reversed if military circumstances required. Nevertheless, he authorized Salinger to release a press statement after this NSC meeting on the plan to withdraw 1,000 military personnel; and at a 31 October news conference he confirmed in public his intention to remove 1,000 military personnel by the end of 1963.[77]

By then reports of another coup plot had reached Kennedy. Back on 5 October in Saigon Major General Duong Van Minh met CIA contact Lieutenant Colonel Lucien Conein, asking what the attitude of the Kennedy administration would be to a coup that replaced Diem with a government more capable of defeating the communist insurgency, and describing the assassination of Diem and Nhu as one way to carry out a coup. The view that Kennedy took was that the United States would not promote such a coup, and in agreement with his CIA director McCone that he could not endorse an assassination plot. However, if Diem neither altered his repressive policies nor improved his military efforts against the communists, then the United States would need to consider the desirability of a new government in South Vietnam; and so the United States should develop contacts with alternative leaders if they emerged. If a coup were to become imminent, Kennedy wanted to conceal from public view any US involvement in or knowledge of such a coup, and to reserve for himself the right to make an a priori assessment of any coup plot and to advise its cancellation if the prospects for its success seemed unpromising. Lodge told Washington that a coup to remove Diem was close at hand and that the White House was in no position to prevent it. It was also likely, added Lodge, that the United States would be blamed for the coup.[78]

Lodge was right: a coup was indeed imminent, and it would begin on the afternoon of 1 November. Two days earlier, though, Kennedy and his advisers had mulled over this scenario; and the divisions which had been to the fore in the late August ExComm 2 meetings re-emerged. Whereas it was Nolting who had taken the lead in August in opposing a coup, this time it was Robert Kennedy, in a manner reminiscent of his stand against the hawks in ExComm during the missile crisis, who played the role of Cassandra. 'To support a coup would be putting the future of Vietnam and in fact all of Southeast Asia in the hands of one man not now known to us,' he warned. 'Diem will not run from a fight or quit under pressure.' 'My view is the minority view,' he conceded. But Taylor and McCone said they agreed with the attorney general. As in late August, State Department officials took the lead in pressing for a coup. This time it was Rusk and Harriman who made that case. Restating a CIA briefing at the start of the meeting that the military forces in support of and opposed to Diem were roughly equal, JFK said that if this were so, 'any attempt to engineer a coup is silly. *If* Lodge agrees with this point of view, then we should instruct him to discourage a coup'. Clearly Jack had found Bobby's arguments on this persuasive (though his comments again revealed a deference to Lodge). These sentiments influenced the telegram drafted by Bundy the following day, 30 October, which instructed Lodge 'to persuade coup leaders to stop or delay' any anti-Diem operation that was not very likely to succeed. But, of course, given Lodge's anti-Diem disposition, that was never going to happen. And the CIA in Saigon retained close contact with the generals planning the coup.[79]

On the morning of 1 November, as generals in Saigon were readying their forces for the coup, Kennedy met again with his advisers. The hope which Kennedy had clung to, both at this point and back in late August, that he could reserve for himself the right to veto any coup attempt that seemed likely to fail, proved forlorn. The generals provided the US embassy with only a four-minute warning before the start of the coup, and then proceeded to cut off telephone contact with the US military advisory group. At the meeting on the 1st Rusk reported that the 'rebel generals' would probably succeed and overthrow Diem. Kennedy asked questions about the progress of the coup; queried the double standard involved in the United States considering recognition of a rebel government in Saigon that would have overthrown a constitutional government when his administration had decided against recognizing a rebel government in Honduras; and – turning to the public-relations dimension of the issue – stressed 'the importance of making clear publicly that this was not a U.S. coup'.[80]

On 1 November Diem phoned Lodge for help, reporting that a rebellion had begun and asking about the attitude of the US government. To this man who had been America's ally for the best part of a decade, Lodge dissembled, saying he was 'not acquainted with all the facts' and that as it was early morning Washington time he could not ascertain the Kennedy administration's view on this. In other words, Lodge was saying Diem would receive no help from the United States in preserving his rule in South Vietnam. That same day rebel army officers assassinated Diem and his brother Nhu.[81]

At a meeting of his advisers on the morning of 2 November, Kennedy was stunned when Michael Forrestal walked in with a cable reporting the death of Diem and Nhu. 'When President Kennedy received the news,' recalled McNamara, 'he literally blanched. I have never seen him so moved.' The coup plotters claimed that they had taken their own lives, but Kennedy was right to doubt whether 'as Catholics the two men would have committed suicide'. Again, he said he wanted to minimize speculation about US culpability for the coup.[82]

Two days later, Monday, 4 November, a reflective Kennedy turned on the tape machine in the Oval Office to record his thoughts on these extraordinary events. In an incongruous juxtaposition of the personal and the geo-strategic, JFK's young children Caroline and John entered the room, and the recording included JFK encouraging three-year-old John to say hello; he obliged. The overthrow of Diem, said Kennedy, was the culmination of 'three months of conversation about a coup'. He noted the deep divisions within his administration on whether to support the coup. His brother Bobby, he said, had been opposed. 'I feel that we must bear a good deal of responsibility for it,' he continued, emphasizing the folly of the 24 August cable that expressed US support for a coup. 'I should not have given my consent to it without a roundtable conference at which McNamara and Taylor could have presented their views. While we did redress that balance in later wires, that first wire encouraged Lodge along a course to which he was in any case inclined.' He had been 'shocked by the death of Diem and Nhu'. Diem had been an 'extraordinary character' who had 'held his country together' for a decade. Kennedy closed by questioning whether the rebel generals could create a stable government – or if it would be 'repressive and undemocratic' and hence soon elicit strong opposition to it. This recording was infused with a strong sense of regret.[83]

In the comments he made to Lodge before he left for Saigon, his description of administration discussions in late August as ExComm meetings, and this thoughtful recording on 4 November, Kennedy conveyed the sense that he understood that this was a watershed moment for US involvement in Vietnam. He was right to identify that 24 August cable as a major error as the green light it gave to the coup plotters led, step by step, to the overthrow of Diem ten weeks later. In those late August meetings with his senior aides, Kennedy could and should have provided clearer, more decisive leadership. That this was not the case was due to his failure to define his precise views on this issue of national security, on which in general he was sure-footed.

Kennedy made two other clear errors on Vietnam in the summer and autumn of 1963. First, he should have seriously considered rather than dismissed the call of French president Charles de Gaulle for negotiations leading to the neutralization and reunification of Vietnam. De Gaulle made this proposal after learning, as Washington had, that via Nhu, Saigon was in contact with the North Vietnamese government. But JFK was sceptical, believing that neutralization was failing in Laos and that in any such settlement South Vietnam would in reality be controlled by the North. In addition, there *was* an element of cynical posturing in North Vietnam's stated interest in neutralization. As one of their leaders later admitted, 'We understood that the United States was not willing to accept our neutralist program, so we used it for propaganda value.' But by the autumn of 1963, columnists as perceptive as Walter Lippmann and James Reston were mulling over the feasibility of neutralization and US withdrawal; and as McNamara argued in a sort of mea culpa in his 1995 memoir *In Retrospect,* JFK and his advisers should have done the same.[84]

Second, Kennedy deferred excessively to Lodge, who had a clear, rigid agenda – regardless of Kennedy's more cautious, nuanced outlook – and that was to promote a coup and overthrow Diem. This is *the* striking oddity of Kennedy's handling of Vietnam. He was a self-confident leader, particularly on foreign policy following the Bay of Pigs fiasco; his handling of the Cuban missile crisis was evidence of that. After the Bay of Pigs he became convinced of the importance of not relying on 'experts' but instead trusting his own judgement. It was incongruous, therefore, that he so often deferred to Lodge in the fall of 1963, even more so in a social sense as he was the sort of Massachusetts WASP Establishment figure that the Irish-Catholic Kennedys had tended to view as untrustworthy rivals. Perhaps Kennedy was being overly political, viewing Vietnam as a mess and thus happy to have a Republican's fingerprints all over it in the run-up to the 1964 election. It may have been more the case that as Kennedy had not imposed himself on the issue of Vietnam before sending Lodge to Saigon, had not defined with precision his own position as he had with other national security issues, he was more disposed to relying on his man on the ground in Saigon. Hence, in the days following the controversial 24 August cable, Kennedy authorized a message to Lodge (and Harkins) asking for advice on whether to carry out the coup against Diem. Lodge constantly avoided seeing Diem, isolating him further, yet Kennedy did not *insist* he meet promptly with the South Vietnamese leader. In his 17 September cable to Lodge, JFK said that all continuing US assistance to Diem would be supplied 'only on your say-so'. The better approach would have been for Kennedy to solicit Lodge's views, consider them alongside those of his senior foreign policy advisers and then instruct his ambassador on the policy he wanted carrying out – rather than giving him such latitude.[85]

Despite these flaws in his leadership on Vietnam, he was right to be cautious and not stridently convinced that the coup was the best thing for American interests, as Lodge did. Whatever the precise significance of NSAM-263, it did suggest that

Kennedy was open to a de-escalation of US involvement in the months to come. It is clear too that he had not conspired in the assassination of Diem. The severity of the dilemma for the United States in Vietnam should also be acknowledged. No president could have devised a neat, politically acceptable solution in 1963. Back Diem and Kennedy would have been accused, as he indeed was, of supporting a reactionary government. Favour a coup in the hope of installing more enlightened leadership and he would be accused, as he has been ever since, of recklessly indulging in regime change. But Kennedy's instincts were right. This was a crucial moment in the history of the United States in Vietnam. The overthrow of Diem destabilized South Vietnam even further, ushering in a series of ephemeral regimes and drawing the United States deeper into the quagmire from which it would not emerge for a decade.

Three weeks after the assassination of Diem, John Kennedy was in an open-top car in downtown Dallas.

Chapter 6

THE CHARACTER QUESTION

On her fourth day working in the White House press office in the summer of 1962, the nineteen-year-old Mimi Beardsley received a phone call from John Kennedy's close aide Dave Powers. He asked whether she would like a lunchtime swim. The White House had a pool a hundred yards from the press office, he explained, and there were plenty of spare bathing suits. A few minutes later Beardsley was relaxing in the pool with two other staffers, Jill Cowan and Priscilla Wear. Powers sat on the edge with his feet in the water which was set at 90 degrees to alleviate the president's back pain.[1]

Kennedy appeared in suit and tie and asked if he could join them. He went to the dressing room and changed into a pair of dark trunks. 'He was remarkably fit' for a 45-year old man, recalled Beardsley, 'flat stomach, toned arms'. Kennedy entered the water and moved towards her. 'It's Mimi, isn't it?' he asked. He proceeded to pepper her with questions about her work in the White House, her relationship with Press Secretary Pierre Salinger and where she was living in Washington. After the swim Beardsley returned to her desk.[2]

In the afternoon Powers called again, inviting her to a staff get-together at 5.30 pm. He collected her and took her to the family residence on the second floor. Cowan, Wear and presidential adviser Kenneth O'Donnell were already there in the West Sitting Hall. Powers poured her a daiquiri, then another. Suddenly JFK entered the room. Everyone stood. After a few minutes he walked over to Beardsley and asked: 'Would you like a tour of the residency, Mimi?' She agreed, expecting the rest of the party to join them. But when she left with the president no one else moved.[3]

Beardsley had long been interested in design and was genuinely curious to see the work undertaken by Jackie Kennedy to restore the White House. But this tour turned out to be more intimate than she could possibly have envisaged. After showing her the family dining room, he walked across the hall to another room. 'This is Mrs. Kennedy's bedroom,' he said. 'Beautiful light, isn't it?' he observed as they gazed out of the window.[4]

She noticed JFK was moving closer to her. She felt his breath on her neck. He touched her shoulder and said, 'This is a very private room.' Then he stood in front of her and stared into her eyes. He put his hands on her shoulders and moved her to the bed. She fell back on her elbows. He began to unbutton her shirtdress and caressed her breasts. He pulled off her panties. She removed her shirtdress but kept her bra on. He lowered his pants and positioned himself above her. Foreplay was rapidly abandoned.[5]

As he began intercourse she offered some resistance. 'Haven't you done this before?' he inquired. 'No.' 'Are you okay?' 'Yes,' she replied. 'He resumed,' recalled Beardsley, 'but more gently.' She nodded when he again asked if she was ok. After climaxing he pulled up his pants, smiled and said to her: 'There's the bathroom if you need it.'[6]

This is the most detailed account we have of a Kennedy seduction. It was provided by Mimi Beardsley, later Mimi Alford, in 2012. What is clear is that this seduction was hardly a unique event, for during his presidency he remained – as he had been before reaching the White House – a philanderer of spectacular proportions. Indeed the sheer hedonism of Kennedy's private life resembled that of Casanova.

The position could be taken that a sober history of the Kennedy years should attach little importance to this and other salacious stories about JFK's private conduct. Tittle-tattle should be confined to the tabloids and not feature in mature scholarship on the man. However, the historian should always respond to the historical debate, and the fact of the matter is that the significance of JFK's private life, especially his sexual behaviour, has become a major theme in Kennedy scholarship. In their 1976 study of the young Kennedy, *In Search of JFK*, Joan and Clay Blair dwelt on his promiscuity. The philandering and macho ethos of the Kennedy men figured prominently in *The Kennedy Imprisonment*, penned in 1982 by one of America's foremost public intellectuals, Garry Wills. A decade later historian Thomas Reeves argued in his bestselling work, *A Question of Character*, that Kennedy's character was flawed, as revealed by his private life, and that this lack of personal morals not only affected but seriously damaged the way he discharged his presidential responsibilities. Award-winning investigative journalist Seymour Hersh was singing from the same hymn sheet in his controversial 1997 work *The Dark Side of Camelot*. 'The central finding' of his book, said Hersh, 'is that Kennedy's private life and personal obsessions – his character – affected the affairs of the nation and its foreign policy far more than has ever been known.' 'This is a book about a man,' he added, 'whose personal weaknesses limited his ability to carry out his duties as president.'[7]

The idea that Kennedy was a terribly flawed human being is a key element in the revisionist critique that has sought to reject the idea that he was a fine president. This warts-and-all examination of Kennedy the man has produced two important arguments: first, his private life showed that his character was shockingly flawed; and second, his private life influenced his role as president. Where one stands in the ongoing debate on the calibre of Kennedy's presidency depends in part on one's response to this damning assessment of his character and personal conduct.

One reaction to this line of argument would be simply to dismiss it – to say Kennedy's private affairs were irrelevant to his handling of the presidency. But these revisionist arguments can only be assessed by considering them carefully. To do that requires a dissection of JFK's behaviour behind closed doors. Dismissing the arguments of Kennedy's critics without that detailed examination is inadequate because it is merely argument by assertion. Moreover, some of JFK's private escapades have a clear prima facie importance. Sleeping with a woman who was close to the head of the Chicago mafia, as Kennedy did with Judith Campbell, *was* a serious matter. So was Kennedy's use of West German prostitute Ellen Rometsch, as she was originally from East Germany and had belonged to communist party organizations. It was neither misguided nor prurient of Wills, Reeves and Hersh to dwell on these sorts of issues. Furthermore, for the historian seeking to understand Kennedy as a man, and not just a politician, that libido was a major part of who he was.

Kennedy's private actions were also important as they produced moments of intense danger to him. They increased the sway of the appalling FBI director J. Edgar Hoover over him, ran the risk of public embarrassment and even threatened his presidency. These issues will be explored later in this chapter. But it was also the case that in the White House Kennedy enjoyed numerous affairs that did not have that significance. They were largely risk-free because of the protection from public and press scrutiny afforded by the walls of the White House, the restrained attitude of the media to the private lives of America's leaders and the loyalty and discretion of the women involved. These relationships provided Kennedy with a constant supply of safe sex – safe in the sense that it was unlikely to jeopardize his presidency. From his perspective, this was a pleasurable diversion, an emotional and physical release from the pressures of leadership. Those relationships shed light on how Kennedy treated others in this compartment of his life. It did not always reflect well on him.

The working women of the White House who became Kennedy's sexual partners constituted a veritable harem. Among others, there were Pamela Turnure and Jill Cowan and Priscilla Wear – and Mimi Beardsley. When Jackie Kennedy was away from the White House, as she often was, these lovers could be called at a moment's notice for a swim or for sex or both.

After losing her virginity to JFK on her fourth day working in the White House press office, Mimi Beardsley became a presidential mistress. Four days after her first sexual encounter with the president, she received a phone call from Powers and said yes when he invited her for another lunchtime swim. She was again joined in the water by Kennedy, Jill Cowan and Priscilla Wear. When Powers phoned later to invite her to the private residence after work, she assumed Cowan and Wear would be there too. They were not. It was only Powers and the president. After some playful banter Powers got up to leave, and so Beardsley did likewise. But JFK did not plan to spend the evening alone. 'Stay for supper, Mimi,' he said. 'The kitchen staff always leaves food in the icebox.' 'And have another daiquiri,' he suggested. It was not long before he was leading her into a bedroom, this time his own rather than his wife's. 'Would you like to take a bath?' he asked. Kennedy said she could close the door and that he would meet her in the bedroom. 'This,' recalls Beardsley, 'was the beginning of our affair.' With Jackie often away with the children that summer in Italy and elsewhere, JFK saw Beardsley at least once a week and often more frequently.[8]

Along with Judith Campbell, Mimi Beardsley is the only mistress of Kennedy when he was president to have provided a detailed account of their affair. Her 2012 memoir is important therefore as it conveys a strong sense of what he was like in this extra-familial compartment of his life. It affords a rare sense of the *texture* of his affairs, or at least of this one.

Sex, of course, was a big part of Kennedy's relationship with Beardsley. Their 'sexual relationship was varied and fun', she remembers. 'Sometimes he would be seductive. Sometimes he was playful. Sometimes he acted as if he had all the time in the world. Other times, he was in no mood to linger.'[9]

Sex, however, was only part of the president's relationship with her. Pleasure, broadly defined, was a key part of Kennedy's credo. It was not, actually, a mindless hedonism. He believed that life was short – having been at death's door on more than one occasion, he knew that to be the case – and hence that it made no sense to deprive oneself of fun, gratification, relaxation, amusement. He was a true hedonist, 'a sensualist', as Beardsley put it. In their oral history for the Kennedy Library, Cowan and Wear were discreet about their relationship with JFK. But Cowan did say that when Kennedy 'was working, he worked terribly hard, and then when he was relaxed, he really relaxed. He thought that women should be in some ways that way, too'.[10]

Jollification, then, characterized the time he spent with Beardsley. As well as swimming together, they listened to music. His tastes were popular, not classical, and he adored Frank Sinatra and Tony Bennett. Beardsley noticed how much enjoyment he derived from listening to Robert Morse's singing on a recording of the musical *How to Succeed in Business Without Really Trying*; his voice 'seemed to light up some pleasure center deep inside his brain'. He also loved spending an inordinate amount of time in the bathtub with her, playing with the numerous rubber ducks along the edge of the tub. She found this playful side of him irresistible. He taught her how to make scrambled eggs. He took her on cruises with his friends on the presidential yacht *Sequoia* along the Potomac. He also got her to pamper him by massaging hair tonic and an ointment into his scalp. So for Kennedy, Beardsley was a provider of sexual gratification but also fun and pleasure more generally.[11]

It is not surprising, therefore, that Beardsley's recollections of the affair forty years on were largely positive. She portrayed him as having been thoughtful, even gracious towards her: he was 'a kind and thoughtful man.... He had true grace when he dealt with people'. As their relationship unfolded, he was 'more attentive, more gentlemanly', she felt. Yet looked at from today's perspective, JFK's relationship with Beardsley seems unsavoury. The power imbalance inherent in a relationship between the most powerful man in the world and a nineteen-year-old intern is clear, and while he generally treated her well, there were at least two times when he abused his power over her.[12]

The first such occasion was in the late summer in the White House swimming pool. Powers was sitting at the side of the pool. Kennedy swam to Beardsley and whispered: 'Mr. Powers looks a little tense. Would you take care of it?' Understanding what JFK had in mind, Beardsley obliged: she swam over to Powers and gave him oral sex. Kennedy watched in silence. Afterwards an embarrassed Beardsley headed straight to the dressing room. She overheard Powers speak to Kennedy with a sternness she had never heard before: 'You shouldn't have made her do that.' 'I know, I know,' said Kennedy. He later apologized to them both. Years later, she would say Kennedy had 'emotionally abused me and debased Dave. For what? To watch me perform for him and to show Dave how much he controlled us?'[13]

A second troubling episode took place in December 1962 when Beardsley joined Kennedy's entourage on his tour of various Western states. During a party at Bing Crosby's Palm Springs house, attended by Hollywood hotshots, one guest handed around some yellow capsules, probably amyl nitrate – commonly known as 'poppers' – that stimulated the heart and supposedly heightened sexual experience. When Kennedy asked Beardsley if she would like to take the drug, she declined. Ignoring her, he popped open the capsule and put it under her nose. Soon Beardsley's heart rate increased and her hands started to shake. She was frightened, began to cry and fled the room. Powers followed her and took her to another part of Crosby's home. He stayed with her for over an hour until the effects of the amyl nitrate wore off. Kennedy did not try the drug himself, despite forcing her to do so.[14]

Any defence of Kennedy's conduct on these two occasions is flimsy. It could be said that he did not force Beardsley to give Powers oral sex, and she herself says that she may have been 'carried away by the spirit of playfulness I felt around him'. Attitudes towards drug use at the start of the 1960s were less censorious than they would later become. Around this time Hollywood legend Cary Grant, for instance, spoke publicly about the benefits of LSD. Those arguments, however, are unpersuasive. In these instances Kennedy displayed an immaturity and a reckless disregard for the feelings of his teenage lover and his most loyal aide. His motivation for getting Beardsley to give Powers oral sex in the pool may have been purely sexual. His use of prostitutes and penchant for threesomes indicated his quest for a variety of sexual experience. This episode probably reflected the same impulse, and from it he probably derived a voyeuristic pleasure. Kennedy may well have viewed the poppers incident as mere schoolyard japes, a playful prank for the amusement of the other partygoers. He probably did not anticipate her physical reaction to the amyl nitrate, and that was badly misjudged. Of course, these juvenile tendencies did not define his character in toto. He could often be thoughtful, gracious and empathetic, but nonetheless there was an irresponsible facet to his character that revealed itself periodically in his private life, though not in his public role as president.[15]

His affair with Beardsley showed how Kennedy was able to live like the legendary Don Juan without scandal. One key factor was the discretion of the media. In the early 1960s the press had a respect for the presidency that the Vietnam War and the Watergate scandal would erode. As in the case of his affair with Pamela Turnure before and during the 1960 presidential campaign, about which her neighbours Florence and Leonard Kater had informed the newspapers, Kennedy relied on the prevalent belief among newspaper editors and journalists that a president's private life was out of bounds. Barbara Gamarekian, who worked in the Press Office alongside Beardsley, knew of this affair. In her interview for the Kennedy Library, she said that Beardsley 'did have sort of a special relationship with the President. I don't know quite what it was'. From what else she said in this interview, she certainly did know. 'It is enough to say,' Gamarekian added, 'that the White House press corps [usually waiting for news just outside the Press Office] and the people working in the White House were very much aware that there were lots of fun and games going on.'[16]

Gamarekian also revealed that

> A lot of the press corps thought that this was going to blow up eventually. This is the sort of thing that legitimate newspaper people don't write about or don't even make any implications about. It was kind of a big joke. Everyone knew about it and there were a lot of sly remarks made. And everyone knew. People talked on two levels all the time. You knew what they were referring to, but of course, I think they jumped to a lot of conclusions on the basis of just putting lots of things together.[17]

A good many journalists, then, knew that Kennedy had affairs. But out of a sense of propriety they did not write about them. Even had they wished to, their editors or newspaper proprietors would not have allowed it; the Katers' failed attempts to get the press to cover JFK's affair with Turnure had made that clear. It is intriguing that some of the nation's scribes, according to Gamarekian, still thought a scandal likely, despite their own professional ethics. Presumably they believed that an irresponsible journalist or editor – or perhaps a conservative paper ideologically opposed to the president – would finally break the silence over JFK's adultery. When the Profumo scandal erupted in Britain, the notion that the same sort of thing could happen in America seemed even more plausible.

Yet that did not happen during the Kennedy years. The judgement made by Kennedy was that the press culture of ignoring presidential shenanigans would persist during his time in the White House. He once remarked that the media could not investigate his private life while he was alive, adding that he did not care what they said on this issue after his death. His judgement on this matter proved sound, and although it might appear to be a cynical attitude on his part, it was also a pragmatic one. This constitutes a point of contrast between two of the presidents with the most notorious sexual lives during their time in the White House. Bill Clinton had a sexual relationship with Monica Lewinsky knowing the press would have no qualms about reporting on his affair. This was quite different from JFK who embarked on his affairs in the almost certain knowledge that journalists would keep quiet. In terms of the likelihood of causing a scandal, this makes Kennedy's sexual conduct very different to Clinton's far riskier behaviour. That should be an important factor in an assessment of JFK's private life in the White House as it serves to contextualize that private life in terms of the relationship between the president and the press prevailing at that time.[18]

Any chance that knowledge of Kennedy's affairs might end up in the public domain, limited anyway by this media deference, was reduced further by the practice Kennedy adopted in organizing the main relationships in his life: strict compartmentalization. Key political advisers such as Ted Sorensen were usually kept separate from his social friendships such as the one he enjoyed with journalist Ben Bradlee. 'I was totally involved in the substantive side of his life,' recalled Sorensen, 'and totally uninvolved in the social and personal side. Except for a few formal banquets, we never dined together during the White House years.' Friendships such as the one with Bradlee did not penetrate the inner sanctum of those men who were privy to, facilitated and sometimes shared his sexual adventures. In the White House, Dave Powers was often the go-between for Kennedy and his lovers. Kennedy could rely on Powers to arrange his trysts with efficiency, discretion and humour. Powers's friend Kenneth O'Donnell, another member of what the press dubbed Kennedy's 'Irish Mafia', and his valet George Thomas also seemed to have 'total, all-hours access to [JFK's private] residence', as Beardsley recalls. Florida senator George Smathers, JFK's Harvard roommate Torbert 'Torby' Macdonald, old pal and Undersecretary of the Navy Paul 'Red' Fay, and railroad lobbyist Bill Thompson were also part of the inner sanctum. Due to their long personal history with him, intense loyalty and, in some cases, their own playboy lifestyle, Kennedy could rely on this group for fun or discretion or both. He was comfortable with them knowing about his flings, certain they would never use this intimate knowledge to tarnish his reputation.[19]

During her affair with the president, Beardsley was struck by how Kennedy organized his life in this way. When she joined the presidential entourage on a trip to the nation's major space and aircraft facilities, Lyndon Johnson suddenly appeared at her seat during the flight from Florida to Houston, and introduced himself. When she later told JFK of the encounter, she noticed that he looked disconcerted. 'Stay away from him,' he ordered Beardsley. She was right to suspect, as she did in later years, that Kennedy 'might have been alarmed that I had slipped out of the private compartment he had put me in'. He certainly did not want his vice president, with whom he had a competitive and at times tense relationship, to acquire information about his private life.[20]

Of the men comprising this tight-knit group, it was Powers who was the most important. At times he resembled the eponymous character played by George Clooney in the 2007 film *Michael Clayton*, the person who would tie up any messy loose ends. When Beardsley thought she was pregnant – JFK never used contraception with her – it was Powers who phoned her college dormitory with the name of a woman who would put her in touch with a New Jersey doctor who could surreptitiously carry out what was then the illegal procedure of abortion. So in this rapidly constructed human chain any abortion would have been hard to trace back to Kennedy. (It turned out to be only a late period.) One other man would end up carrying out this sort of clean-up operation for JFK, albeit on a grander scale: Robert Kennedy.[21]

Kennedy's affair with Beardsley drew to a close in 1963 when she began to date a young man she would go on to marry. In a way, the fact of his affair with her is banal, as his adulteries were so frequent. It is the detail of his affairs that surprise. In this case two facts astonish: Beardsley never called him by his first name – she always said 'Mr President', even during coitus – and he never kissed her, not even when having sex. That first detail speaks to the power imbalance in their relationship; the second reveals a president behaving like a prostitute who is happy to have sex with others but will kiss only their partner or spouse – so for JFK, Jackie Kennedy.[22]

Mimi Beardsley was but one member of the White House staff who slept with Kennedy. The others included two very close friends Jill Cowan and Priscilla Wear. Inspired by JFK during the 1960 campaign, they had left Goucher College to work for him at the Democratic National Convention in Los Angeles. One associate recalled that Cowan, described as a 'sexy little girl' by another colleague, hitchhiked her way to California to volunteer for JFK. During the Democratic Convention Wear, whose childhood nickname was Fiddle, and Cowan, who became known as Faddle, worked with Kennedy's press secretary Pierre Salinger and others on a daily newspaper. Ostensibly impartial, it was in fact designed to promote Kennedy's candidacy. After the Convention Cowan and Wear were based in Washington, though Cowan recalled joining Kennedy on the campaign trail sometimes.[23]

When JFK decamped to Palm Beach after the election to work on his transition, Cowan and Wear joined his staff there. Asked later whether his back was hurting during his stay in Florida, Cowan and Wear's answers were suggestive, to say the least. 'When he first arrived down there, he was quite vigorous,' said Cowan. 'He was in very good shape.' 'Physically he was in good shape,' agreed Wear. 'His back wasn't bothering him at all.' It would be instructive to know how exactly Cowan and Wear knew that.[24]

In the new administration these two close friends became part of Kennedy's White House staff. Wear worked as an assistant to JFK's personal secretary Evelyn Lincoln, while Cowan joined Salinger's staff in the Press Office. Cowan often took wire-service ticker tape to Kennedy in the Oval Office. On a daily basis he dropped by the Press Office where he saw Cowan. That office was just across the hall from the Oval Office. Lincoln's office, where Wear worked, was just outside the Oval Office. The proximity of Kennedy to Cowan and Wear meant those lunchtime swims described by Beardsley, as well as their sexual encounters, were easy for him to arrange.

As well as assisting Evelyn Lincoln and Pierre Salinger, Cowan and Wear helped Kennedy process the countless autograph requests he received by signing his name. In early 1962 they achieved a certain fame when the editors of *Look* magazine decided to publish an article on them entitled 'Fiddle & Faddle'. It included lots of photographs. Kennedy liked the pictures of them with his children and was gratified that the article did not embarrass him. The rumour mill about the nature of their relationship with the president was active though. A junior military aide to Kennedy revealed, 'We had heard about Fiddle and Faddle.' *Time* correspondent Hugh Sidey also knew of JFK's affair with them. Jackie Kennedy herself suspected that an affair with Wear was taking place. When giving a tour of the White House to a reporter for *Paris Match* she entered Lincoln's office where Wear was working. The First Lady turned to the journalist and said in French, 'This is the girl who supposedly is sleeping with my husband.' Wear knew enough French to understand the comment.[25]

The relationship of Cowan and Wear to JFK was similar to that of Beardsley. Like the young intern, they spent time with him frolicking in the White House pool. Like Beardsley, they escorted him on trips away from Washington. Cowan went with him to Nassau and to Berlin and Ireland, and both of them accompanied him to Costa Rica. Wesley Hagood, a historian of the presidents' sex lives, draws the not unreasonable conclusion that 'Since Jack was fond of *ménage-à-trois* liaisons, it seems safe to assume that they participated in this type of sexual activity'. Indeed Lyndon Johnson's press secretary George Reedy has said that Wear and Cowan swam naked with JFK and did have three-way sex with him.[26]

When Gamarekian noticed the sense of intimacy, shared secret knowledge and playfulness in the relationship between Beardsley and some other young women at the White House, she must have been referring to Cowan and Wear. 'The thing that amazed me so,' said Gamarekian,

> was that these two or three girls were great friends and bosom buddies and gathered in corners and whispered and giggled, and there seemed to be no jealousy between them, and this was all one great big happy party and they didn't seem to resent any interest that the President or any other men might have in any of the girls. It was a marvelous example of sharing, which I found very difficult to understand as a woman! I just think that I would have found it difficult to enter into this kind of a relationship if I had been at all emotionally involved without having some very normal feelings of jealousy and possessiveness. But apparently this didn't enter into the relationship. They were the best of friends, and they all seemed to share the same [outlook].[27]

In her memoir, Beardsley describes Wear and Cowan as 'playful and carefree young women who were extremely comfortable in the President's company – and vice versa'. Beardsley claims she was unaware at the time that Kennedy had any other lovers. Although Wear was friendly to her, she said, she never discussed her relationship with JFK. That does not square with Gamarekian's characterization of the Wear-Cowan-Beardsley relationship, with its giggling and whispering and palpable lack of jealousy. Ellen Rometsch, a prostitute who was one of JFK's sexual partners in 1963, spoke of swimming-pool parties at the White House that were essentially orgies. That observation, in conjunction with the intimacy between Beardsley, Wear and Cowan, raises the possibility of whether the three young women did participate in sex parties with not only Kennedy but his kith and kin. Beardsley giving Powers oral sex suggests this was a possibility, as does a letter she sent to JFK's brother-in-law, Hollywood actor and bon vivant Peter Lawford, which was released in 2013: 'I hope New York was a great success and that you and Milt faired the plane trip well and recovered from that unforgettable night. I must say I still don't quite believe it! Please do come to Boston in January. I hope I see you soon.' In another letter to Lawford, Beardsley expressed the hope that 'we left your wife's clothes in wearable condition.'[28]

As with Beardsley, it is clear that Kennedy's relationship with Cowan and Wear involved more than just sex. He enjoyed the time he spent with them, as can be seen from the way he opened up to the two young women, disclosing some of his innermost secrets, including his surprisingly ambivalent feelings about his own family. In their March 1965 interview for the Kennedy Library, they discussed his deep depression after the Bay of Pigs, how JFK said he would prefer a sudden death at the peak of his career to aging gradually like his father, his admiration for his deceased sister Kathleen, and his feeling that he had never received the attention he needed from his parents or siblings as theirs had been such a large family. Most surprisingly, he opened his heart to them about his father. 'I think his relationship with his father was very strained,' said Wear. 'He once said that he could never be around his father for more than three days without having to get away. His father was terribly dictatorial always giving him advice on things. I think he just never felt relaxed around him.' It is inconceivable that Kennedy would reveal these things to Wear in front of Evelyn Lincoln or to Cowan in front of her Press Office colleagues. These must have been discussions in their private moments that preceded or followed their sexual encounters. Kennedy must have found them stimulating young women to talk to, not only to sleep with. In later life they would go on to have distinguished careers.[29]

Kennedy's White House harem did not end there, as he continued the affair he had begun before reaching the presidency with Pamela Turnure, who had worked in his Senate office. At JFK's insistence, she became the First Lady's press secretary. She was spotted taking the lift to Kennedy's private quarters shortly after JFK had left a White House reception. With an uncanny resemblance to Jackie, she remained on good terms with the First Lady, but by all accounts her affair with Jackie's husband continued during his presidency.[30]

Whereas liaisons with his White House staff neither threatened his presidency nor had a bearing on his policies, Kennedy's affair with Californian socialite Judith Campbell did. Introduced to her by Frank Sinatra in February 1960, he began a sexual relationship with her a month later, one that persisted through the presidential campaign. Recklessly, Kennedy continued that affair despite knowing of her growing friendship with Chicago mobster Sam Giancana. Given that Sinatra had introduced her to Giancana after getting her together with JFK, it would be reasonable to suspect that Sinatra would have informed Giancana that she was close to Kennedy – and hence, knowing Campbell would give the mobster intimate and potentially compromising knowledge of the presidential candidate's private life. His well-known association with and deference to Giancana and other mobsters mean that Sinatra's motivation for ingratiating himself in this way to the Chicago crime boss is obvious.[31]

After his election victory over Nixon, Kennedy decided to carry on this dangerous affair with Campbell. Busy with the preparations for the start of his administration, he still took the time to phone her and invite her to his inauguration. As Campbell felt uncomfortable attending with his wife and family there, she declined the offer. According to the interview she gave in 1988 to *People* magazine, which is consistent on this matter with the account in her 1977 autobiography, President Kennedy initially had little time for her. Affairs of state took precedence over his sexual affairs during the first three months of his presidency. After the Bay of Pigs, however, he resumed his relationship with Campbell.[32]

Kennedy's motivations for doing so were no doubt largely carnal. Campbell was both very beautiful and very sexy, a sort of eroticized version of Jackie Kennedy. Johnny Roselli, the Las Vegas mobster and Giancana's close associate, once described her as 'prettier than Elizabeth Taylor'. 'I know Liz', he told Giancana, 'and I'm telling you this gal has it all over her'.[33]

Despite Campbell's almost irresistible charms, Kennedy should have resisted. By sleeping with a woman so close to Giancana, he was leaving himself vulnerable to blackmail by the Mob. Giancana could have used his knowledge of JFK's affair with Campbell to compromise the investigations of Bobby Kennedy's Justice Department into organized crime. He could even have threatened his entire presidency by arranging for the story of the Kennedy–Campbell affair to be revealed in the public domain. Carrying on with Campbell was dangerous enough when JFK had been a presidential candidate, even more so once he was in the White House. Although the affair with Campbell did not destroy his presidency, it could have done. For that reason, it represents one of the two great misjudgements in his private life as president. The other was his use of prostitute Ellen Rometsch in 1963. There was an additional reason why his relationship with Campbell was such a serious matter: it increased the hold of J. Edgar Hoover over him, though this would not become clear to JFK until the spring of 1962.

Just the fact that Kennedy was sleeping with Campbell, who was seeing Giancana, meant that this astonishing triangular relationship was fraught with danger to Kennedy. According to the account she gave in 1988, however, Kennedy's inappropriate intimacy with the Mob went beyond his affair with her. For what should have been the cause for concern for Kennedy about Campbell, namely her close ties to the most notorious gangster in the land, was for him an opportunity firstly to assist his presidential campaign in 1960 and then to advance his foreign policy agenda as president – that is, if Campbell was telling the truth.[34]

It was in that *People* magazine interview that Campbell supplemented the original account she had given in her memoir by claiming that in addition to being Kennedy's lover she served as courier between JFK on the one hand and Giancana and Roselli on the other. Moreover, she said that she arranged meetings between JFK and Giancana during the 1960 campaign and the Kennedy presidency. In an interview with Seymour Hersh for his 1997 book *The Dark Side of Camelot*, Campbell fleshed out this account of how Kennedy had consorted with criminals. If Campbell's recollections of this are accurate, then his relationship with her was even more dangerous than it originally appeared.[35]

Campbell claimed that at Kennedy's request she set up a meeting between him and Giancana in April 1960 in the run-up to the West Virginia primary because he said he needed Giancana's 'help in the campaign'; she arranged 'several more meetings' between Kennedy and Giancana after the Democratic Convention in July 1960; she not only set up meetings but couriered envelopes and satchels, beginning in April 1960 when JFK asked her to take around $250,000 in cash to the Chicago crime boss; between the election and inauguration Kennedy instructed her to take to Giancana documents in an envelope about the 'elimination' of Castro; she made at least another ten trips in 1961 to Giancana and Roselli to deliver envelopes from Kennedy; Bobby Kennedy was involved as he sometimes brought the envelope for JFK and Campbell to the White House, usually when they were having a post-coital dinner; she thought the envelopes were not from the FBI but the CIA; and that the last time she delivered an envelope for JFK was in late 1961.[36]

It behoves the historian to examine Campbell's evidence with a critical eye, not simply to assume her bona fides. The fact that she was paid around $50,000 for the 1988 interview with Kitty Kelley, in which she first revealed her role as courier between Kennedy and the Mob, needs to be considered. This means that there was at least an implicit pressure on Campbell to provide startling revelations in order to justify the money she was being paid. That is not to say that her version of events was necessarily skewed, but it does mean she had a motivation to embroider the truth.[37]

The fact that Campbell told different stories at different times also needs to be pondered. None of this information about the envelopes and the meetings between Kennedy and Giancana appeared in her 1977 memoir *My Story*. She said to Kelley that she had concealed this information in the 1970s as she feared for her life if she told the whole story, and that she was finally telling the truth as she had been diagnosed with terminal cancer and so no longer had anything to fear. Assuming this to be a frank explanation of the inconsistencies between her 1977 and 1988 accounts, it would not explain why she provided new and crucial information to Seymour Hersh that was absent from her *People* magazine interview. Why did she make no mention of Bobby Kennedy's key role, as she did to Hersh, if she felt able to be candid in 1988? Likewise, why did she not mention to Kelley, as she did to Hersh, that Kennedy had asked her after the election but before the inauguration to deliver to Giancana documents about the assassination of Castro? Similarly, she told Hersh that she had delivered a huge sum of money from Kennedy to Giancana in April 1960, but failed to mention this astonishing information to Kelley. If Campbell's varying accounts were evaluated according to the evidentiary standards of a court of law, she would be regarded as an unreliable witness. Given the many inconsistencies in her various versions of events, and that the original allegation that she had set up meetings and conveyed envelopes between Kennedy and Giancana was made in an interview for which she was paid a lot of money, historians must consider the possibility that Campbell's claim on this matter is entirely fictitious.[38]

That issue can also be explored by considering the *reasonableness* of her account given what is known about the personalities and working habits of not only John and Bobby Kennedy, but Giancana as well. Gangsters like Giancana were not in the habit of corresponding with anyone. It was not Mob custom and practice to participate in any correspondence of letters or documentation that could be compromising or incriminating.

It is not only Sam Giancana's known methods of doing business that make Campbell's claims appear fanciful, but also Bobby Kennedy's role as brother-protector. As his aide John Seigenthaler put it, the most important priority for

Bobby in his political career, more than his later senatorial responsibilities for New York and his own presidential ambitions, was serving his elder brother with fanatical loyalty. 'I honestly believe Bobby would have taken a bolt of lightning for Jack,' said Seigenthaler. This fraternal devotion explains Bobby's insistence that the drugs used by the quack doctor Max Jacobson to treat JFK be sent to FBI and Food and Drug Administration laboratories for testing, and the speed with which he dispatched presidential lover Ellen Rometsch, whose prostitution became known to the press, back to West Germany. To be sure, Bobby was determined after the Bay of Pigs to work for Castro's overthrow as revenge for the way that bungled invasion had humiliated his brother. That could be viewed as motivation enough for Bobby to participate in underhand dealings with the Mob aimed at the assassination of the Cuban leader. Yet his tenure as attorney general is well known and well regarded for the determination he showed in trying to prosecute the Mafia. Cooperating with gangsters on what was essentially American foreign policy would have been inconsistent with his effort to put them behind bars. More importantly, Bobby would surely have realised that any sort of correspondence between the White House and the Mob would have compromised his brother as it would have left him vulnerable to blackmail by Giancana and Roselli. As his overriding objective was *always* to protect his brother, it is implausible to think he would have allowed his brother to correspond with the Mafia. For this reason, Campbell's allegation that Robert Kennedy sometimes brought envelopes to the White House for her to take to Mob leaders must be a canard. He would never have exposed his beloved brother in that way. If this part of her account is unreliable, her entire story about passing mail and arranging meetings between JFK and the Mafia should be viewed in the same way.[39]

Campbell's other extraordinary claims need to be viewed with a sceptical eye. In 1988 she said that after the Bay of Pigs catastrophe JFK phoned her to request that she collect an envelope from Roselli in Las Vegas to take to Giancana in Chicago. There she arranged a meeting between Kennedy and Giancana at the Ambassador East Hotel on the evening of 28 April 1961. She stayed in the bathroom while the two men spoke in private. After that JFK instructed her to go to Florida to see Giancana and Roselli to pick up another envelope, which she brought to the president on 5 May. After making love in the White House the next day, Kennedy gave her an envelope to give Giancana. On 8 August 1961, Campbell also claimed, Giancana turned up at her hotel room in Washington and told her that he had just come from a meeting with JFK. Given the many inconsistencies in her various accounts and the financial inducements for the interview she gave *People* magazine, the most plausible conclusion is that these numerous personal meetings and extensive correspondence did not take place.[40]

There is another troubling inconsistency in Campbell's recollections of her role in 1961. She told *People* magazine that she had no idea at the time of what the information in the envelopes was about. It was only in 1975 when the US Senate investigated CIA assassination plots against foreign leaders that 'It finally dawned on me that I was probably helping Jack orchestrate the attempted assassination of Fidel Castro with the help of the Mafia'.[41]

Compare this to the account she gave a few years later to Seymour Hersh. Prior to his inauguration JFK gave her documents in an envelope to take to Giancana, and told her they were to do with getting rid of the Cuban leader. 'I knew what they [the documents] dealt with,' she said. 'I knew they dealt with the "elimination" of Castro and that Sam and Johnny [Roselli] had been hired by the CIA. That's what Jack explained to me in the very beginning.' Both of these accounts cannot be accurate. That increases the doubts about the plausibility of Campbell's role as go-between.[42]

The independent evidence supporting Campbell's allegations on this matter is slim. It appears to consist of only two anecdotes, presented by Hersh. The first is the claim by Martin Underwood, an operative for Chicago Mayor Richard Daley, that Kennedy aide Ken O'Donnell asked him in April 1960 to take the same train from Washington to Chicago as that taken by Campbell; and that he saw her hand a satchel (full of cash) to Giancana on her arrival in Chicago. The second is the recollection of reporter Johnny Grant, who had known Campbell when she was a teenager, of an episode in March 1963. He said that running into her in Palm Springs, she confided in him about her relationship with Kennedy and Giancana, including her role as courier between the president and the Mob.[43]

This evidence needs to be taken seriously. On the other hand, both recollections came more than thirty years after the Kennedy–Campbell affair. Given the passage of time, the vagaries of memory, what Giancana's own relatives said about the implausibility of him participating in this sort of correspondence, Bobby's role in protecting and minimizing any threats to his brother, and the recognition that this does not constitute contemporaneous corroboration of Campbell's claims, the two anecdotes provided by Hersh are slim reeds on which to rest the argument that Campbell's extraordinary revelations about passing correspondence and setting up meetings between JFK and Giancana are credible.

While Campbell's account of Kennedy's relationship with Giancana is unreliable, she remains one of only two presidential mistresses (along with Mimi Beardsley) to provide a detailed account of her affair with JFK. As with Beardsley, she sheds light on what he was like in this private, extramarital compartment of his life. There were differences in Kennedy's relationship with Campbell and with Beardsley. For one thing, Campbell called him Jack and not, as Beardsley did, Mr President. For another, JFK often kissed Campbell, whereas – bizarrely – he had sex with Beardsley but never kissed her. Campbell always resisted Kennedy's pressure to get her to swim with him in the White House pool. Unlike Beardsley, she never spent a full night with him. Whereas JFK designated Dave Powers as the go-between with Beardsley, he used his secretary, Evelyn Lincoln, to liaise with Campbell by phone.[44]

Beyond those differences, however, Kennedy struck Campbell in much the same way he did his teenage-intern lover: charming, attentive, playful and attractive. 'I couldn't resist him,' she said. 'You can't believe his charm when he wanted to turn it on.' Her inability to resist him was due not only to his charm but to his good looks and erotic appeal. Mimi Beardsley was struck by his handsomeness. Marilyn Monroe would comment on it too. Likewise with Judith Campbell. 'Some women would have done anything to get near him,' she said. 'He had sex appeal. And he knew it.' On their first date together she had been dazzled 'by his good looks. He seemed so young and virile, so dashing'. What is surprising about her recollections is the insecurity he revealed. He constantly quizzed her as to his appearance. The self-doubt he expressed indicated that it was not just vanity. 'He needed the confidence that comes from reassurance,' she noticed. Beneath the veneer of complete confidence lay surprising insecurities, perhaps connected to his early years with a favoured, handsome, stronger elder brother, as well as the sequence of debilitating illnesses that must have made him question his own virility. Another sign of that insecurity was that he was often jealous of her relationships with other men, despite her apparent fidelity. In her final testimony – a 1997 *Vanity Fair* interview two years before succumbing to long-term cancer – she said she never slept with anyone else during her affair with JFK. He could hardly have said the same thing.[45]

Like Beardsley, Campbell found his playfulness appealing. When he visited her in California in December 1961, he relished joining in a spoof historical tour of her apartment. 'Hark! What have we here?' he proclaimed on seeing her bedroom. 'A mysterious contraption designed for the dubious pleasures of our ancient leader,' she replied.[46]

Rather than acting like a crass, Harvey Weinstein–type rogue, he was usually gentle and thoughtful. What would be said about that other presidential philanderer, Bill Clinton – that he was an exceptionally good listener – was often articulated by those close to Kennedy, including Campbell. 'When you talked to him, you felt you were the only person on the planet, much less just in the room,' she said. 'He never forgot anything…. He didn't just pretend to be listening to you – he listened to you. He absorbed everything.' His thoughtfulness was apparent in his sexual life with her. The first time he made love to her, on 7 March 1960, 'He couldn't have been more loving, more concerned about my feelings, more considerate, more gentle,' she recalled. He often sent her a dozen red roses (though in this he would be outdone by the regular delivery of five dozen yellow roses from Sam Giancana). White House telephone logs showed there were at least seventy phone conversations between JFK and Campbell; so this was no casual love affair. He once gave her two $1,000 bills so that she could buy a mink coat (but she deposited the cash); and on another he gave her a beautiful 18-carat gold brooch with rubies and diamonds. Once he asked her: 'Do you think you could love me?' So Kennedy enjoyed the romance, as well as the sex, with Campbell. The one anomalous and, from her point of view, distasteful exception to the consideration he usually displayed was when at the July 1960 Democratic National Convention in Los Angeles he arranged for a young woman to join them for a ménage-à-trois. As she had once with Sinatra when he tried the same thing, she angrily refused the proposition.[47]

How Kennedy conducted his affair with Campbell sheds light on two other features of the modus operandi of his private life. First, he continued to rely on the discretion of the media, and did so with confidence. When he met her for lunch in Las Vegas the day after they were introduced, he was in the middle of a press conference. She was surprised when he called out nonchalantly, 'Judy, I'll be right with you, we're just finishing up.' All the journalists turned to look at her. Kennedy seemed unfazed. Second, the compartmentalization of his life which Mimi Beardsley noticed was apparent to Campbell too. In August 1961 she had a row with Kennedy when, in the company of Dave Powers at the White House, he accused her of speaking to others about his attempt at a threesome with her. (He was right: she had told a few friends.) For JFK, Campbell taking umbrage at a proposed threesome was one thing; passing on that information beyond his immediate circle was another. When Kennedy broached the matter with her, he described it as 'quite serious'.[48]

The beginning of the end of Kennedy's affair with Campbell came on 22 March 1962 when at a White House luncheon J. Edgar Hoover informed the president that the FBI knew about his relationship with Campbell and her ties to Giancana and Roselli. With her connection to these gangsters, Hoover warned Kennedy of the danger to him of blackmail by the Mob. It is sensible to assume that Hoover – not close to the Kennedys and now under the watchful eye of Bobby as attorney general – was making a shrewd power play. In effect he was telling JFK that his position as FBI director could not be questioned because he knew all about the president's dangerous affair with Campbell. Hoover reinforced the point both in public and private. Before this meeting with JFK, he put in writing, in a memorandum to Bobby Kennedy, the FBI's knowledge of Campbell's contacts with Giancana and Roselli, and the fact that she had phoned Evelyn Lincoln twice in one week. Then on 9 May 1962 Hearst's preferred gossip columnist Walter Winchell wrote that 'Judy Campbell of Palm Springs and Bevhills is Topic No. 1 in Romantic Political Circles'. Campbell herself read the Winchell item in the *Los Angeles Herald-Examiner*. Records show that Hoover had phoned an executive at the Hearst newspapers shortly after his luncheon with JFK on 22 March. It was his way of reinforcing the point that Kennedy was beholden to him, that any time he wished to he could threaten the president with public exposure.[49]

It was at this moment in the spring of 1962 that Kennedy's private life reached crisis point. His ill-judged affair with Campbell had not only brought him dangerously close to the Mob but had also increased Hoover's power over him. After Hoover's intervention Kennedy had less contact with Campbell. But they stayed in touch. According to her interview with *Vanity Fair*, she visited him one last time in the White House. They made love. She became pregnant. When she phoned to tell him, Kennedy said, 'What are you going to do?' before correcting himself: 'I'm sorry. What are *we* going to do?' He asked if she wanted to keep the baby, and said that it was 'an option…. We can arrange it'. With his high profile and the FBI's interest in them, she did not think having the child was a good idea. She claimed that Kennedy called her back later to suggest she ask Giancana to arrange the abortion. Giancana was enraged by Kennedy's cavalier conduct, and said she could keep Kennedy's child and that he would marry her. So moved was she by Giancana's concern that she made love to the Mob boss that evening, for the one and only time in their relationship. Giancana arranged the abortion for

Campbell at Chicago's Grant Hospital in January 1963. After that she saw JFK only once more.[50]

Too many historians have fallen into one of two traps when considering the significance of Kennedy's affair with Campbell: some writers have devoted little attention to her, apparently on the grounds that this was a personal matter fundamentally unrelated to his presidency; others have simply believed everything she said, including her role as courier between JFK and the Mob, despite the inconsistencies in her various accounts and the implausibility of some of her claims. The sounder approach is to treat this as a serious matter as an affair between a president and a woman close to the Mafia constituted that, but to evaluate the reliability of the available evidence with due care and attention. Adopting that approach, it should be concluded that her claim to have passed correspondence and set up meetings between JFK and Mob leaders is unconvincing. Nevertheless, an affair lasting more than two years, when he was presidential candidate and then president, undoubtedly did take place. That left him vulnerable to blackmail by Giancana and increased Hoover's sway over him. And that was bad enough.

Whereas Kennedy's affair with Judith Campbell exposed his connections to the Mafia, his relationship with Mary Meyer raises another important character issue, one which had potentially grave consequences – his drug use. His affair with her had other intriguing dimensions to it. She was interested in politics, especially international affairs, and yearned for a world of peace rather than Cold War tensions. Historians have speculated on whether she influenced the progressive thrust of his foreign policy in 1963, including his American University speech and Nuclear Test Ban Treaty. As her ex-husband Cord Meyer was a senior CIA official and as she was gunned down in Washington, a year after JFK's slaying, in what appeared to be a clinical assassination, the Kennedy–Meyer affair also raises the issue of the secret state's role in keeping tabs on his life. Furthermore, this relationship is important to Kennedy's emotional history, for this *was* a true love affair. In that sense this was the most important affair of his presidential years. He may have loved Mary Meyer more than any woman, including possibly Jackie Kennedy, since his wartime relationship with Inga Arvad.

Part of the reason for the intensity of his feelings for Meyer was the fact that their affaire de coeur was the culmination of an intermittent, but quarter-century-long, flirtation. There was also a strong sense of sympatico. They were of the same generation, from the same upper-class background, with many of the same friends. At the same time there was always something of the bohemian about Meyer, despite her Establishment credentials, that was apparent in her work as an avant-garde artist and her curiosity about drugs as a means to self-enlightenment. For Kennedy, the unconventional no doubt made Meyer a touch uncontrollable and thus more alluring. Also the fact that she loved him knowing what he was, a playboy with self-gratification top of his personal agenda, created a depth to their relationship and his feelings for her. This was quite unlike those many other affairs where a mistress remained oblivious to his philandering with other women.

The teenage Kennedy met Mary Pinchot, a beautiful, elegant blonde from a family on the social register, at a winter dance at Choate School in 1936. Her date for the evening, William 'Bill' Attwood, was vexed to discover he had a rival for her affections. As he was dancing with her, JFK 'cut in' – tapping him on the shoulder and replacing Attwood as her dancing partner. He continued to 'cut in' to dance with her throughout the evening. He was clearly smitten.[51]

In the years which followed Mary Pinchot endured the suicide of her half-sister Rosamund, broke with her critical and abusive father, and attended Vassar College where she displayed an independent streak and a penchant for the arts. As he dated various women who were Pinchot's contemporaries at Vassar, Kennedy remained part of the social world she inhabited. She met and married Cord Meyer. Although he would later become a senior official at the CIA, he was – when she met him – an idealist desperate for world peace. Mary encountered JFK again at the 1945 San Francisco conference which launched the United Nations. She accompanied her husband who was part of the American delegation; Kennedy attended as a journalist for the Hearst newspapers. Kennedy was as attracted to Mary as he had been a decade earlier at that Choate dance. Noticing JFK's interest in his wife, a furious Meyer snubbed him by refusing an interview with the young Bostonian for an article he was writing.[52]

As Cord Meyer began to do the dirty work of the Cold War for the CIA in the 1950s, his idealistic values changed and this drove a wedge between himself and Mary. On a trip to Europe in 1954 with her sister Tony, she had an affair. In the fall of 1956 she told her husband that she wanted a divorce. Her increasing sense of independence was apparent from her interest in the contemporary art scene. She took lessons and began to paint.[53]

By 1957 Mary Meyer had settled in Georgetown, only a few blocks from the new home of Jack and Jackie Kennedy. When she headed to Nevada a year later to finalize her divorce, JFK asked if Pamela Turnure, who had worked in his Senate office, could stay at her house. Knowing that Turnure must have been his mistress, as she indeed was, the broad-minded Meyer agreed.[54]

The Turnure episode contributed to Meyer's view of Kennedy as a self-indulgent playboy. One source told author Leo Damore that 'Mary had been aware of Jack's womanizing since college. She wasn't interested in becoming another notch on Jack's gun. She was a serious person of quality, not frivolity. He had always been enamored by her, but she saw through his superficiality with women, and he knew it, though she always admitted to some remote attraction to him'. However, Meyer's then lover, artist Kenneth Noland, suspected she rendezvoused with JFK in the summer of 1959 at a cabin she had rented in Provincetown, Massachusetts. One source disclosed that JFK revealed his marital problems and that she scolded him with a candour (that was characteristic of her) for his philandering. 'At one point, Mary said he was almost in tears,' the source added. 'He was so unhappy, and alone, she told me. Mary wasn't about to get involved with him then, though she told me she held him tenderly that day.' Apparently nothing sexual occurred.[55]

The information we have about the affair which took place between Meyer and Kennedy during his presidency comes chiefly from a 1976 *National Enquirer* article. That would seem a disreputable outlet for such an important revelation, but in fact the source who gave the *Enquirer* the vital information for this piece, James

Truitt – a respected journalist and ex-vice president of the *Washington Post* – was perfectly credible. Truitt, along with his wife Anne, had been good friends of Meyer who confided in them about her affair with JFK. The conscientious journalist that he was, Truitt took copious and precise notes of what she said.[56]

According to Truitt, Mary Meyer rejected a sexual advance from Kennedy at a White House dinner-dance on the evening of 11 November 1961. But on 22 January 1962, with Jackie away at the Virginia estate Glen Ora, Meyer became his lover. Her frequent visits to the White House in the summer and fall of 1962, as revealed by White House logs, suggest Kennedy and Meyer made full use of the opportunity afforded by the three-month vacation that Jackie took. In addition to her private White House meetings with JFK, Meyer attended numerous dinner dances, luncheons and small dinner parties given by the Kennedys at 1600 Pennsylvania Avenue. Jack and Mary also enjoyed secret trysts in Georgetown at her home and the house of JFK's journalist friend Joseph Alsop. There is an alternative chronology to the Meyer–Kennedy romance. Ken O'Donnell, who was very close to Kennedy, told Leo Damore that Meyer came to the White House shortly after the inauguration, and frequently thereafter in 1961. Her entry to the White House was recorded in the Secret Service logs as 'Dave Powers plus one'. There are numerous such entries throughout 1961. So perhaps the affair had started in the first year of his presidency, though the more reasonable conclusion is that Truitt's chronology, as it was based on Meyer's own account, is accurate.[57]

Much more than Judy Campbell or Marilyn Monroe, or indeed any of his lovers during his time in the White House, Kennedy's affair with Meyer had meaningful depth. Meyer's status in Kennedy's presidential life was different to that of any of his other lovers. She was far more visible; he did not seek to conceal her importance to him. She was 'almost part of the furniture', according to White House counsel Myer Feldman. Kennedy would discuss policy with her. When he was ready to resume atmospheric nuclear testing in spring 1962, she challenged his decision, encouraging him to avoid a spiralling arms race with Russia. He also showed an emotional dependence on her that was absent from his other presidential affairs. When he could not reach her by phone, he was observed pacing 'feverishly' around the Oval Office.[58]

The truth was profound: Kennedy loved Mary Meyer. The evidence for this is substantial and persuasive. First, journalist Charles Bartlett, a Kennedy friend who had introduced him to Jackie, told Mary Meyer biographer Peter Janney: 'That was a dangerous relationship. Jack was in love with Mary Meyer. He was certainly smitten by her, he was heavily smitten. He was very frank with me about it, that he thought she was absolutely great.' Second, Ken O'Donnell revealed to Damore the depth of Kennedy's feelings for Meyer. 'Jack confided to Kenny he was deeply in love with Mary,' said Damore, 'that after he left the White House he envisioned a future with her and would divorce Jackie.' Third, an unsent note written by JFK to Meyer a month before his assassination, which surfaced at a 2016 auction, showed his tender feelings for her: 'Why don't you leave suburbia for once – come and see me – either here – or at the Cape next week or in Boston on the 19th. I know it is unwise, irrational, and that you may hate it – on the other hand you may not – and

I will love it. You say that it is good for me not to get what I want. After all of these years – you should give me a more loving answer than that. Why don't you just say yes.'[59]

How did Meyer succeed in eliciting not only Kennedy's lust, in ample supply with lots of other women, but his love? Part of the answer does lie with her true understanding of what Kennedy was: an emotionally complex and brazenly promiscuous man. That understanding was due in part to how she brought to bear a kind of therapeutic but critical empathy when he opened up to her. There is the account of their rendezvous in Provincetown in 1959 when he spoke of his marital unhappiness, and she both scolded him for his womanizing and, as he was close to tears, held him tenderly. That unsent October 1963 note, in which Kennedy cited her argument that he should not always get what he wanted, suggests she did not always do his bidding. Her willingness to hold up a mirror to his true nature, warts and all, was implicit in his comment at a February 1962 White House dinner-dance to his journalist friend and Meyer's brother-in-law Ben Bradlee that 'Mary would be rough to live with'. Rough, presumably, because she challenged and criticized rather than mollycoddled him. Kennedy's comment was significant too in a literal sense: he had obviously given thought to what it would be like to live with her.[60]

The most notorious aspect of Kennedy's affair with Meyer was their use of drugs. According to what Meyer told Truitt, they smoked marijuana at the White House on the evening of 16 July 1962. When she brought out a box containing six marijuana cigarettes, JFK said: 'Let's try it.' Sitting on the bed together, Kennedy initially felt nothing but then started to laugh, observing, 'We're having a White House conference on narcotics here in two weeks!' After sharing a second joint with her he lay down for a long time with his eyes closed and then said that he was hungry. He went to get soup and chocolate. Then they shared a third joint. But he declined a fourth. 'No more,' he told her. 'Suppose the Russians did something now!' 'This isn't like cocaine,' he added. 'I'll get you some of that.' A month later Kennedy said he wanted to smoke pot with her again, but it never happened.[61]

In addition to smoking pot with Meyer on this occasion, it has been alleged that they 'took a mild acid [LSD] trip together, during which they made love'. That claim was made by CIA counterintelligence chief Jim Angleton in an interview which C. David Heymann says he gave for his biography of Jackie Kennedy. But no record of this Heymann–Angleton interview exists, and the allegation of Kennedy's acid use with Meyer cannot be verified. It is instructive to note that drug guru Timothy Leary, who claimed to have mentored Meyer, said he did not know that Meyer took LSD in the White House with Kennedy – meaning Meyer had never told him this was the case. Just as historians should be careful in accepting at face value all of Judy Campbell's claims, so they should refrain from believing all of the rumours surrounding his affair with Mary Meyer.[62]

As with his adulteries, Kennedy's drug use must be put in its proper historical context. He had affairs knowing the press culture of the day meant that journalists would not report his indiscretions and hence his trysts were essentially a political irrelevance. With the issue of drug use, it should be recalled that the disapproval of narcotics that became widespread in later years was not so entrenched at the time of Kennedy's election as president. In a magazine article the year before Hollywood legend Cary Grant had extolled the virtues of LSD as a promoter of self-enlightenment and inner peace. The general view of drugs as a social evil, and indeed the explicit criminality of drug use on the statute books, followed the Kennedy years and therefore could not have influenced JFK's thinking.[63]

That is not to dismiss Kennedy's drug use as irrelevant to an examination of his presidency or to condone it. It was ill-advised as anything that could compromise the lucidity of his thinking is of concern. But to contextualize his conduct in the prevailing attitudes of the early 1960s does call into question to some degree his apparent recklessness. In that sense, was his one-off use of marijuana of any greater concern than Richard Nixon's more regular heavy drinking as president?[64]

Kennedy's infamous relationship with Dr Max Jacobson should be viewed in the same light: it was ill-advised but needs to be understood not only in terms of contemporary attitudes towards drug use but also Kennedy's ill-health. His friend Charles Spalding introduced him to Jacobson, known for the state of mind his treatments induced as 'Dr Feelgood', during the 1960 campaign. Jacobson treated him for stress, and beginning in spring 1961 the young president began to see Jacobson frequently, sometimes several times a week. For instance, JFK requested the eccentric doctor's services before his meetings with French leader Charles de Gaulle and Khrushchev as he had hurt his back during a tree-planting ceremony in Canada. It is reputed that Jacobson treated him during such events as the 1962 University of Mississippi civil rights crisis.[65]

The reason why Kennedy's relationship with Jacobson is controversial is because of the nature of those treatments: he gave Kennedy injections of 'speed' (amphetamines) and steroids. From a medical point of view, Jacobson's approach was as unwise as it appears. Small wonder he was never affiliated with the American Medical Association, and that in 1975 the New York Board of Medicine revoked his license.[66]

For Kennedy, his motivation was clear and to some extent understandable. His Addison's disease and back problems often left him in considerable pain, and so to live for the first time a pain-free existence, at least for periods of time, was for him a blessed relief. What may well have enlarged Kennedy's sense that using Jacobson's services was a good idea was the fact that his patients included many other distinguished individuals, from Winston Churchill to playwright Tennessee Williams. In addition, Jackie Kennedy became a patient, and JFK knew that his wife was invariably careful, not reckless, in personal matters.[67]

What did reflect poorly on JFK's judgement was the way he disregarded warnings from reputable sources about Jacobson. Bobby Kennedy was concerned enough to send Jacobson's medications to FBI scientists who reported a high concentration of speed and steroids, an assessment confirmed by the Food and Drug Administration. JFK was unmoved by what should have been troubling news. 'I don't care if it's horse piss,' he said. 'It works.'[68]

Kennedy's dealings with Jacobson were like some other facets of his private life, such as his relationships with Judy Campbell and Ellen Rometsch, where there was a clear distinction between the actual and potential damage done to his presidency. A convincing case cannot be made that his use of Jacobson's speed–steroid concoctions had any discernible impact on his decision-making. For instance, his handling of the University of Mississippi crisis was generally adept. But given the addictive nature of these drugs, there was a conceivable scenario whereby Jacobson's treatments rendered him unfit to be president. Consider the fate of Mark Shaw, another Jacobson patient. The celebrated photographer for *Life* magazine died at forty-seven with a suspected heart attack. When the autopsy was carried out, however, no sign of heart disease could be identified. What was discovered was a coating of amphetamines on Shaw's organs and heavy scarring of his veins. That could have been John Kennedy's story.[69]

As well as the issue of Kennedy's drug use raised by his affair with Mary Meyer, there is also the question of whether she influenced the progressive thrust of his final year in the White House. The case can be made – as I have in this work – that after a generally hard-line approach to the Cold War and a cautious approach to civil rights, Kennedy changed after the missile crisis to prioritize peace and equal rights, with his test ban treaty and civil rights bill as examples of that. It makes sense to view the Kennedy presidency in this way as a story of change and growth.

What has been claimed by some is that Mary Meyer influenced this shift in Kennedy's political thinking. Meyer's biographer Peter Janney argues that the progressive politics promoted by the president was influenced by his lover and their shared hallucinatory experiences: 'If some part of his [political] transformation was catalysed by a horizon-altering psychedelic excursion with Mary Meyer, then so be it. He wouldn't have been the first iconic figure in human history to partake, nor would he be the last. Stepping out of the proverbial box of normal perception … has, in fact, changed the course of events and perspectives for many respected notables.'[70]

Strengthening the inclination to gauge Meyer's influence on Kennedy in this way is the evidence presented by drug guru Timothy Leary. In his 1983 memoir *Flashbacks*, he claimed that Meyer showed up, unannounced, at his Harvard University office in April 1962, and asked his advice on 'how to run an LSD session' as she had a friend who was 'a very important man' and 'wants to try it himself'. She explained that she wanted to use drugs in this way to promote world peace. 'I've heard [Beat poet] Allen Ginsberg on radio and TV shows,' she allegedly told Leary, 'saying that if Khrushchev and Kennedy would take LSD together they'd end world conflict'. This, claimed Leary, was the first of several meetings with Meyer in which she picked his brains on how women from Washington's social elite could run LSD sessions in order to influence senior political figures. Viewed in this way, Kennedy's peace overtures in 1963 came only after and thus could have been influenced by the Meyer–Leary plot to 'turn on' political leaders, including JFK.[71]

So guided by Leary, did Meyer supervise psychedelic sessions that altered Kennedy's mindset and put him on the path to brotherly love and world peace? Once again, the evidence must be considered circumspectly. No one has ever verified Leary's claims about his dealings with Meyer. Leary's biographer Robert Greenfield has said *Flashbacks* is not wholly accurate. Put bluntly, historians should resist the temptation to regard as reliable the evidence of a man who for much of the time was 'off his head'. His reliability is also called into question by his failure even to mention Meyer in his earlier books. Perhaps the final word on his soundness as a source in terms of his own ability to recall the past easily in a complete, unbroken fashion is provided by Leary himself in the title of his memoir: *Flashbacks*. As with aspects of Judy Campbell's story, the accuracy of Leary's version of events should not be assumed. In this case the dubious reliability of the source and lack of corroborating evidence means Leary's claims must be regarded as spurious.[72]

It makes more sense to interpret Kennedy's peace overtures in 1963 in the context of his ongoing reflections on international affairs in light of his own political and not personal experiences. In particular, it was the visceral experience of striving to prevent the Third World War during the Cuban missile crisis that convinced him of the dire need to reduce Cold War tensions. To attribute the important changes in Kennedy's leadership of the nation to Leary's incredible claims is to trivialize JFK's mature engagement with world affairs, and his commendable open-mindedness in reviewing his approach to the Cold War and changing his rhetoric and policies accordingly.

It may well have been the case that Kennedy's affair with Meyer was winding down by 1963 anyway. In January 1963 the hard-drinking owner of *The Washington Post* Philip L. Graham blurted out in public at a Phoenix dinner for the Associated Press board of directors that Kennedy was sleeping with Meyer. Soon afterwards Graham was hospitalized. A few months later he committed suicide. It may have been the case that following Graham's indiscretion, even though newspapers had not reported it, Kennedy and Meyer, or one of them, decided it best to end the romance. At the very least the friendship remained, as Meyer continued to see Kennedy socially and at the White House. Oddly, at Kennedy's funeral on 25 November 1963 Meyer, according to her sister Tony, 'didn't seem very upset. It puzzled me'.[73]

In sexual affairs, there has long been talk of femme fatales. But Kennedy was the ultimate homme fatale. Witty, charming, attentive he may have been, but for so many women the consequences of their love for him were catastrophic. For Jackie Kennedy, she had to cope with the humiliation of his constant infidelity. Judy Campbell spent the rest of her life with a gun under her pillow, fearful that her intimate knowledge of Kennedy and the Mob had put her life in danger. Mimi Beardsley's confession of her affair with Kennedy to her fiancé doomed her subsequent marriage. Another Kennedy lover, West German Ellen Rometsch, was thrown out of the country. But the greatest price may well have been paid by Mary Meyer. Eleven months after JFK's assassination, she was murdered on 12 October 1964, as she walked along the Chesapeake and Ohio Canal towpath in the nation's capital. She was heard shouting out: 'Someone help me.' In an eerily clinical, professional manner, she was shot twice – once to the head, and once to the shoulder blade. That second shot ripped into her aorta, cutting off the blood flow to her heart. The lingering suspicion is that this was an intelligence operation aimed at silencing the woman with secret and troubling knowledge of the private Kennedy that had been recorded in a diary that would subsequently be confiscated.[74]

Kennedy's affair with Meyer is important to a personal history of his presidency. The extent of his drug-taking with her may well have been exaggerated, and certainly Timothy Leary's claims should be disregarded. The notion that Meyer was responsible for Kennedy's more conciliatory policies towards Moscow in the final months of his presidency is fanciful too. But she *was* important because Kennedy loved her far more than his other presidential mistresses. In understanding President Kennedy the man, that is important enough.

As with so many of his lovers, Marilyn Monroe paid a high price for her fling with John Kennedy: together with her affair with Bobby Kennedy, it can have only deepened the emotional instability that helped bring about her death in the summer of 1962. Monroe was JFK's most famous mistress. For the public she is the first name that springs to mind when Kennedy's long list of lovers is considered. Indeed the Kennedy–Monroe affair has become one of the best-known stories in twentieth-century popular culture.

The details of that affair are contested. To a great extent Monroe's biographers have relied on interviews, conducted decades after her death in 1962, in constructing her life story, including her relationship with JFK. The differences in the various accounts of Kennedy's relationship with Monroe relate not least to the question of timing – namely, when did their affair begin? Despite this and other points of dispute, the weight of evidence makes clear that this affair – despite the occasional denial by some writers – *did* take place.[75]

The historical significance of Kennedy's dalliance with Monroe lies chiefly in the way it shaped his public image. The identity of Kennedy's other presidential mistresses – not knowledge of these affairs, but simply the existence of these women – was largely unknown to the American people. Marilyn Monroe, however, was, along with Elizabeth II, the most famous woman in the world. What she did in public, including her dealings with Kennedy, mattered as the media reported her activities obsessively to a public with an insatiable appetite for stories about her. Specifically, her performance of 'Happy Birthday' at Kennedy's 19 May 1962 birthday celebration at Madison Square Garden was important for the way it bolstered his own image as a sex symbol. Other implications of his affair with the Hollywood star can be considered. Biographer Anthony Summers, for instance, has speculated on whether the affair of not only JFK but also Bobby Kennedy with Monroe left the Kennedy brothers vulnerable to blackmail by the Mob. Nevertheless, the unique feature of JFK's affair with Monroe was her remarkable celebrity and connection with him in the public sphere, and this can be said despite his probable flings with other actresses such as Angie Dickinson and Jayne Mansfield.[76]

Though it will be a bitter pill for the millions who still idolize Marilyn Monroe, Kennedy's liaison with her was insignificant in terms of his emotional history. This was not like his relationship with Mary Meyer, which was a genuine love affair. With Marilyn Monroe, the evidence suggests that while she attached great importance to the affair, Kennedy did not. For him, she was a fantasy sexual experience, but nothing more than that. That was in spite of the fact that he had lusted after her for years before becoming her lover.

Since the early 1950s JFK salivated over Marilyn as did millions of other Americans after the publication of a nude picture of her in the first issue of *Playboy* magazine. In autumn 1954 he was confined to a hospital bed following his back surgery. Easing his recovery was a poster of Monroe in blue shorts stuck on the wall upside down so that her legs, spread wide, were up in the air in an erotically provocative manner.[77]

Some suggest that Kennedy's affair with Monroe started in the 1950s during his trips to the West Coast. But many of her biographers say the affair began in the early 1960s, certainly by 1961 and possibly during the presidential campaign. Kennedy's brother-in-law, the British actor and Rat-Pack member Peter Lawford, played the key role in facilitating the Kennedy–Monroe affair. His third wife Deborah Gould revealed that Lawford had told her 'Jack … had always wanted to meet Marilyn Monroe; it was one of his fantasies. Could Peter arrange for that? He did – he would do anything he was asked to do'. Thereafter Kennedy's assignations with Marilyn often took place at Lawford's Santa Monica home. His wife Patricia liked the vulnerable actress and in 1960 had begun to invite her to their beach house. The other setting for their trysts was Kennedy's Big Apple base, the Carlyle Hotel. There is no record of him meeting her at the White House, which makes sense as her celebrity would have sparked rumours that he would have wanted to avoid.[78]

Kennedy fascinated Monroe. Part of it was his good looks and winning personality, qualities prized by any Hollywood star. 'She was so impressed by Kennedy's charm and charisma,' said one Kennedy aide who observed them together at close quarters, 'that she was almost starry-eyed.' During the 1960 campaign she told British journalist W. J. Weatherby that it would be very satisfying to have a young, handsome leader in the White House should Kennedy win.[79]

Kennedy impressed Marilyn with not only his star quality but also his gifts as a political leader. Ever since her marriage to playwright Arthur Miller she had been interested in politics. Her views were on the Left, identifying with the poor, impassioned about civil rights, and troubled by the nuclear arms race. She wanted Kennedy to defeat Nixon, and was thrilled when he did so. Thereafter Weatherby, who continued to see Marilyn, was struck by her enthusiasm for Kennedy's presidency. When he questioned JFK's support for Martin Luther King around the time of his inauguration, she rebuked him: 'The President will go all the way…. You just wait and see.' 'I think he's going to be another Lincoln,' she told Weatherby on another occasion. Deference as well as admiration characterized her view of JFK. 'Marilyn Monroe is a soldier,' she told her psychiatrist. 'Her Commander in Chief is the greatest and most powerful man in the world. The first duty of a soldier is to obey her Commander in Chief. He says "do this." He says "do that." You do that.'[80]

For his part, Kennedy's feelings for Marilyn were less profound. He was 'very fond' of her, an associate recalled, and he was very attracted to her. But there is nothing to suggest any greater emotional involvement. An account of his approach to lovemaking with her is suggestive. According to reporter James Bacon, who knew Marilyn well, 'She said he wouldn't indulge in foreplay, because he was on the run all the time.' Even Mimi Beardsley had more fun with JFK than that. And if his performance in bed with Marilyn was that perfunctory, she probably resorted to the strategy she had employed for most of her sexual life: faking orgasms. She once told her psychiatrist: 'Speaking of Oscars, I would win overwhelmingly if the Academy gave an Oscar for faking orgasms. I have done some of my best acting convincing my partners I was in the throes of ecstasy.'[81]

If privately it meant little more to him than another notch on his belt, Kennedy's association with Marilyn was important for its impact on his image. Her rendition of 'Happy Birthday' at Madison Square Garden served to enhance his own sex-symbol status. A procession of stars performed for the president that night, including Maria Callas and Ella Fitzgerald, but Marilyn stole the show.

Figure 6.1 John and Robert Kennedy chat with Marilyn Monroe at a New York party following her famous rendition of 'Happy Birthday' on the occasion of JFK's birthday celebrations at Madison Square Garden in May 1962. His affair with her would contribute to the emphasis placed by some historians on his private life and character. (*Source*: Wikimedia, public domain, Search media – Wikimedia Commons.)

Her impact on the audience, posterity and JFK's image was due in large part to the dress she wore. Made by the celebrated designer Jean Louis, it aimed at showcasing the most famous body in the world in the most striking, alluring way possible. 'It was nude,' said the designer, 'very thin material, embroidered with rhinestones, so she would shine in the spotlight. She wore nothing, absolutely nothing, underneath.' In fact modesty demanded a body stocking. So figure-hugging was the dress that she needed to be sewn into it.[82]

Introduced by Peter Lawford, a tipsy Monroe tiptoed towards the podium. Kennedy watched his lover from the presidential box, smoking a cigar. At the podium Marilyn removed her ermine jacket. The audience audibly gasped. With the dress flesh-coloured and her voluptuous, hour-glass figure so conspicuous, they thought – at least for a second or two – that she was naked. With his intimate knowledge of her body Kennedy certainly enjoyed the illusion. But she did too. As a child she had fantasized about being nude before her admirers, in public, without shame. To the Madison Square Garden crowd, she looked stunning. Simply put, she was the embodiment of sex.[83]

Her vocal performance accentuated her erotic impact. 'Happy birthday, Mr.Pres-id-ent' might sound trivial and erotically neutral but not in the sensual, breathy, suggestive style in which she sang the words. She added some lyrics, penned by Richard Adler, which referenced his political battle with U.S. Steel, before encouraging the crowd to join her in a reprisal of 'Happy Birthday'. Coming to the microphone, a charming, ironic Kennedy announced: 'I can now retire from politics after having had 'Happy Birthday' sung to me in such a sweet, wholesome way.' Marilyn's performance elicited much comment from the print media. 'The figure was famous,' reported *Time* magazine. 'And for one breathless moment, the 15,000 people in Madison Square Garden thought they were going to see all of it.'[84]

Monroe's celebrated performance at Madison Square Garden bolstered Kennedy's image as a sex symbol. The dynamic of having the world's greatest sex symbol using her body and talents as an artist for JFK's pleasure added to his allure. His own beauty and glamour made him appear a worthy recipient of her attentions. The sense conveyed by her performance for him was the appropriate linking of two stars.

After the concert John and Bobby Kennedy attended a party at the home of movie producer Arthur Krim, as did Marilyn Monroe. Bobby, Adlai Stevenson and Arthur Schlesinger competed for her attentions. When he saw the Kennedys and Marilyn, the official White House photographer took a picture. It is the only photograph of JFK and Monroe together. As the photographer clicked, the president turned away so that his face was largely concealed. The picture makes one thing clear: Kennedy had something to hide.[85]

In the final year of his presidency, the Kennedy affair most fraught with danger was the one he conducted with a prostitute: Ellen Rometsch. Despite the protection afforded by a deferential Fourth Estate, his fling with Rometsch almost did become public knowledge. It also increased his dependence on J. Edgar Hoover. Most troublingly, the Rometsch affair highlighted the risks to US national security entailed by his playboy lifestyle.

These national-security implications were due to Rometsch's backstory, about which Kennedy was ignorant when he began to use her services that, he would divulge, included the best oral sex he had ever received. Married to a West German air-force sergeant working in Washington for the German Embassy, Rometsch had evidently become dissatisfied with her husband's economic status and so became an upmarket prostitute servicing Washington's movers and shakers, including John Kennedy. What JFK did not know was that Rometsch came not from West Germany but what, by the time she was a young girl, was Communist East Germany. She joined two Communist Party organizations before leaving for the West in 1955. As sexual compromise was a standard espionage technique, Rometsch's relationship with Kennedy raises an important issue: Was she a communist spy and hence did JFK's affair with her threaten national security?[86]

Rometsch came to Kennedy's attention because of his friendships with railroad executive and fellow playboy Bill Thompson and Secretary to the Senate Democrats Bobby Baker whose ethical sense did not preclude securing federal contracts for friends or attractive young women for politicians. Baker had supplied JFK with women during his time as a Massachusetts senator. Shortly after becoming president, a candid Kennedy informed Baker that 'I get a migraine headache if I don't get a strange piece of ass every day'. Baker was happy to continue providing Kennedy with women when in the spring of 1963 at his base of operations in Washington, the Quorum Club, Thompson asked: 'who is that good-looking girl? That woman looks like Elizabeth Taylor.' Baker explained that she was a German whose husband worked at the German Embassy, and that all the men who used her services had been more than satisfied. When Thompson asked if she would be willing to meet the president, Baker assured him she would. So it was that Thompson collected Rometsch from her apartment and escorted her to the White House. Both the president and the prostitute reported to Baker on the encounter that ensued. She described Kennedy as a 'really fun guy and [said] how delighted she was to be with him'. He told Baker 'she was the most exciting woman that he had been with'. The reasons for his satisfaction with her were not hard to fathom: she was an immaculately dressed, well mannered, carnally skilled, sexy, stunning brunette. Kennedy requested her services on at least ten occasions. Sometimes these encounters took place as part of what were essentially White House orgies; Rometsch told Baker of naked pool parties there attended by numerous men but many more women.[87]

Before the Rometsch affair came close to exposing Kennedy's womanizing, another story almost revealed his private recklessness to the world: the Profumo scandal. John Profumo, Harold Macmillan's Minister of War, had been sleeping with a young woman Christine Keeler, who had also been having an affair with Russian naval attaché Yevgeny Ivanov. An issue of great concern was whether Profumo had disclosed national security secrets to Ivanov via Keeler. In June 1963 this story was reported in the press, scandalizing the British public and so tarnishing the reputation of Macmillan's government that the prime minister resigned four months later.[88]

Kennedy devoured every detail of the Profumo scandal as it unfolded. Ben Bradlee observed that 'It combined so many things that interested him: low doings in high places, the British nobility, sex, and spying'. He soon instructed the US ambassador at the Court of St. James, David Bruce, to send all of his cables on the affair directly to him. 'His cables are just fantastic,' said a prurient president to Bradlee.[89]

Kennedy's interest in the scandal was heightened by the fact that two prostitutes connected him to Profumo: a Chinese woman Suzy Chang and a blonde Czech Maria Novotny. They had attended parties with Profumo and Keeler, but had also known JFK socially and biblically. Prior to the presidency he had dined with Chang at the New York restaurant 21. According to Novotny's subsequent disclosures, she and Chang had been hired to have sex with Kennedy both before and after the November 1960 election. When the names of Chang and Novotny were reported in press accounts of the Profumo affair, JFK must have been troubled by the possibility that he would become embroiled in the scandal should journalists find out that he had slept with prostitutes who knew Profumo.[90]

To check whether a link had been established between Kennedy and those individuals who were part of the Profumo affair, J. Edgar Hoover ordered the FBI legal attaché in London, Charles Bates, to find out whether allegations were being made about the involvement of any Americans. CIA director McCone instructed the CIA station in London to do the same thing. One CIA official there said he had learned from the FBI that the White House was behind the order from Hoover to look into the Profumo affair. The CIA's Deputy Chief of Station in London worked alongside MI5 on Profumo, but fortunately he unearthed no evidence linking any senior US official to the scandal.[91]

Two American journalists, however, did learn of JFK's connection to Profumo. On 29 June 1963 an article by James D. Horan and Dom Frasca, entitled 'High U.S. Aide Implicated in V-Girl Scandal', appeared in the Hearst newspaper, the *New York Journal-American*. Horan and Frasca wrote that 'a man who holds a "very high" elective office' in the Kennedy administration had a fling with a 'Chinese girl' involved in the Profumo affair. Maria Novotny was quoted in support of this claim. Horan and Frasca had constructed this account on the basis of information from journalist Peter Earle of the *News of the World*, the British tabloid which had paid Novotny for her story. As a result of Bobby Kennedy's intervention, the Hearst paper pulled this story after only one edition. His cleaning-up operation included a meeting two days later with Horan and Frasca, in which he chided the two journalists for writing this incendiary story with – in his view – such little evidence.[92]

If JFK thought he had emerged that summer with his personal reputation unsullied by public scandal, he was soon disabused of that notion, for on 3 July Hoover told Bobby Kennedy that senior US government officials had been sexually involved with a woman, Ellen Rometsch, who was originally from Communist East Germany and had worked for East German leader Walter Ulbricht. The implication of JFK's involvement in this scandal would not have been lost on Bobby who alluded to rumours about Hoover's own sexuality by observing that 'there always are allegations about prominent people that they are either homosexuals or promiscuous'. Despite his apparent lack of concern, Robert Kennedy carefully noted down Rometsch's name and then took decisive action to protect his brother's reputation: on 21 August she was deported back to West Germany, following a State Department request. LaVern Duffy, who knew Bobby Kennedy well and was in love with Rometsch, escorted her. There is some evidence that suggests her subsequent silence – after more than half-a-century she has remained taciturn about her extraordinary Washington life in 1963 and her relationship with JFK – was bought with money, presumably at the behest of the Kennedys.[93]

Rometsch may have been out of the country, but she continued to pose a danger to John Kennedy. That fall the Bobby Baker scandal broke out. A media storm erupted over his dodgy financial dealings. His secret life at the Quorum Club as a procurer of women for politicians became known. The Senate Rules Committee started an investigation into Baker. The Republicans on the committee soon learned about Ellen Rometsch. Then on 26 October 1963 Clark Mollenhoff published a piece in the *Des Moines Register* reporting that the Rules Committee was about to investigate Rometsch and the strange story of her expulsion from the country. Mollenhoff also revealed that the committee would evaluate allegations that Rometsch had been involved with not only senators and staff but also 'several high executive branch officials'. Mollenhoff emphasized Rometsch's background in Communist East Germany, and the concern that her activities in Washington were espionage-related, especially as some of her sexual partners were of high rank.[94]

More than any of his other affairs, JFK's relationship with Rometsch threatened to smash through the barriers erected by traditional media discretion when it came to the private lives of the nation's leaders, and so alert the American people as to the true nature of his personal life. Once again he would rely on his brother to prevent that nightmare scenario from taking place. In this instance, however, he also needed the intervention of a man with whom his relations were frosty: J. Edgar Hoover. Bobby Kennedy spoke to Hoover aide Courtney Evans and then by phone and in person with Hoover, conveying the president's concern over the damage that could be caused by a congressional investigation into Rometsch. He asked for Hoover's help. In particular he requested that the FBI director meet with Mike Mansfield and Everett Dirksen, the Democratic and Republican leaders in the Senate, to urge them to abandon the investigation of Rometsch. Reluctantly Hoover obliged, and his intervention with Mansfield and Dirksen did the trick. As the Rometsch investigation was jettisoned, JFK's reputation was protected.[95]

That came at a price for the Rometsch affair increased Kennedy's dependence on Hoover. A key issue in the debate on Kennedy's character is whether his private life influenced his political role as president. In general it did not. He was reckless in his personal life; usually sensible and measured in his political life. But the Rometsch affair was one of the few instances when there was a connection between the two. He probably would have liked to dismiss the FBI director. On this his judgement was sound. Hoover was nothing less than one of the most corrupt, nefarious figures in the political life of twentieth-century America, as his despicable efforts to undermine Martin Luther King and the Civil Rights

Movement showed. But Kennedy most likely felt his hands were tied as Hoover had in his possession a substantial file on his own indiscretions, going all the way back to Inga Arvad. So he decided after the 1960 election to retain Hoover as his FBI director. Any freedom for manoeuvre in terms of JFK being able to remove Hoover was curtailed first of all by the director's knowledge of the JFK–Campbell affair and, second, by his reliance on Hoover for quashing the Rometsch story. For the first time in eight months JFK paid homage to Hoover by inviting him to lunch at the White House, no doubt to thank him for his vital help in this affair. Kennedy's indebtedness to Hoover was clear.[96]

For JFK, there were still loose ends to be tied. Congressional exposure of his relationship with Rometsch had been prevented, but there remained a chance that the media might spotlight it. To shape the story should the press report further on it, Kennedy indulged in a spot of media management by inviting his journalist-pal Ben Bradlee to a private dinner. He used the occasion to frame the Rometsch story in terms of indiscretions on Capitol Hill rather than in the White House. 'Boy, the dirt he [Hoover] has on those senators,' he told Bradlee. 'You wouldn't believe it.' He went on to say Hoover had brought along a photograph of Rometsch, which showed she was a 'really beautiful woman'. Misleadingly, Kennedy was implying he had never seen her in the flesh. One thing JFK said should have given Bradlee pause for thought: he kept referring to her as 'Elly', suggesting a personal knowledge of the woman that did not square with the rest of his account.[97]

The most important aspect of the Rometsch affair was the way it highlighted the risks run by Kennedy's presidential philandering to national security. Sexual compromise is and has long been a standard espionage technique, as Donald Trump is alleged to have discovered in a urinary encounter with prostitutes in a Moscow hotel room during the 2013 Miss Universe beauty pageant. Two years before Kennedy's election as president, Russian intelligence had arranged for the French ambassador in Moscow to be sexually compromised. Rometsch was almost certainly not a spy; Stasi files, available since the Berlin Wall came down, make no mention of her. That would seem improbable if she had been involved in espionage. But hailing from Communist East Germany, she could have been a spy. His sexual relationship with her showed therefore the dangers posed by his reckless private life. Along with his affair with the Mob-connected Judy Campbell, Ellen Rometsch represented the most serious misjudgement of his private life when president. For the way it ran the risk of endangering national security, it was the sequel to his affair with Inga Arvad two decades earlier.[98]

A Mafia moll, a Hollywood superstar, a German communist, a drug-taking artist, a teenage intern – small wonder that many Kennedy scholars have examined JFK's private life and character through the prism of his sexual conquests. But in that historians have erred, for in focusing on his affairs they have displayed the same obsession with sex that they attribute to Kennedy. That view of Kennedy the man, however, is narrow and unpersuasive. It obscures the complexity inherent in anyone's character. In other words, Kennedy's character comprised numerous traits, one of which was a penchant for sexual indulgence. But there was so much more to him than that. Not all of it was commendable. He could be petty, even vindictive. Note the malicious newspaper story he planted about Adlai Stevenson, only weeks after he had helped JFK in the missile crisis by defending at the United Nations America's stance against the Russian missile deployment in Cuba. Two years earlier he had tried to sully the reputation of his rival in the 1960 Democratic primaries, Hubert Humphrey, by pressuring Ben Bradlee to investigate his military service, or rather lack of it, during the Second World War.[99]

Yet there was much about Kennedy's character that impressed, and it is these admirable qualities that renders the idea of him as a 'bad man' who lacked a moral compass as an unsatisfying, two-dimensional caricature. Kennedy had courage. During the Second World War, his leadership of *PT 109* was valiant. That leadership helped save the lives of his crew. That courage, as well as stoicism, was evident in the way he dealt with life-threatening Addison's disease and spinal surgery. 'He had a tremendous amount of courage, never complaining [about the pain], always calm,' recalled one confidant. Courage was a virtue he had extolled in *Profiles in Courage*. He liked to cite Hemingway's definition of courage as 'grace under pressure'. In his private life, Kennedy exhibited courage himself.[100]

He also displayed personal growth. When he first arrived on Capitol Hill, he was a fairly indolent congressman who prioritized his active social life over his legislative responsibilities. As his congressional career unfolded, he became increasingly serious-minded and conscientious. Economist John Kenneth Galbraith, who knew and advised Kennedy during these years, noticed his growing sense of professional application. He said at first JFK would ask his advice on how to vote on economic legislation. After a time, he asked him to explain the background to the issues connected to legislation. Then there came a time when he no longer called as he had become so well informed he did not require Galbraith's academic expertise. As president, Kennedy remained diligent. That is not a presidential given, as Ronald Reagan's occasional laziness demonstrated.[101]

Contrary to what Thomas Reeves and others have argued, a strong sense of morality did guide Kennedy's approach to the presidency, and where it really mattered – public policy. Most political issues do not have a clear-cut morality. Take defence expenditures, for example. It could be argued that the ethical position on this would be to cut military spending so as not to escalate a dangerous arms race. On the other hand, it could be argued that given the horrors of communist rule apparent in the Soviet Union and China – tens of millions killed in the Purges and the Cultural Revolution – a stronger stance in the Cold War, including greater military preparedness on the part of the West, was the more ethical position.

There was one issue, however, that certainly did have a clear moral significance: civil rights. At root, it was a question of whether a leader believed in equality or not. More than any previous president in the twentieth century, Kennedy met that moral challenge. In his landmark 11 June 1963 address, he defined civil rights as not just a legal or political issue, but a moral one. In doing so – as argued earlier – he put his presidency on the line, as he knew the price to be paid: the loss of support from many white Southerners. This was a serious matter politically as his bid for re-election as president was only a year away.[102]

Compare the moral authority Kennedy brought to bear in June 1963 with the ethically questionable leadership provided by Dwight Eisenhower. After the 1956 presidential campaign he did not need to worry that a strong stance on civil rights would compromise his re-election prospects. It cannot be argued that civil rights was not high on the national agenda during the Eisenhower years, not after the 1954 Supreme Court decision against segregation in schools, the Montgomery Bus Boycott and the Little Rock crisis. The bottom line is that Eisenhower lacked the moral commitment to racial equality that Kennedy displayed in 1963. For Ike, it was not an urgent matter. He did not use his immense prestige and popularity to urge the American people to support civil rights. He was more concerned about not alienating his White Southern friends and his political allies by imposing change on the South than by the discrimination suffered by Black Americans. When it came to the profound moral test of civil rights, Eisenhower failed and Kennedy, ultimately, passed. This matter was so much more important than Kennedy's dalliances with Marilyn Monroe, Mimi Beardsley and his other mistresses. Those affairs affected the lives of usually two people, his wife and his lover. Civil rights affected the lives of millions, and the progress made in advancing equality was of fundamental importance to the very fabric of American society.[103]

JFK's commitment to civil rights revealed another Kennedy virtue: empathy. He came from a privileged background of wealth and social rank, but he was acutely aware of the discrimination suffered by Irish-Americans. His father had been excluded from the most prestigious clubs at Harvard due to his Irish-Catholic background. The anti-immigrant backlash of the 1920s against Irish Catholics had been severe. JFK's 1960 campaign, in which so much attention had been paid to the question of whether his Catholicism should disqualify him from the presidency, reminded him on the eve of his election as president of the force of irrational prejudice in American life. With the issue of Black equality, there was a strong sense with Kennedy that he had an empathetic understanding of the hurt caused by discrimination.[104]

Many of the major works on Kennedy since the 1970s, notably those by Garry Wills, Thomas Reeves and Seymour Hersh, have dwelt on his personal excesses in developing their harsh interpretations of his presidency. This effort to discredit Kennedy's historical reputation by attacking his private life and character must be rejected. His playboy lifestyle did not represent the totality of his character. He was also courageous, stoical, empathetic, increasingly conscientious and, in the stance he took at the end of his life on equal rights in America, *moral*. Moreover, there were very few ways in which his private conduct influenced his presidential role. He probably felt unable to sack Hoover because of the FBI director's knowledge of his affairs, including those with Judy Campbell and Ellen Rometsch. But the significance of that is limited, in a comparative sense, given that no president from the 1920s until Hoover's death in 1972 felt able to dismiss him. Kennedy's affair with Campbell is relevant to his policy on Cuba as the CIA sought to assassinate Castro by hiring Giancana, and she was seeing him as well as sleeping with JFK. But the inconsistencies in her accounts, her implausible claims and her commercial inducements to sensationalize mean that her more outlandish allegations about a frequent correspondence and numerous meetings between Kennedy and Giancana should be dismissed.

There was one occasion when Kennedy's womanizing did influence the way he met his responsibilities for national security. He once attended a party in New York to rendezvous with various women and in doing so became separated from his Secret Service agents who carried the codes needed to fire nuclear weapons. A Kennedy aide recalled, 'It suddenly hit me. Jack was off getting laid and the Bagman with the black satchel had been left behind. The Russians could have bombed us to hell and back, and there would have been nothing we could have done about it.' Apart from these rare instances, Kennedy's private life had little bearing on his presidency. A negative assessment of Kennedy that rests on the idea that his character was dreadful and that his personal life seriously damaged his presidency should be rejected.[105]

That position becomes even sounder when the hypothetical that his personal life influenced his presidency is tested. Doing so makes clear the disconnection between the public and private spheres of his life; for if he was as macho and reckless in public affairs as he was in his private conduct then why did he not use force to ensure Castro's overthrow when the Bay of Pigs invasion began to fail? Why did he always refuse to send troops to Vietnam, despite being urged to do so by a number of his top aides? Why did he reject a military strike on Cuba in favour of the more cautious approach of a blockade during the missile crisis? Kennedy's private conduct was risky. In his decision-making as president, he was careful and restrained.

If it is a disconnection that characterizes the relationship between Kennedy's private life and public role, in contrast to what many of his critics have claimed, why would that be the case? The reason why his personal and public behaviour were so different is that the roots of his conduct in these spheres were different. Formative familial experiences account for his treatment of women and risk-taking proclivities: his brazenly unfaithful, alpha-male father, his somewhat cold, distant mother and his heightened sense of mortality arising from a sequence of illnesses that began in childhood. His approach to policy, however, derived not from early psychological influences but from a lengthy intellectual process in which Kennedy dwelt on America's role in world affairs, dating back to the writing of *Why England Slept*, as well as domestic-policy issues. The process of refining his views as he reflected on public affairs continued throughout his presidency. The missile crisis modified his stance on the Cold War, and the Birmingham crisis changed his outlook on civil rights. This shift in his policies took place as his private behaviour remained unchanged, again suggesting a disconnect between his private life and his presidential leadership.

Despite all of this, Kennedy's private life did involve risk. Two affairs, in particular, were dangerous and misguided. His relationships with Mafia moll Judy Campbell and the former East German Communist Ellen Rometsch showed how he made himself vulnerable to blackmail from the Mob and hostile secret services from behind the 'iron curtain'. No actual damage to his presidency occurred, but it could have done – and that was a risk Kennedy should never have taken.

Historians have been right to highlight character in assessing John Kennedy's presidency. His character did matter. But it did not damage his presidency in the way his critics have claimed. Rather, it was precisely why he was such a fine president. The moral leadership he showed on civil rights in 1963 reflected an admirable sense of fairness and compassion. His excellent leadership in October 1962 in ending the most dangerous nuclear confrontation of the Cold War had been due to various impressive character traits, including the strength to stand up to his own generals. And the capacity he showed for reflection, change and growth over the course of his presidency was commendable too.

Chapter 7

HOLLYWOOD ALLURE

The coming of television to America in the 1950s had profound implications for the nation's politics: the *visual* mattered more than ever before. It always had made a difference. Cartoonists, photographers and artists had influenced the way the American people viewed a succession of presidents. But the impact of TV, with its capacity to transmit footage of a president into the households of tens of millions of Americans, was so much greater. This changed what was required for political success. It may have been the case that the lanky, lugubrious Abraham Lincoln, with his high-pitched voice, would have struggled to win a presidential election in the modern era. In the televisual age what would be ideal was a politician who looked like a movie star. John Kennedy fitted the bill perfectly.

JFK's unprecedented emphasis on image is apparent when comparing him to his predecessors in the White House, Harry Truman and Dwight Eisenhower. As implausible as it seems nowadays, Truman cared hardly a jot about crafting an appealing image of himself for the public. 'During his nearly eight-year presidency,' writes historian Sean Savage, 'Harry S. Truman seemed to be indifferent about his presidential image and status in public opinion polls.' As for Eisenhower, his image as a military hero was an important ingredient in his political success. But his attitude, for instance, towards televised press conferences was less enthusiastic than Kennedy's would be. The argument has been made that Eisenhower's often woeful syntax at news conferences was a deliberate strategy to confuse journalists, concealing his meaning and political purposes by speaking without clarity or coherence. There was an element of truth in that. But it was more the case that Eisenhower, despite his considerable intelligence, was less fluent and assured than Kennedy when sparring with the nation's scribes before the television cameras.[1]

The contrast between the appetite of Truman and Eisenhower on the one hand and JFK on the other for appearing on television was stark. That contrast reflected a broader difference between Kennedy and his presidential predecessors, namely the greater importance that he attached to image. As an element in the modern presidency, image could be viewed, by definition, as a superficial issue, reflecting on how a leader presents himself rather than what surely has to be the more important matter of the substance of his policies. That being the case, Kennedy could be criticized for paying too much attention to his own image.

This view of Kennedy's leadership is naïve and unpersuasive. It was to his credit that he grasped the ever-increasing importance of image in the televisual age. It reflected his political acumen. It was not Kennedy's fault that television transformed American popular culture after the Second World War. He had to deal with the world as it was. It was sensible that he pondered the implications of television for his life in politics. Again, it was to his credit that he worked hard at developing his performative skill in front of camera. Talented as he was in this regard, there was a learning curve for JFK. Footage from his 1952 Senate campaign shows him practising a statement for a television ad and – to his chagrin – getting it wrong time after time. The way he prioritized television performance as president, and his ability to make such a favourable impression in front of the cameras, showed his talent, diligence, prescience and sense of pragmatism. He deserves praise not censure for this.[2]

Image was indeed a crucial part of Kennedy's political success. His ability to construct a dazzling image as man of letters, war hero, sex symbol and symbol of the family had been a major factor in his political rise to the point where a presidential bid was feasible. Again, image was vital to his victory in the 1960 election, especially when considering the impact of the Kennedy–Nixon television debates.[3]

Despite his wafer-thin margin of victory over Nixon, Kennedy enjoyed high poll ratings throughout his presidency. In fact his average approval rating, 70.1 per cent, is higher than any other president in recorded history (since Harry Truman). Only two others, Eisenhower and George H.W. Bush, achieved an overall average of more than 60 per cent. Kennedy's high ratings were due in large part to a positive perception of his presidential performance. His adroit handling of the 1961 Berlin crisis and the Cuban missile crisis, for example, boosted his popularity. But it was not *just* a matter of policy. Note his remarkably high poll ratings even after the disastrous Bay of Pigs invasion and his failure to secure passage of some key pieces of legislation. This suggests that the way his image enchanted the American people was a major reason for his popularity.[4]

Kennedy's rise to power, election as president, popularity and therefore credibility in the White House, iconic status in death – none of this can be explained without consideration of his image. Hence image is not merely useful to a history of Kennedy's life in politics, it is indispensable. Biographies of him that say little on this subject are deficient.

That being the case, a key issue is *how* Kennedy succeeded in fashioning such a potent presidential image. A key part of his appeal was sex. This was an example where his private life was connected to his public role as president. It was his lover Judy Campbell who, in saying that Kennedy had sex appeal and knew it, articulated what many of the women who knew JFK personally thought. In the image he projected to the American people, it was a case of Kennedy transmitting, whether by photographic image or television footage or by other means, that same sex appeal.[5]

This was an example of Kennedy using the White House to enhance his pre-presidential image. From his first campaign in 1946, he had been viewed as a sex symbol. Before marrying Jackie he was described as the most eligible bachelor in the country, and in the 1950s he was judged to be the most attractive politician in Washington. The 1960 campaign had played a major role in bolstering his erotic credentials. Exposure in those television debates increased his allure. The atmosphere on the campaign trail after the first debate with Nixon was febrile, with reports of women swooning unexaggerated. He had become the Elvis of American politics.

The bully pulpit of the presidency, as Theodore Roosevelt famously described it, would be used by Kennedy to bolster support not only for his policies but for his image as well, including his sex-symbol status. A subjective matter, to be sure, but as an attractive man Kennedy was in an advantageous position to highlight his physical allure in the image he projected. But he worked at it too. He thought about his appearance no less than did Cary Grant. Recent presidents have often had advisers for this sort of thing, but Kennedy had no need for guidance on fashion. He acquired an encyclopedic knowledge on issues such as whether a well-dressed man should wear jackets with two buttons or three, the appropriate size of a jacket lapel, what colour sock should be worn in order to complement a particular suit. Small wonder that magazines such as *Esquire* published in-depth articles on Kennedy's taste in fashion. It was the sort of press coverage appropriate for a Hollywood actor or a model. But here it was being bestowed on the president of the United States, and without a hint of irony.[6]

Nor was his concern for his appearance confined to his wardrobe for his hair, which had elicited much praise from his early days in politics, was pampered extravagantly. He sourced the finest hair tonic on the market from a New York company, Frances Fox. One day his serious-minded National Security Adviser McGeorge Bundy and a colleague entered the Oval Office to find a pretty young woman massaging his hair with lotion. When Bundy rebuked the president of the United States for devoting precious time to such fripperies, Kennedy quipped that Bundy and his colleague clearly took a cavalier attitude to matters follicle: they both had receding hairlines. Perfecting an image required this sort of fastidious attention to his appearance.[7]

Association was an important means by which Kennedy's sex-symbol status was enhanced. Linked to other sex symbols, this had the effect of increasing his own erotic appeal. In particular, Kennedy became connected to three of the great sex symbols of the age, both real and fictional: Marilyn Monroe, Anita Ekberg and James Bond. His marriage to Jackie Kennedy also accentuated his glamour.

Marilyn Monroe was the most celebrated sex symbol in the world. From a *Playboy* cover in 1953 to films such as *Gentlemen Prefer Blondes*, *The Seven Year Itch* and *Some Like It Hot*, she had come to embody female sensuality to millions of people across America and throughout the world. It was perhaps that combination of voluptuousness and a vulnerability linked to her devastating childhood that created her unique allure.[8]

Perhaps it was fitting that the greatest sex symbol from the world of showbusiness and the greatest sex symbol from the word of politics became lovers. Monroe is on record as saying that she found Kennedy very attractive. But she was also impressed by him as a political leader. At the time of his election, as explained earlier, she was convinced that he would prove to be an outstanding president.[9]

When Monroe stepped onto the stage at New York's Madison Square Garden on 19 May 1962 to perform for the president at a gala celebrating his forty-fifth

Figure 7.1 JFK attends a ball held on the occasion of his inauguration as president on 20 January 1961. His sartorial elegance reflected the Hollywood style that would characterize his time in the White House. (*Source*: Wikimedia, public domain, Search media – Wikimedia Commons.)

birthday, therefore, she did so with an intimate knowledge of the private Kennedy and an admiration for his presidency. This iconic occasion is discussed in Chapter 6, but it is worth considering it further. In her performance Monroe conveyed a sense of forbidden knowledge of Kennedy. There was, in retrospect, an authenticity to her public flirtation with the president.

Marilyn Monroe performing for JFK was an event that would inevitably attract considerable attention from the press and public alike. But what gave the occasion its iconic status was the overt sexuality of her performance. Singing 'Happy Birthday' would seem to have been innocent and trivial, but not the way Monroe dressed and moved. In a Jean Louis-designed, flesh-coloured dress, she appeared to be nude as she reached the microphone – hence the gasps from the audience. When she urged the audience to join her in another refrain of 'Happy Birthday', she did so with such gusto that her breasts heaved. The greatest sex symbol in the world had delivered one of her sexiest performances. She had done so in honour of a young president whose own glamour made him appear a worthy recipient of Monroe's flatteringly seductive performance. This increased his own allure.[10]

That *Esquire* magazine decided to adorn its January 1963 cover with an image that set a photograph of a dripping-wet Kennedy, clad only in shorts, on a Santa Monica beach, alongside a picture of the voluptuous, sexy Swedish actress Anita Ekberg, in the Trevi Fountain scene from the iconic Italian film *La Dolce Vita*, directed by Federico Fellini, said much about the authenticity of Kennedy's sex-symbol status. Substitute Lyndon Johnson or Richard Nixon or Joe Biden for Kennedy on this *Esquire* cover, and it seems utterly risible. But with Kennedy, not at all.[11]

Esquire designed this cover so that it seemed as if Ekberg was staring admiringly at Kennedy. He is surrounded by his own admirers who are clearly excited to be near him. A sense was conveyed of Ekberg, herself one of the world's most famous sex symbols after *La Dolce Vita*, giving her seal of approval to Kennedy's good looks. The image makes it appear that Ekberg was intrigued by JFK and fancied him. As with Monroe, Kennedy's public association with Anita Ekberg bolstered his erotic credentials. It demonstrated one other aspect of the construction of his image: although he was able to control this process to a remarkable extent, he could not do so entirely. Others had agency too, including the media. In this case, though, the Fourth Estate portrayed him in a way that flattered, adding to his sex appeal.

The attractive woman with whom Kennedy was most associated was his wife. The way he was presented with Monroe and Ekberg, and some other stars such as Grace Kelly, was striking and notable, but they were one-offs. By contrast, the public was bombarded by images of Jack and Jackie during their years in the White House. Her appeal was of a different sort to that of the bombshells Monroe and Ekberg. She was elegant, 'classy', immaculately dressed and coiffed – and there was an intriguing element of mystery about her that derived from the importance she attached to her own privacy. The presentation of Jackie Kennedy as a chic, desirable woman to the American people had been going on long before she became First Lady, with images of her – sometimes alone, sometimes with JFK – on the cover of magazines such as *Life* and *Time*. At the inaugural ball in January 1961 she looked more like a European princess than a traditional First Lady in the mould of Bess Truman or Mamie Eisenhower. Right from the outset of the Kennedy presidency, Jackie's glamour was to the fore.[12]

Photography was a key medium for the portrayal of Jackie as an exceptionally attractive First Lady, sometimes regal, sometimes coquettish. Major magazines often put her on their covers and wrote her up in articles which included numerous photographs of her. But television too played an important role in presenting her to the American people. As a dutiful and eye-catching spouse, she enhanced his status as a symbol of the family, and as a lover of the arts she added to his reputation as a leader of cultural sophistication. But her glamour, by association, increased JFK's own. As First Lady, Jackie became a fashion icon. Many American women began to wear the sleeveless dresses that she preferred, and there were even stories of some women having plastic surgery so as to make their noses look like Jackie's, and imitating her voice. Her attractiveness elicited much comment. A July 1961 *Look* magazine article lauded her beauty, saying that she was 'as willowy as a fashion model'. Kennedy's sex appeal predated his relationship with Jackie. But by the time of his presidency it was part of his individual appeal but also an aspect of his glamorous marriage.[13]

Jackie, Marilyn and Anita added to JFK's sex appeal. So did the fictional British spy James Bond. In 1961 Ian Fleming's literary creation became linked in the public mind with John Kennedy when he told *Life* magazine that *From Russia with Love* was one of his favourite books. Such was the impact of this news that sales of the James Bond novels soared.[14]

Prior to his presidency, Kennedy had read and enjoyed the Bond novels. But what increased his interest was his meeting with Fleming in spring 1960, as he was battling for the Democratic presidential nomination – as described at the start of this book. A mutual friend asked JFK if she could bring the writer to a dinner party at the Kennedys' Washington home; Kennedy was happy to oblige. During the dinner, Fleming dispensed advice on how best to handle Castro. He came up with an array of fantastical schemes that would not have looked out of place in a Bond novel. Fleming stayed in touch with JFK, sending him signed copies of his books. Fleming intrigued Kennedy who would pump British journalist Henry Brandon for gossip about the writer. Fascinated by Fleming, enthralled by his espionage stories, Kennedy was being candid when he said that *From Russia with Love* was one of his favourite books. After that Kennedy was linked by the media and the public to James Bond. Newspapers and magazines commented on the Bond–Kennedy connection, including at the time of the October 1962 release in Britain of the first Bond movie, *Dr. No*, starring Sean Connery. That the film of *Dr. No*, which told the story of a Caribbean despot intent on disrupting America's missile programme, opened in the same month that the Cuban missile crisis took place strengthened that sense of connection between JFK and Bond.[15]

Kennedy's admiration for Fleming's books, then, linked him to Bond in the public mind. But it was the overlap between the mission and persona of Bond and of JFK that made the parallel credible. Both were charged with defending the 'free world' against totalitarian menace. Both had their mettle tested by crises, whether in Berlin or the missile crisis on Kennedy's part, or in confronting an assortment of megalomaniacs bent on world domination on the part of Bond.

Kennedy and Bond also shared a prodigious sex appeal. A hedonist, the debonair Bond moved from lover to lover in Fleming's novels. But his philandering was highlighted even more in the film franchise. Simply put, Bond was sexy. That too was the case with Kennedy, and his association with the playboy Bond served to augment his own sex-symbol credentials.

JFK's image as a sex symbol had ideological implications for his presidency. Throughout his political career he had sought to distance himself from liberals and what could be perceived as their naivety, particularly in meeting the communist challenge. A deficit in masculinity had become an implicit but important part of the GOP critique of Democratic politicians. They were 'soft' on communism, alleged Republican critics. Over time 'soft' on crime and 'soft' on welfare cheats would become a regular Republican characterization of Democratic policies. From this point of view, the abundance of masculinity suggested by Kennedy's sex appeal and his association with the likes of Marilyn Monroe and James Bond was politically useful. Kennedy's opponents could say many things about him but suggesting that he was another 'soft' liberal like Stevenson would never be persuasive. Sex was not a trivial feature of Kennedy's image. Its political benefits were considerable.

It was in the 1970s that Kennedy's womanizing became widely known. Details of his affairs with Marilyn Monroe, Judith Campbell and Mary Meyer were reported in the media and then discussed in historical works. It was to be expected that this new information would sully his reputation. Yet it did not. In public opinion polls Americans continued to rate JFK as one of their greatest presidents. What explains this paradox is the importance of sex to his image during his lifetime. That Kennedy had enjoyed numerous affairs was in a sense consistent with this emphasis on his erotic appeal. Rather than undermine his glorious image, therefore, the revelations of his playboy exploits actually reinforced a key aspect of it – that he was a sex symbol.

In later years one of his lovers, Mimi Beardsley, recalled his playfulness. 'Part of him,' she said, 'seemed to be still an adolescent teenager at Choate.' He loved taking long baths with her, creating – she remembered – 'our own mini-spa.' One day Beardsley noticed that there was a row of yellow ducks along the side of the bathtub. A present from one of his friends, they referenced a comedy record by Vaughn Meader, *The First Family*, which had sold huge numbers and reached number one in the charts. Meader was a Kennedy impersonator, and in one skit he had JFK enumerate the toys which were his daughter Caroline's and those which were John, Jr.'s before declaring: 'The rubber duck is mine.' With Beardsley's input, Kennedy named the ducks after his kith and kin, devised stories about them and had duck races along the length of the tub. In *The First Family*, Meader had spotlighted JFK's relationship with his family, for comic effect, and the president had relished it.[16]

Meader's hit record demonstrated how the American people viewed Kennedy through the prism of family, in fact more so than any chief executive in American history, despite the illustrious Adams and Roosevelt clans that had supplied several previous presidents. When the public looked at Kennedy in the White House, they saw not an individual politician but the symbol of a family and, as time went on, the head of a political dynasty.

Put alongside his sex appeal, his resonance as a symbol of family life gave his presidential image a powerful duality. It meant that he appeared modern and traditional at the same time, with his family-man credentials hewn from the rock of Eisenhower's 1950s America, and his dangerous sexuality very much of its time, the decade of the 1960s in which the sexual revolution changed American society and culture. Kennedy had both an avant-garde and a traditionalist appeal. It was an irresistible combination.

The way JFK as president came to symbolize the family was again linked to his pre-presidential image, which was influenced by the fact that so many Kennedy family members were prominent. Prior to the presidency, Americans had come to know Joe Kennedy, Sr. – star of Wall Street, FDR's ambassador in London and once one of the men tipped by the press to succeed Roosevelt in the White House. As the daughter of Boston mayor 'Honey Fitz' Fitzgerald, Rose Kennedy was well known in her own right, especially in New England.

The 1960 campaign and its aftermath brought more Kennedys to the fore. As JFK's campaign manager, attorney general and his closest adviser in the administration, Bobby Kennedy became a familiar figure to Americans. Newspaper and magazine articles drew attention to his important role. He was centre stage during most of the crucial episodes in his brother's presidency, not least those to do with civil rights. Beyond the carefully constructed JFK image and the slick, modern, media-savvy Kennedy political machine, there was something elemental about the president's appeal, to which millions of Americans could relate: he was very close to his brother. Their love and support for each other was clear and admirable.

That this was a remarkable political dynasty, not just a notable family, became even more apparent with the meteoric rise of Edward Kennedy. Joe Kennedy in particular was determined that his youngest son would run for and win the Senate seat vacated by JFK on winning the presidency. That is precisely what happened. The primary race in 1962 was a bruising encounter with Edward McCormack, the nephew of Speaker of the House John McCormack. The younger McCormack decried Teddy's lack of experience as well as the brazen dynastic ambitions of the Kennedys. He had a point on both counts, but his accusation that the Kennedys were creating a dynasty added to the sense of JFK as the head of an exceptional family. McCormack's attack came to naught. Teddy won the Democratic primary and then the election in November. By 1963 three brothers were senator, attorney general and the president of the United States.[17]

It was the First Lady who did the most to strengthen JFK's credentials as a symbol of the family. Such a stark contrast to Bess Truman and Mamie Eisenhower, she received enormous media attention as First Lady. Without a political purpose akin to that of Eleanor Roosevelt, there was much focus on her role as a young mother to two adorable, photogenic children. All of this meant that Americans looked at John Kennedy and saw not only their president but a son, a brother, a husband, a father.

The link between family and the Kennedy presidency was established right from the start of the new administration. The inauguration was used by JFK to showcase not only his approach to policy, as expressed in his inaugural address, but his family as well. As Kennedy was sworn in as president, 16 members of his family were on the platform. The familial implications of JFK's inauguration were not lost on the press. In his column Charley Knickerbocker said, 'His ascension to power is more than just a change-over of administration and a party victory; it is the proclamation of a new American dynasty – the Kennedys.'[18]

Figure 7.2 The American people were bombarded by images of familial bliss in the White House during the Kennedy years. Here his children Caroline and John Jr. play with JFK in the Oval Office. (*Source*: Wikimedia, public domain, Search media – Wikimedia Commons.)

The inauguration not only entrenched the notion of JFK as a symbol of the family but also created the associated idea of Kennedy as royal and of the Kennedys as America's royal family. The description of the Kennedys as the nation's royal family is commonplace today. But the birth of that idea can be dated precisely to 20 January 1961. The pageantry of Kennedy's inauguration evoked European monarchical traditions. Inviting the august poet Robert Frost to recite his verse was consistent with the British practice of the royal family appointing a Poet Laureate to write poems for special occasions. Such was the sartorial splendour of Jack and Jackie that they seemed more like a royal than a political couple. Jackie's dress at the inaugural ball, in particular, looked regal. Working from Jackie's own sketches and ideas, Ethel Frankau of Bergdorf Custom Salon designed an 'off-white sleeveless gown of silk chiffon . . . encrusted with brilliants and embroidered with silver thread', which she wore with a matching cape. In short, Jackie looked like a princess – and, by implication, JFK appeared to be prince-like. This view of the Kennedy inauguration as a royal affair was not an ex post facto interpretation of the occasion. Journalists spoke in these terms at the time, with one scribe stating that 'there was an unmistakable aura of pseudo-monarchical dynasty [about the inauguration]'.[19]

After the inauguration the print media and television transmitted to the American people the image of the new president as anchored in a family setting. The First Family always attracts a lot of attention from the Fourth Estate. Journalists know that their readers are curious about the private life and thus the family life of their president. But with their youth and Hollywood glamour, the Kennedy family were grist to the mill of reporters more than any previous First Family had been. The media focus on JFK and his family, however, was due not only to newspaper and magazine editors with their sights set on ever-greater sales but to the president himself who prioritized the projection of a positive image of himself and his family via the media. He was often involved in the selection of friendly journalists and leading photographers for articles on his family. Promoted in effect by both the president and the press, the Kennedy family acquired a prominence in popular culture.[20]

An article in *Look* magazine on 28 February 1961 was a good example of how the print media presented an idealized version of the president in a family setting. For the pictures, Audrey Hepburn's favourite photographer Richard Avedon was selected. The journalist who wrote up the article, Laura Bergquist, had known the Kennedys for several years and was well disposed. Hence JFK knew the coverage of his family would be gushing, and that the photographs would be gorgeous. That proved to be the case. The Avedon photograph on *Look*'s front cover showed a smiling Jack and Jackie with their young daughter Caroline holding the baby, John Jr., in the Floridian sunshine. Stripped of the trappings of political office, JFK appeared here as part of a happy, well-to-do family. The photos included alongside Bergquist's article showed other charming, touching images of the Kennedys, such as the two children at play, and Jackie and Caroline chatting with JFK looking on. Bergquist's article waxed lyrical about Kennedy's skills as a father, Jackie's spousal and maternal devotion, and Caroline's intelligence. This sort of irresistible portrait of a seemingly perfect American family compelled the public to think of JFK in the context of family.[21]

Television, as well as the print media, transmitted beguiling images of the Kennedy family into the living rooms of millions of Americans. A notable example of this was Jackie Kennedy's tour of the White House, filmed by CBS and broadcast to a large television audience on Valentine's Day in 1962. In this hour-long TV special, Jackie showed correspondent Charles Collingwood various rooms in the White House which she had restored in a historically credible and aesthetically pleasing way. Her intelligence and impressive knowledge of the arts were apparent, as was her commitment to improving the White House on behalf of her husband. A sense of dutiful spouse, as well as well-informed culture vulture, was conveyed. At the end of her tour the television audience got to see a proud JFK paying tribute to the work undertaken by his wife.[22]

Just before Kennedy's assassination, *Look* magazine printed an article, 'The President and His Son', which focused on JFK's role as a father. Included were photographs of John, Jr., with a number showing him at play with his dad. One of them, which would become among the most enduring images of the 'Camelot' reign of the Kennedys, showed John, Jr., in the Oval Office playing beneath the desk as JFK worked away. In what turned out to be the final days of the Kennedy presidency, the American people were reminded of how the nation's leader combined his political role with his family responsibilities.[23]

The way he symbolized the family gave JFK a traditional appeal that resonated with many Americans. Adding to this traditional component of his image was the attention paid to his religious faith. His Catholicism had been a major issue in the 1960 campaign, and this established the idea of him as a man of faith. There was an authenticity to this part of his image as, despite his hedonistic lifestyle, JFK's faith was important to him (as it was to another complex, libidinous president, Bill Clinton). He prayed and attended church regularly. Whenever back in Massachusetts, he got in touch with Archbishop of Boston Richard Cardinal Cushing to discuss Catholicism. Cushing once described Kennedy as 'the greatest representative of [the Catholic] brotherhood . . . that we had among the laity'. As president-elect, then president he was photographed in religious settings: at prayer during the christening of his baby John Jr., chatting with a group of nuns, attending a christening with Jackie at Westminster Cathedral in London. Kennedy embodied cutting-edge change: the youngest ever elected president and a sex symbol whose erotic appeal meshed with the broader cultural changes of the 1960s. But as president he also personified tradition: family and faith, as well as military service. That increased his appeal to many Americans.[24]

Prior to the presidency Kennedy's scholarly achievements had set him apart from other politicians. Two books and a winner of the Pulitzer Prize constituted a record of intellectual distinction that rivals such as Lyndon Johnson and Hubert Humphrey, as well as the darling of the liberal-intellectual set Adlai Stevenson, could not match. It could be claimed that this comparison was misleading as *Why England Slept* was merely an able undergraduate thesis that might never have seen print had it not been for Joe Kennedy's connections (though in the view of this author it was much more than that), and *Profiles in Courage* had not – for the most part – even been written by JFK. But in terms of his image all of that was irrelevant. It was the appearance that mattered, and what Kennedy seemed to be was a political leader with admirable literary credentials. As with the other elements of his image, his reputation as a man of letters influenced his life in politics, for it implied he was a politician with a commendable *sophistication*. That was helpful as this was what Kennedy wished to suggest about his policy ideas. Put another way, the cleverness of his political thinking could be inferred from the cleverness evident in his literary success.

That literary success was expanded as an element in Kennedy's presidential image into the idea that he was a leader with a wide-ranging cultural sophistication. In this, he was indebted to his wife. While his knowledge of the arts was limited – due in part to an upbringing in which success, showbusiness, sports and sex, along with public affairs, were emphasized, but not the arts – Jackie was the definitive culture vulture. Painting, literature, foreign languages, classical music, interior design – she loved it all. The White House became a great patron of the arts thanks to Jackie's cultural interests. But her husband would be the beneficiary of her role as the 'unofficial Minister of Culture', as *The New York Times* put it. The general assumption was that the president shared the First Lady's penchant for the arts as his earlier literary achievements made this seem probable, and because he was an active participant in so many of the cultural events that she organized. This was where the alpha-male aspects of his image as sex symbol and war hero were important. Had a hypothetical Adlai Stevenson presidency brought so many artists into the White House, this would have been portrayed by his critics as a reflection of his egg-head proclivities that showed he was out of touch with ordinary Americans, and an effete intellectualism that cast doubt on his ability to man up to the Russians. As a sex symbol and war hero, Kennedy was immune from any such criticism of the emphasis placed on the arts during his presidency.[25]

His inauguration made clear from the outset of his administration that he and Jackie would foster close ties with America's most illustrious artists. Leonard Bernstein composed a special *Fanfare* for the occasion and conducted the National Symphony Orchestra in a performance of it at a pre-inaugural concert. At the inauguration itself the great contralto Marian Anderson sang 'The Star-Spangled Banner' and Robert Frost read his poetry. The Kennedys invited more than 150 artists and scientists to the inauguration, including playwrights Arthur Miller and Tennessee Williams.[26]

This was a sign of things to come as the Kennedys proceeded to host a series of high-profile cultural events. These included White House dinners in April 1962 for Nobel Prize winners from the Western Hemisphere and a month later for the Frenchman on whom Jackie had an intellectual crush, André Malraux, a distinguished novelist and art critic and Charles de Gaulle's minister for cultural affairs. But the most celebrated of these occasions was the White House concert given by Pablo Casals on 13 November 1961. This was a coup for JFK as the great Spanish cellist had long refused to play in any country which recognized General Franco's dictatorship. The last time he had performed in the White House, Teddy Roosevelt was president. But Kennedy courted Casals, writing a letter in which he praised him as 'one of the world's greatest artists'. Numerous composers and other artists attended the Casals concert. The event attracted enormous attention. NBC and ABC broadcast the concert on radio. Newspapers gave the event extensive coverage. Columbia released a record of the concert.[27]

To the American people it was clear that that they had a cultured leader in the White House. Before the Casals concert he spoke to the audience of his respect for artistic endeavour. He linked freedom of artistic expression to his own role as a protector of freedom in the political arena: 'We believe that an artist, in order to be true to himself and his work, must be a free man or woman, and we are anxious to see emphasized the tremendous artistic talents we have available in this country.' More Americans, he argued, should be aware of the work of their nation's musicians, painters and architects. Privately, Kennedy confessed, 'Pablo Casals? I didn't know what the hell he played – someone had to tell me,' and this philistinism was not the only example of Kennedy's ignorance on such matters. He had never heard of Aaron Copland or Samuel Barber until the White House social secretary enlightened him just before these two stars of American classical music attended a White House soirée. This was the part of Kennedy's image where the gap between appearance and reality was greatest. He *was* a war hero, a credible sex symbol and an interesting symbol of the family. But the gap between his apparent cultural sophistication and the reality was wide. He read historical works extensively and had some interest in architecture. And of course he was a published author. But his knowledge of theatre, opera, classical music and painting was slight. As the American people remained unaware of his limited interest in the arts, this did not sully his reputation. The truth was that he had no idea who Pablo Casals was, despite his status as one of the great international stars in the performing arts. But the *apparent* truth, которая served to burnish his image, was that he was an admirer of Casals and happy to use the office of the presidency to showcase his artistic genius; and that was a worthy undertaking as it enriched the cultural life of the nation.[28]

The Casals concert was one of three major cultural events during the Kennedy years that dazzled America and shaped JFK's image in the process. The second was Jackie Kennedy's televised White House tour. The third was the loan by the French government of the most famous painting in the world, Leonardo da Vinci's *Mona Lisa*, to the United States in early 1963.

Jackie's White House tour was a notable example of how her engagement with matters aesthetic added sheen to her husband's image. On visiting Mamie Eisenhower just before the transfer of presidential power, Jackie was disappointed by the White House. There was too much contemporary furniture, she thought, and the mix of styles bequeathed by previous presidents made for an unappealing mishmash. The new First Lady set to work restoring the White House. She replaced contemporary with historical furniture from the White House basement and warehouse. She established a White House Fine Arts Committee and a Special Committee for White House Paintings to encourage well-heeled Americans to make donations to aid in the restoration.[29]

CBS came up with the idea for a televised tour of the White House in which the First Lady explained the work she had done in restoring it. Jackie agreed, and in *A Tour of the White House with Mrs. John F. Kennedy* she moved from room to room explaining to correspondent Charles Collingwood the changes that she had made. Broadcast on Valentine's Day 1962 by CBS and NBC and later by ABC, the viewing figures in the United States were remarkable. It was subsequently screened in more than a hundred countries.[30]

Towards the end of the programme JFK made an appearance. He expressed his pride in his wife's efforts in restoring the White House and his hope that Americans would visit the presidential home to see first-hand the work she had undertaken. 'Anything which dramatizes the great story of the United States,' he said, 'as I think the White House does, is worthy of the closest attention and respect by Americans who live here and who visit here and who are part of our citizenry.' The idea transmitted to the American people by this television extravaganza was that their president and his wife had a refinement that was evident in this excellent restoration of the White House.[31]

In the identification of the Kennedy White House with the arts and the life of the mind, more was to come. Once again, it was a case of Jackie Kennedy boosting her husband's image; for it was due to her indefatigable efforts that the French government agreed to loan the *Mona Lisa* to Washington's National Gallery of Art and New York's Metropolitan Museum of Art. The loaning of the *Mona Lisa* turned out to be *the* cultural event of the Kennedy presidency. More than 1.6 million Americans went to see it as 'Mona Mania' gripped the Big Apple and the nation's capital.[32]

It was during André Malraux's visit to Washington in spring 1962 that Jackie seized the opportunity to suggest to de Gaulle's minister for culture that the French loan some of their masterpieces to the United States. 'I would love to see the *Mona Lisa* again,' she told Malraux, 'and show her to the Americans.' Malraux said he would look into it. Charmed by the Francophile First Lady, he wanted to do her bidding and before his Washington trip was over he promised her that he would send da Vinci's painting to America. Seven months later the *Mona Lisa* crossed the Atlantic, arriving in New York on 19 December. Media coverage of the event was vast.[33]

Again Jackie's handiwork and the staging of a major cultural event added lustre to Kennedy's image as a sophisticate. On 8 January 1963 the *Mona Lisa* was unveiled in a special ceremony at the National Gallery of Art. A large audience of luminaries was in attendance. The event was broadcast live by satellite to Europe. After Malraux had spoken, Kennedy addressed the audience. He praised France as the world's 'leading artistic power' but pledged to nourish America's own artistic endeavours. He proceeded to link the values represented by Leonardo da Vinci's work, including a commitment to individual liberty, and those which America's leaders were duty bound to defend. 'We here tonight,' declared Kennedy, 'among them many of the men entrusted with the destiny of this Republic, also come to pay homage to this great creation of the civilization which we share, the beliefs which we protect, and the aspirations toward which we together strive.' What JFK was suggesting was a unity of purpose and thus a meaningful connection between himself as leader of the 'free world' and this titan of the Renaissance.[34]

After the prestige garnered by bringing the *Mona Lisa* to America, Kennedy continued to highlight his administration's commitment to the arts. To that end, he signed Executive Order 11112, which established the President's Advisory Council on the Arts. The purpose of this committee was to make recommendations to JFK on how to boost cultural activities throughout the nation.[35]

Then a month before the assassination in Dallas, Kennedy delivered his most important presidential address on the arts. Speaking in his home state on 26 October 1963 at Amherst College, he emphasized – as he had in his address at the unveiling of the *Mona Lisa* – the importance of freedom to the artist and hence, by implication, the link between his political role as president and the cultural vibrancy of the nation. He spoke of the need to balance the pursuit of military power and wealth with an appreciation of 'grace and beauty' in protecting the environment and the architectural heritage of America. With lofty rhetoric that stirred the assembled audience of students and academics, Kennedy said:

> I look forward to an America which will reward achievement in the arts as we reward achievement in business or statecraft. I look forward to an America which will steadily raise the standards of artistic accomplishment and which will steadily enlarge cultural opportunities for all of our citizens. And I look forward

to an America which commands respect throughout the world not only for its strength but for its civilization as well.[36]

Kennedy's Amherst address represented the rhetorical apex of his campaign to promote the arts. To be sure, much of what was done in this area was the product of his wife's handiwork: those White House soirées, the Valentine's Day tour of the newly restored White House, the loaning of the *Mona Lisa*. But in terms of appearances, all of this was of a piece with how the American people perceived Kennedy prior to his presidency. With his books and Pulitzer Prize, he seemed both politician and man of letters. The cultural activism of the Kennedy White House, which took place despite his personal disinterest in the arts, strengthened this part of Kennedy's image. The pre-presidential man of letters now appeared to Americans, more broadly, as a cultural sophisticate. Safeguarded by his credentials as a war hero and sex symbol from accusations of liberal eggheadism, JFK's image as a cultured leader indicated to the American people, very usefully, that here was a president whose rich cultural hinterland suggested a sophistication in his approach to policy as well.

During his presidency, Kennedy's status as a military hero was also highlighted. First, journalist Robert Donovan commenced research after the inauguration for a book on JFK's *PT 109* exploits, which was published before the year was out by McGraw-Hill. His book was always intended to be a tribute, but ensuring that this would be the case was the author's willingness to submit the manuscript to JFK for his approval. On publication the book sold impressively.[37]

Second, Warner Brothers decided to make a movie on Kennedy's wartime heroism, believing it had strong commercial potential. As with the Donovan book, Kennedy got involved to ensure that this portrayal of his younger self was to his liking. He made known to Warner Brothers his views on casting (he tried, unsuccessfully, to persuade young, glamorous Warren Beatty to play himself), who should direct the film, and on the script to which he insisted on various changes. Even the United States Navy was put at the disposal of the film-makers to assist in their shooting of *PT 109*. Starring Cliff Robertson as JFK, the movie was released in June 1963 to mixed reviews, and its box office performance disappointed Warner Brothers and Kennedy himself. Nevertheless, moviegoers in what would be the last summer of his life were reminded that their president had been a genuine war hero. To Americans, their leader in the White House had brawn as well as brains.[38]

Donovan's book and this Hollywood film highlighted Kennedy's heroism in the Second World War. The heroic was indeed an element in his presidential image, in part due to these *PT 109* reminders, but more fundamentally because he succeeded in completing a narrative which he had begun in 1940 with *Why England Slept*. America needed bold leadership, he had argued then, that would bolster the nation's military power as it confronted Adolf Hitler. Sixteen years later he again called for courageous leadership in *Profiles in Courage*: US politicians needed to have the strength and independence to put the national interest ahead of the wishes of their constituents. As president he was able to come across as the embodiment of the heroic leadership he had written about as he had to deal with not one but two of the most dangerous crises of the Cold War: the Berlin crisis of 1961 and the Cuban missile crisis. The Russians had threatened America's presence in the key German city and then, apparently, its very existence with nuclear weapons in Cuba. The stakes were so high. But, like the hero in a Hollywood movie, Kennedy had prevailed, compelling Khrushchev to back down.

A key part of Kennedy's appeal was the belief that he was so much more than an ordinary politician: a sex symbol, a literary figure but also a genuine hero, indeed a star. Crucial to the promotion of the idea that he was a presidential star was his exposure on television. It would be easy to castigate Kennedy for an excessive reliance on TV: doing the nation's business, not public relations, should have been the bedrock of his presidency.

With what has transpired in politics since the Kennedy years, be it ceaseless polling, 'spin' and the Trumpian use of Twitter, this is an attractive line of argument – and, at first glance, an ethically compelling one. But it does not hold water. For one thing, the relationship between image-building and the crafting of policy is not inversely proportional. Just because Kennedy devoted time to and was skilled at projecting an appealing image did not mean he lacked the ability to devise policy that was in the national interest. Conversely, a president unconcerned with image is not inevitably an impressive policymaker. It is perfectly possible for a president to be adept (or incompetent) at both image-building and policymaking.

Second, rather than representing a shortcoming in leadership, Kennedy's consideration of his image was justified given the broad changes that had taken place in American culture in the 1950s. Harry Truman's dismissive attitude towards the issue of presidential image was just about feasible in the aftermath of the Second World War. But television transformed US popular culture in the 1950s. Almost nine out of ten Americans had one by the end of the decade. Suddenly, the visual mattered more in politics than it ever had before. If anyone was in any doubt as to the profound impact of television on politics then the Kennedy–Nixon TV debates in the 1960 presidential campaign settled the matter. It was to Kennedy's credit that he grasped the importance of TV to politics, and it reflected well on his talent and skill as a politician that he was able to master the television medium.[39]

Third, Kennedy's focus on developing an attractive presidential image was merited as this influenced his credibility with the American people. If he appeared persuasive, decisive, inspirational, sympathetic, trustworthy – and a television presence and compelling image could help with all of those things – that bolstered his credibility with the electorate. That in turn fortified his political position, including the perceived strength of his position in relation to Congress. Richard Neustadt has written persuasively of the importance of credibility to presidential success, and more than ever before image in a televisual age played a major role in shoring up credibility. Kennedy understood that.[40]

It would have been troubling, however, if Kennedy had defined policy on the basis of what best served his image rather than the national interest. Yet there were no occasions during his presidency when this was the case. As with all presidents, he considered how policy influenced his administration's credibility. But he never altered policy from what he thought would be in the national interest in order to enhance his personal image.

It was his press secretary, Pierre Salinger, who grasped how television could be used to boost JFK's presidency as it had so aided his 1960 campaign. Hence he came up with the idea of live televised press conferences to exploit the telegenic appeal of the new president. Eisenhower had permitted his press conferences to be filmed but only on the understanding that his press secretary could edit not only the transcript from which journalists could quote but the actual footage of the news conference as well. Salinger, however, believed that Kennedy could discard those precautions and permit his press conferences to be broadcast live into the homes of millions of Americans. Worried about over-exposure and vexing a print media that would feel marginalized by the new television medium, Kennedy nonetheless approved Salinger's plan. His self-confidence precluded the concern felt by some of his aides that a live broadcast of a news conference would run too great a risk of a humiliating gaffe.[41]

So polished and assured were JFK's live televised press conferences, the first of which took place only five days after his inauguration, that they burnished his image. They were in effect pieces of televisual theatre, highly performative. As with Broadway or the West End, there were rehearsals, consideration of the staging, attention to costume and hair, the performance itself, the reaction of the audience, and then the reviews. Kennedy's mastery of his stagecraft was no less complete than Laurence Olivier's.[42]

His preparation was meticulous. A committee coordinating the work of numerous government departments briefed Kennedy before his press conferences. This included the precise wording of answers to questions on sensitive topics; so Kennedy had his script which he rehearsed. On the morning of the news conference, Salinger, Sorensen, McNamara, Bundy and Rusk assisted him in anticipating questions and framing answers to them. Kennedy would ask for extra information on the questions he thought most likely to be asked. Salinger, Sorensen and Bundy passed on that information to him an hour before the news conference, after waking him from the afternoon nap he took to ensure that he was well rested for his encounter with the Fourth Estate. As befitting his Hollywood sense of style, Kennedy always selected an elegant, well-cut suit, and his hair was coiffed to perfection. To make sure the sense of theatrical spectacle was maximized, partitions were used at the back of the State Department auditorium, where his press conferences took place, to make it look like the room was full, even if less of the nation's scribes were in attendance than usual. The morning after a press conference, the newspapers would review Kennedy's performance. But the most important reviewer, and certainly the most forensic in his analysis, was JFK himself. He scrutinized footage of each news conference, making mental notes on how his performance could be improved in terms of the cogency of his answers, camera angles and lighting.[43]

Kennedy's accomplished performances at his press conferences were due to his natural aptitude for this sort of challenge but also the skill he developed through careful preparation. His assured and detailed responses to questions from journalists convinced many Americans that their young president was well informed, on top of things. Not all presidents – Reagan and Trump are cases in point – have convinced on this score. Important, however, was the way Kennedy interspersed his answers with charm and humour. When asked about a Republican resolution on the inadequacy of his leadership, he quipped: 'I am sure it was passed unanimously.' These lighter touches indicated that Kennedy was no policy-wonk dullard. He would never come across as say Jimmy Carter could: a president prone to explanations with a soporific density. Those who met Kennedy have testified to his irresistible charm. As one friend and adviser put it, he had an exceptional ability to be liked immediately. The live press conferences, with their sense of immediacy and intimate presentation of Kennedy's personality, enabled him to transmit his personal charm to millions of Americans via television. There was a parallel here with the way FDR utilized radio to deliver his 'fireside chats': he was able to convey his personal charm, warmth and confidence – so evident in his one-on-one conversations with friends and advisers – to millions of Americans in the early sixties.[44]

Of course an important factor in Kennedy's television performances, in comparison to Roosevelt's radio addresses, was the visual. In this, all the factors which had helped make JFK a sex symbol contributed to the aesthetic impact of his press conferences: his good looks, immaculate grooming and fabulous hair. In short, he looked like a film star, and that was exceedingly helpful for what was a performance for the television cameras. His film-star appearance was in marked contrast to the aesthetics of other presidents in the post-war era – Truman, Ike, LBJ and Nixon. He had a glamour they lacked, and that enabled him to seduce the American people, via the intimate gaze of television, in a way they could not.

One other factor facilitated Kennedy's bravura performances at these news conferences: a media deference that future presidents would not enjoy. Before the Vietnam War and Watergate and the demands of the 24/7 news cycle in a cable television era, journalists were more respectful. They refrained from reporting on a president's private life. What a profound difference that would have made to Bill Clinton's presidency. What a profound difference it made to JFK as it protected him from scandal. Journalists were also less relentless in their probing of presidential shortcomings. They said little when at the first news conference since the Bay of Pigs Kennedy refused to answer questions about that catastrophe. Some journalists were even willing accomplices in helping presidents to get their message across to the American people. In Kennedy's case, Salinger planted questions with compliant journalists before JFK's news conferences, telling them that if they asked a particular question, they would receive from Kennedy a very interesting response. Thus sometimes Kennedy answered questions which, in effect, he was asking himself. All of this meant that the favourable impression made by his press conference performances was not eroded by ceaseless questions of a prurient or hostile nature. Put in theatrical terms, Kennedy's live audience and his reviewers were, for the most part, on his side; and that allowed him to shine, adding yet further lustre to his fulgent image.[45]

Kennedy's focus on television did not come at the expense of a sustained effort to court the print media. Helpful here was Kennedy's own experience as a journalist for the Hearst newspapers at the end of World War II. He knew their business, what made them tick. His close friendships with journalists, such as Benjamin Bradlee of *Newsweek*, deepened his knowledge of the workings of the Fourth Estate.[46]

During his presidency, Kennedy devoured numerous newspapers, including *The New York Times*, *The Washington Post*, *Chicago Tribune* and the *Boston Globe*, and magazines such as *Life*, *Time* and the *New Yorker*. Most days he met twice with his press secretary, Pierre Salinger, to monitor the newspaper coverage of his leadership. This effort derived from a sensible recognition on Kennedy's part that many Americans formed an impression of his presidency on the basis of how newspapers and magazines reported his actions; and that in turn affected his popularity and credibility with the American people.[47]

For the most part, Kennedy did an excellent job at creating a slick White House press operation that did much to produce laudatory coverage in the written press. Other presidents, notably Theodore and Franklin Roosevelt, had been adroit in handling journalists, but no previous president matched the efficiency and effectiveness of Kennedy's management of the media.

Recognition, consultation, praise, friendliness and unprecedented accessibility were the techniques used by Kennedy to generate goodwill among journalists and hence favourable column inches. Reporters were flattered by the attention he lavished on them. He often phoned them to discuss a particular piece they had written. He gave personal briefings to such luminaries as Walter Lippmann, James Reston and Drew Pearson, and arranged for advisers like Ted Sorensen to update them on administration policy. Kennedy even used some eminent media figures as ad hoc advisers, thus making unlikely their criticism of an approach or policy which they had helped shape. For instance, on the issue of whether China should be permitted to join the United Nations, JFK solicited the advice of media tycoon Henry Luce.[48]

Accessibility and amiability increased media goodwill towards Kennedy. Journalists found the Kennedy team to be friendlier and more communicative than Eisenhower and his aides. Kennedy ensured that reporters had considerable access to him and his advisers. 'I let it be known,' said Salinger, 'that ... the White House would be an open beat. Any reporter could interview any staffer on any subject and without clearing with me.' Moreover, Salinger held two daily press briefings, demonstrating his own availability to reporters.[49]

Kennedy showed the same sort of commitment himself. In addition to the numerous briefings he gave journalists, he held White House luncheons, during which he took questions from editors and publishers from across the nation. During his winter vacation in Palm Beach, he scheduled lengthy meetings with White House correspondents to review the year's events and to discuss future developments. Even on holiday, Kennedy was available to reporters; and they appreciated that. This made the press coverage he received more positive than it would otherwise have been.[50]

More robust tactics, as well as this consideration and civility, characterized Kennedy's approach to journalists. If vexed by a critical article, he did not keep his feelings under wraps. The offending journalist or his or her editor would receive an indignant phone call in which JFK would make the case that the article was misguided or ill-informed. He was prepared to resort to more extreme measures if he felt particularly aggrieved. When Ben Bradlee said in an August 1962 *Look* magazine article that it was hard to compose an article that was flattering enough to satisfy the Kennedys, JFK treated him as a pariah for three months. From access to the president several times a week, he was totally cut off. Kennedy was letting him know that the exceptional White House access he had enjoyed, of enormous benefit to his journalistic career, had to be reciprocated by unceasingly positive coverage if that favourable treatment were to continue. It was a striking example of the coercive media management used by Kennedy in his quest for flattering news stories on his presidency.[51]

In understanding JFK's unique appeal, an additional point should be made: His image seemed different to other presidents in part because of a certain Frenchness that suggested style and sophistication. In many ways this aspect of the Kennedy White House was rooted in Jackie's intense Francophilia, which had been nourished by her junior year abroad as a Vassar student at the University of Grenoble, then at the Sorbonne. When she completed her studies at George Washington University in 1951, she took into adult life a passion for French language, literature, painting – indeed French culture in general. In this way, she was cut from the same cloth as another notable White House resident, Thomas Jefferson.[52]

This influenced the style of the Kennedy White House and hence JFK's image. As discussed earlier, Jackie organized one of the Kennedys' lavish state dinners for the French Minister of Culture Malraux in spring 1962. It was her friendship with Malraux that resulted in the highlight of the Kennedy presidency in terms of the arts: the loaning of the *Mona Lisa* to the United States. And the locus for the entrance of Jack and Jackie on the world stage as president and First Lady was Paris when they visited de Gaulle in the late spring of 1961. Famously, the Kennedys, especially the elegant, French-speaking First Lady, dazzled Parisians during their visit.[53]

The French sensibilities of the Kennedy White House went beyond all of that. To ensure the success of luncheons and state dinners, Jackie hired the chef René Verdon, first on an ad hoc basis, then permanently. His debut in the White House kitchen came with the luncheon in April 1961 for British prime minister Harold Macmillan. Verdon was credited with bringing fine dining to a White House whose culinary standards had hitherto often left a lot to be desired. Though based in New York when Jackie recruited him, Verdon had been born and raised in France and trained at a number of restaurants in Paris. When the likes of conductor/composer Leonard Bernstein waxed lyrical about the excellence of White House dinners during the Kennedy years, the style of cooking he (and others) so enjoyed was French.[54]

So was the fashion style of the First Lady that elicited so much comment at the time and ever since, and shaped the aesthetics of Camelot. She loved Chanel but when criticized for extravagant shopping excursions she solved the problem of having to appear patriotic while indulging her preference for French style by patronizing Chez Ninon, a Manhattan boutique which for three decades had copied French designs for its well-heeled clients. Even the iconic pink suit worn by Jackie on the day of JFK's assassination, though made by Chez Ninon, was a copy of a 1960 Chanel design, duplicating exactly the patterns and materials of the French fashion house. After JFK's election Jackie appointed Oleg Cassini as her personal couturier. A playboy whose love interests overlapped with JFK's (notably Hollywood star Gene Tierney), Cassini had been born in Paris to Russian aristocrats and raised in Florence. As a designer his style was heavily influenced by European trends. When Americans looked at their chic First Lady, what they were admiring to a great extent was French style. This multiplicity of connections to French culture infused the image of the Kennedy White House with elegance and sophistication, setting it apart from other presidencies.[55]

A way of gauging the exceptional power of John Kennedy's image is to apply a branch of film scholarship known as star theory, developed in particular by Richard Dyer. Dyer explored how certain Hollywood actors achieved star status. Building on the work of other scholars, notably Orrin E. Klapp, he argued that stars tended to conform to certain types: the Good Joe, the Tough Guy and the Pin-up. Alternative types were discernible too, including the Rebel, personified by the likes of Marlon Brando. Applying star theory to Kennedy helps explain the remarkable potency of his image as he came across as all of these types to the American people. His Good-Joe credentials were created by his sympathetic style, his image as a family man of religious faith, and policies such as the Peace Corps and his civil rights address of 11 June 1963 in which he made the moral case for equal rights. His status as a *PT 109* war hero, as well as all those stories of games of touch football on the White House lawn, presented him as a Tough Guy; and standing up to the Russians in Berlin and during the missile crisis further bolstered that part of his image. His sex-symbol status, furthered by his sartorial elegance and links to the likes of Marilyn Monroe and James Bond, made him a very plausible Pin-up. The sense of breaking the rules conveyed by Kennedy – no one that young elected president, no other Catholic had reached the White House, no previous president with his Hollywood style – made him a certain type of Rebel. Amalgamate the images of Bing Crosby, Sean Connery, Robert Redford (as male Pin-up) and Marlon Brando and an approximate sense of the stupefying star power of JFK is apparent.[56]

The construction of such a dazzling image was an important achievement. Kennedy could not totally control this process as others, especially those in the media, influenced the development of his image by the way they portrayed him. But to a large extent he was able to shape his own image – powerful, multifaceted, compelling. The political benefits of that were considerable. Not only did it aid his political rise and election as president, it helped ensure his popularity and credibility with the American people during his White House years. The highest average poll ratings of any president in modern recorded history say something, not only about the perceived efficacy of his leadership but also the brilliance of his image. Image-building is an essential part of the art of politics in the modern era. In a Western democratic context, Kennedy was better at it than anyone.

Chapter 8

WITHOUT DALLAS

What if the most famous murder in history had not taken place? With a life and a presidency ended prematurely by an assassin's bullets, historians have understandably considered what would have happened to Kennedy had he lived beyond Dallas. They have done so in a way that bolsters their interpretation of Kennedy's presidency. His Camelot supporters, including Arthur Schlesinger and Theodore Sorensen, said he would have achieved great things. Schlesinger wrote: 'He had so little time: it was as if Jackson died before the nullification controversy and the Bank war, as if Lincoln had been killed six months after Gettysburg or Franklin Roosevelt at the end of 1935 or Truman before the Marshall Plan.' Robert Dallek has argued that JFK would have played a commendable role in reducing Cold War tensions. Kennedy's detractors take a different view. 'The dark side of the president's personal and official activities,' claimed Thomas Reeves, 'might have ruined Kennedy's second term and brought the nation another kind of grief and mourning than that which tragically did ensue.' This book has considered JFK's political life, private life and life as a cultural icon. This chapter discusses his afterlife in the sense of what would probably have happened to a Kennedy presidency had he lived. It is an important issue as it sheds light on the consequences of his murder for America.[1]

The first issue to be resolved is the likely duration of a hypothetical Kennedy presidency. Would he have been a one- or two-term president? This is significant as it influences considerably his probable legacy. In the modern era, say from the 1930s onwards, successful presidents – Dwight Eisenhower, Ronald Reagan and arguably Barack Obama and Bill Clinton – have generally served two full terms. (George W. Bush, given his dismal poll ratings towards the end of a presidency mired in war and financial crisis, is an exception to that rule.) By contrast, presidents who have failed to win re-election (or election) – Gerald Ford, Jimmy Carter and George Bush Sr. – have been perceived as failures as the American people showed their disapproval at the ballot box of a presidential record. Again, that rule is open to interpretation. It may well be the case, for instance, that in future years a consensus will crystallize around the idea that George H.W. Bush's record of a successful prosecution of the first Gulf War, skilful management of the ending of the Cold War and a politically brave attempt to deal with Reagan's legacy of debt by raising taxes (despite his 1988 campaign promise not to do so) merits a positive assessment of his presidency. Nevertheless, in general the rule holds: two-term presidents are more likely to be successful, and perceived to be successful by the American people and ultimately historians, than one-term presidents.

In Kennedy's case, serving two full terms would have required victory in the 1964 election. We know that Kennedy's successor, Lyndon Johnson, did win this election in a landslide, crushing the Republican candidate, Arizona senator Barry Goldwater, by 16 million votes. Would Kennedy have enjoyed such a triumph?

Several factors bear on this issue. One is the calibre and nature of the Republican opposition that Kennedy would have faced. By the time Reagan was in the White House it was clear that Goldwater had been an important figure in the redefinition and resurgence of modern conservatism. What had seemed outside of the ideological mainstream in Goldwater's 1964 campaign had become the mainstream in Reagan's America.[2]

In the context of the early 1960s, however, when Franklin Roosevelt's New Deal coalition remained intact, and when the only Republican in more than a third of a century able to capture the White House, Dwight Eisenhower, had been a five-star general and national hero who would have been elected had he run as a Democrat (as some Democrats had wanted him to), Goldwater's identification with the right-wing of the Republican Party was a liability. Saying, as he did during the campaign, that the use of extremism to defend liberty was no vice and that he wished to lob a nuclear warhead into the men's toilets at the Kremlin may have excited his Republican base, but it alienated moderate voters.[3]

Goldwater's perceived extremism would, therefore, have aided Kennedy's bid for re-election. It is instructive to note JFK's own assessment in 1960 of the field of possible GOP presidential candidates. The Republican he feared most was the moderate (and on some issues liberal) New York governor Nelson Rockefeller. Candidates for the presidency can adopt one of two basic strategies: focus on energizing the party's base, its core voters, or on occupying the political centre to attract moderate swing voters. Not just in 1960 but throughout his political career, Kennedy subscribed to the latter philosophy. He believed, his aide Walt Rostow recalled, that 'the balance of feeling in the electorate lay with a "moderate, decent, conservative margin," which a Democratic candidate had to reach'. Accordingly, Kennedy feared Republicans from the right of the party, including Richard Nixon, less than those from the moderate wing. For that reason, it was a possible Rockefeller candidacy that had troubled JFK most in 1960. 'Nobody ever had any doubt he could beat me in 1960,' he told Ben Bradlee. 'I knew that.' The Republican Kennedy really wanted to face in 1964 was Goldwater. So Kennedy himself, an astute analyst of American politics, believed his prospects for re-election would be enhanced if the Republicans nominated Goldwater for president. That was a sound assessment.[4]

An important factor affecting Kennedy's chances of victory in 1964 would have been his ability as a campaigner. It is axiomatic that the greater the campaigning skill of a candidate, the more likely he or she is to be elected. As has been argued earlier, Kennedy was an exceptional campaigner: charismatic, indefatigable, strategically adept and with great televisual flair. Inspiring speeches from his brilliant wordsmith Ted Sorensen and vast campaign funds would also have helped JFK in 1964 as they did in 1960. As he had in 1960, Kennedy would have used these manifold strengths in 1964 to build a formidable campaign, one that Goldwater would have found exceedingly difficult to resist.

Of the various issues which Kennedy and Goldwater would have contested, the one of potentially decisive importance was the economy. Election results over the course of the previous century suggest that economic factors have been of paramount significance. Economic downturns in 1920, 1932, 1960, 1980, 1992 and 2008 saw a change of party in the White House, bringing Harding, FDR, JFK, Reagan, Clinton and Obama to power. Conversely, an apparently strong or improving economy in 1924, 1936, 1956, 1984, 1996 and 2012 saw incumbent presidents returned to office. By 1964 the US economy was in rude health. Indeed by some estimates Kennedy's economic record has been the most impressive among US presidents since the Second World War. This boded well for his re-election prospects.[5]

In foreign policy too Kennedy could boast of a striking success: the Cuban missile crisis. He had shown both toughness and diplomatic finesse in standing up to the Russians and defusing the most dangerous crisis of the Cold War era. His handling of the missile crisis would have inoculated Kennedy from attempts by Goldwater to portray his Democratic rival as 'soft' or inept in foreign affairs.

The most notable impediment to Kennedy's chances for re-election was the strong and impressive stance that he had taken on civil rights in 1963: his stirring speech on 11 June in which he told Americans that racial equality was a moral issue and the civil rights bill he had introduced to end segregation. Commendable and courageous, that stance came with a political price: diminishing popularity among White Southerners, as his declining poll ratings in the last few months of his presidency revealed. On the other hand, his national poll ratings stood at around 60 per cent shortly before his assassination, still high. His strong support for civil rights would have energized the liberal base of the Democratic Party, the group prior to 1960 which had felt ambivalent about this son of the appeaser Joe Kennedy and friend of Red-baiting Joe McCarthy. Furthermore, Lyndon Johnson's success in passing Kennedy's civil rights bill did not prevent his landslide victory over Goldwater. Hence, JFK's stance on civil rights would not have irreparably damaged his prospects for re-election.[6]

Had Kennedy not been murdered in Dallas, therefore, the most plausible scenario is that he would have been re-elected. The perceived extremism of his opponent, his skill as a campaigner, the strength of the economy and his credibility-enhancing triumph in the Cuban missile crisis suggest that Kennedy would have won the 1964 election and by a far greater margin of victory than in 1960. Without the tragedy of Dallas, the overwhelming likelihood is that JFK would have remained president until January 1969.

The major international issues Kennedy would have had to tackle certainly include America's role in Vietnam and its relationship with Russia. By 1965 Lyndon Johnson had to decide whether to send US troops to the Dominican Republic to prevent the left from seizing power. Kennedy would have faced the same dilemma. On the domestic front the immediate challenges would have included securing passage in Congress of his civil rights bill. It is a reasonable assumption that the nature of JFK's private life, particularly his philandering, would have stayed the same. Whether his adultery would have become public knowledge, thus damaging his presidency, needs to be considered. The projection of a powerful and seductive image was a major aspect of Kennedy's time in the White House. It would have been a prominent feature of a post-Dallas Kennedy presidency too.

Of all the issues which would have determined Kennedy's legacy and reputation had he lived, the most important is Vietnam. Lyndon Johnson, twenty months after becoming president, took the United States to war there. This ultimately destroyed his presidency. Beyond the issue of Vietnam, Johnson's achievements were so remarkable – the Civil Rights Act, Voting Rights Act, Medicare and Medicaid – it is no exaggeration to say that without the disaster of the Vietnam War he may have ended up on Mount Rushmore. But entering a war in Vietnam that divided America, cost tens of thousands of lives and that he could not win eroded his credibility and compelled his decision at the end of March 1968 to bow out of his re-election campaign. Thus, the key hypothetical question is whether Kennedy would have gone to war in Vietnam, as Johnson did, with the same catastrophic consequences for his presidency.

That question divides into two parts. First, did Kennedy have concrete plans for US policy in Vietnam? And, second, if not, what would he have most likely done in Vietnam? As for long-term plans, there is no evidence – as discussed earlier – that Kennedy had made a decision on whether to fight a full-scale land war there. In a sense, this was of a piece with the proclivity he had shown at times, particularly early on in his presidency, to pay insufficient attention to how events might play out in the medium- or long-term: authorizing the Bay of Pigs invasion and other anti-Castro initiatives without thinking hard enough about how Khrushchev might respond (which turned out to be by the deployment of missiles in Cuba).

Grafted on to this issue of Kennedy's tendency at times to avoid dwelling on the long term is the growth he displayed as a leader in his White House years. That he became a more sophisticated and progressive thinker on relations with Russia and civil rights begs the question of whether a part of that growth was a greater ability to consider long-term developments. How he reflected in 1963 on the future of Soviet–American relations as well as race relations in the United States suggests he *did* improve as a leader in this regard. Still, on Vietnam his long-term thinking remained unclear.[7]

Kennedy's open mind on the future direction of American policy in Vietnam was revealed by those statements to the press, including his 2 September interview with Walter Cronkite, in which he said, 'In the final analysis, it is their [the South Vietnamese] war. They are the ones who have to win it or lose it'. This indicated that Kennedy was unlikely to bolster the South Vietnamese army with US ground troops given that it was *their* war. Yet in the same interview he said, 'I don't agree with those who say we should withdraw' from Vietnam as it was 'a very important struggle'. This suggested that Kennedy was ready to stay the course in Vietnam, and presumably this strong commitment would have included US troop deployments if required in order to defeat the communists. Kennedy could have been thinking of public relations: he wanted to assure the American people that somehow he would not tolerate a defeat in Vietnam *and* that he would keep America out of a protracted war there. On the other hand, his contradictory statements may have reflected the ambiguity of his outlook on Vietnam, that he was genuinely undecided about the future course he would steer.[8]

The counter-argument made by some Kennedy acolytes to the claim that he had not made up his mind, and hence that a Kennedy war in Vietnam was a possibility, is to draw attention to NSAM-263, the directive issued by JFK in October 1963 authorizing the withdrawal of 1,000 US military personnel from South Vietnam by the end of the year. Historian John Newman has attached great importance to this, claiming it signified Kennedy's intention to pull out of Vietnam – an argument which influenced director Oliver Stone's 1991 film on the assassination, *JFK*. The argument that NSAM-263 constituted an unequivocal decision on JFK's part to withdraw from Vietnam is an overstated one. There is evidence that Kennedy viewed NSAM-263 in part as a way of indicating US displeasure at Diem's policies and of pressuring him to increase his effectiveness in governing and on the battlefield. Logevall asserts, 'No further withdrawals were envisioned [after NSAM-263]; more advisers could be sent in the future, if the situation demanded.' In other words, NSAM-263 was not part of a definite Kennedy plan to pull out of Vietnam. Moreover, although Kennedy insiders said in various publications that Kennedy had indeed planned to withdraw from Vietnam, these memoirs came out after the Vietnam War had turned into a disaster. '*Johnny, We Hardly Knew Ye*', penned by close aides Ken O' Donnell and Dave Powers at the start of the 1970s, is a case in point. However, the earlier memoirs, published before the war had become calamitous – such as those by Schlesinger and by Sorensen in 1965 – made no such lofty claims about the significance of NSAM-263. And that is telling. On the other hand, NSAM-263 can and should be viewed as evidence that Kennedy was open to the idea of US de-escalation in Vietnam; and O'Donnell and Powers may well have recalled accurately JFK's comments on US withdrawal from the country.[9]

As Kennedy had made no definite decision as to his future course in Vietnam, the question of what he might have done must be considered. On this, there are factors suggesting he would not have fought a war in Vietnam. But there are other considerations indicating the opposite.

For various reasons, it is sound to think of Kennedy as a different sort of leader to Lyndon Johnson, as one who would not have acted in the same way in Vietnam. For one thing, Kennedy would not have had the same difficulty as Johnson did after Dallas in succeeding a martyr whose popularity had only increased in death. In a poll after the assassination two out of three Americans claimed to have voted for Kennedy in 1960. It had actually been less than one in two. In her interview with Theodore White for *Life* magazine, Jackie Kennedy ensured that layers of Camelot mythology implying JFK's greatness soon enveloped the memory of her late husband.[10]

Succeeding a legend created a terrible pressure on Johnson. He had to prove that he was a worthy successor to a mythical figure. Historian Paul Henggeler has written cogently about how Johnson felt overshadowed in the White House by the Kennedy legacy and mythology. In foreign policy, proving his mettle meant above all else preventing a communist victory in Vietnam. Hence the vow made in private by LBJ two days after Kennedy's assassination: 'I will not lose in Vietnam.' Three days later, in a speech before Congress, in which he assured the nation of continuity between the new administration and JFK's, he promised to keep Kennedy's commitments in South Vietnam. He may well have been thinking of the precedent of Republicans attacking Harry Truman for the 'loss' of China in 1949. He did not want his credibility compromised in the same way. The whole dynamic of Johnson's policies in Vietnam being constrained by the expectations created by JFK's assassination would not have existed for Kennedy had he lived.[11]

A second difference between Kennedy and Johnson lay in their attitude to the military. During his presidency, Kennedy developed a healthy scepticism towards the top brass. Even during the early days of his presidency, this became an issue when a senior military figure briefed against the new administration's defence policies. Kennedy felt compelled to muzzle his own military: any of their statements to the press had to receive prior White House approval.[12]

It was the Bay of Pigs, however, that markedly increased Kennedy's suspicions as the military approved a CIA operation that turned out to be a disaster, inflicting on him the greatest humiliation of his presidency. As the generals urged him eighteen months later to handle the missile crisis by bombing Cuba, even after a consensus emerged in the administration in favour of the more prudent option of a naval blockade, those concerns about his military intensified. Kennedy's suspicion that the military could be dangerously gung-ho – could not see beyond its raison d'être to fight – was confirmed by the response of General Curtis LeMay and Admiral George Anderson to the diplomatic settlement of the missile crisis: they were disappointed, even angry. 'The greatest defeat in our history,' groused LeMay who called for a quick invasion of Cuba. Kennedy felt nothing but contempt for such a nonsensical attitude. The Berlin crisis in the summer of 1961 had also made him wary about the stridently hard-line advice he received in the midst of a very dangerous superpower confrontation.[13]

The result of all this was that JFK came to view his military's outlook on foreign affairs with not just a pinch of salt but a fistful of it. For all the hyperbole of Oliver Stone's 1991 film *JFK*, one theme it develops which is sound is the tension between Kennedy and his generals. Lyndon Johnson's attitude towards the military leadership was far less sceptical. He was shrewd and certainly not the crassly belligerent president of macho Texan stereotype that his most severe critics claim. But he did not bring to bear the critical faculties sharpened by a presidential catastrophe like the Bay of Pigs that had been caused in part by sloppy advice from the generals, and by a feeling of being let down by them again in the most dangerous crisis of the nuclear age. It is thus reasonable to assume that when in the early summer of 1965 General William Westmoreland called for the deployment of a huge US military force in South Vietnam, Kennedy would have been more prepared than Johnson to reject that advice.[14]

Another factor suggesting that Kennedy would have handled Vietnam differently than did LBJ is the Cuban missile crisis. In a crisis which brought America and the world closer to nuclear war than they had ever been, he faced down the Russians. He had compelled Khrushchev to withdraw Soviet missiles from Cuba and had done so without making inordinately great concessions. No one could credibly claim, in the wake of the missile crisis, that Kennedy was incompetent in foreign policy and too weak to handle the Communists.

He had proved his mettle as a major statesman in a way that Johnson had not before deciding to go to war in Vietnam in July 1965. Influencing that decision was a need he felt to demonstrate his robustness and credibility in foreign affairs, especially as a politician who had a bravura reputation in domestic but not foreign policy. Credibility would have been a consideration for Kennedy too in the summer of 1965, but less of one. He had already established his foreign policy credentials in the gravest crisis of the Cold War.

The way Lyndon Johnson's fervent commitment to the Great Society shaped his approach to the war in Vietnam is another difference to a post-Dallas Kennedy presidency. Various scholars have shown that Johnson viewed Vietnam through the prism of his cherished reform programme. He believed that he needed to prevail in Vietnam as defeat there would so erode his credibility that support in Congress and the country for his Great Society reforms would evaporate. 'If I don't go in now and they show later I should have gone,' he said, 'then they'll be all over me in Congress. They won't be talking about my civil rights bill or education or beautification. No, sir. They'll be pushing Vietnam up my ass every time. Vietnam. Vietnam. Vietnam.' Johnson got this wrong: Vietnam and the Great Society were connected but not in the way he thought. Rather than preserving the Great Society, the war in Vietnam weakened it. Funds which would have been spent on domestic programmes went instead on the war. The nation's focus was diverted to Vietnam and away from issues of social justice. As the war went badly, the credibility of LBJ and his policies at home was compromised.[15]

With Kennedy, there were domestic reforms he wanted to enact, notably his civil rights bill. But his domestic-policy vision was less sweeping than Johnson's and less central to his idealized conception of his presidency. Kennedy would not have felt obliged to prosecute the war in Vietnam for reasons of domestic policy, in the way that Johnson did.

The shift in Kennedy's foreign policy during the final year of his life also indicates an approach to Vietnam in 1964–5 that would have been different to LBJ's. While continuing to believe in the importance of meeting the communist challenge, the emphasis in JFK's foreign policy after the missile crisis had changed so that accommodation with Moscow became prioritized, as argued in the previous chapter. The Nuclear Test Ban Treaty, his American University speech and his consideration in autumn 1963 of various types of cooperation with the Russians (including a collaborative moon project) revealed the shift in his approach to the Cold War. Living through the Cuban missile crisis when the fate of mankind rested on his shoulders (and Khrushchev's) had left him with a visceral fear that the Cold War might spiral out of control with dire consequences.

If one extrapolates Kennedy's post–missile crisis foreign policy, with its hallmark of conciliation rather than confrontation, America would have had a president with a different mindset to Johnson's, one more reluctant to use force to fight a war in Southeast Asia.[16]

A final reason for believing that Kennedy would have charted a different course in Vietnam than Johnson did is the fact that JFK had rejected specific advice to send in US combat troops (and hence to go to war there). He had ignored just such advice in the fall of 1961 when Walt Rostow and General Maxwell Taylor returned from Saigon recommending that JFK dispatch 8,000 US troops to South Vietnam. When George Ball, the famous State Department dissenter on Vietnam, advised JFK in a private conversation that the implementation of the Taylor–Rostow proposals would lead to a nightmarish, interminable US war in that country, Kennedy responded: 'George, you're just crazier than hell. That just isn't going to happen.' Kennedy's comment could have meant that he did not think a US war in Vietnam would end badly or that the scenario described by Ball would not materialize as he had no intention of fighting a full-scale land war in Vietnam. The fact that JFK rejected the advice from Rostow and Taylor on dispatching troops suggests the latter interpretation is the sounder. This does not prove he would have rejected such bellicose recommendations in 1965, but it does highlight a prudence and capacity to think independently on Kennedy's part that indicate he would have been just as careful when considering subsequent proposals for war in Vietnam.[17]

This cluster of considerations point to a hypothetical history in which Kennedy would not have made the same catastrophic decision as Johnson to go to war. But there are other factors that suggest an alternative scenario. One is the impact of the coup against Diem in November 1963, for what happened in South Vietnam as a result, which made policymaking in Vietnam so difficult for LBJ as it would have done for Kennedy in 1964–5, was chronic political instability. Diem had been corrupt and nepotistic – hardly the model progressive leader Washington would have liked to champion – but at least he had provided continuity of leadership for the best part of a decade. With Diem's death, a series of ephemeral governments in Vietnam followed (something JFK feared would happen, in the last few weeks of his life). This was significant for the American role in two ways. First, it meant the US was drawn further into the conflict as it struggled to prop up increasingly fragile governments in Saigon. Second, Washington's consideration of and intermittent willingness to countenance a coup in the late summer and autumn of 1963 made some policymakers believe that they had a responsibility to support the regimes that followed in South Vietnam. This dynamic of the United States being stuck ever deeper in the quicksands of Vietnam due to Diem's overthrow may well have existed too in a post-Dallas Kennedy presidency.[18]

A second factor pointing to a Kennedy decision to go to war is the influence of the 1964 presidential election. Johnson did not want to emphasize Vietnam in that campaign. He understood that it was a tricky issue for the Democrats. What exactly did he plan to do there? And did it not represent an opportunity for the Republicans to question his effectiveness as a Cold War leader? To the extent that he did discuss the issue in the campaign, he demonstrated his moderation in comparison to Goldwater by saying he would not send American soldiers to fight and die in Vietnam. At the same time, he was determined to prevent Goldwater from using the issue to claim that his administration was 'soft' on communism. This partly explains his reaction to the two alleged attacks by the North Vietnamese on American ships in the Gulf of Tonkin in August 1964 (though the evidence now suggests that the second attack never took place). He responded to this episode by introducing on Capitol Hill the Tonkin Gulf Resolution, which gave him a blank cheque to 'take all necessary measures to repel any armed attack against the forces of the United States and to prevent further aggression' in Southeast Asia. It was the closest to an actual US declaration of war during the Vietnam conflict. Nicholas Katzenbach was not the only one to believe that LBJ had secured congressional approval of the Tonkin Gulf Resolution (at least in part) to undercut GOP claims in the presidential campaign that he was weak in combatting communism.[19]

Kennedy may have done essentially the same thing in 1964: to commit more explicitly to the war in Vietnam for politically motivated reasons. Adding weight to that idea is JFK's track record of moving to the right of Republican opponents during campaigns to protect himself from the charge that he was yet another Democrat who could not be trusted on national security. He did that in earlier congressional campaigns, such as his 1952 Senate race against Henry Cabot Lodge, and the 1960 presidential campaign in which he described the Eisenhower–Nixon failure to prevent Castro from coming to power as abysmal and promised to be tougher than Nixon in handling the Cuban leader. This strategy was linked to Kennedy's belief that a Democrat needed to appeal to the centre rather than to the left wing of the political spectrum. Assuming he would have campaigned in 1964 as he had earlier in his career, JFK may have made the sort of commitments on Vietnam that Johnson did with the Tonkin Gulf Resolution; and ultimately this may have deepened Kennedy's involvement in Vietnam as it did with LBJ.[20]

JFK's record of escalation in Vietnam can also be seen as indicating that he would have gone to war. Despite his caution when dealing with international crises and his refusal to send combat troops to South Vietnam, Kennedy did escalate American involvement there. Around 700 US military personnel were in South Vietnam when he was inaugurated; on his death there were roughly 16,000. Those numbers were still a long way from the more than half-million combatants that Johnson would send to Vietnam. Nor does the escalation authorized by Kennedy mean that he would have made the fateful decision to move from the deployment of military personnel to troops. Still, the pattern of escalation in the Kennedy years can be extrapolated to a post-Dallas Kennedy presidency to make the case that he would have escalated yet further to the deployment of ground troops in South Vietnam.[21]

Another factor pointing to the same scenario is Kennedy's view of dissent. It is easy to think that when it came to contrary voices in his administration he was more receptive than Johnson proved to be. Famously, Johnson had a King Lear–like revulsion for dissent within his circle of advisers. He equated it with disloyalty. Although he at least listened to George Ball's warnings on the dangers of escalation in Vietnam, he did not want the dissent to go beyond Ball. When Vice President Hubert Humphrey objected in early 1965 to further escalation, Johnson cut him out of key administration discussions on Vietnam thereafter.[22]

Kennedy could give the impression of being more tolerant. The ExComm meetings during the Cuban missile crisis generated a lively debate between those officials who advocated the use of force and those who favoured a naval blockade. But there are several instances of how dissent could provoke his ire. When Chester Bowles's opposition to the Bay of Pigs operation was reported in the press, Kennedy viewed the disclosure as disloyalty and took his revenge by demoting his undersecretary of state to a more minor position in the State Department. The key dissenter in the missile crisis was Adlai Stevenson with his heartfelt plea for negotiations and mutual concessions. In a spiteful act of revenge, Kennedy planted a hostile account of Stevenson's performance in the missile crisis, describing it as 1930s-style appeasement, with two friendly journalists who wrote up the story for the *Saturday Evening Post*. The result, as Kennedy had intended, was humiliation for Stevenson.[23]

There was little which vexed JFK more than being preached to by liberals, as Stevenson did once in a conversation on nuclear testing. This was rooted in the historic tension between Kennedy and the liberal wing of the Democratic Party, which had become acute after his failure to take a stand against Joe McCarthy. In 1964–5 some of those dissenters in an unrestricted administration debate on Vietnam in a Kennedy second term would have been liberals. (We know that Stevenson, shortly before his death from a heart attack on a street in London in July 1965, opposed US escalation in Vietnam, as LBJ's UN ambassador.) Would Kennedy have dismissed, as he did with Bowles with the Bay of Pigs and Stevenson in the early days of the missile crisis, liberal sanctimony. On the other hand, by pushing the peace agenda and civil rights in 1963 Kennedy was singing more from the liberal hymn sheet at the end of his presidency than he had at the start. So he might have been more willing to side with the likes of Stevenson and Ball in the summer of 1965 than he had been a few years earlier.[24]

Another consideration pointing to a Kennedy war in Vietnam is how the situation there changed decisively in 1965. Prior to that, US presidents had essentially three alternatives: to go to war to defeat the communists; admit defeat and withdraw; pursue a middle course of supplying more aid and advisers to the government of South Vietnam. No president wanted to go to war, especially after the stalemate of Korea, or to lose another country to the communists. Eisenhower, Kennedy and Johnson in the early part of his presidency followed that middle path. The problem for LBJ by the summer of 1965 was that the South Vietnamese government seemed as though it was about to fall to the communists. Those triple alternatives had become a binary dilemma: fight or lose. To argue that in this situation Kennedy would have plumped for the latter course is to claim that he would have been willing to tolerate what some would have regarded as an ignominious Cold War defeat.

One more factor casts doubt over Kennedy's capacity to reject the path of war in 1965: his record of rejecting negotiations as a means of ending the Vietnam conflict. When de Gaulle called publicly in August 1963 for negotiations to resolve the Vietnam issue, the Kennedy administration was unsympathetic. When they learned that Nhu had contacted the North Vietnamese communists in search of an accommodation, they were unimpressed. Given the fragility of the Saigon government and the momentum behind the communists, Kennedy and his advisers worried that the South Vietnamese would enter any discussions in a weak bargaining position. In the end diplomacy would have probably been required to avoid a US war in Vietnam. On this, Kennedy's record was unpromising.[25]

Various factors can be identified, therefore, to support the argument that Kennedy would have either avoided or prosecuted a war in Vietnam. It is the judgement made on the precise influence exerted by these factors which determines a final assessment of this issue. Kennedy's manifest capacity to reject his military's hawkish advice, his shift towards a more conciliatory foreign policy in 1963 and his enhanced credibility in international affairs due to his successful management of the Cuban missile crisis (and hence the limited pressure he would have felt to prove in Vietnam that he could cut the mustard on the world stage) indicate that Kennedy would probably have decided against going to war in Vietnam. His default approach to politics and policy was caution, in contrast with the lack of it in his private life. Putting his presidency on the line by fighting a land war in Southeast Asia would not ultimately be a decision he could have made with equanimity.

In terms of his general approach to the Cold War, and in particular his relationship with Moscow, JFK would most likely have continued to implement the more accommodating policy he had come to favour in the final year of his life. The missile crisis changed Kennedy. The Test Ban Treaty and his American University speech were clear signs of a shift away from confrontation with Moscow. Kennedy had urged his audience at American University and the American people to 're-examine our attitude toward the Soviet Union'. It is unthinkable that Kennedy would have used this sort of rhetoric early in his presidency. The argument here should not be overstated. Kennedy had not gone from Cold Warrior to peacenik. He still regarded the Soviet Union as a major adversary. But the *emphasis* of his Cold War policies had changed.[26]

Khrushchev, with whom he had developed this more harmonious relationship, would still have been ousted from power in the autumn of 1964. In addition, Kennedy would have had to contend with the decision made by the Soviet leadership later in the 1960s to embark on a military build-up to narrow the huge lead enjoyed by the United States in nuclear weaponry. This would have given Kennedy pause for thought about the significance of this development for future Soviet-American relations. But he would probably have continued in some form the propitiatory approach towards Moscow that he had adopted since the missile crisis. This trend towards superpower accommodation initiated by Kennedy (and Khrushchev) did, in fact, continue during the Johnson years. In 1967–8 LBJ signed the Outer Space Treaty with the Soviets, which prohibited nuclear weapons in the earth's orbit or in space; signed the Nuclear Non-proliferation Treaty, which banned the assisting of other nations in acquiring nuclear weapons; and cooperated with Moscow in defusing tensions in the Middle East after the Arab–Israeli War.[27]

Figure 8.1 John F. Kennedy lying in state in the Capitol Rotunda, following the assassination in Dallas. In the years which followed, many Americans pondered the price paid for this tragedy in terms of the future direction of the country, including US policy in Vietnam. (*Source*: Wikimedia, public domain, Search media – Wikimedia Commons).

In April 1965 Johnson intervened in Latin America by sending more than 20,000 US troops to the Dominican Republic. His aim was to quell an uprising aimed at restoring Juan Bosch, the left-wing politician who had been elected in 1962, and to back instead the right-wing leader Reid Cabral. Intervention in Cuba at the Bay of Pigs could be seen as a precedent for how Kennedy would have handled the crisis in the Dominican Republic. On the other hand, precisely because the Bay of Pigs represented his greatest foreign policy disaster he would have been wary about again putting his credibility on the line by interfering in Latin America. The humiliation of the Bay of Pigs suggests that Kennedy would not necessarily have intervened in the Dominican Republic. As Johnson had not suffered the catastrophe which Kennedy had in April 1961, he felt less constrained than Kennedy would have in intervening in the Dominican Republic in 1965. Even if Kennedy had interceded, as LBJ did, with the same outcome – it would not have had a substantial impact on his credibility, as it did not with Johnson, though it was deeply unpopular in Latin America. Compared to Vietnam, the Dominican Republic was very much a sideshow for American foreign policy.[28]

In domestic affairs, Lyndon Johnson's presidency was defined by the Great Society, his programme of sweeping reform. Freed from the constraints of seeking re-election as senator for Texas and then the powerlessness of the vice presidency, Johnson was able to give full expression to his progressive instincts in a way that took him back to his New Deal roots. But the reform programme he championed went even beyond what his political hero Franklin Roosevelt had achieved, particularly in the field of civil rights. Indeed, no president had ever introduced and enacted such a plethora of legislation. Medicare, Medicaid, elementary and secondary and higher education innovations, farm reform, immigration reform, drug controls, National Foundation on the Arts and Humanities, water and air pollution control, highway beautification, the War on Poverty, traffic safety, child nutrition, tire safety, urban mass transit, drug rehabilitation – as well as the landmark Civil Rights Act and Voting Rights Act – represented a mere fraction of Johnson's legislative achievements.[29]

The scope of the Great Society proved a double-edged sword in a political sense. To be sure, Johnson carried out essential and morally significant reforms. He made America a more equal society with his civil rights policies, and his healthcare initiatives brought the country more in line with progressive traditions in other Western countries. But the seemingly endless conveyor belt of new policies under the Great Society played into the conservative critique that was developed during and after Johnson's presidency, which contributed to the shift to the right in US politics signified by the election of Richard Nixon as president in 1968, that the Democrats were promoting an insidious 'big government' approach that was antithetical to American traditions of self-reliance, individual freedom and the free market. Johnson presided over liberalism's greatest achievements but also the collapse of the New Deal consensus that had been in place since Franklin Roosevelt's presidency.

This raises the issue of whether Kennedy would have done a better job at sustaining that New Deal consensus. He was committed to reform. The legislative programme he had unveiled at the start of his presidency had included housing, Medicare, raising the minimum wage, aid-to-depressed areas and important educational policies. After the Birmingham crisis in the spring of 1963, he had become strongly committed to civil rights. His introduction of the civil rights bill to end racial segregation was the result of this increased resolve. Influenced by Michael Harrington's 1962 book *The Other America*, which exposed the extent of poverty in the country, JFK – in the latter part of his presidency – instructed his advisers to address the issue of deprivation. The Kennedy administration's deliberations on this issue influenced Lyndon Johnson's subsequent War on Poverty, a key element in his Great Society. On the other hand, Kennedy had a keen sense of the limits of reform, of the need not to alienate moderate voters by promoting a legislative programme that was too radical or extensive. It seems likely that Kennedy would have endorsed some of the changes that Johnson came to enact, but not all of them. This may have enabled him to retain the New Deal consensus rather than sowing the seeds of its demise, as Johnson arguably did.[30]

The major legislation which Johnson inherited from Kennedy and got passed in Congress included the civil rights bill. Whether Kennedy would have succeeded in passing this legislation would have shaped his legacy, particularly as the latter was one of the most important pieces of legislation in twentieth-century American history. What did Kennedy's legislative record suggest about the likelihood that he would have got this bill enacted? By reputation JFK is viewed as a less adroit legislator than Lyndon Johnson whose skills in dealing with Congress were honed in the 1950s during his period as Senate majority leader. Yet Kennedy's overall legislative record, as political scientist Irving Bernstein argued, supersedes that of most modern US presidents. A clear majority of his proposals were approved by Congress; so in a strict mathematical sense Kennedy's legislative numbers stack up. Moreover, the idea that Kennedy's domestic endeavours were constrained by a lack of focus or application is unpersuasive. Despite his greater pre-presidential interest in foreign affairs, Kennedy was often compelled in the White House to focus on domestic-policy issues. On the other hand, his record in passing his most important pieces of legislation was less impressive. His key bills included the ones on education and Medicare; he failed to secure pass of either.[31]

With JFK's civil rights bill, the issue is not clear-cut. There were Republican objections but some of the most vociferous opposition to Kennedy's civil rights bill came from the liberals in Congress who thought that it needed strengthening. This resulted in Kennedy's bill being bolstered in the House Judiciary subcommittee in a way that made it less palatable to Republicans and conservative Democrats. But a compromise bill was negotiated, and by the time of the assassination, it had moved on to the House Rules Committee where the chairman Howard Smith appeared to have no plans to move it on to the full House of Representatives. The progress made on the bill thereafter was due in large part to the tactical skills of Lyndon Johnson. He pressured Smith by winning support among House members for a 'discharge petition', which would have compelled the bill to be passed out of the Rules Committee. Seeing the writing on the wall, Smith buckled and at the end of January 1964 allowed the bill to be sent to the full House. In the Senate, Johnson broke the Southern filibuster, led by his old mentor Richard Russell, by various means, including the use of Senator Hubert Humphrey to work on the Republican Leader in the Senate Everett Dirksen so as to ensure the votes for cloture. One estimate is that Johnson's personal pressure influenced the votes of a dozen senators.[32]

Whether Kennedy would have got his civil rights bill passed is highly debatable. He would have needed to push the bill through both the House and Senate, requiring the circumvention of the House Rules Committee and then ending the filibuster in the Senate. It is the most difficult of all the hypothetical issues to resolve, even more so – in the view of this author – than Vietnam. But Kennedy had invested considerable political capital in the passage of the civil rights bill, and to his credit had used the moral authority of the presidency to promote it. He was becoming a more adroit leader as his presidency unfolded. There were moderate Republicans who could be expected to give their support. My view, then, is that the most likely scenario is that Kennedy would have got the civil rights bill through Congress. This would have stood alongside the resolution of the Cuban missile crisis as one of the great achievements of his presidency.

It is safe to assume that the nature of Kennedy's private life, including the almost countless infidelities, would have remained the same after Dallas. A key factor as to why this had been a political irrelevance during Camelot was a Fourth Estate that did not define a prurient interest in the president's private life as an important obligation. That is why Kennedy was certain the press would not report on his sex life. During Lyndon Johnson's presidency, this informal understanding between the press and the presidency endured. It is noteworthy that LBJ was almost as libidinous as his predecessor. He once claimed to have had more women by accident than Kennedy had on purpose. He used White House secretaries as his private harem, and his wife Lady Bird Johnson once caught him in flagrante with one of them. He had a decades-long affair with Alice Glass, and a twenty-one-year affair with Madeleine Brown, who claimed to have given birth to his illegitimate son. As aide George Reedy said, Johnson 'may have been just a country boy from the central hills of Texas, but he had the instincts of a Turkish sultan in Istanbul'. An expert on the private lives of American presidents has concluded that apart from JFK, Johnson had 'the most active extramarital sex life of any American president'. Johnson is not known to have had affairs with Mafia molls or prostitutes with communist backgrounds, but he was a philanderer of spectacular proportions. Again, as with Kennedy, Johnson's affairs represented a non-issue politically as the press did not report on them. It is most likely, therefore, that Kennedy's private life – despite its capacity to shock later generations – would not have damaged his presidency had he lived. Rather than scandal and even impeachment, as Thomas Reeves has suggested, he would have seen out his two terms as president.[33]

One other factor would have influenced a post-Dallas Kennedy presidency as it did his actual presidency: his ability to project an impossibly beguiling image to the American people (and the world). Prior to his election as president, Kennedy had constructed that powerful image as war hero, man of letters, sex symbol and symbol of family life. Added to that during the 1960 campaign was the idea of him as a man of religious faith (due to the emphasis on his Catholicism) and then as royal. The greatest image polisher in American political history, JFK had used the presidency to burnish that image.

Kennedy's potent image had political significance. It increased his popularity with the American people, endeared him yet further to his political allies, made him seem more formidable to his detractors. However effective his presidency was, it was more successful than it would have been otherwise because of his dazzling image. This would have been the case too in a post-Dallas presidency in a way that would have contrasted with the less glamorous Lyndon Johnson.

The assassination in Dallas abruptly terminated the presidency of John Kennedy. In the end, the ongoing debate about the merits of his leadership must centre on the specifics of his record in the White House on such matters as the Bay of Pigs, civil rights, the Berlin crisis, the missile crisis and Vietnam. But the question of how a Kennedy presidency would have played out had there been no assassination is important as it sheds light on the consequences for America of Kennedy's murder. We know what did happen during the Johnson years. To what extent would the course charted by Kennedy have differed had he remained at the helm?

What this chapter suggests is that the United States probably did pay a price for Kennedy's demise. Most likely a two-term president, factors such as his inveterate distrust of his own military and the trajectory of his foreign policy towards accommodation in the Cold War mean that he would have probably avoided the decision made by Johnson to go to war in Vietnam. He would have been more sceptical about military intervention in the Dominican Republic, and the cooperation with the Soviets that took place during the Johnson years would have been evident too in an elongated Kennedy presidency – and most likely intensified. Kennedy would have espoused a progressive domestic agenda, symbolized by his commitment to equality with his civil rights bill, but it would have been less expansive and less vulnerable to the conservative claim that an out-of-control, wasteful 'big government' approach, contrary to America's traditions of self-reliance and free-market entrepreneurship, had been foisted on the country. Factors such as White opposition in the South to Democratic civil rights legislation and the impact of the urban riots in the mid- and late 1960s on public attitudes towards liberalism would still have been influential. Nevertheless, without the assassination of John Kennedy, the New Deal coalition and era of Democratic Party domination of the presidency would have been more likely to endure.

CONCLUSION

The fluctuations in John F. Kennedy's historical reputation have been dramatic: from the claim of greatness made by Arthur Schlesinger and Theodore Sorensen, which, if accepted, would place Kennedy in the presidential pantheon with Washington, Lincoln and FDR, to the revisionist depiction of him as a leader with an atrocious character and a dangerously belligerent foreign policy. Indeed the critique of his character has been a key component of the attack on his reputation made by biographers such as Thomas Reeves and Seymour Hersh. How one views the character issue is, therefore, an important element in one's overall assessment of JFK.

This book argues that revisionists have been justified in drawing attention to Kennedy's character, not least because of the extraordinary nature of his private life. We know that character can have a decisive impact on a presidency – think Richard Nixon or Donald Trump. The attack on Kennedy's character has focused on his sexual life, but while that can certainly be regarded as a component of character it does not define it in toto. Character comprises a multiplicity of traits, including courage, calmness in the face of extreme pressure, the capacity to think independently, the ability to change and grow, confidence, stoicism, resilience, appropriate cautiousness, empathy and in the context of his political life taking a stand on issues with a clear moral dimension – and Kennedy, to his credit, possessed all of those qualities. In fact it was his *strength of character* that helps account for both his political rise and his most important presidential successes. Crucial to his rise to power were the independence he showed as a young man to the views on the appeasement of Hitler held by his domineering father Joseph P. Kennedy in the writing of *Why England Slept*; the courage and ingenuity he showed when his *PT 109* boat was rammed by a Japanese destroyer in the Second World War; his stoic refusal to allow his terrible ill-health to end his ambition to play a role in public life; his confidence in taking on the seemingly unbeatable Senator Lodge in 1952 when no one thought he could win.

Preventing the Third World War, quite possibly a nuclear conflict, in the most dangerous episode of the Cold War era, the Cuban missile crisis, was the most important foreign policy accomplishment of his presidency. Analyse his leadership during that crisis and it becomes clear that his success in defusing it (without triggering a superpower war or making unacceptably great concessions) was due, fundamentally, to his character strengths: keeping an open mind on how to respond to the missiles in Cuba when the initial consensus in the ExComm group of presidential advisers was in favour of an air strike on the Soviet missile sites; the backbone to stand up to his trigger-happy generals; caution in not overreacting to provocation, notably when the US U-2 plane was shot down over Cuba; and, throughout, a remarkable calmness under the most extraordinary pressure. Likewise, the strong commitment he made on behalf of civil rights in June 1963, defining it as a moral issue in his landmark address on the 11th and introducing the historic civil rights bill to end segregation, was founded to a considerable extent on his understanding of the moral necessity of equal rights. Doing this despite knowing that it would damage his popularity in the South in the run-up to his 1964 presidential re-election campaign also reflected well on his character. The overall trajectory of his presidency, excessively hard-line on Cold War issues and inordinately cautious on civil rights at first, but determined by 1963 to push for equal rights and to make the United States more secure and the world safer by reducing superpower tensions, demonstrated his ability to learn by his experiences in the White House, particularly the missile crisis and the Birmingham civil rights crisis, and that too reflected well on his character.

Image, as well as character, is crucial to an understanding of Kennedy's political rise and how the American people perceived his presidency. In his congressional years, he was an impressive politician. But he failed to take a stand on the key issue in US politics in the early 1950s: McCarthyism. His legislative record paled in comparison to the likes of Lyndon Johnson. On matters of policy it is difficult to make the case that he was a more well-informed and sophisticated thinker than Hubert Humphrey or Adlai Stevenson. Where he was peerless was in his ability to craft an image more powerful and seductive than any politician not only of his generation but in American history – and quite possibly any democratic leader in world history. Man of letters, war hero, sex symbol, family man, man of faith and royal, he seemed to have it all. Part of the power of his image came from that multifacetedness; but it was also the way he personified traditional values such as military service, religious faith and family, but at the same time an exciting sense of youth, cutting-edge change and erotic appeal. Each time a formidable political rival came up against him, whether Lodge in 1952 or Humphrey then Nixon in 1960, they were simply outdazzled. An important factor in his political ascent, his televisual image, was key to his besting of Nixon in the 1960 TV debates and hence his election as president. His luminous image, polished by both himself and Jackie as a glamorous First Lady and 'unofficial minister of culture', was important to his presidential popularity and thus credibility. This is reflected in the fact that he has the highest average approval ratings of any president since the Second World War. Image is not of tangential but rather of fundamental importance to Kennedy's life in politics. My view, therefore, is that biographers need to consider this issue more fully. I have presented in this book my thoughts on the construction and significance of Kennedy's image. Hopefully other historians will also dwell on this issue so as to develop further our understanding of this crucial issue. In a televisual age, image is more important than it has ever been in politics. Hence, it is a crucial element in the art of modern politics. His dazzling image represented, therefore, a major political achievement on Kennedy's part.

So how should Kennedy be rated as president? This aspect of presidential historiography – the ratings game – might seem rather facile and trite. But, actually, it is linked to a key part of citizenship, which is assessing at election time the respective merits of various candidates and making a wise choice as to the candidate who would best serve the national interest. So it is an important matter. As with any president, his record was a mixture of successes and failures. One's overall view should be determined by weighing the one against the other. The failures included, notably, the Bay of Pigs fiasco, but also legislative disappointments such as his inability to secure passage of his education and Medicare bills. His successes, it seems to me, far outweigh those failures: his adroit handling of the 1961 Berlin crisis, his manifestly effective management of the Cuban missile crisis, the Test Ban Treaty, his historic rhetorical and legislative commitment to civil rights in June 1963 – and one can add to that his innovative and popular establishment of the Peace Corps and his outstanding record on the economy. Vietnam constitutes the most ambiguous part of JFK's presidential legacy. It is difficult to discern his precise thinking on an issue to which he did not devote sustained attention until the final few months of his life. However, there is enough in his record and his comments on Vietnam to indicate a caution, evident in his consistent refusal to deploy US combat troops in South Vietnam, that suggests he would not have escalated to a full-scale land war in Southeast Asia, in the way that Lyndon Johnson did.

This is not to indulge in Camelot hyperbole, for it would be unpersuasive to make the case, as Schlesinger and Sorensen suggested, that Kennedy deserves to be ranked as a 'great' president alongside Lincoln and FDR. Saving the Union, abolishing slavery, pulling the US through the Great Depression, building a welfare state, defeating fascism and winning the Second World War – Kennedy's achievements cannot be said to match those. But my argument is that he was the finest president of his generation. He did not suffer presidency-defining catastrophes as Lyndon Johnson did with Vietnam and Richard Nixon did with Watergate. A key development in scholarship in recent decades has been the emergence of Eisenhower revisionism, the idea that Ike was a hugely impressive leader. In polls of academic opinion, he is now consistently rated higher than his successor in the White House. This notion is fanciful and should be rejected. Eisenhower has received some credit for things that should be a given, namely that he knew what was going on and was not dominated by his advisers. Although economic issues have not been a focus for this study, it is worth pointing out that three recessions took place during the Eisenhower years. There is a whole raft of policy initiatives in US policy towards Castro – the Bay of Pigs invasion, contingency planning for military action against Cuba, assassination plots against Castro, economic sanctions and diplomatic pressure – for which Kennedy has received substantial criticism. The planning for all of those anti-Castro policies in fact began in the Eisenhower years, but they have not been used to dent his overall presidential reputation. That constitutes an interpretative double standard. Moreover, Eisenhower lacked Kennedy's moral compass when it came to equal rights. He was intent on making sure the law was carried out, but it is unimaginable that Eisenhower would ever have delivered the sort of impassioned speech on civil rights that JFK did in June 1963. Kennedy has been criticized for his role in the coup against Diem in 1963, clearly a milestone on the road to full US involvement in the war in Vietnam; but no less significant was Eisenhower's decision after the division of the country in 1954 to back the South Vietnamese government (a commitment which both JFK and Lyndon Johnson felt obliged to uphold) and then to connive in the cancellation of the scheduled nationwide elections in 1956 (which would have reunified the country and in that way have prevented the disastrous US war in Vietnam that ultimately ensued). It is worth noting that the academic reputations of Eisenhower and Kennedy have been inversely proportional; that is to say, as Ike's reputation soared in the 1970s and 1980s, JFK's suffered. That suggests these two developments were linked. Implicitly, the idea was that if Eisenhower had been a more impressive president than previously assumed, he was most probably better than other presidents in that era, including JFK. The evidence of their presidential records does not support such an idea.

Paradoxically, no one did more damage to Kennedy's reputation than did Camelot biographers. Their praise was so extravagant that it made inevitable the backlash in historical writing evident in the work of Garry Wills, Thomas Reeves, Seymour Hersh and others. In order to refute the extreme Camelot arguments in favour of Kennedy, revisionist or counter-Camelot writers felt compelled to be just as extreme in their criticisms of him. This resulted in a caricatured, two-dimensional view of him as a depraved man and a dangerously belligerent leader. While the extremes of Camelot praise and revisionist censure should be avoided, a cogent case can and should be made that Kennedy was a very impressive leader. He advanced the cause of a more equal society and generally managed with finesse the international challenges of one of the most dangerous periods in world history. That was no small achievement.

NOTES

Introduction

1 'Fame and Fortune,' *The Age*, 14 December 1966, http://news.google.com/newspapers?nid=1300&dat=19661214&id=Aq9PAAAAIBAJ7sjid=aZMDAAAAIBAJ&pg=3280,2525882 [all internet citations accessed between 2008 and 2023].
2 Ibid.; Michael R. Beschloss, *The Crisis Years: Kennedy and Khrushchev, 1960-1963* (New York: Edward Burlingame, 1991), 134–5.
3 Christine Bold, 'Under the Very Shirts of Britania: Re-Reading Women in the James Bond Novels,' in Christoph Lindner, ed., *The James Bond Phenomenon: A Critical Reader* (Manchester: Manchester University Press, 2003), 179; John F. Kennedy Miscellaneous Information, John F. Kennedy Library, Boston, MA, www.jfklibrary.org/Research/Ready-Reference/JFK-Miscellaneous-Information.aspx; James Chapman, *License to Thrill: A Cultural History of the James Bond Films*, 2nd edn (London: IB Tauris, 2007), 44; newspaper clipping, 'James Bond Qualities for the U.S. Guerrilla Fighter,' *The Times* (London), 27 April 1961, President's Office Files, box 115, John F. Kennedy Library, Boston, MA.
4 Simon McKay, *The Man with the Golden Touch: How the Bond Films Conquered the World* (London: Aurum Press, 2008), 36–7.
5 Mark J. White, *Missiles in Cuba: Kennedy, Khrushchev, Castro and the 1962 Crisis* (Chicago: Ivan R. Dee, 1997); Kennedy, commencement address at American University, 10 June 1963, *Public Papers of the Presidents of the United States: John F. Kennedy, 1963*, www.presidency.ucsb.edu/ws/?pid=9266.
6 Kennedy, radio and television report to the American people on civil rights, 11 June 1963, *Public Papers of the Presidents*, www.presidency.ucsb.edu/ws/index.php?pid=9271&st=old+as+the+scriptures&st1.
7 David Halberstam, 'Introduction,' in *The Kennedy Presidential Press Conferences* (New York: E.M. Coleman Enterprises, 1978), iii; Joan Blair and Clay Blair, *The Search for JFK* (New York: Berkley, 1976), 482–3.
8 Garry Wills, *The Kennedy Imprisonment: A Meditation on Power* (Boston: Little, Brown, 1982), 72–83.
9 Wills, *Kennedy Imprisonment*; Thomas C. Reeves, *A Question of Character: A Life of John F. Kennedy* (New York: Free Press, 1991); Seymour Hersh, *The Dark Side of Camelot* (Boston: Little, Brown, 1997).
10 Hersh, *Dark Side of Camelot*, 387–90, 398–406; Van D. Banse, L.-M. Nagel, and U. Muller, 'John F. Kennedy und seine Geliebte aus der DDR,' *Die Welt*, 29 December 2013, www.welt.de/vermischtes/article123373410/John-F-Kennedy-und-seine-Geliebte-aus-der.DDR.html.
11 Arthur M. Schlesinger, Jr., *A Thousand Days: John F. Kennedy in the White House* (London: Mayflower-Dell reprint, 1967); Theodore C. Sorensen, *Kennedy* (New York: Harper, 1965); William Manchester, *The Death of a President* (New York: Harper & Row, 1967 paperback edn); Theodore H. White, 'An Epilogue: For President Kennedy,'

Life 55 (6 December 1963), pp. 158–9; Nigel Hamilton, 'The Rise and Fall of Camelot,' *New England Journal of History* 52 (Fall 1995), pp. 91–108; Sam Kashner, 'A Clash of Camelots,' *Vanity Fair* (October 2009), www.vanityfair.com/politics/features/2009/10/death-of-a-president200910. Michael J. Hogan, *The Afterlife of John Fitzgerald Kennedy* (Cambridge: Cambridge University Press, 2017), provides excellent analysis of the establishment of the Kennedy Camelot legend after his death.

12 Wills, *The Kennedy Imprisonment*; Reeves, *A Question of Character*; Hersh, *The Dark Side of Camelot*.

13 Herbert S. Parmet, *Jack: The Struggles of John F. Kennedy* (New York: Dial, 1980), and *JFK: The Presidency of John F. Kennedy* (New York: Penguin, 1984 paperback edn); James N. Giglio, *The Presidency of John F. Kennedy* (Lawrence: University Press of Kansas, 1991); Nigel Hamilton, *JFK: Reckless Youth* (London: Arrow, 1993 paperback edn).

14 Robert Dallek, *John F. Kennedy: An Unfinished Life* (London: Penguin, 2004 paperback edn); Fredrik Logevall, *JFK* (London: Penguin, 2021 paperback edn).

15 Beth Cherryman, 'James Bond author Ian Fleming's Roots in Dundee,' *Evening Telegraph*, 15 February 2014, www.eveningtelegraph.co.uk/news/local/james-bond-author-ian-fleming-s-roots-in-dundee-1.221618.

Chapter 1

1 Judith Exner, *My Story* (New York: Grove Press, 1977), pp. 135–6.
2 Rose Fitzgerald Kennedy, *Times to Remember* (London: Pan Books, 1975 paperback edn), pp. 119–23, 195–200.
3 Reeves, *A Question of Character*, pp. 29–30, 40; Hamilton, *JFK*, passim; Kennedy, *Times to Remember*, pp. 90–1, 100–1. For an excellent and sympathetic portrayal of Rose, see Barbara A. Perry, *Rose Kennedy: The Life and Times of a Political Matriarch* (New York: Norton, 2013).
4 Kennedy, *Times to Remember*, pp. 109, 146–7, 153–4, 221; PBS documentary, *The Kennedys* (1992); oral history of Jill Cowan and Priscilla Wear, p. 16, Kennedy Library.
5 Reeves, *A Question of Character*, passim.
6 Hamilton, *JFK*, pp. 51–2, 83.
7 Ibid., p. 18; Michael O'Brien, *John F. Kennedy: A Biography* (New York: Thomas Dunne, 2005), p. 29; Kennedy, *Times to Remember*, pp. 70–1.
8 Hamilton, *JFK*, pp. 63–9, 211–12.
9 Logevall, *JFK*, pp. 99–102, 128, 151–2; oral history of K. LeMoyne Billings, no. 1, pp. 11–12, Kennedy Library.
10 Reeves, *A Question of Character*, p. 41.
11 Ibid., p. 171; Robert Dallek, 'The Medical Ordeals of JFK,' *Atlantic Monthly*, December 2002, https://www.theatlantic.com/magazine/archive/2013/08/the-medical-ordeals-of-jfk/309469/.
12 Dallek, 'Medical Ordeals of JFK.'
13 Dallek, *John F. Kennedy*, pp. 73–6.
14 Dallek, 'Medical Ordeals of JFK.'
15 Dallek, *John F. Kennedy*, p. 81.
16 PBS documentary, *The Kennedys* (1992); Dallek, 'Medical Ordeals of JFK.'

17 Dallek, *John F. Kennedy*, pp. 61-2; James MacGregor Burns, *John Kennedy: A Political Profile* (New York: Avon, 1960 paperback edn), p. 56.
18 Oral history of Arthur Krock, p. 5, and oral history of Henry Luce, pp. 1-2, both Kennedy Library.
19 Oral history of Payson Wild, pp. 1-2, 6, Kennedy Library.
20 Oral history of Edward A. Crane, pp. 1-2, Kennedy Library; oral history of Wild, p. 2; Hamilton, *JFK*, p. 50.
21 Dallek, *John F. Kennedy*, p. 66; Reeves, *A Question of Character*, p. 50; S.T. Williamson, 'Why Britain Slept While Hitler Prepared for War,' *New York Times* (Sec VI), 11 August 1940, copy in Papers of Theodore C. Sorensen, box 8, Kennedy Library.
22 U.S. Department of State, *Foreign Relations of the United States* (hereafter cited as FRUS), *1940* (Washington, DC: US Government Printing Office, 1958), pp. 35, 37 (all FRUS citations are via https://history.state.gov/historicaldocuments/kennedy); John F. Kennedy, *Why England Slept* (New York: W. Funk, 1961 edn), p. 229.
23 Oral history of Wild, p. 12.
24 Kennedy, *Why England Slept*, pp. 215-31.
25 Dallek, *John F. Kennedy*, pp. 83-4.
26 Hamilton, *JFK*, p. 423.
27 For a more extensive discussion of Mary Meyer's relationship with JFK, see Chapter 6.
28 Hamilton, *JFK*, pp. 428-9.
29 Ibid., pp. 429-32.
30 Parmet, *Jack*, p. 90; Hamilton, *JFK*, p. 422.
31 Blair and Blair, *Search for JFK*, pp. 132-3.
32 Dallek, *John F. Kennedy*, p. 84; Hamilton, *JFK*, p. 454; Blair and Blair, *Search for JFK*, p. 142.
33 Blair and Blair, *Search for JFK*, pp. 134, 139 142; Hamilton, *JFK*, pp. 441, 443, 457.
34 Parmet, *Jack*, p. 90; Hamilton, *JFK*, pp. 454-5; Logevall, *JFK*, p. 309; J.R. Ruggles letter to J. Edgar Hoover, 23 February 1962, in Athan G. Theoharis, *From the Secret Files of J. Edgar Hoover* (Chicago: Ivan R. Dee, 1993 paperback edn), p. 26.
35 Hamilton, *JFK*, pp. 426-7; Hoover letter to McKee, 24 December 1941, and Hoover to Biddle, 21 January 1942, in Theoharis, ed., *From the Secret Files of J. Edgar Hoover*, pp. 17-18, 19-20.
36 Hamilton, *JFK*, pp. 438-9, 456.
37 Ibid., pp. 474-6.
38 Ibid., pp. 473-4.
39 FBI transcript, Wire Tape Conversation, JFK to Arvad, 6 March 1942, 10.15 pm, in Theoharis, ed., *From the Secret Files of J. Edgar Hoover*, pp. 28-9.
40 Hamilton, *JFK*, p. 478.
41 Blair and Blair, *Search for JFK*, p. 144; Theoharis, ed., *From the Secret Files of J. Edgar Hoover*, p. 31.
42 Dallek, *John F. Kennedy*, pp. 87-90; Ernest Heitkamp, 'Navy Grads Here Cross Section of U.S.,' *Chicago Herald-American*, 25 September 1942, copy from the Kennedy Library.
43 Critics of Kennedy regarding PT 109 include Reeves, *A Question of Character*, pp. 63, 66-8, and Blair and Blair, *Search for JFK*, pp. 234-5.
44 Stephen Plotkin, 'Sixty Years Later, the Story of PT-109 Still Captivates,' *Prologue Magazine* 35 (Summer 2003), https://www.archives.gov/publications/prologue/2003/summer/pt109.html; John Hersey, 'Survival,' *New Yorker*, 17 June 1944, copy from Kennedy Library.

45 Blair and Blair, *Search for JFK*, p. 331; Dallek, *John F. Kennedy*, pp. 95–6, makes very persuasive arguments on these matters; Hamilton, *JFK*, p. 570; Logevall, *JFK*, p. 340.
46 Plotkin, 'Sixty Years Later.'
47 Ibid.
48 Logevall, *JFK*, p. 350; Hersey, 'Survival,' and 'Survival,' *Reader's Digest,* August 1944, Kennedy Library; Hamilton, *JFK*, pp. 652–3.
49 Hamilton, *JFK*, pp. 34–5.
50 Logevall, *JFK*, pp. 392–5, 414; Reeves, *A Question of Character*, pp. 76, 85.
51 Hamilton, *JFK*, pp. 460–1; oral history of Charles Bartlett, no. 1, p. 3, Kennedy Library.
52 Oral history of Mark Dalton, no. 1, p. 11, Kennedy Library; Logevall, *JFK*, pp. 422–3.
53 Dalton's comments in PBS documentary, *The Kennedys* (1992); oral history of Samuel Bornstein, p. 3, Kennedy Library.
54 Oral history of Peter Cloherty, p. 11; oral history of Thomas Broderick, pp. 18-19; oral history of K. LeMoyne Billings, no. 4, p. 268 – all from the Kennedy Library.
55 Dallek, *John F. Kennedy*, p. 123.
56 Parmet, *Jack*, pp. 145, 159; Blair and Blair, *Search for JFK*, pp. 441, 466; oral history of Dalton, pp. 1–2; oral history of Billings, no. 4, pp. 268–9.
57 Oral history of Bornstein, p. 8, Kennedy Library; Hamilton, *JFK*, p. 767; oral history of Joseph A. DeGuglielmo, p. 7, Kennedy Library.
58 Blair and Blair, *Search for JFK*, pp. 482–3; Reeves, *A Question of Character*, p. 83.
59 Oral history of Dalton, p. 14, Kennedy Library; Parmet, *Jack*, p. 159; Blair and Blair, *Search for JFK*, pp. 468–73.
60 Parmet, *Jack*, pp. 157, 160.
61 Logevall, *JFK*, pp. 425, 435.
62 Oral history of Broderick, pp 40–1, Kennedy Library.
63 See, for example, the cover of *Esquire Magazine,* October 1968.
64 William E. Leuchtenburg, *In the Shadow of FDR: From Harry Truman to Ronald Reagan*, rev. ed. (Ithaca: Cornell University Press, 1985), pp. 64, 74.
65 For Joe Kennedy's relationship with FDR, see Michael R. Beschloss, *Kennedy and Roosevelt: The Uneasy Alliance* (New York: Norton, 1980).
66 W.W. Rostow, *The Diffusion of Power: An Essay in Recent History* (New York: Macmillan, 1972), p. 129; Bill Clinton, *My Life* (New York: Knopf, 2004), passim.
67 Leuchtenburg, *In the Shadow of FDR*, pp. 64, 75, 77.
68 JFK, remarks at University of North Carolina, Chapel Hill, 27 March 1947, and remarks in the House of Representatives, 20 November 1947 – both from the Kennedy Library Digital (via https://www.jfklibrary.org/archives/search-collections/browse-digitized-collections).
69 JFK, remarks in Salem, MA, 30 January 1949, Kennedy Library Digital.
70 *Congressional Record*, 82nd Congress, 2nd session, p. 3871, and 82nd Cong., 1st sess., pp. 10179, 10185–6.
71 Parmet, *Jack*, pp. 465–78.
72 JFK, report on his trip to the Middle and Far East, 14 November 1951, Pre-Presidential Papers, box 95, Kennedy Library.
73 For the impact of *Sputnik* during the Eisenhower years, see Yanek Mieczkowski, *Eisenhower's Sputnik Moment: The Race for Space and World Prestige* (Ithaca: Cornell University Press, 2013).
74 Kennedy, remarks in the Senate, 14 August 1958, Kennedy Library Digital.

Chapter 2

1. Parmet, *Jack*, pp. 234–5; oral history of Edward C. Berube, p. 12, Kennedy Library; oral history of Broderick, p. 57.
2. Oral history of John T. Burke, pp. 2–4, 6, Kennedy Library; Ralph M. Blagden, 'Cabot Lodge's Toughest Fight,' *Reporter*, 30 September 1952, p. 10, copy from the Kennedy Library; Logevall, *JFK*, pp. 506–7, 525–6, 527–8.
3. Oral history of Burke, p. 7; Kenneth P. O'Donnell and David F. Powers, *'Johnny, We Hardly Knew Ye': Memories of John Fitzgerald Kennedy* (Boston: Little, Brown, 1972 paperback edn), pp. 77–8; Logevall, *JFK*, p. 531.
4. Oral history of Burke, p. 5.
5. Dallek, 'Medical Ordeals of JFK'; O'Donnell and Powers, *'Johnny, We Hardly Knew Ye'*, p. 79.
6. Oral history of Burke, pp. 4–5, 8–9.
7. Dallek, *John F. Kennedy*, p. 175; oral history of Berube p. 22; Logevall, *JFK*, p. 521.
8. Logevall, *JFK*, p. 511.
9. Parmet, *Jack*, pp. 239, 253
10. Logevall, *JFK*, p. 530; Dallek, *John F. Kennedy*, p. 175.
11. Logevall, *JFK*, pp. 560–3; oral history of Bartlett, p. 22.
12. Oral history of Billings, no. 2, pp. 65, 68.
13. Oral history of Bartlett, pp. 20–2; Kim Bielenberg, 'How did Jackie's Private Letters to an Irish Priest Get Put up for Sale?,' *Irish Independent*, 14 May 2014, https://m.independent.ie/irish-news/how-did-jackies-private-letters-to-an-irish-priest-get-put-up-for-sale/30272207.html; Logevall, *JFK*, pp. 534–5, 558–9.
14. Bielenberg, 'Jackie's Private Letters to an Irish Priest'; PBS documentary, *The Kennedys* (1992).
15. Bielenberg, 'Jackie's Private Letters to an Irish Priest'; Logevall, *JFK*, p. 557.
16. Gunilla von Post, *Love, Jack* (New York: Crown, 1997), passim.
17. Ibid., p. 68.
18. Reeves, *A Question of Character*, pp. 137–8.
19. 'Life Goes A-Courting with a U.S. Senator,' *Life*, 20 July 1953, pp. 96–9 and the cover image, and 'John Kennedy's Lovely Lady,' *Life*, 24 August 1959, including the cover image – copies of both from the Kennedy Library.
20. 'A Debut into a Burgeoning Family,' *Life*, 21 April 1958, including the cover image, Periodical File, box 3, Kennedy Library.
21. Larry Tye, *Demagogue: The Life and Long Shadow of Senator Joe McCarthy* (Boston: Mariner Books, 2020) is an excellent study of McCarthy.
22. Oral history of Charles Spalding, p. 35, Kennedy Library.
23. Parmet, *Jack*, pp. 367–9, 462–4; excerpt, Eleanor Roosevelt, 'On My Own,' *Saturday Evening Post*, 8 March 1958, in the Eleanor Roosevelt Papers, via https://erpapers.columbian.gwu.edu.
24. Parmet, *Jack*, pp. 304–6, 482.
25. Oral history of Alastair Forbes, no. 1, p. 5, Kennedy Library; oral history of George A. Smathers, no. 3, p. 2G, Kennedy Library.
26. Logevall, *JFK*, pp. 476–7, 590; Dallek, *John F. Kennedy*, p. 191.
27. Dallek, *John F. Kennedy*, p. 162; Parmet, *Jack*, pp. 211–12; oral history of Robert Armory, Jr., no. 1, p. 3, Kennedy Library.
28. O'Donnell and Powers, *'Johnny, We Hardly Knew Ye'*, pp. 96, 108.

29. Parmet, *Jack*, p. 251.
30. Dallek, *John F. Kennedy*, p. 190.
31. Burns, *John Kennedy*, pp. 141–2; Dallek, *John F. Kennedy*, p. 189.
32. Parmet, *Jack*, pp. 304–5.
33. Ibid., pp. 305–6.
34. O'Donnell and Powers, '*Johnny, We Hardly Knew Ye*', p. 79; Dallek, 'Medical Ordeals of JFK'; T. Glenn Pait and Justin T. Dowdy, 'John Kennedy's Back: Chronic Pain, Failed Surgeries, and the Story of its Effect on his Life and Death,' *Journal of Neurosurgery* 27 (11 July 2017), p. 249.
35. Oral history of Jean McGonigle Mannix, p. 21, Kennedy Library; oral history of Jack L. Bell, p. 15, Kennedy Library.
36. Parmet, *Jack*, pp. 310; *Time Magazine*, 24 October 1960.
37. Oral history of Alastair Forbes, no. 1, p. 5. For a detailed account of the damage inflicted on the American people by McCarthyism, see Richard M. Fried, *Nightmare in Red: The McCarthy Era in Perspective* (New York and Oxford: Oxford University Press, 1990).
38. Parmet, *Jack*, p. 329; Thomas T. McAvoy, review of *Profiles in Courage*, *Review of Politics* 18 (July 1956), p. 364; Reeves, *A Question of Character*, p. 128.
39. John F. Kennedy, *Profiles in Courage* (New York: Harper Perennial, 2006 edn).
40. Parmet, *Jack*, pp. 324–6; oral history of Krock, p. 25.
41. Burns, *John Kennedy*, p. 159.
42. Oral history of Clark Clifford, no. 1, pp. 4–6, Kennedy Library.
43. Oral history of Clifford, p. 4; oral history of James MacGregor Burns, pp. 31–2, Kennedy Library.
44. Parmet, *Jack*, pp. 326–33.
45. Michael Korda, 'Prompting the President,' *New Yorker*, 6 October 1997, p. 88.
46. Dallek, John F. Kennedy, passim; O'Donnell and Powers, '*Johnny, We Hardly Knew Ye*', pp. 127–9.
47. Mark J. White, *Against the President: Dissent and Decision-making in the White House* (Chicago: Ivan R. Dee, 2007), p. 181.
48. Ibid., pp. 175–7.
49. Theodore H. White, *The Making of the President 1960* (New York: Atheneum, 1961 paperback edn), pp. 128, 371; Sorensen, *Kennedy*, p. 180.
50. Exner, *My Story*, pp. 90–2; JFK, address to the Houston ministers conference, 12 September 1960, Kennedy Library Digital.
51. *New York Times*, 7 October 1960, p. 20, and 21 October 1960, p. 18.
52. White, *Making of the President 1960*, passim. See, also, Christopher Matthews, *Kennedy and Nixon: The Rivalry that Shaped Postwar America* (New York: Simon & Schuster, 2011).
53. Transcript, First Kennedy-Nixon Presidential Debate, 26 September 1960, www.debates,org/index,php?page=september-26-1960-debate-transcript; White, *Making of the President 1960*, pp. 309, 324–5. 328–9; 1960 Presidential Debates, http://cgi.cnn.com/ALLPOLITICS/1996/debates/history/1960.
54. White, *Making of the President, 1960*, pp. 329–30; Gallup polls on presidential trial heat, 25 September and 12 October 1960 (with the latter, the polling was actually done in the days following the debate), in George H. Gallup, ed., *The Gallup Poll: Public Opinion, 1935-1971* (New York: Random House, 1972), vol. 3, pp. 1685, 1687.
55. Cari Beauchamp, 'Two Sons, One Destiny,' *Vanity Fair*, December 2004, www.vanityfair.com/news/2004/12/kennedy-200412.

Chapter 3

1. Todd S. Purdum, 'From That Day Forth,' *Vanity Fair*, October 2013, https://archive.vanityfair.com/article/2013/10/from-that-day-forth.
2. Ted Sorensen, *Counselor* (New York: Harper Perennial, 2009 paperback edn), pp. 226–7; Kennedy, inaugural address, 20 January, 1961, American Presidency Project (this and other citations from this collection are via www.presidency.ucsb.edu).
3. Kennedy, inaugural address.
4. Ibid.
5. Ibid.
6. There are various insightful studies of JFK's foreign policy, including Stephen G. Rabe, *John F. Kennedy: World Leader* (Washington, DC: Potomac Books, 2010).
7. Memorandum of conversation between Khrushchev and Harriman, 23 June 1959, President's Office Files (POF), box 126, Kennedy Library; Khrushchev, 'Khrushchev Reviews 81-Party Moscow Conference', *Current Digest of the Soviet Press* 13 (22 February 1961), pp. 8, 9, 11; Maxwell D. Taylor, *Swords and Plowshares* (New York: Norton, 1972), p. 200.
8. Arthur Krock memorandum, 26 May 1960, Papers of Arthur Krock, box 31, Mudd Library, Princeton University, Princeton, NJ; George W. Ball, *The Past Has Another Pattern: Memoirs* (New York: Norton, 1982), p. 158.
9. David Halberstam, *The Best and the Brightest* (New York: Penguin reprint, 1983), pp. 188–9; oral history of Robert S. McNamara, p. 7, Kennedy Library; oral history of Adam Yarmolinsky, no. 1, p. 23, Kennedy Library.
10. For overviews of the careers and views of Stevenson and Bowles, see John Bartlow Martin, *Adlai Stevenson and the World: The Life of Adlai E. Stevenson* (Garden City, NY: Doubleday, 1977), and Chester Bowles, *Promises to Keep: My Years in Public Life, 1941-1969* (New York: Harper & Row, 1971).
11. Oral history of W. Averell Harriman, no. 2, p. 37, Kennedy Library; Stevenson to Kennedy, 22 November 1960, and television conversation with JFK, 13 January 1961, in Walter Johnson, ed., *The Papers of Adlai E. Stevenson* (Boston: Little Brown, 1977), VII, pp. 585, 615–17.
12. Trumbull Higgins, *The Perfect Failure: Kennedy, Eisenhower, and the CIA at the Bay of Pigs* (New York: Norton, 1989), pp. 70–1, 79–80; Mark J. White, *The Cuban Missile Crisis* (London and Basingstoke: Macmillan, 1996), p. 24.
13. Kennedy, annual message to the Congress on the State of the Union, 30 January 1961, American Presidency Project.
14. Editorial Note (No. 22), US Department of State, *FRUS, 1961-1963* (Washington, DC: US Government Printing Office, 1997), vol. X, Cuba (all citations from FRUS are via https://history.state.gov/historicaldocuments/kennedy).
15. Stephen G. Rabe, 'Eisenhower Revisionism: A Decade of Scholarship,' *Diplomatic History* 17 (Winter 1993), pp. 97–115; C-SPAN Presidential Historians Survey 2021, www.c-span.org/presidentsurvey2021/?page=overall.
16. Bundy, memorandum of discussion on Cuba, 28 January 1961, National Security Files, box 35A, Kennedy Library.
17. Robert F. Kennedy, *Thirteen Days: A Memoir of the Cuban Missile Crisis* (New York: Norton, 1969), p. 90; memorandum of meeting with JFK, 8 February 1961, National Security Files, box 35A, Kennedy Library; Editorial Note 80 and Bowles memo for Rusk, 31 March 1961, *FRUS, 1961-1963*, X; Bowles, *Promises to Keep*, pp. 327–8; Dean Rusk, *As I Saw It* (New York: Norton, 1990), p. 209.

18 Oral history of Dean G. Acheson, pp. 13–14, Kennedy Library; oral history of Harlan Cleveland, pp. 21–3, Kennedy Library; White, *Cuban Missile Crisis*, pp. 33-4.
19 Bundy, memorandum of discussion on Cuba, 28 January 1961; Foreign Office to Washington, 28 April 1961, FO 371/156181, National Archives, Kew; Schlesinger to JFK, 'Joseph Newman on Cuba,' 31 March 1961, Papers of Arthur M. Schlesinger, Jr., box WH-5, Kennedy Library.
20 Memorandum of meeting with JFK, 8 February 1961, Editorial Note 59, and Editorial Note 65 – all in *FRUS, 1961-1963*, X.
21 JCS memo for McNamara, 3 February 1961, in *FRUS, 1961-1963*, X.
22 Higgins, *Perfect Failure*, pp. 126–49.
23 Clark Clifford with Richard Holbrooke, *Counsel to the President: A Memoir* (New York: Random House, 1991), p. 349; Khrushchev letter to Kennedy, 18 April 1961, in *FRUS, 1961-1963* (Washington, DC: US Government Printing Office, 1996), vol. VI; 5 May 1961 Gallup poll, in Gallup, *The Gallup Poll*, vol. 3, p. 1717.
24 Richard N. Goodwin, *Remembering America: A Voice from the Sixties* (Boston: Little, Brown, 1988), p. 187.
25 JFK, address before the American Society of Newspaper Editors, 20 April 1961, American Presidency Project; Richard M. Nixon, *RN: The Memoirs of Richard Nixon* (London: Sidgwick & Jackson, 1978), pp. 234–5.
26 Goodwin, *Remembering America*, p. 188; Bowles to Kennedy, 20 April 1961, Papers of Chester Bowles, box 297, Sterling Library, Yale University, New Haven, CT.
27 Stevenson to Kennedy, 'Some lessons from Cuba,' 23 April 1961, Papers of Adlai E. Stevenson, box 830, Mudd Library, Princeton University, Princeton, NJ.
28 National Security Action Memorandum No. 2422, 'U.S. Policy Toward Cuba,' 5 May 1961, National Security Files, box 313, Kennedy Library.
29 Schlesinger, *A Thousand Days*, pp. 289–91.
30 Stevenson letter to Philip Noel-Baker, 6 July 1961, in Walter Johnson, ed., *The Papers of Adlai E. Stevenson*, vol. VIII (Boston: Little, Brown, 1979), p. 91; Hope M. Harrison, 'Ulbricht and the Concrete "Rose": New Archival Evidence on the Dynamics of Soviet-East German Relations and the Berlin Crisis, 1958-61,' Working Paper No. 5, Woodrow Wilson Center's Cold War International History Project (May 1993), p. 35.
31 Oral history of McGeorge Bundy, pp. 50–1, Kennedy Library; Bundy, notes on discussion, 11 February 1961, *FRUS, 1961-1963* (Washington, DC: US Government Printing Office, 1998), vol. V; Kennedy letter to Khrushchev, 22 February 1961, *FRUS, 1961-1963*, VI.
32 Burdett, memo of conversation, 5 April 1961, *FRUS, 1961-1963*, vol. XIV.
33 Lawrence Freedman, *Kennedy's Wars: Berlin, Cuba, Laos, and Vietnam* (New York and Oxford: Oxford University Press, 2000), pp. 53–4; C. David Heymann, *A Woman Named Jackie* (New York: Lyle Stuart, 1989), pp. 300–1.
34 Memorandum of conversation between Kennedy and Khrushchev, 3 June 1961, 12.45 pm, POF, box 126, Kennedy Library. (The citations in the following notes for the transcripts of the Vienna summit meetings are from the same box.)
35 Ibid.; Reeves, *A Question of Character*, p. 299.
36 Memorandum of conversation between Kennedy and Khrushchev, 3 June 1961, 3 pm.
37 Memorandum of conversation between Kennedy and Khrushchev, 4 June 1961, 10.15 am.

38 Ibid.
39 Ibid.
40 Memorandum of conversation between Kennedy and Khrushchev (during lunch), 4 June 1961.
41 Memorandum of conversation between Kennedy and Khrushchev, 4 June 1961, 3.15 pm.
42 Ibid.
43 Ibid.; Nikita S. Khrushchev, *Khrushchev Remembers: The Last Testament* (Boston: Little, Brown, 1974), pp. 499–500.
44 Oral history of Foy Kohler, p. 4, Kennedy Library.
45 Beschloss, *Crisis Years*, p. 234; I.F. Stone, 'The Brink,' *New York Review of Books*, 14 April 1966, https://nybooks.com/articles/1966/04/14/the-brink/; diary entry for 11 June 1961, in Peter Catterall, ed., *The Macmillan Diaries*, vol. II (London: Macmillan, 2011), p. 390; McGeorge Bundy, *Danger and Survival: Choices About the Bomb in the First Fifty Years* (New York: Random House, 1988), p. 363.
46 JFK, radio and television report to the American people on returning from Europe, 6 June 1961, American Presidency Project.
47 Beschloss, *Crisis Years*, p. 235.
48 Bundy memo for JFK, 10 June 1961, *FRUS, 1961-1963*, XIV.
49 Ibid.
50 Oral history of Acheson, pp. 19–20; Truman letter to Acheson, 7 July 1961, in Robert H. Ferrell, ed., *Off the Record: The Private Papers of Harry S. Truman* (New York: Harper & Row, 1980), p. 395.
51 Oral history of Martin J. Hillenbrand, pp. 4–5, Kennedy Library; record of meeting of the Interdepartmental Coordinating Group on Berlin contingency planning, 16 June 1961, and Editorial Note 47, *FRUS, 1961-1963*, XIV.
52 JFK press conference, 28 June 1961, Kennedy Library Digital.
53 Dean Acheson report, 28 June 1961, FRUS, 1961-1963, XIV; diary entry, 6 July 1961, in Drew Pearson, *Washington Merry-Go-Round* (Lincoln: Potomac Books, 2015), p. 89.
54 NSC memorandum for the record, undated but 29 June 1961, *FRUS, 1961-1963*, XIV.
55 Beschloss, *Crisis Years*, p. 245.
56 Ibid., p. 246; Schlesinger, *A Thousand Days*, p. 325.
57 Schlesinger, *A Thousand Days*, pp. 323–5.
58 Ibid., p. 325. Around this time JFK received a memo from Stevenson who urged him not 'to create the impression we expect general war in the fall,' while convincing Moscow of 'our determination to maintain our Berlin position.' See Johnson, ed., *Papers of Adlai E. Stevenson*, VIII, p. 89.
59 Memo of discussion in the NSC, 13 July 1961, *FRUS, 1961-1963*, XIV.
60 Ibid.; Schlesinger, *A Thousand Days*, p. 325.
61 Memo of discussion in the NSC, 13 July 1961.
62 Beschloss, *Crisis Years*, p. 255.
63 Sorensen memo for JFK, 17 July 1961, document 2184, National Security Archive collection on *The Berlin Crisis, 1958-1962* (Alexandria, VA: Chadwyck-Healey, 1991) – hereafter cited as the NSA Berlin Collection; memorandum of meeting on Berlin, 17 July 1961, memorandum of conversation, 18 July 1961, and memorandum of meeting on Berlin, 18 July 1961 – all in *FRUS, 1961-1963*, XIV.
64 Memorandum of minutes of the NSC Meeting, 19 July 1961, *FRUS, 1961-1963*, XIV; 14 July 1961 Gallup poll in Gallup, *The Gallup Poll*, vol. 3, p. 1726.

65 Thomas C. Schelling Paper, 5 July 1961, *FRUS, 1961-1963*, XIV.
66 Kennedy, radio and television report to the American people on the Berlin crisis, 25 July 1961, American Presidency Project.
67 Ibid.
68 Ibid.
69 Ibid.
70 Ibid.
71 Ibid.
72 Beschloss, *Crisis Years*, p. 261.
73 Schlesinger, *A Thousand Days*, p. 329.
74 Schlesinger, *A Thousand Days*, pp. 327–8; Salinger memo for JFK, 8 August 1961, document 2276, Berlin NSA Collection.
75 Oral history of Hillenbrand, p. 16; Schlesinger, *A Thousand Days*, p. 329.
76 Beschloss, *Crisis Years*, p. 264; Bundy, *Danger and Survival*, p. 682 fn. 15; Kennedy news conference, 10 August 1961, Kennedy Library Digital.
77 Freedman, *Kennedy's Wars: Berlin, Cuba, Laos, and Vietnam*, p. 75.
78 Beschloss, *The Crisis Years*, pp. 266–7.
79 Schlesinger, *A Thousand Days*, p. 330; Khrushchev, *Khrushchev Remembers: The Last Testament*, p. 506; Clifford, *Counsel to the President*, p. 356.
80 Beschloss, *Crisis Years*, p. 272; oral history of Kohler, p. 5.
81 Beschloss, *Crisis Years*, p. 273; oral history of Lucius D. Clay, p. 3, Kennedy Library.
82 JFK memo for Rusk, 14 August 1961, document 2299; Robert Kennedy memo for JFK, 17 August 1961, document 2329; JFK memo for McNamara, 14 August 1961, document 2301 – all from the NSA Berlin Collection.
83 Schlesinger, *A Thousand Days*, p. 330; letter from US government to Soviet government, 17 August 1961, in Martin W. Sandler, ed., *The Letters of John F. Kennedy* (London: Bloomsbury, 2013), pp. 247–9; O'Donnell and Powers, '*Johnny, We Hardly Knew Ye*', p. 303.
84 Brandt letter to JFK, 16 August 1961, and JFK letter to Brandt, 18 August 1961, in *FRUS, 1961-1963*, XIV; JFK memo for Lyndon Johnson, 18 August 1961, document 2351, NSA Berlin Collection; oral history of Willy Brandt, p. 1, Lyndon B. Johnson Library, www.discoverlbj.org/item/oh-brandtw-nd-1-03-07; Schlesinger, *A Thousand Days*, pp. 330–1; 6 September 1961 Gallup poll, in Gallup, *The Gallup Poll*, vol. 3, p. 1734.
85 Pearson, *Washington Merry-Go-Round*, p. 98.
86 Even after JFK had succeeded in protecting West Berlin that summer, Acheson for some unfathomable reason believed that Kennedy was about to give Berlin to the Russians. See Ferrell, ed., *Off the Record*, pp. 396–7.
87 Irving Bernstein, *Promises Kept: John F. Kennedy's New Frontier* (New York and Oxford: Oxford University Press, 1991); Giglio, *Presidency of John F. Kennedy*, p. 120.
88 Giglio, *Presidency of John F. Kennedy*, pp. 97–104 provides fluent coverage of these domestic-policy initiatives.
89 Andrew Soergel, 'Which Presidents Have Been Best for the Economy?' *U.S. News & World Report*, (28 October 2015); Giglio, *Presidency of John F. Kennedy*, pp. 106, 135–9.
90 Giglio, *Presidency of John F. Kennedy*, pp. 129–33; Benjamin C. Bradlee, *Conversations with Kennedy* (New York: Pocket, 1976 paperback edn), p. 77; JFK news conference, 11 April 1962, Kennedy Library Digital.
91 Carl M. Brauer, 'Kennedy, Johnson and the War on Poverty,' *Journal of American History* 69 (June 1982), pp. 98–119.

92 Shauna Shames and Pamela O'Leary, 'JFK, a Pioneer in the Women's Movement,' *Los Angeles Times*, 22 November 2013, https://www.latimes.com/opinion/la-xpm-2013-nov-22-la-oe-shames-kennedy-women-20131122-story.html; Giglio, *Presidency of John F. Kennedy*, p. 142; Terry O'Neill, 'JFK's Contribution to Women's Rights – and What He Might Want US to Do Next,' *National Organization for Women*, 22 November 2013, https://now.org/blog/jfks-contribution-to-womens-rights-and-what-he-might-want-us-to-do-next/.
93 JFK's inaugural address, 20 January 1961, American Presidency Project.
94 Nick Bryant, *The Bystander: John F. Kennedy and the Struggle for Black Equality* (New York: Basic Books, 2006), pp. 261–2; oral history of James L. Farmer, no. 1, p. 5, Kennedy Library; Raymond Arsenault, *Freedom Riders: 1961 and the Struggle for Racial Justice* (New York: Oxford University Press, 2006), p. 4.
95 Bryant, *Bystander*, pp. 262–3; oral history of Farmer, no. 1, pp. 6–7.
96 Bryant, *Bystander*, pp. 263–4; Harris Wofford, *Of Kennedys and Kings: Making Sense of the Sixties* (New York: Farrar, Straus, Giroux, 1980), pp. 151–2.
97 Nicholas deB. Katzenbach, *Some of It Was Fun: Working with RFK and LBJ* (New York and London: Norton, 2008), pp. 43–4; Wofford, *Of Kennedys and Kings*, p. 152.
98 Bryant, *Bystander*, p. 264; Wofford, *Of Kennedys and Kings*, p. 153.
99 Wofford, *Of Kennedys and Kings*, pp. 152–4; Bryant, *Bystander*, pp. 268–9.
100 Arsenault, *Freedom Riders*, p. 220; Bryant, *Bystander*, pp. 269–73; Katzenbach, *Some of It Was Fun*, pp. 44–6.
101 JFK, statement by the president concerning interference with the "Freedom Riders" in Alabama, 20 May 1961, American Presidency Project.
102 Wofford, *Of Kennedys and Kings*, pp. 125–6.
103 Bryant, *Bystander*, pp. 276–8; oral history of Farmer, no. 1, p. 7.
104 JFK, special message to the Congress on urgent national needs, 25 May 1961, American Presidency Project; Bryant, *Bystander*, p. 279.
105 JFK press conference, 19 July 1961, Kennedy Library Digital.
106 Katzenbach, *Some of It Was Fun*, pp. 46–7; Wofford, *Of Kennedys and Kings*, p. 157.
107 Katzenbach, *Some of It Was Fun*, p. 47; oral history of Farmer, no. 1, p. 7.

Chapter 4

1 Goodwin to JFK, 22 August 1961, Papers of Theodore C. Sorensen, box 48, John F. Kennedy Library, Boston, Massachusetts; Goodwin, *Remembering America*, pp. 195–202.
2 US Senate Select Committee to Study Governmental Operations with Respect to Intelligence Activities, interim report, S. Rept. 94-465, 94th Congress, 1st session, *Alleged Assassination Plots Involving Foreign Leaders*, passim.
3 Ibid.
4 Ibid.
5 Ibid.; oral history of Smathers, interview 1, tape 2, pp. 6–7.
6 *Alleged Assassination Plots*, passim; Beschloss, *Crisis Years*, pp. 134–5; Wofford, *Of Kennedys and Kings*, p. 362.
7 Thomas Parrott, memorandum for the record, 5 October 1961, National Security Files, Countries Series, Cuba, General, 6/61–12/61, Kennedy Library.
8 Ibid.

9   National Security Action Memorandum No, 2422, 'U.S. Policy Toward Cuba,' 5 May 1961, National Security Files, box 313, Kennedy Library.
10 Goodwin, *Remembering America*, pp. 187–8; CIA Paper on Covert Actions Against Cuba, undated, *FRUS, 1961-1963*, X.
11 *Alleged Assassination Plots*, p. 141.
12 John Kennedy, memorandum to Rusk, McNamara et al, 30 November 1961, President's Office Files, Countries Series, Cuba, Security, 1961, Kennedy Library; National Security Council meeting, 18 January 1962, National Security Files, box 313, Kennedy Library; Richard Helms, memorandum for John McCone, 19 January 1962, *FRUS, 1961-1963*, X.
13 William Craig, memorandum for Edward Lansdale, 2 February 1962, John F. Kennedy Assassination Records Collection, National Archives and Records Administration, College Park, MD.
14 Taylor, Guidelines for Operation Mongoose, 14 March 1962, *FRUS, 1961-1963*, X.
15 Ibid., p. 771n.
16 White, *Missiles in Cuba*, pp. 22, 28–9.
17 'Big Maneuver Opens,' *New York Times*, 10 April 1962; 'President Sees Atlantic Fleet Hunt and Destroy "Enemy" Submarine,' *New York Times*, 15 April 1962.
18 White, *Missiles in Cuba*, p. 40. For the Soviet side of the superpower confrontation over Cuba in 1962, Aleksandr Fursenko and Timothy Naftali, *'One Hell of a Gamble': Khrushchev, Castro, and Kennedy, 1958-1964* (New York: Norton, 1997) is excellent.
19 As an example of this literature, see Thomas G. Paterson, 'Fixation with Cuba: The Bay of Pigs, Missile Crisis, and Covert War against Fidel Castro,' in Paterson, ed., *Kennedy's Quest for Victory: American Foreign Policy, 1961-1963* (New York: Oxford University Press, 1989).
20 White, *Missiles in Cuba*, pp. 31–4.
21 Ibid., pp. 35–6.
22 As an example of Eisenhower revisionism, see Stephen E. Ambrose, *Eisenhower: The President* (New York: Simon and Schuster, 1984).
23 White, *Missiles in Cuba*, p. 53.
24 Kenneth Keating speech, *Congressional* Record, 87th Congress, 2nd session, pp. 18358-18359; Republican Congressional Committee, 'The Cuban Issue: A Chronology,' May 1963, Papers of John Sherman Cooper, box 551, University of Kentucky Library, Lexington, Kentucky.
25 Theodore Sorensen, memorandum for the files, 6 September 1962, *FRUS, 1961-1963*, X; McCone memorandum, 'Soviet MRBMs in Cuba,' 31 October 1962, in Mary S. McAuliffe, ed., *CIA Documents on the Cuban Missile Crisis 1962* (CIA: Washington DC, October 1992), pp. 13–17; White, *Missiles in Cuba*, p. 57.
26 White House news conference with Pierre Salinger, 4 September 1962, National Security Files, box 36, Kennedy Library; presidential news conference, 13 September 1962, US National Archives and Records Service, *Public Papers of the Presidents of the United States: John F. Kennedy, 1962* (Washington, DC: US Government Printing Office, 1963), pp. 674–5.
27 Taylor, memorandum for Kennedy, 17 August 1962, National Security Files, Meetings and Memoranda Series, Special Group (Augmented), Operation Mongoose, 8/62, Kennedy Library; McCone, memorandum of Mongoose meeting, 4 October 1962, US Department of State, *FRUS, 1961-1963* (Washington, DC: US Government Printing Office, 1996), vol. XI, *Cuban Missile Crisis and Aftermath*.
28 Taylor, memorandum for Kennedy, 17 August 1962.

29 Kennedy, memorandum for McNamara, 21 September 1962, *FRUS, 1961-1963*, X.
30 McCone, memorandum of meeting with Kennedy, 11 October 1962, *FRUS, 1961-1963*, XI; James G. Hershberg, 'Before "The Missiles of Cuba": Did Kennedy Plan a Military Strike against Cuba?' *Diplomatic History* 14 (spring 1990), pp. 163–98.
31 White, *Missiles in Cuba*, p. 76.
32 Chronology for The Cuban Missile Crisis, 1962 collection, National Security Archive (NSA), Washington, DC; Frank Sieverts, internal Kennedy administration history, 'The Cuban Crisis, 1962,' 22 August 1963, p. 34, document no. 3154, NSA; Elie Abel, *The Missile Crisis* (Philadelphia: Lippincott, 1966), pp. 43–4; White, *Missiles in Cuba*, p. 79.
33 Transcript, ExComm meeting, 11:50 am-12.57 pm, 16 October 1962 (hereafter ExComm transcript, First Meeting), p. 27, and transcript, ExComm meeting, 6.30 pm-7.55 pm, 16 October 1962 (hereafter ExComm transcript, Second Meeting), pp. 18–19 – both in Presidential Recordings, Kennedy Library; oral history of Roswell L. Gilpatric, p. 50, Kennedy Library.
34 ExComm transcript, Second Meeting, pp. 11–15, 25, 35, 36; ExComm transcript, First Meeting, p. 1, 13, 21–2.
35 Transcript, ExComm meeting, 6.30–8.00 pm, 16 October 1962, in Timothy Naftali and Philip Zelikow, eds., *The Presidential Recordings: John F. Kennedy: The Great Crises* (New York and London: Norton, 2001), vol. II, p. 437; ExComm transcript, 6.30 pm, 16 October 1962, in Ernest R. May and Philip D. Zelikow, *The Kennedy Tapes: Inside the White House during the Cuban Missile Crisis* (Cambridge, MA, and London: Belknap Press of Harvard University, 1997) p. 114.
36 ExComm transcript, 6.30 pm–8.00 pm, 16 October 1962, *Presidential Recordings: Kennedy*, II, p. 466; ExComm transcript, 11.00 am, 18 October 1962, *Kennedy Tapes*, p. 143; ExComm transcript, 11.10 am–1.15 pm, 18 October 1962, *Presidential Recordings: Kennedy*, II, pp. 545, 547.
37 Robert Kennedy, *Thirteen Days*, p. 25.
38 ExComm transcript, 11.10 am–1.15 pm, 18 October 1962, *Presidential Recordings: Kennedy*, II, pp. 538, 547, 581, 589, 593; ExComm transcript, 11:00 am, 18 October 1962, pp. 144–6.
39 Oral history of Acheson, p. 24, and Dean G. Acheson, 'Dean Acheson's Version of Robert Kennedy's Version of the Cuban Missile Affair: Homage to Plain Dumb Luck,' *Esquire* 71 (February 1969), pp. 44, 46, 76–7; memorandum of conversation between Kennedy and Gromyko, 18 October 1962, National Security Files, Countries Series, USSR, Gromyko Talks, Kennedy Library.
40 Transcript, meeting between JFK and the Joint Chiefs, 9:45 am, 19 October 1962, *Kennedy Tapes*, pp. 174–5, 178–9, 183, 186; transcript, meeting between JFK and the Joint Chiefs, 9.45–10.30 am, 19 October 1962, *Presidential Recordings: Kennedy*, II, pp. 581, 589, 593.
41 White, *Missiles in Cuba*, pp. 94–5; Meeker, minutes of ExComm meeting, 11.00 am, 19 October 1962, document no. 699, The Cuban Missile Crisis, 1962, collection, NSA.
42 Minutes of the 505th meeting of the National Security Council, 2.30–5.10 pm, 20 October 1962, in *FRUS, 1961-1963*, XI.
43 Ibid.
44 O'Donnell and Powers, '*Johnny, We Hardly Knew Ye*', pp. 325–6.
45 McNamara, notes on meeting with JFK, 21 October 1962, *FRUS, 1961-1963*, XI.
46 JFK, radio and television report to the American people on the Soviet arms build-up in Cuba, 22 October 1962, *Public Papers of the Presidents, 1962*, pp. 806–9;

transcript, ExComm meeting, 3 pm, 22 October 1962, *Kennedy Tapes*, pp. 230–44; memorandum of meeting between JFK and the Congressional leadership on 22 October, 24 October 1962, *Kennedy Tapes*, pp. 247–75.
47 Rusk, *As I Saw It*, p. 235; Kennedy to Khrushchev, 22 October 1962, *FRUS, 1961-1963*, XI.
48 JFK, radio and television report to the American people on the Soviet arms build-up in Cuba, 22 October 1962.
49 Ibid.
50 Ibid.
51 White, *Missiles in Cuba*, p. 111; Mimi Alford, *Once Upon A Secret: My Hidden Affair with JFK* (London: Arrow, 2013), pp. 91–2.
52 J. Hoberman, 'When Dr No Met Dr Strangelove,' *Sight and Sound* 3 (December 1993), p. 18.
53 'Show Business,' *Time* magazine, 19 October 1962, *Dr. No* microjacket, British Film Institute, London.
54 White, *Missiles in Cuba*, p. 103.
55 Ibid., p. 114.
56 Robert Kennedy, *Thirteen Days*, p. 40.
57 Kennedy to Khrushchev, 23 October 1962, *FRUS, 1961-1963*, XI; White, *Missiles in Cuba*, p. 118.
58 JFK, proclamation 3504: interdiction of the delivery of offensive weapons to Cuba, 23 October 1962, *Public Papers of the Presidents, 1962*, pp. 809–11; May and Zelikow, eds, *Kennedy Tapes*, p. 347; Robert Kennedy, memorandum for JFK, 24 October 1962, President's Office Files, Cuba Security, Kennedy Library.
59 Kennedy, *Thirteen Days*, pp. 47–8.
60 Ibid., pp. 49–50; O'Donnell and Powers, '*Johnny, We Hardly Knew Ye*', p. 332.
61 Khrushchev to Kennedy, 24 October 1962, President's Office Files, Cuba, Kennedy Library; Executive Committee Record of Action, 10.00 am, 25 October 1962, Summary Record of NSC Executive Committee meeting no. 5, 5.00 pm, 25 October 1962, unauthored memorandum, 'Political Path,' 25 October 1962, unauthored and undated memorandum, 'Scenario for Airstrike against offensive missile bases and bombers in Cuba' – all of these are in National Security Files, box 315, Kennedy Library. See, also, Rostow memorandum, 'The Possible Role of a Progressive Economic Blockade Against Cuba,' 25 October 1962, National Security Files, box 36, Kennedy Library; and McCone memorandum, 'Meeting of the NSC Executive Committee, 25 October, 5:00 P.M.,' 26 October 1962, in McAuliffe, ed., *CIA Documents*, p. 309.
62 Dean to Foreign Office, 25 October 1962, FO 371/162387, National Archives, Kew.
63 White, *Missiles in Cuba*, p. 127; Adlai E. Stevenson and Valerian A. Zorin, 'Has the U.S.S.R. Missiles in Cuba? United Nations Debate,' *Vital Speeches of the Day* 29 (15 November 1962), pp. 80–2.
64 Transcript, ExComm meeting, 10.00 am, 26 October 1962, *Kennedy Tapes*, pp. 443–71 (and p. 685).
65 Ibid., pp. 463–4. See, also, for Stevenson's role in the missile crisis Sheldon M. Stern, *The Cuban Missile Crisis in American Memory: Myths versus Reality* (Stanford: Stanford University Press, 2012), pp. 129–33.
66 Khrushchev to Kennedy, 26 October 1962, Department of State Records, National Archives and Records Administration, College Park, MD; Kennedy, *Thirteen Days*, pp. 68–9; Bruce J. Allyn et al., eds, *Back to the Brink: Proceedings of the Moscow*

Conference on the Cuban Missile Crisis, January 27-28, 1989 (Lanham, MD: University Press of America, 1992), pp. 112–14, 117–18.
67 Khrushchev to Kennedy, 27 October 1962, *FRUS, 1961-1963*, XI.
68 Fursenko and Naftali, *"One Hell of a Gamble"*, pp. 273–4.
69 Kennedy, *Thirteen Days*, p. 75; Kennedy to Khrushchev, 28 October 1962, *FRUS, 1961-1963*, XI; Castro to Khrushchev, 26 October 1962, in Laurence Chang and Peter Kornbluh, eds, *The Cuban Missile Crisis, 1962: A National Security Archive Documents Reader* (New York: New Press, 1992), p. 189.
70 Transcript, ExComm meeting, 4.00 pm, 27 October 1962, *Kennedy Tapes*, pp. 563, 566; undated Lyndon Johnson notes on NSC meeting [apparently written on 27 October], Vice Presidential Security Files, box 8, Lyndon B. Johnson Library, Austin, Texas.
71 Kennedy, *Thirteen Days*, pp. 79–80.
72 Allyn et al., eds, *Back to the Brink*, p. 93; transcript, ExComm meeting, 10.00 am, 27 October 1962, *Kennedy Tapes*, pp. 497–9. For a critique of Robert Kennedy's *Thirteen Days*, see Stern, *The Cuban Missile Crisis in American Memory*, pp. 32–9.
73 Transcripts, ExComm meetings, 10.00 am and 4 pm, 27 October 1962, *Kennedy Tapes*, pp. 498, 501, 512, 548.
74 Kennedy, *Thirteen Days*, pp. 84–7; Dobrynin, cable to Soviet Foreign Ministry, 27 October 1962, in Woodrow Wilson International Center, *Cold War International History Project Bulletin* 5 (Spring 1995), pp. 79–80; Kennedy to Khrushchev, 27 October 1962, *FRUS, 1961-1963*, XI.
75 Transcript, ExComm meeting, 4.00 pm, 27 October 1962, *Kennedy Tapes*, p. 568; Rusk, *As I Saw It*, pp. 240–1. See, also, Philip Nash, *The Other Missiles of October: Eisenhower, Kennedy, and the Jupiters, 1957-1963* (Chapel Hill: University of North Carolina Press, 1997), pp. 144–5.
76 Wesley O. Hagood, *Presidential Sex: From the Founding Fathers to Bill* Clinton (New York: Grove, 1997), p. 176; Alford, *Once Upon A Secret*, p. 93.
77 Alford, *Once Upon a Secret*, pp. 87–8.
78 Ibid., 93–4.
79 Ibid., 94–5.
80 Ibid., p. 95; White, *Missiles in Cuba*, pp. 142–4.
81 Khrushchev to Kennedy, 28 October 1962, *FRUS, 1961-1963*, XI; Kennedy, *Thirteen Days*, p. 88; Dobrynin, telegram to Soviet Foreign Ministry, 28 October 1962, in *Cold War International History Project Bulletin* 5 (Spring 1995), p. 76.
82 Transcript, ExComm meeting, 11.10 am, 28 October 1962, National Security Files, Meetings and Memoranda Series, Executive Committee, Vol. I, Meetings 6-10, Kennedy Library; White, *Missiles in Cuba*, pp. 144–5.
83 Kennedy, *Thirteen Days*, p. 88.
84 Ibid., p. 88.

Chapter 5

1 William Burr and Hector L. Montford, eds, 'The Making of the Limited Test Ban Treaty, 1958-1963,' 8 August 2003, National Security Archive (NSA), https://nsarchive2.gwu.edu/NSAEBB/NSAEBB94/index.htm [hereafter cited as NSA Test Ban Collection]; Martha Smith-Norris, 'The Eisenhower Administration and the Nuclear Test Ban Talks,, 1958-1960: Another Challenge to "Revisionism", *Diplomatic*

     History 27 (September 2003), pp. 503–41; PBS documentary, *The Kennedys*; Ormsby-Gore quoted in Thurston Clarke, *JFK's Last Hundred Days: An Intimate Portrait of a Great President* (London: Allen Lane, 2013), p. 7.
2. JFK, television and radio interview: 'After Two Years – a Conversation with the President,' 17 December 1962, American Presidency Project.
3. Oral history of Bundy, p. 47; Stephen G. Rabe, 'After the Missiles of October: John F. Kennedy and Cuba, November 1962 to November 1963,' *Presidential Studies Quarterly* 30 (December 2000), pp. 714–26.
4. Editorial Notes 251, 254 and 262, and memorandum of conversation, 9 January 1963, *FRUS, 1961-1963* (Washington, DC: US Government Printing Office, 1995), *Arms Control and Disarmament*, vol. VII; NSA Test Ban Collection.
5. See Kennedy's press conferences on 21 February, 6 March, 21 March and 24 April 1963, Kennedy Library Digital; McNamara memo for Kennedy, 16 February 1963, NSA Test Ban Collection.
6. Robert Kennedy memo for JFK, 3 April 1963, as summarised in Editorial Note 270, *FRUS, 1961-1963*, VII; Theo Zenou, 'John F. Kennedy and the Summer of Peace, 1963,' PhD thesis, University of Cambridge (2023), p. 11; Richard Reeves, *President Kennedy: Profile of Power* (New York: Simon and Schuster, 1993), p. 510.
7. Reeves, *President Kennedy*, p. 510; memorandum of conversation, 9 January 1963 and Editorial Note 262, *FRUS, 1961-1963*, VII; Dallek, *John F. Kennedy*, p. 613.
8. Reeves, *President Kennedy*, pp. 510–11.
9. Kennedy to Macmillan, 28 March 1963, Macmillan to Kennedy, 3 April 1963, Kennedy to Macmillan, 11 and 15 April 1963, Kennedy and Macmillan to Khrushchev, 15 April 1963, Kennedy to Khrushchev, 11 April 1963, Khrushchev to Kennedy, 8 May and 8 June 1963 – all in *FRUS, 1961-1963*, VII.
10. NSAM No. 239, 6 May 1963, *FRUS, 1961-1963*, VII.
11. Reeves, *President Kennedy*, pp. 511–12. It must have followed Cousins's plea to JFK for a great speech but McGeorge Bundy recalled that a month or so before this address, Kennedy, Sorensen and himself 'reached a reasonable agreement that we needed to make a speech on peace, that we had that University engagement coming and that it would be then'. See oral history of Bundy, p. 44.
12. Schlesinger, *A Thousand Days*, pp. 693–4; Sorensen, *Counselor*, p. 326.
13. Sorensen, *Counselor*, p. 326; Proctor memorandum for the record, 8 June 1963, *FRUS, 1961-1963*, VII; Zenou, 'John F. Kennedy and the Summer of Peace, 1963,' p. 35.
14. Beschloss, *Crisis Years*, p. 599.
15. JFK, commencement address at American University, 10 June 1963, American Presidency Project.
16. Ibid.
17. Ibid.
18. Ibid.
19. Ibid.
20. Ibid.
21. Zenou, 'John F. Kennedy and the Summer of Peace, 1963,' p. 233.
22. JFK, commencement address at American University, 10 June 1963.
23. Beschloss, *Crisis Years*, p. 602; Kennedy news conference, 12 December 1962, Kennedy Library Digital.
24. Bunn, memorandum of conversation, 14 June 1963, CIA National Intelligence Estimate, 28 June 1963, Glenn Seaborg, journal entry, 21 June 1963, Editorial Note 297 – all in *FRUS, 1961-1963*, VII.

25 Oral history of Carl Kaysen, #2, pp. 117–19, 121, Kennedy Library; Beschloss, *Crisis Years*, p. 601; Kennedy to Khrushchev, in Bundy telegram for Harriman, 12 July 1963, *FRUS, 1961-1963*, VII; Schlesinger, *A Thousand Days*, p. 697; CIA Information Report on 'Soviet Reaction to 10 June Speech of President Kennedy', 11 June 1963, NSA Test Ban Collection; Beschloss, *Crisis Years*, p. 601.
26 Editorial Note 309, *FRUS, 1961-1963*, VII; Ball memo for Kennedy, 'Analysis of Language of Khrushchev speech regarding test ban and NATO Warsaw Pact', 2 July 1963, NSA Test Ban Collection; Beschloss, *Crisis Years*, p. 618.
27 Editorial Note 309; Rusk to Schroeder, 3 July 1963; instructions for Harriman, 10 July 1963 – all in *FRUS, 1961-1963*, VII.
28 Summary record of the 515th NSC meeting, 9 July 1963, *FRUS, 1961-1963*, VII.
29 Kennedy to Khrushchev, in Bundy telegram for Harriman, 12 July 1963.
30 Andreas Wegner and Marcel Gerber, 'John F. Kennedy and the Limited Test Ban Treaty', *Presidential Studies Quarterly* 29 (June 1999), p. 478; Reeves, *President Kennedy*, p. 545.
31 Schlesinger, *A Thousand Days*, pp. 697–9; Freedman, *Kennedy's Wars*, pp. 272–4; oral history of Kaysen, #2, pp. 129–30; Kohler to Rusk, 24 July 1963, NSA Test Ban Collection.
32 Schlesinger, *A Thousand Days*, p. 700; Clarke, *JFK's Last Hundred Days*, p. 9.
33 Schesinger, *A Thousand Days*, p. 700; Rusk, *As I Saw It*, p. 256; Beschloss, *Crisis Years*, p. 628.
34 Diary entry, 10 September 1963, in Pearson, *Washington Merry-Go-Round*, p. 196; Kennedy, radio and television address to the American people on the Nuclear Test Ban Treaty, 26 July 1963, American Presidency Project; Wegner and Gerber, 'John F. Kennedy and the Limited Test Ban Treaty', p. 479; Clarke, *JFK's Last Hundred Days*, p. 22; Zenou, 'John F. Kennedy and the Summer of Peace, 1963,' pp. 14–15; Gallup poll on the Test Ban Treaty, 1 September 1963, in *The Gallup Poll*, vol. 3, p. 1837.
35 JCS memo for McNamara, 10 April 1963, *FRUS, 1961-1963*, VII.
36 Wegner and Gerber, 'John F. Kennedy and the Limited Test Ban Treaty', p. 478; Freedman, *Kennedy's Wars*, p. 275; Schlesinger, *A Thousand Days*, p. 703.
37 Clarke, *JFK's Last Hundred Days*, pp. 25–6, 30–1.
38 Rusk, *As I Saw It*, p. 257; Beschloss, *Crisis Years*, pp. 628–9; Zenou, 'John F. Kennedy and the Summer of Peace', 1963, p. 14.
39 Rusk, *As I Saw It*, p. 259.
40 Stevenson letter to Steinbeck, 15 August 1963, in Johnson, ed., *Papers of Adlai E. Stevenson*, p. 445; Beschloss, *Crisis Years*, pp. 646–7, 658–9.
41 Oral history of Smathers, no. 3, p. 6F; Wofford, *Of Kennedys and Kings*, p. 168; oral history of Roy Wilkins, pp. 23–4, Kennedy Library.
42 Reeves, *President Kennedy*, p. 468; oral history of Wilkins, p. 20; Bryant, *Bystander*, pp. 370–6.
43 Taylor Branch, *Pillar of Fire: America in the King Years, 1963-65* (New York: Simon and Schuster, 1998), passim, for detailed coverage of the Birmingham protests; Bryant, *Bystander*, p. 381.
44 Aldon D. Morris, 'Birmingham Confrontation Reconsidered: An Analysis of the Dynamics and Tactics of Mobilization,' *American Sociological Review* 58 (October 1993), p. 628; Branch, *Pillar of Fire*, pp. 46–9.
45 Stephen Levingston, 'Children have Changed America before, Braving Fire Hoses and Police Dogs for Civil Rights,' *Washington* Post, 23 March 2018; Bryant, *Bystander*, pp. 386–9.

46 Bryant, *Bystander*, p. 385; oral history of Burke Marshall, no. 5, pp. 97–102, Kennedy Library. For the skill shown by Marshall in these negotiations, see Victor S. Navasky, *Kennedy Justice* (New York: Atheneum, 1971), pp. 218–19.
47 JFK press conference, 8 May 1963, Kennedy Library Digital; diary entries, 9 and 12 May 1963, in Pearson, *Washington Merry-Go-Round*, pp. 181–2; Bryant, *Bystander*, pp. 390–3; Navasky, *Kennedy Justice*, pp. 208, 218.
48 Navasky, *Kennedy Justice*, p. 441; Wofford, *Of Kennedys and Kings*, p. 171; Schlesinger, *A Thousand Days*, pp. 739–40; Giglio, *Presidency of John F. Kennedy*, p. 179.
49 JFK press conferences, 8 and 22 May 1963, Kennedy Library Digital; Bryant, *Bystander*, p. 417; Katzenbach, *Some of It Was Fun*, pp. 109, 111, 114; Sorensen, *Counselor*, p. 278.
50 *Robert Kennedy: In His Own Words*, pp. 149, 173; Bryant, *Bystander*, pp. 397, 401; JFK press conferences, 8 and 22 May 1963; Katzenbach, *Some of It Was Fun*, p. 118; Wofford, *Of Kennedys and Kings*, p. 172.
51 Oral history of Marshall, no. 5, pp. 108–9; *Robert Kennedy: In His Own Words*, pp. 175–7; Robert Drew, *Crisis: Behind a Presidential Commitment* documentary (1963); Wofford, *Of Kennedys and Kings*, p. 173; Sorensen, *Counselor*, p. 279.
52 *Robert Kennedy: In His Own Words*, p. 176; oral history of Marshall, #5, pp. 109–10; Bryant, *Bystander*, p. 422; Sorensen, *Counselor*, p. 280.
53 JFK, radio and television report to the American people on civil rights, 11 June 1963, American Presidency Project.
54 Ibid.
55 Ibid.; Bryant, *Bystander*, pp. 423–4; Wofford, *Of Kennedys and Kings*, p. 173.
56 Oral history of Marshall, no. 5, p. 110; entry for 17 June 1963, President's Appointments Book, Kennedy Library.
57 *Robert Kennedy: In His Own Words*, pp. 203–5, 216–18; Katzenbach, *Some of It Was Fun*, pp. 118–29.
58 Katzenbach, *Some of It Was Fun*, p. 125; oral history of John R. Lewis, p. 2, Kennedy Library; oral history of Farmer, p. 20; Kennedy press conference, 17 July 1963, Kennedy Library Digital; Reeves, *President Kennedy*, pp. 580–1, 584.
59 Gallup polls on Integration (July 10) and Integration (July 14) in *The Gallup Poll*, vol. 3, pp. 1827, 1828, 1836.
60 Gallup polls, 1 March and 20 September 1963, in *The Gallup Poll*, vol. 3, pp. 1807, 1840.
61 Robert D. Schulzinger, *A Time for War: The United States and Vietnam, 1941-1975* (New York: Oxford University Press, 1997), is an insightful history of US involvement in Vietnam, including during the Kennedy years; George C. Herring, *America's Longest War: The United States and Vietnam, 1950-1975* (New York: McGraw-Hill, 1996 edn.), pp. 95–9; John Dumbrell, *Rethinking the Vietnam War* (Basingstoke: Palgrave Macmillan, 2012), p. 38; Dallek, *John F. Kennedy*, p. 665.
62 *Robert Kennedy: In His Own Words*, pp. 394–5; Rusk, *As I Saw It*, p. 435.
63 Robert S. McNamara, *In Retrospect: The Tragedy and Lessons of Vietnam* (New York: Random House, 1995), pp. 37, 40, 41; Herring, *America's Longest War*, p. 92 ; Dallek, *John F. Kennedy*, p. 668; Sorensen, *Counselor*, pp. 356–7.
64 Mark Perry, 'MacArthur's Last Stand Against a Winless War,' *American Conservative*, 3 October 2018, www.americanconservative.com/macarthurs-last-stand-against-a-winless-war/.
65 *Robert Kennedy: In His Own Words*, p. 288.
66 O'Donnell and Powers, '*Johnny, We Hardly Knew Ye*', pp. 15–16.

67 See Kennedy news conferences, Kennedy Library Digital, passim.
68 Kennedy news conferences, 22 May and 17 July 1963, Kennedy Library Digital; McNamara, *In Retrospect*, pp. 48–9; Fredrik Logevall, *Choosing War: The Lost Chance for Peace and the Escalation of War in Vietnam* (Berkeley: University of California Press, 2001 paperback edn), p. 34; Heinz, memorandum for the record of the secretary of defense conference, 6 May 1963, *FRUS, 1961-1963* (Washington, DC: US Government Printing Office, 1991), *Vietnam, January-August 1963*, vol. III.
69 Transcription of Kennedy-Lodge meeting tape, 15 August 1963, in 'New Light in a Dark Corner: Evidence on the Diem Coup in South Vietnam, November 1963,' 1 November 2020, National Security Archive, https://nsarchive.gwu.edu/briefing-book-vietnam/2020-11-01/new-light-dark-corner-evidence-diem-coup-november-1963; Dumbrell, *Rethinking the Vietnam War*, p. 38; Luke A. Nichter, *The Last Brahmin: Henry Cabot Lodge Jr. and the Making of the Cold War* (New Haven: Yale University Press, 2020); George Fujii, H-Diplo Roundtable XXII-30, 8 March 2021, https://networks.h-net.org/node/28443/discussions/7380841/h-diplo-roundtable-xxii-30-nichter-last-brahmin-henry-cabot-lodge.
70 John Prados, Introduction, 'JFK and the Diem Coup,' 5 November 2003, National Security Archive (NSA) Electronic Briefing Book No. 101, https://nsarchive2.gwu.edu/NSAEBB/NSAEBB101/; McNamara, *In Retrospect*, p. 51; Ball, *Past Has Another Pattern*, p. 370; *Robert Kennedy: In His Own Words*, p. 404.
71 Ball telegram to Lodge, 24 August 1963, document 2, NSA Briefing Book No. 101; McNamara, *In Retrospect*, pp. 52–4; Ball, *Past Has Another Pattern*, pp. 371–2; Rusk, *As I Saw It*, pp. 437–8; *Robert Kennedy: In His Own Words*, pp. 396–7.
72 McNamara, *In Retrospect*, pp. 52, 56; Clarke, *JFK's Last Hundred Days*, p. 106; memo of conversation/conference with the president, 26 August 1963, 12 noon, 27 August 1963, 4 pm, 28 August 1963, 12 noon, and 29 August 1963, 12 noon – all in NSA Briefing Book No. 101; *Robert Kennedy: In His Own Words*, p. 397.
73 Bromley Smith notes of White House meeting, 28 August 1963, 4 p.m., 'New Light in a Dark Corner,' 1 November 2020, National Security Archive; memo of conference with the president, 29 August 1963, 12 noon, and cable from Rusk to Lodge, 29 August 1963, both in NSA Briefing Book No. 101; Dallek, *John F. Kennedy*, p. 675.
74 Memo of conversation, 27 August 1963, 4 pm, and memo of conference with the president, 28 August 1963, 12 noon.
75 Transcript of broadcast with Walter Cronkite inaugurating a CBS television news programme, 2 September 1963, and transcript of broadcast on NBC's 'Huntley-Brinkley Report,' 9 September 1963, American Presidency Project.
76 Hilsman, memorandum of conversation, 10 September 1963, *FRUS, 1961-1963* (Washington, DC: US Government Printing Office, 1991), *Vietnam, August-December 1963*, vol. IV; McNamara, *In Retrospect*, pp. 65–8, 73–7.
77 Taylor and McNamara memo for JFK, 2 October 1963, summary record of 519th NSC meeting, 2 October 1963, and NSAM No. 263, 11 October 1963, *FRUS, 1961-1963*, IV; McNamara, *In Retrospect*, pp. 80–1; JFK news conference, 31 October 1963, Kennedy Library Digital. Marc J. Selverstone's view is that Kennedy's stated plan to withdraw constituted political cover which enabled him to continue to provide military support to the Saigon government. See *The Kennedy Withdrawal: Camelot and the American Commitment to Vietnam* (Cambridge, MA: Harvard University Press, 2023).
78 CIA telegram, 5 October 1963, *FRUS, 1961-1963*, IV; McNamara, *In Retrospect*, p. 81.

79 Memo of conference with the president, 29 October 1963, 4.20 pm, and Bundy to Lodge, 30 October 1963, both in NSA Briefing Book No. 101; Herring, *America's Longest War*, p. 117.
80 Prados, Introduction, 'JFK and the Diem Coup'; memorandum of conference with the president, 1 November 1963, NSA Briefing Book No. 101.
81 John M. Dunn, memorandum for the record (of Diem-Lodge phone conversation), 1 November 1963, NSA Briefing Book No. 101.
82 McNamara, *In Retrospect*, p. 84; memorandum of conference with the president, 2 November 1963, 9.15 am, NSA Briefing Book No. 101.
83 Transcript, JFK's memoir dictation on the assassination of Diem, 4 November 1963, Miller Center, https://millercenter.org/the-presidency/educational-resources/jfk-memoir-dictation-assassination-of-diem.
84 McNamara, *In Retrospect*, pp. 51, 62, 71; quoted in Dumbrell, *Rethinking the Vietnam War*, p. 41.
85 McNamara, *In Retrospect*, pp. 59, 63, 66.

Chapter 6

1 Alford, *Once Upon A Secret*, pp. 39–43.
2 Ibid., pp. 43–4.
3 Ibid., pp. 45–8.
4 Ibid., pp. 48–9.
5 Ibid., pp. 49–50.
6 Ibid., p. 50.
7 Blair and Blair, *Search for JFK*; Reeves, *A Question of Character*; Wills, *Kennedy Imprisonment*; Hersh, *Dark Side of Camelot*, p. ix.
8 Alford, *Once Upon A Secret*, pp. 61–4.
9 Ibid., p. 65.
10 Ibid., p. 65; oral history of Cowan and Wear, p. 17.
11 Alford, *Once Upon A Secret*, pp. 66–7, 77–9.
12 Ibid., pp. 62, 65.
13 Ibid., pp. 101–3.
14 Ibid., pp. 99–101.
15 Ibid., p. 102; Richard Gehman, 'Ageless Cary Grant,' *Good Housekeeping*, September 1960, p. 64.
16 Oral history of Barbara Gamarekian, pp. 17, 19, Kennedy Library.
17 Ibid., pp. 28–9.
18 Hagood, *Presidential Sex*, p. 139; Andrew Morton, *Monica's Story* (New York: St. Martin's Press, 1999).
19 Sorensen, *Counselor*, p. 114; Bradlee, *Conversations with Kennedy*; Alford, *Once Upon A Secret*, pp. 67, 79; Hersh, *Dark Side of Camelot*, pp. 388–90.
20 Alford, *Once Upon A Secret*, pp. 84–5.
21 Ibid., p. 104.
22 Ibid., pp. 51, 78, 82.
23 Oral history of Cowan and Wear, pp. 2–3; oral history of Edwin R. Bayley, interview no. 2, p. 118, Kennedy Library; oral history of Pierre E.G. Salinger, interview no. 1, pp. 66–7, Kennedy Library.
24 Oral history of Cowan and Wear, p. 9.

25 Oral history of Cowan and Wear, p. 1; Laura Bergquist, 'Fiddle and Faddle,' *Look* 26 (2 January 1962), pp. 30–3, 35; Alford, *Once Upon A Secret*, p. 73; oral history of Gamarekian, pp. 31–2.
26 Alford, *Once Upon A Secret*, pp. 42–3; oral history of Cowan and Wear, pp. 23, 25; Hagood, *Presidential Sex*, p. 151.
27 Oral history of Gamarekian, p. 21.
28 Alford, *Once Upon A Secret*, pp. 57, 72–3; Hersh, *Dark Side of Camelot*, pp. 389–90; James Gordon, 'The Gushing Letters of JFK's Three Young Intern Lovers,' *Daily Mail*, 10 November 2013, https://www.dailymail.co.uk/news/article-2497991/Letters-White-House-interns-JFK-allegedly-affairs-with.html.
29 Oral history of Cowan and Wear, pp. 13, 16, 17, 22, 28.
30 Hagood, *Presidential Sex*, pp. 148–9.
31 Exner, *My Story*, pp. 86–7, 99–103, 116–20; interview with Judith Campbell Exner in Kitty Kelley, 'The Dark Side of Camelot,' *People*, 29 February 1988, https://people.com//archive/cover-story-the-dark-side-of-camelot-vol-29-no-8/.
32 Exner, *My Story*, pp. 197, 204; Kelley, 'The Dark Side of Camelot.'
33 Exner, *My Story*, pp. 215–16.
34 Kelley, 'The Dark Side of Camelot.'
35 Ibid.; Hersh, *Dark Side of Camelot*, pp. 294–325.
36 Kelley, 'The Dark Side of Camelot'; Hersh, *Dark Side of Camelot*, pp. 303, 307–8.
37 Gerri Hirshey, 'Kelley, Women and the Power of Pay Dirt,' *Washington Post*, 1 November 1988, https://www.washingtonpost.com/archive/lifestyle/1988/11/01/kelley-women-and-the-power-of-pay-dirt/2ae07f1f-cdf6-4ff4-1938-5822d17c55a73/?utm_term=.9d04d87331a3.
38 Kelley, 'The Dark Side of Camelot.'
39 PBS documentary, *The Kennedys* (1992); Hersh, *Dark Side of Camelot*, pp. 237, 399. The classic biography on Robert Kennedy is Arthur M. Schlesinger, Jr., *Robert Kennedy and His Times* (London: Andre Deutsch, 1978).
40 Kelley, 'The Dark Side of Camelot.'
41 Ibid.
42 Hersh, *Dark Side of Camelot*, p. 307.
43 Ibid., pp. 304–5, 324–5.
44 Exner, *My Story*, pp. 98, 100–1, 217, 219, 243.
45 Interview with Judith Campbell Exner in Liz Smith, 'The Exner Files,' *Vanity Fair*, January 1997, pp. 30–43, *passim*; Exner, *My Story*, pp. 90, 111, 136.
46 Exner, *My Story*, p. 247.
47 Hersh, *Dark Side of Camelot*, p. 299; Exner, *My Story*, pp. 104–5, 123, 131, 149, 164–6; US Senate interim report, *Alleged Assassination Plots Involving Foreign Leaders*, 94th Congress, 1st session, p. 129 (incl. footnote 2).
48 Exner, *My Story*, pp. 89–90, 231–3.
49 Hersh, *Dark Side of Camelot*, p. 312; Smith, 'The Exner Files.'
50 Smith, 'The Exner Files,' pp. 42–3.
51 Peter Janney, *Mary's Mosaic: The CIA Conspiracy to Murder John F. Kennedy, Mary Pinchot Meyer, and their Vision for World Peace* (New York: Skyhorse Publishing, 2016 paperback edn), p. 151.
52 Ibid., pp. 153–6, 166, 170–2.
53 Ibid., pp. 180–2, 184, 187, 189, 201, 204–5; Nina Burleigh, *A Very Private Woman: The Life and Unresolved Murder of Presidential Mistress Mary Meyer* (New York: Bantam, 1998), pp. 147–9, 152.

54 Janney, *Mary's Mosaic*, pp. 189, 200.
55 Ibid., pp. 206–7.
56 Bernie Ward and Granville Toogood, 'Former Vice President of Washington Post Reveals JFK 2-Year White House Romance,' *National Enquirer*, 2 March 1976, p. 4.
57 Ibid.; Janney, *Mary's Mosaic*, p. 226.
58 Janney, *Mary's Mosaic*, pp. 228, 232.
59 Ibid., pp. 230–1; Erin Blakemore, 'A Steamy Letter From JFK Is up for Auction,' *Smithsonian Magazine* (3 June 2016), https://www.smithsonianmag.com/smart-news/steamy-letter-jfk-auction-180959310/.
60 Bradlee, *Conversations with Kennedy*, p.54.
61 Ward and Toogood, 'Former Vice President of Washington Post Reveals JFK 2-Year White House Romance.'
62 Janney, *Mary's Mosaic*, p. 224.
63 Gehman, 'Ageless Cary Grant,' p. 64.
64 John A. Farrell, 'The Year Nixon Fell Apart,' *Politico*, 26 March 2017, https://www.politico.com/magazine/story/2017/03/john-farrell-nixon-book-excerpt-214954.
65 Heymann, *A Woman Named Jackie*, pp. 296–308, 313–14. Jacobson's widow gave Heymann access to her late husband's papers.
66 Ibid., pp. 296, 301, 309–11.
67 Ibid., p. 297n.
68 Ibid., pp. 311–13.
69 Ibid., pp. 541, 544.
70 Janney, *Mary's Mosaic*, p. 257.
71 Timothy Leary, *Flashbacks: An Autobiography* (Los Angeles: J.P. Tarcher, 1983), pp. 128–30.
72 Janney, *Mary's Mosaic*, p. 222.
73 Deborah Davis, *Katharine the Great: Katharine Graham and Her Washington Post Empire* (New York: Sheridan Square Press, 1991), p. 164; Sally Bedell Smith, *Grace and Power: The Private World of the Kennedy White House* (New York: Random House, 2004), p. 454.
74 Kelley, 'The Dark Side of Camelot'; Alford, *Once Upon A Secret*, pp. 133–5; Burleigh, *A Very Private Woman*, pp. 11–12.
75 Sarah Churchwell, *The Many Lives of Marilyn Monroe* (London: Granta, 2005), p. 223.
76 Anthony Summers, *Goddess: The Secret Lives of Marilyn Monroe* (London: Phoenix, 2000 paperback edn), pp. 307–9.
77 Reeves, *A Question of Character*, p. 124.
78 Summers, *Goddess*, pp. 291–2, 300–1. Monroe's attendance at a luncheon with JFK at Peter Lawford's home is confirmed by FBI sources. See memorandum for J. Edgar Hoover on Marilyn Monroe Security Matter, date unclear, pp. 18–19, FBI file on Marilyn Monroe, Part I, https://vault.fbi.gov/MarilynMonroe/MarilynMonroePart1of2/view.
79 Summers, *Goddess*, pp. 292, 294; W.J. Weatherby, *Conversations with Marilyn* (London: Robson Books, 1976), pp. 53, 55. See, also, Stanley Buchtal and Bernard Comment, *Fragments: Poems, Intimate Notes, Letters by Marilyn Monroe* (London: HarperCollins, 2010), pp. 220–1.
80 Memorandum for J. Edgar Hoover, 27 April 1956, FBI file on Marilyn Monroe, Part I (on how the FBI kept tabs on her left-wing views and associations); Weatherby, *Conversations with Marilyn*, pp. 171–2, 206; Milner's transcript of Monroe Tapes for Dr Ralph Greenson, www.jcrows.com/marilynbeyondthegrave.html.
81 Summers, *Goddess*, pp. 292, 302; Milner's transcript of Monroe Tapes for Dr. Ralph Greenson.

82 Summers, *Goddess*, p. 364.
83 Ibid., p. 365; Marilyn Monroe: Happy Birthday Rehearsal and Extended Performance, www.youtube.com/watch?v=t4bHRMaLoZM; Donald Spoto, *Marilyn Monroe: The Biography* (New York: HarperCollins, 1993), p. 578.
84 Marilyn Monroe: Happy Birthday Rehearsal and Extended Performance; 'Happy Birthday,' *Time*, 1 June 1962, www.time.com/time/printout/0,8816,938361,00.html.
85 Schlesinger, *Robert Kennedy and His Times*, p. 590; Cecil Stoughton photograph, John and Robert Kennedy and Marilyn Monroe, 19 May 1962, Kennedy Library.
86 Dirk Banse, L.-M. Nagel, and Uwe Muller, 'John F. Kennedy and his lover from the GDR,' *Die Welt*, 29 December 2013, https://www.welt.de/vermischtes/article123373410/John-F-Kennedy-und-seine-teliebte-aus-der-DDR.html; Hersh, *Dark Side of Camelot*, pp. 387–8.
87 Ibid., pp. 388–90.
88 For an insightful examination of the Profumo affair, see Richard Davenport-Hines, *An English Affair: Sex, Class and Power in the Age of Profumo* (New York: HarperCollins, 2012).
89 Bradlee, *Conversations with Kennedy*, pp. 227–8.
90 Hersh, *Dark Side of Camelot*, p. 391.
91 Ibid., pp. 391–2.
92 Ibid., pp. 394, 396–7.
93 Ibid., pp. 398–400.
94 Clark Mollenhoff, 'US Expels Girl Linked to Officials,' *Des Moines Register*, 26 October 1963, p. 1.
95 Hersh, *Dark Side of Camelot*, pp. 402–4
96 Clarke, *JFK's Last Hundred Days*, p. 275.
97 Bradlee, *Conversations with Kennedy*, pp. 225–6.
98 Banse, Nagel and Muller, 'John F. Kennedy and his lover from the GDR'; Beschloss, *Crisis Years*, p. 612.
99 Stewart Alsop and Charles Bartlett, 'In Time of Crisis,' *Saturday Evening Post*, 18 December 1962, pp. 16–20; White, *Cuban Missile Crisis*, p. 167.
100 Oral history of Richard Cardinal Cushing, p. 12, Kennedy Library.
101 PBS documentary, *The Kennedys* (1992).
102 John Kennedy, radio and television report to the American People on civil rights, 11 June 1963.
103 David A. Nichols, in his book *A Matter of Justice: Eisenhower and the Beginning of the Civil Rights Revolution* (New York: Simon and Schuster, 2007), tries to rehabilitate Ike's reputation on civil rights.
104 Parmet, *Jack*, p. 6.
105 Heymann, *A Woman Named Jackie*, p. 291.

Chapter 7

1 Sean J. Savage, 'Truman: The Everyman,' in Iwan Morgan and Mark White, eds, *The Presidential Image: A History from Theodore Roosevelt to Donald Trump* (London and New York: IB Tauris/Bloomsbury, 2020), pp. 75–92; Ambrose, *Eisenhower: The President*, pp. 52–3.
2 PBS documentary, *The Kennedys* (1992).

3   With previous examinations of JFK's image, among the most insightful are John Hellmann, *The Kennedy Obsession: The American Myth of JFK* (New York: Columbia University Press, 1997), and Michael J. Hogan, *The Afterlife of John Fitzgerald Kennedy: A Biography* (Cambridge: Cambridge University Press, 2017).
4   Gallup, 'Presidential Approval Ratings – Gallup Historical Statistics and Trends,' https://news.gallup.com/poll/116677/presidential-approval-ratings-gallup-historical-statistics-trends.aspx.
5   Exner, *My Story*, p. 111.
6   'The Monogram on This Man's Shirt is J.F.K.,' *Esquire,* January 1962, copy from Kennedy Library.
7   Rich Lowry, 'Never Mind the Chippies,' *New York Post*, 10 February 2012, https://nypost.com/2012/02/10/camelot-never-mind-the-chippies/; Beschloss, *Crisis Years*, p. 254.
8   Perceptive biographies of Monroe include Churchwell, *The Many Lives of Marilyn Monroe*; Spoto, *Marilyn Monroe*; Summers, *Goddess*.
9   Summers, *Goddess*, p. 298; Buchtal and Comment, *Fragments*, pp. 220–1; Mark White, *Kennedy: A Cultural History of an American Icon* (London and New York: Bloomsbury, 2013), pp. 69–70.
10 White, *Kennedy: A Cultural History of an American Icon*, pp. 70–1.
11 *Esquire* front cover, January 1963, www.esquire.com/cover/cover-detail?year=1963&month=1.
12 Photograph, JFK and Jackie arrive at Inaugural Ball, 20 January 1961, JFKWHP-AR6281-D, Kennedy Library Digital.
13 Laura Bergquist, 'Jacqueline Kennedy: What You Don't Know about Our First Lady,' *Look* 25 (4 July 1961), pp. 62, 72.
14 Chapman, *License to Thrill*, p. 44; Michael Denning, 'Licensed to Look: James Bond and the Heroism of Consumption,' in Lindner, ed., *James Bond Phenomenon*, p. 56.
15 'Fame and Fortune,' *The Age*, 14 December 1966; 'Show Business,' *Time*, 19 October 1962.
16 Alford, *Once Upon A Secret*, pp. 65–6; Margalit Fox, 'Vaughn Meader, Star as Kennedy Mimicker, Dies at 68,' *New York Times*, 30 October 2004, www.nytimes.com/2004/10/30/us/vaughn-meader-star-as-kennedy-mimicker-dies-at-68.html.
17 For an account of Ted Kennedy's 1962 campaign, see Joe McGinniss, *The Last Brother* (New York: Simon and Schuster, 1993), pp. 253–6, 296–310, 316–17.
18 Reeves, *President Kennedy*, p. 35; quoted in Victor Lasky, *J.F.K.: The Man and the Myth* (New York: Macmillan, 1963), pp. 11–12.
19 Reeves, *President Kennedy*, pp. 35–6; 'Jacqueline Kennedy's Inaugural Gown, 1961,' Smithsonian's National Museum of American History, 9 March 2016, https://www.si.edu/newdesk/photos/jacqueline-kennedys-inaugural-gown-1961; Lasky, *J.F.K.*, p. 12.
20 Hamilton, *JFK*, pp. 211–12 for the historical roots of the Kennedys' interest in positive press.
21 Laura Bergquist, 'An Informal Visit with Our New First Family,' *Look* 25 (28 February 1961), pp. 100–6 (and front cover); Pamela Fiori, 'All About Audrey,' *Harper's Bazaar,* 23 January 2013, www.harpersbazaar.com/fashion/photography/a1349/audrey-hepburn-richard-avedon-0213/; oral history of Laura Bergquist Knebel, interview 1, pp. 1–3, Kennedy Library.
22 DVD, *A Tour of the White House with Mrs. John F. Kennedy* (Field Museum, 2004).
23 Laura Bergquist, 'The President and His Son,' *Look* 27 (3 December 1963), pp. 26–34, 36.
24 Oral history of Richard Cardinal Cushing, pp. 2, 7; 'The High Point in Notable Week,' *Life* 49 (19 December 1960), p. 29; photograph, JFK greeting a group of

nuns, April 1961, Photograph Collection, Kennedy Library; photograph, President John F. Kennedy and his wife attend a christening at Westminster Cathedral, 1961, www.alamy.com/president-john-f-kennedy-and-his-wife-attend-a-christening-at-westminster-cathedral-london-1961-artist-unknown-image262760349.html.
25 Quoted in Reeves, *President Kennedy*, p. 475.
26 Purdum, 'From That Day Forth'; Lasky, *J.F.K.*, pp. 15–16.
27 JFK, remarks at a dinner honouring Nobel Prize winners of the Western Hemisphere, 29 April 1962, www.jfklink.com/speeches/jfk/publicpapers/1962/jfk161_62.html and JFK, toast at a dinner for André Malraux, 11 May 1962, www.jfklink.com/speeches/jfk/publicpapers/1962/jfk184_62.html [both accessed on 15 August 2012]; Nina Totenberg, 'At Kennedy Center, An Arts Legacy Alive At 50,' www.npr.org/2011/01/25/133178585/at-kennedy-center-an-arts-legacy-alive-at-50; Parmet, *JFK*, p. 129; letter from JFK to Pablo Casals, 10 October 1961, www.jfklink.com/speeches/jfk/publicpapers/1961/jfk431_61.html; Elise K. Kirk, 'Music at the White House,' Kennedy Library.
28 JFK, remarks of welcome at the White House concert by Pablo Casals, 13 November 1961, American Presidency Project; Reeves, *A Question of Character*, p. 316; oral history of Letitia Baldrige Hollensteiner, pp. 86-7, Kennedy Library.
29 'Rear Window: The First Lady, 14 February 1962,' *Independent on Sunday*, 10 February 2008, p. 48; Margaret Leslie Davis, *Mona Lisa in Camelot* (New York: Da Capo, 2008), pp. 20–2; Giglio, *Presidency of John F. Kennedy*, pp. 272–3.
30 DVD, *A Tour of the White House with Mrs. John F. Kennedy*; Barbara A. Perry, *Jacqueline Kennedy: First Lady of the New Frontier* (Lawrence, KS: University Press of Kansas, 2004), p. 125.
31 DVD, *A Tour of the White House with Mrs. John F. Kennedy*.
32 Margaret Leslie Davis, 'The Two First Ladies,' *Vanity Fair*, November 2008, https://archive.vanityfair.com/article/2008/11/the-two-first-ladies; Perry, *Jacqueline Kennedy*, p. 132.
33 Davis, 'The Two First Ladies.' For a fuller account of the bringing of the Mona Lisa to the US, see Davis, *Mona Lisa in Camelot*.
34 Perry, *Jacqueline Kennedy*, pp. 130, 132; Kennedy, remarks at the National Gallery of Art upon opening the Mona Lisa exhibition, 8 January 1963, American Presidency Project.
35 Executive Order 11112 creating the President's Advisory Council on the Arts, 12 June 1963, Schlesinger Papers.
36 Kennedy, remarks at Amherst College upon receiving an honorary degree, 26 October 1963, American Presidency Project.
37 Robert J. Donovan, *PT 109: John F. Kennedy in World War II* (New York: McGraw Hill, 1961); oral history of Robert J. Donovan, pp. 17, 26–9, Kennedy Library.
38 Nicholas J. Cull, 'Anatomy of a Shipwreck: Warner Bros., The White House, and the Celluloid Sinking of PT-109,' in J.E. Smyth, ed., *Hollywood and the American Historical Film* (Houndmills, Basingstoke: Palgrave Macmillan, 2011), p. 139; Donovan, *PT 109*.
39 Savage, 'Truman: the Everyman,' pp. 75–92; Perry, *Jacqueline Kennedy*, p. 126.
40 Richard E. Neustadt, *Presidential Power and the Modern Presidents* (New York: Free Press, 1991 edn).
41 Pierre Salinger, *With Kennedy* (Garden City, NY: Doubleday, 1966), pp. 53–4, 56; James Reston, *Deadline* (New York: Random House, 1991), p. 289.
42 Kennedy news conference, 25 January 1961, American Presidency Project.

43 Salinger, *With Kennedy*, pp. 135–8, 140; Sorensen, *Kennedy*, pp. 323–4.
44 PBS documentary, *The Kennedys*. For examples of JFK's use of charm and humour at press conferences, see Sorensen, *Kennedy*, pp. 314, 324.
45 Kennedy news conference, 21 April 1961, American Presidency Project; Salinger, *With Kennedy*, p. 141.
46 Logevall, *JFK*, pp. 392–8. For JFK's relationship with Bradlee, see Bradlee, *Conversations with Kennedy*.
47 Salinger, *With Kennedy*, pp. 117–18, 121–2; Sorensen, *Kennedy*, p. 316; Schlesinger, *A Thousand Days*, p. 563; oral history of Luce, p. 25.
48 Salinger, *With Kennedy*, p. 120; oral history of Luce, pp. 27–9.
49 Stewart Alsop, *Stay of Execution: A Sort of Memoir* (Philadelphia and New York: Lippincott, 1973), pp. 87–8; Salinger, *With Kennedy*, pp. 127–8.
50 Salinger, *With Kennedy*, pp. 129–30; Sorensen, *Kennedy*, pp. 327–8.
51 Bradlee, *Conversations with Kennedy*, pp. 21–4.
52 Ann Mah, 'A Year in Paris That Transformed Jacqueline Kennedy Onassis,' *New York Times*, 23 June 2019, www.nytimes.com/2019/06/23/travel/paris-jacqueline-bouvier-kennedy-onassis-college.html.
53 Letitia Baldrige memo for John Walker, 14 April 1962, White House Social Files (Folder: John Walker), Kennedy Library; draft schedule, visit of André Malraux, Schlesinger Papers, box WH-15; Davis, *Mona Lisa in Camelot*, passim; Beschloss, *Crisis Years*, pp. 183, 186.
54 William Grimes, 'René Verdon, French Chef for the Kennedys, Dies at 86,' *New York Times*, 5 February 2011, www.nytimes.com/2011/02/05/us/05verdon.html; oral history of Leonard Bernstein, p. 7, Kennedy Library.
55 'Fashion: Sophie & Nona,' *Time*, 23 March 1962, https://content.time.com/time/subscriber/article/0,33009,829128,00.html; Jess Cartner-Morley, 'Jackie Kennedy's Pink Wool Suit and the Dark Side of First Lady Fashion,' *Guardian*, 17 January 2017, www.theguardian.com/fashion/2017/jan/17/jackie-kennedy-pink-wool-suit-dark-side-first-lady-fashion-dallas-glamour-power; Heymann, *A Woman Named Jackie*, pp. 250–1; Reeves, *A Question of Character*, p. 83.
56 Richard Dyer, *Stars* (London: British Film Institute, 1998 edn), pp. 47–59.

Chapter 8

1 Schlesinger, *A Thousand Days*, pp. 785–6; Reeves, *A Question of Character*, p. 420; Robert Dallek, 'JFK's Second Term,' *The Atlantic*, June 2003, https://www.theatlantic.com/magazine/archive/2003/06/jfks-second-term/302734/. For a view on this issue from beyond academe, see television journalist Jeff Greenfield's work, *If Kennedy Lived: The First and Second Terms of President John F. Kennedy: An Alternate History* (New York: G.P. Putnam's, 2013).
2 See Barry M. Goldwater, with Jack Casserly, *Goldwater* (New York: St. Martin's Press, 1988).
3 Walter R. Mears, 'Goldwater was Outspoken, Untamable,' *Washington Post*, 29 May 1998, https://www.washingtonpost.com/wp-srv/politics/daily/may98/goldremember.htm.
4 Rostow, *Diffusion of Power*, p. 129; Bradlee, *Conversations with Kennedy*, p. 116.
5 Soergel, 'Which Presidents Have Been Best for the Economy,' https://www.usnews.com/news/blogs/data-mine/2015/10/28/which-presidents-have-been-best-for-the-economy.

6. John Kennedy, radio and tv report to the American people on civil rights, 11 June 1963, American Presidency Project; Andrew Kohut, 'From the Archives: JFK's America,' *Pew Research Center*, 5 July 2019, https://www.pewresearch.org/fact-tank/2019/07/05/jfks-america/.
7. Various historians identify this maturation in Kennedy's presidential leadership. See, for instance, Giglio, *Presidency of John F. Kennedy*, p. 287.
8. Transcript of Broadcast with Walter Cronkite, 2 September 1963, The American Presidency Project.
9. John M. Newman, *JFK and Vietnam: Deception, Intrigue, and the Struggle for Power* (New York: Warner Brothers, 1992); telegram from the Department of State to the Embassy in Vietnam, 5 October 1963, *FRUS, 1961-1963*, IV; Fredrik Logevall, 'Vietnam and the Question of What Might Have Been,' in Mark J. White, ed., *Kennedy: The New Frontier Revisited* (New York: New York University Press, 1998), pp. 26–7; O'Donnell with Powers, '*Johnny, We Hardly Knew Ye*', pp. 13–18.
10. Documentary, *The Kennedys* (PBS, 1992); Theodore H. White, 'An Epilogue: For President Kennedy,' *Life* 55 (6 December 1963), pp. 158–9. See, also, Theodore White, typed notes of conversation with Jackie Kennedy on 29 November 1963, 19 December 1963, Personal Papers of Theodore H. White, box 59, Kennedy Library.
11. Paul R. Henggeler, *In His Steps: Lyndon Johnson and the Kennedy Mystique* (Chicago: Ivan R. Dee, 1991); quoted in Logevall, *Choosing War*, p. 77; Lyndon Johnson, address before a Joint Session of Congress, 27 November 1963, American Presidency Project.
12. Robert Dallek, 'JFK vs the Military,' *The Atlantic* (Fall 2013), https://www.theatlantic.com/magazine/archive/2013/08/jfk-vs-the-military/309496/.
13. Ibid.
14. Oliver Stone and Zachary Sklar, *JFK: The Book of the Film* (New York: Warner Brothers, 1992).
15. Dumbrell, *Rethinking the Vietnam War*, pp. 54–5; documentary, *LBJ* (PBS, 1991).
16. Rusk, *As I Saw It*, pp. 255–9; John Kennedy, address before the 18th General Assembly of the United Nations, 20 September 1963, Kennedy Library Digital; oral history of James E. Webb, interview I, pp. 23–4, Lyndon Baines Johnson Library, Austin, Texas, http://www.lbjlibrary.net/collections/oral-histories/webb-e.-james.html.
17. Dumbrell, *Rethinking the Vietnam War*, p. 37; Ball, *Past Has Another Pattern*, p. 366; David L. DiLeo, *George Ball, Vietnam, and the Rethinking of Containment* (Chapel Hill and London: University of North Carolina Press, 1991), p. 56.
18. John Prados, 'JFK and the Diem Coup,' 5 November 2003, National Security Archive, https://nsarchive2.gwu.edu/NSAEBB/NSAEBB101/index.htm.
19. Lyndon Johnson, remarks in Memorial Hall, Akron University, 21 October 1964, American Presidency Project; John Prados, '40th Anniversary of the Gulf of Tonkin Incident,' 4 August 2004, National Security Archive, https://nsarchive2.gwu.edu/NSAEBB/NSAEBB132/essay.htm; Johnson, radio and television report to the American people following renewed aggression in the Gulf of Tonkin, 4 August 1964, American Presidency Project.
20. Kennedy, Senate campaign announcement, 5 October 1952, Pre-Presidential Papers, Kennedy Library, Kennedy Library Digital; Goodwin, *Remembering America*, pp. 124–5.
21. Gary R. Hess, *Vietnam: Explaining America's Lost War*, 2nd ed. (Chichester: Wiley Blackwell, 2015), p. 51.
22. Memorandum for the record by McGeorge Bundy, 20 September 1964, *FRUS, 1964-1968* (Washington, DC: US Government Printing Office, 1992), I, *Vietnam, 1964*;

Hubert H. Humphrey, *The Education of a Public Man: My Life and Politics* (Garden City, NY: Doubleday, 1976), pp. 319, 327.

23. ExComm transcripts in May and Zelikow, *The Kennedy Tapes*; Rusk, *As I Saw It*, pp. 209, 212; Stewart Alsop and Charles Bartlett, 'In Time of Crisis,' *Saturday Evening Post*, 8 December 1962, pp. 15–20; entry for 11 November 1962, President's Appointment Book, Kennedy Library; Bartlett to Kennedy, 29 and 31 October 1962, President's Office Files, box 28, Kennedy Library; Johnson, ed., *Papers of Adlai E. Stevenson*, VIII, pp. 351–2.

24. Reeves, *President Kennedy*, pp. 226–7; Reeves, *A Question of Character*, pp. 120–4; Harlan Cleveland, 'On a World-Scale Roller Coaster: Adlai Stevenson at the UN, 1961-65,' in Alvin Liebling, ed., *Adlai Stevenson's Lasting Legacy* (New York and Basingstoke: Palgrave Macmillan, 2007), pp. 139–40.

25. Logevall, 'Vietnam and the Question of What Might Have Been,' pp. 32–3.

26. John Kennedy, commencement address at American University in Washington, 10 June 1963, American Presidency Project. For an example of JFK's more hard-line rhetoric early in his presidency, see Kennedy, address before the American Society of Newspaper Editors, 20 April 1961, American Presidency Project.

27. For a perceptive examination of Lyndon Johnson's role on the world stage apart from the Vietnam War, see H.W. Brands, ed., *The Foreign Policies of Lyndon Johnson beyond Vietnam* (College Station: Texas A & M University Press, 1999).

28. See Abraham F. Lowenthal, *The Dominican Intervention* (Baltimore: Johns Hopkins University Press, 1995 edn); it is a classic study of Johnson's policies in the Dominican Republic.

29. Robert Dallek, *Flawed Giant: Lyndon Johnson and His Times, 1961-1973* (New York: Oxford University Press, 1998), passim.

30. Bernstein, *Promises Kept*, passim; Michael Harrington, *The Other America: Poverty in the United States* (New York: Macmillan, 1962).

31. Bernstein, *Promises Kept*, passim; Reeves, *President Kennedy*, p. 276.

32. Schlesinger, *A Thousand Days*, p. 747; and, for a lucid summary of both Johnson's promotion of the civil rights bill and the historical literature on it, see Michael O'Donnell, 'How LBJ Saved the Civil Rights Act,' *The Atlantic*, April 2014, https://www.theatlantic.com/magazine/archive/2014/04/what-the-hells-the-presidency-for/358630/.

33. Hagood, *Presidential Sex*, pp. 139, 188–95.

SELECTED BIBLIOGRAPHY

Bernstein, Irving. *Promises Kept: John F. Kennedy's New Frontier*. New York and Oxford: Oxford University Press, 1991.

Beschloss, Michael R. *The Crisis Years: Kennedy and Khrushchev, 1960-1963*. New York: Edward Burlingame, 1991.

Blair, Joan and Clay. *The Search for* JFK. New York: Berkley, 1976.

Bryant, Nick. *The Bystander: John F. Kennedy and the Struggle for Black Equality*. New York: Basic Books, 2006.

Clarke, Thurston. *JFK's Last Hundred Days: An Intimate Portrait of a Great President*. London: Penguin, 2014 paperback edn.

Dallek, Robert. *John F. Kennedy: An Unfinished Life*. London: Penguin, 2004 paperback edn.

Freedman, Lawrence. *Kennedy's Wars: Berlin, Cuba, Laos, and Vietnam*. New York: Oxford University Press, 2000.

Giglio, James N. *The Presidency of John F. Kennedy*. Lawrence: University Press of Kansas, 1991.

Hamilton, Nigel. *JFK: Reckless Youth*. London: Arrow, 1993 paperback edn.

Hersh, Seymour. *The Dark Side of Camelot*. Boston: Little, Brown, 1997.

Kennedy, John F. *Why England Slept*. New York: W. Funk, 1961 edn.

Kennedy, Robert F. *Thirteen Days: A Memoir of the Cuban Missile Crisis*. New York: Norton, 1969.

Kennedy, Rose Fitzgerald. *Times to Remember*. London: Pan Books, 1975 paperback edn.

Logevall, Fredrik. *JFK*. London: Penguin, 2021 paperback edn.

O'Brien, Michael. *John F. Kennedy: A Biography*. New York: Thomas Dunne, 2005.

O'Donnell, Kenneth P., and Powers, David F. *"Johnny, We Hardly Knew Ye": Memories of John Fitzgerald Kennedy*. Boston: Little, Brown, 1972 paperback edn.

Parmet, Herbert S. *Jack: The Struggles of John F. Kennedy*. New York: Dial, 1980.

Parmet, Herbert S. *JFK: The Presidency of John F. Kennedy*. New York: Penguin paperback edn, 1984.

Paterson, Thomas G., ed. *Kennedy's Quest for Victory: American Foreign Policy, 1961-1963*. New York: Oxford University Press, 1989.

Perry, Barbara A. *Jacqueline Kennedy: First Lady of the New Frontier*. Lawrence, Kansas: University Press of Kansas, 2004.

Reeves, Thomas C. *A Question of Character: A Life of John F. Kennedy*. New York: Free Press, 1991.

Rusk, Dean. *As I Saw It*. New York: Norton, 1990.

Salinger, Pierre G. *With Kennedy*. Garden City, NY: Doubleday, 1966.

Schlesinger, Jr., Arthur M. *A Thousand Days: John F. Kennedy in the White House*. London: Mayflower-Dell reprint, 1967.

Sorensen, Ted. *Counselor*. New York: Harper Perennial, 2009 paperback edn.

Sorensen, Theodore C. *Kennedy*. New York: Harper, 1965.

White, Theodore H. *The Making of the President, 1960*. New York: Atheneum, 1961.
Wills, Garry. *The Kennedy Imprisonment: A Meditation on Power*. Boston: Little, Brown, 1982.
Wofford, Harris. *Of Kennedys and Kings: Making Sense of the Sixties*. New York: Farrar, Straus, Giroux, 1980.

INDEX

Abernathy, Ralph   139
Acheson, Dean G.   64, 69, 76–80, 82, 86, 108
Adams, John Quincy   51
Adams, Sherman   135
Adenauer, Konrad   68
Adler, Richard   183
Alabama Christian Movement for Human Rights   137
Alford, Mimi   158
Alliance for Progress aid programme   60
Alsop, Joseph   76, 175
Amagiri, Japanese destroyer   24
An American Life (Reagan)   51
Anderson, George   220
Anderson, Marian   204
Anderson, Rudolf   116
Angleton, Jim   163, 176
anti-Diem protests   147, 153
anti-immigrant backlash   189
anti-poverty planning   89
Appeasement at Munich   14
Army–McCarthy hearings (1954)   47
Arvad, Inga   8, 13, 17–23, 26, 39, 41, 173, 187
Attwood, William 'Bill'   174
Avedon, Richard   202

Bacon, James   182
Baker, Bobby   184
Baldwin, James   139
Ball, George W.   107, 108, 149, 150, 222–4
Barber, Samuel   204
Bartlett, Charles   26, 39, 175
Bates, Charles   185
Bay of Pigs operation (1961)   1, 2, 4, 17, 54, 60, 61, 63–7, 69, 70, 73, 79, 82, 86, 90, 91, 95, 97, 99–102, 107, 108, 123, 126, 128, 134, 145, 147, 155, 166, 167, 169, 190, 194, 210, 218, 220, 224, 226, 229, 233
Beardsley, Mimi   6, 103, 111, 118, 119, 157–61, 163–5, 170–2, 179, 182, 189, 199
Behind a Presidential Commitment (Drew)   141
Belafonte, Harry   93
Bell, Jack   48
Bennett, Tony   160
Benton, Thomas Hart   51
Bergquist, Laura   202
Berlin Airlift (1948–49)   86
Berlin crisis (1961)   68–72, 74–6, 82–7, 95, 123, 124, 127, 151, 194, 208, 220, 229, 233
    US military planning   78, 80, 85
Berlin Task Force   76, 85
Bernstein, Irving   87, 228
Bernstein, Leonard   204, 212
Beschloss, Michael R.   128
Bevel, James   138
Biddle, Francis   20
Billings, LeMoyne K.   11, 21, 22, 27, 32, 39
Birmingham crisis (1963)   4, 60, 95, 138, 139, 142, 190, 227
Bissell, Richard   99
Black Muslims   139
Black voter registration   90
Blair, Clay   158
Blair, Joan   158
Bohlen, Charles   45, 64, 69
Bolshakov, Georgi   70
Bond, James   61
Bosch, Juan   226
Bouvier, Jacqueline (Jackie). *See* Kennedy, Jacqueline
Bouvier, John Vernou   41
Bowen, Lester   28

Bowles, Chester   61, 62, 64–7, 224
Boynton v. Virginia case (1960)   91
Bradlee, Benjamin   89, 163, 176, 187, 211, 212, 216
Brando, Marlon   53
Brandt, Willy   86
Brinkmanship   61
Broderick, Thomas   27, 35
Brown, Madeleine   229
Brown v. Board of Education (1954)   91
Bruce, David   185
Bucharest   113
Bundy, McGeorge   62, 74–6, 78, 81, 84, 106, 113, 117, 124, 128, 150, 153, 195, 209, 250 n.11, 262 n.22
Bunyan, John   7
Burke, John T.   36
Burns, James MacGregor   50, 51
Bush, George H.W.   108, 194, 215

Cabral, Reid   226
Callas, Maria   182
Campbell, Judith   3, 7, 53, 159, 166–73, 175–7, 179, 187, 189, 190, 194, 199
Capehart, Homer   103
Carter, Jimmy   210, 215
Cassini, Oleg   213
Castro, Fidel   1, 2, 5, 54, 60, 62–7, 97–101, 103, 105, 107, 111, 114–16, 119, 124, 136, 168–70, 189, 190, 198, 223, 233
  assassination planning for   97, 98
Castro, Raúl   97
To Catch a Thief (Hitchcock)   43
Celler, Emanuel   143
Chamberlain, Neville   14
Chang, Suzy   185
Chayes, Abram   78
children's crusade (in Birmingham, 1963)   138
Chinese policy   68, 133
Churchill, Winston   13, 17, 33, 50, 177
CIA   17, 63–7, 85, 97–9, 108, 131, 148, 150, 152, 168–70, 173, 174, 176, 189, 220
CIA–Mafia alliance   97
Citizens' Committee for a Nuclear Test Ban   134
Civil Rights Act (1964)   87, 218, 227

Civil Rights Movement   90, 136, 186–7
Clay, Lucius   86
Cleveland, Grover   11
Clifford, Clark M.   50, 51, 66
Clinton, Bill   30, 42, 53, 162, 171, 210, 215, 217
Clinton, Hillary   42, 43
Clooney, George   163
Coerr, Wymberley   98
Coffee with the Kennedys (1952 campaign TV programme)   37
Cohn, Roy   45, 47, 52
Collingwood, Charles   202, 205
Conant, James   45
Conein, Lucien   152
Congress of Racial Equality (CORE)   90
Connery, Sean   112, 213
Connor, Bull   138
Coolidge, Calvin   11
Copland, Aaron   204
Cordier, Andrew   114, 118
Cowan, Jill   157, 159, 160, 164–6
Cox, William Harold   136
Craig, William   100, 246 n.13
Crane, Edward   15
Cromwell, Oliver   75
Cronkite, Walter   151, 218
Crosby, Bing   213
Cuban missile crisis (1962)   2, 4, 17, 29, 60, 62, 68, 75, 76, 81, 101, 106, 110, 120, 121, 123, 124, 127, 151, 155, 179, 194, 198, 208, 217, 221, 224, 225, 228, 231, 233
Cushing, Richard Cardinal   39, 46, 203

Daley, Richard   170
Dallek, Robert   6, 11, 36, 145, 215
Dalton, Mark   26
Damore, Leo   174, 175
The Dark Side of Camelot (Hersh)   158, 167
Davids, Jules   51
da Vinci, Leonardo   205
DEFCON 2   113
de Gaulle, Charles   84, 155, 177, 204, 206, 212, 225
Democratic National Convention   52, 54–5, 61, 164, 167

Democratic Party   30, 44, 45, 47, 52, 55, 69, 87, 136, 217, 224, 230
Dever, Paul   46
Dickinson, Angie   180
Diem, Ngo Dinh   123, 144, 145, 147–56, 219, 222, 234
Dillon, C. Douglas   62, 114, 115
Dirksen, Everett   134, 135, 186, 228
Dobrynin, Anatoly   110, 113, 118, 120, 126
Donovan, Robert   207
Drew, Robert   141
Dr. No (James Bond movie)   112
Duc, Thich Quang   147
Duffy, LaVern   186
Dulles, Allen   1, 62, 64, 65, 104, 105, 113, 153, 185
Dulles, John Foster   61, 70
Dyer, Richard   213

Earle, Peter   185
Eisenhower, Dwight D.   11, 30, 33, 35, 52, 54, 61–5, 68, 88, 101, 102, 121, 124, 134, 135, 141, 144, 145, 189, 193, 194, 209–11, 215, 216, 233
Eisenhower, Mamie   197, 200, 205
Ekberg, Anita   195, 197, 198
Elizabeth II   180
Equal Pay Act (1963)   89
Evans, Reginald   25
Executive Committee of the National Security Council (ExComm)   106–10, 114–17, 119, 120, 151, 153, 154, 224, 231

Fanfani, Amintore   83
Farmer, James   90, 91, 94, 95
Fay, Paul 'Red'   27, 163
Fejos, Paul   18, 20
Feklisov, Aleksandr   115, 116
The Feminine Mystique (Friedan)   89
The First Family (Meader)   199
First World War   7, 25
Fitzgerald, Ella   182
Fitzgerald, John F. 'Honey Fitz'   7, 10
Flanders, Ralph   47
Flashbacks (Leary)   178, 179
Fleming, Ian   1, 2, 6, 17, 18, 98, 100, 106, 112, 198

Forbes, Alastair   45, 49
Ford, Gerald   215
Formosa Resolution (1955)   49
Fox, Frances   195
Frasca, Dom   185
Freedom Rides (1961)   4, 90–5, 123, 129, 136, 139
Friedan, Betty   89
From Russia with Love   1, 2, 198
Frost, Robert   201
Fulbright, J. William   64, 84, 110
Funk, Wilfred publishers   14
Fursenko, Aleksandr   116

Galbraith, John Kenneth   146, 188
Gamarekian, Barbara   161, 162, 165
game theory   81
Gary Powers's U-2 reconnaissance incident (1960)   124
Giancana, Sam   3, 97, 166–8
Giglio, James   87, 88, 140
Gilpatric, Roswell   146, 150
Ginsberg, Allen   178
Goldwater, Barry   103, 216, 217
Goodwin, Richard N.   64, 65, 67, 97, 124
Gorbachev, Mikhail   101
Gould, Deborah   181
Graham, Philip L.   179
Grant, Cary   161, 177, 195
Grant, Johnny   170
Great Depression   233
Greene, Graham   99
Greenfield, Robert   178
Gribkov, Anatoly   101
Gromyko, Andrei A.   108, 133
Guevara, Che   97
The Guns of August (Tuchman)   113

Hagood, Wesley O.   165
Halberstam, David   2, 149, 150
Halleck, Charles   143
Hamilton, Nigel   6, 8, 18
Harriman, W. Averell   61–3, 69, 131–4, 149, 150, 153, 251 n.25
Harrington, Michael   227
Harrison, William Henry   11
Harvey, William   97, 98
Hearst, William Randolph   22
Heller, Walter   88, 89

Henggeler, Paul 219
Hepburn, Audrey 119, 202
heroic leadership 17, 50, 54, 121, 207
Hersey, John 25, 28, 37
Hersh, Seymour 3, 5, 158, 159, 167, 168, 170, 189, 231, 234
Hershberg, James 105
Heymann, C. David 176
Hillenbrand, Martin 76
Hilsman, Roger 64
Hiss, Alger 46
Hitchcock, Alfred 43
Hitler, Adolf 207
Hood, James 140
Hoover, J. Edgar 17, 18, 20, 21, 23, 91, 159, 167, 172, 173, 183, 185–7, 189
Horan, James D. 185
Houston, Sam 50
Humphrey, Hubert H. 33, 52, 53, 56, 137, 188, 203, 224, 228, 232
Huntley-Brinkley Report 151
Husted, John G.W. 39

I'm for Roosevelt (1936 book by Joseph P. Kennedy) 10
In Search of JFK (Joan and Clay Blair) 158
Interstate Commerce Commission (ICC) 94

Jacobson, Max 70, 169, 177, 178
Janney, Peter 178
Jefferson, Thomas 212
JFK. *See* Kennedy, John F. (JFK)
JFK: Reckless Youth (Hamilton) 6, 8
John F. Kennedy: An Unfinished Life, 1917-1963 (Dallek) 6
Johnson, Lady Bird 229
Johnson, Lyndon 4, 11, 28, 52, 55, 56, 64, 79, 86–8, 117, 134, 141, 145, 147, 163, 165, 197, 203, 216–30, 232–4
Jupiter missiles 101, 104, 108, 109, 112, 114, 115, 117

Kansas–Nebraska bill (1854) 50
Katzenbach, Nicholas deB 91, 94, 140, 143, 223
Keating, Kenneth 103

Keeler, Christine 184
Kefauver, Estes 44, 52
Kelley, Kitty 168
Kelly, Grace 41, 43, 197
Kennan, George 69
Kennedy, Edward M. 28, 200
Kennedy, Jacqueline 1, 4, 5, 28, 39–43, 51, 70, 78, 157, 159, 164, 166, 167, 173–7, 179, 194, 195, 197, 198, 201–6, 212, 213, 219, 232
Kennedy, John F. (JFK)
    1946 campaign 27, 28, 35
    1952 campaign 35, 37, 38, 43
    1960 presidential campaign 6, 7, 11, 45, 53, 55, 56, 62, 63, 70, 81, 87, 89, 92, 97, 98, 136, 142, 161, 164, 167, 177, 181, 189, 194, 200, 203, 208, 209, 223, 229
    academic performance 7
    analysis of US foreign policy 33
    assassination 1, 4, 29, 89, 179, 202, 206, 213, 217, 219, 220, 226
    Catholicism 39, 54, 189, 203
    character of James Bond 1, 3
    character strengths 32, 35
    civil rights 49, 94, 123, 136–9, 142–4, 189, 228
    crisis management 70, 138
    economic policies 88
    FBI director 18, 172
    in first TV debate (1960) 56
    five 'must' bills 87, 90
    marriage 39–43
    medical battles 6, 11, 13, 25, 27, 36, 48, 57, 190
    moral leadership 49, 93, 191
    Navy and Marine Corps Medal 25
    New Frontier 88
    officer training 23
    private life 3–5, 17, 21, 53, 158, 159, 161–3, 166, 167, 171, 172, 177, 186–90, 194, 202, 210, 215, 218, 225, 229, 231
    PT 109 leadership 23–5, 35, 37, 57, 188, 207, 213, 231
    Pulitzer Prize winner 49, 50
    social life 39, 45, 188
Kennedy, Joseph P. Jr. 13–15, 25, 26

Kennedy, Joseph P. Sr.   8–10, 13, 14, 18, 21, 25, 26, 29, 32, 35–7, 42, 45, 46, 50, 51, 200, 203, 217
Kennedy, Kathleen   20
Kennedy, Patrick J.   9, 10
Kennedy, Robert F.   18, 28, 32, 35, 37, 45, 47, 53, 54, 62, 64, 66, 67, 70, 74, 80, 85, 91–4, 99, 100, 104, 107–9, 112, 113, 117, 118, 120, 121, 126, 135, 138–41, 144, 151, 153, 154, 167–70, 172, 177, 180, 183, 185, 186, 200
Kennedy, Rose Fitzgerald   7–9, 28, 37, 38, 200
The Kennedy Imprisonment (Wills)   158
Kennedy–Nixon TV debate (1960)   53, 55, 193, 208
Khrushchev, Nikita S.   54, 60–3, 66–86, 91, 101–3, 105–7, 109–11, 113–20, 124–7, 130–3, 177, 178, 208, 218, 221, 225
  demands on Berlin   72
  leadership style   102
King, Martin Luther   29, 54, 90, 92, 137, 139, 142, 181, 186
Kipling, Rudyard   7
Kissinger, Henry   78
Klan, Ku Klux   139
Klapp, Orrin E.   213
Knickerbocker, Charley   200
Kohler, Foy   73, 76, 85, 133
Krim, Arthur   183
Krock, Arthur   10, 14, 19, 50
Krulak, Victor   151
Kuznetsov, Vasiliy   125

Landis, James   51
Lansdale, Edward   64, 99
Lantphibex-1-62 (1962)   100, 101
Lawford, Peter   10, 165, 181, 183
Leary, Timothy   178–80
Leiter, Marion   1
LeMay, Curtis E.   109, 220
Leonard, Joseph Fr.   39, 41
Lewinsky, Monica   162
Lincoln, Abraham   120, 142, 193
Lincoln, Evelyn   164, 166, 170, 172, 181
Lippmann, Walter   76, 155, 211
Little Rock crisis (1957)   189

Lodge, Henry Cabot   35–9, 46, 47, 148–55, 223, 231, 232
Logevall, Fredrik   6, 26, 36, 219
Louis, Jean   183, 196
Luce, Henry   14, 211

MacArthur, Douglas   24, 146, 148
Macdonald, Torbert 'Torby'   163
Macmillan, Harold   69, 73, 74, 124, 127, 130, 133, 184, 212
Malone, Vivian   140
Malraux, André   204, 206
Manchester, William   4, 5
Mannix, McGonigle Jean   48
Manpower Development and Training Act (1962)   88
Mansfield, Jayne   180
Mansfield, Mike   147, 186
The Man with the Golden Gun (Fleming)   1
Mao Tse Tung   71
Marshall, Burke   90, 138, 140–3
Marshall Plan (1947)   31, 37, 215
Martin, Louis E.   90, 139, 142
Marvin, Langdon Parker Jr.   22
McCarran Internal Security Act (1950)   46
McCarthy, Joseph   13, 17, 30–2, 36, 43–50, 56, 87, 217, 224
McCarthyism   30, 44, 47–50, 56, 232
McCloy, John   83
McCone, John A.   1, 62, 104, 105, 113, 115, 134, 149, 150, 153, 185
McCormack, Edward   200
McCoy, Ronald   19
McCulloch, William M.   143
McMahon, Patrick   24
McMillan, Priscilla Johnson   41
McNamara, Robert S.   62, 63, 77–80, 85, 105, 107, 118, 120, 126, 128, 132, 146, 148–50, 152, 154, 155, 209, 253 n.77
Meader, Vaughn   199
Medicaid   218, 227
Medicare   218, 227
Mendenhall, Joseph   152
Menshikov, Mikhail   80
Meyer, Cord   173, 174

Meyer, Mary   3, 18, 173–80, 199
Miller, Arthur   181, 204
Minh, Duong Van   152
Minh, Ho Chi   144
'missile gap'   33, 54, 121
Mollenhoff, Clark   186
Mona Lisa (da Vinci)   205–7, 212
Monroe, Marilyn   3, 10, 170, 175, 180, 181, 183, 189, 195–7, 199, 213, 256 n.78
Montgomery Bus Boycott (1955–1956)   189
Morse, Robert   160
Murrow, Edward   64

National Association for the Advancement of Colored People (NAACP)   137
National Security Action Memorandum No. 263 (NSAM-263)   148, 152, 155, 219
Nehru, Jawaharlal   32
Neustadt, Richard   208
Neville, Michael J.   28
Nevins, Allan   51
New Deal coalition   216, 230
Newman, John   219
Newman, Paul   53
Nhu, Madame   148, 149
Nhu, Ngo Dinh   148, 152, 154, 155, 225
Nitze, Paul   117
Nixon, Richard M.   53–6, 67, 103, 166, 177, 181, 194, 195, 197, 210, 216, 223, 227, 231–3
Noland, Kenneth   174
Nolting, Frederick   150
North Atlantic Treaty Organization (NATO)   32, 68, 69, 71, 76, 108, 118, 131, 132
Novotny, Maria   185
Nuclear Test Ban Treaty (1963)   2, 29, 32, 62, 123, 124, 126, 127, 130–3, 135, 147, 148, 173, 178, 221, 225, 233

Obama, Barack   87, 215
O'Brien, Lawrence F.   88, 141
O'Donnell, Kenneth P.   48, 90, 112, 141, 147, 157, 163, 170, 175, 219
Olivier, Laurence   209
Onassis, Aristotle   41

Operation Anadyr   103
Operation Mongoose   2, 17, 60, 66, 67, 99–102, 104, 105, 107
Ormsby-Gore, David   124
Oswald, Lee Harvey   2
The Other America (Harrington)   227
Outer Space Treaty (1967)   225

Parmet, Herbert   5, 48, 51
Parrott, Thomas   98
Patterson, John   92, 93
Peace Corps   29, 60, 93, 213, 233
Pearson, Drew   50, 51, 77, 86, 139, 211
Perkins, Frances   89
Pinchot, Mary   173, 174
Polonik, Mikhail   113
Pope Pius XII   39
Powers, David F.   48, 118, 119, 147, 148, 157, 159–61, 163, 165, 170, 172, 175, 219
President's Commission on the Status of Women   89
Presley, Elvis   53
Profiles in Courage (Kennedy)   1, 15, 17, 25, 33, 45, 49–51, 54, 121, 188, 203, 207
Profumo, John   184, 185
Promises Kept (Bernstein)   87

The Quiet American (Greene)   99

Randolph, Philip   143
Reader's Digest article on JFK and PT 109 (Hersey)   25, 28, 37
Reagan, Ronald   51, 83, 188, 210, 215–17
Redford, Robert   213
Red Scare   43, 45, 49
Reedy, George   165, 229
Reeves, Thomas C.   3, 5, 44, 158, 159, 188, 189, 215, 229, 231, 234
Reston, James   74, 155, 211
Robertson, Cliff   207
Rockefeller, Nelson   137, 216
Rockwell, Norman   43
Roman Holiday   118, 119
Rometsch, Ellen   159, 165, 167, 169, 177, 179, 183–5, 186
Roosevelt, Eleanor   30, 42, 44, 45, 52, 61, 87, 89, 200

Roosevelt, Franklin D.   3, 5, 8, 10, 11, 13, 29, 42, 49, 87, 88, 211, 215, 216, 227
Roselli, Johnny   167
Ross, Edmund   51
Rosselli, John   97
Rostow, W.W.   84, 85, 93, 145, 216, 222
Rusk, Dean   62, 64, 78, 79, 84, 85, 107, 110, 113, 128, 131–5, 145, 149, 150, 153, 209, 244 n.82, 246 n.12
Russell, Richard   110, 133, 228
Russo, Joseph   26

Salinger, Pierre G.   104, 152, 157, 164, 209–11, 246 n.26
Saloschin, Robert   94
SANE Nuclear Policy   126
Scali, John   115
Schelling, Thomas C.   81
Schine, David   47
Schlesinger, Arthur M. Jr.   4, 5, 51, 64, 65, 78, 79, 128, 183, 215, 219, 231, 233
Second World War   53, 57, 112, 120, 129, 131, 188, 193, 207, 208, 217, 231–3
Seigenthaler, John   92, 168, 169
Senator Joe McCarthy (Rovere)   45
Shaw, Mark   178
Shuttlesworth, Fred   137
Sidey, Hugh   164
Sinatra, Frank   3, 27, 160, 166, 171
Smathers, George A.   42, 45, 98, 136, 163
Smith, Howard K.   91, 228
Smith, Jerome   139
Social Security Act (1935)   87
Sorensen, Theodore C.   4, 5, 47, 48, 50, 51, 59, 80, 90, 112, 117, 128, 133, 140, 141, 146, 162, 163, 209, 211, 215, 216, 219, 231, 233
Southeast Asia Treaty Organization (SEATO)   145
Southern Christian Leadership Conference   137
Soviet Union   31, 46, 71, 73, 101–3, 108, 119, 124, 126, 129, 130, 148, 188, 225
Spalding, Charles   2, 29, 44, 177
Sputnik (1957)   33, 54
Stalin, Joseph   102
star theory   213
steel industry crisis   89

Steinbeck, John   135, 136
Stevenson, Adlai E.   30, 32, 35, 41, 52, 59, 61–5, 67, 68, 109, 110, 114, 115, 135, 136, 183, 188, 199, 203, 204, 224, 232
Stevenson, Robert Louis   7
Stone, Oliver   219
Stowe, Harriet Beecher   7
Swanson, Gloria   8, 10
Sweeney, Walter   110
Szulc, Tad   98, 99

Taft, Robert   45, 51
Taylor, Maxwell D.   78, 79, 98–100, 104, 108, 110, 117, 128, 132, 134, 145, 150, 152–4, 222
Taylor, Zachary   11
Taylor–Rostow recommendations (1961)   146, 147
'Third Way' ideology   30
Thirteen Days (Robert Kennedy)   117
Thomas, George   163
Thompson, Bill   163, 184
Tierney, Gene   10, 28, 213
Tonkin Gulf Resolution (1964)   223
Trade Expansion Act (1962)   88
Trafficante, Santos   97
Truitt, James   175
Truman, Bess   197
Truman, Harry S.   30–2, 43, 46, 49, 68, 76, 105, 121, 133, 145, 193, 208, 210, 215, 220
Truman Doctrine (1947)   31
Trump, Donald   187, 231
Tuchman, Barbara   112
Turnure, Pamela   159, 161, 162, 166, 174

Ulbricht, Walter   69, 84, 185
Underwood, Martin   170
University of Alabama desegregation (1963)   129, 140–2
University of Mississippi crisis (1962)   123, 178
U Thant   118

Verdon, René   212
Vienna summit (1961)   70, 74, 75, 77, 91
Vietnam, US policy in   5, 60, 103, 144–9, 151–6, 217–26, 229, 230, 233, 234

von Post, Gunilla   41
Voting Rights Act (1965)   87, 218, 227

Wallace, George   140
Wallace, Henry   125
Wallace, Mike   50
Walsh, David I.   35
Warner Brothers   207
War on Poverty   89
WASP-Irish distrust   9
Wear, Priscilla   9, 157, 159, 160, 164, 165
Wear-Cowan-Beardsley relationship   165
Weatherby, W.J.   181
Webster, Daniel   50
Weinstein, Harvey   171
Westmoreland, William   220
White, Byron   92
White, John   19

White, Theodore   4, 55, 219
Why England Slept (John Kennedy)   4, 7, 8, 13–17, 19, 22, 23, 25, 31–3, 37, 49, 50, 54, 57, 59, 68, 70, 81, 82, 87, 111, 113, 121, 190, 203, 207, 231
Wild, Payson   14, 15
Wilkins, Roy   90, 137
Williams, Mennen 'Soapy'   61
Williams, Tennessee   177, 204
Wills, Garry   3, 5, 6, 158, 159, 189, 234
Wilson, Woodrow   7, 11, 29, 35, 128
Winchell, Walter   21, 172
Wofford, Harris   90, 92–4
Woodward, Robert   98

Yalta conference (1945)   31

Zorin, Valerian   114